"A Hideous Bit of Morbidity"

ALSO BY JASON COLAVITO

Knowing Fear: Science, Knowledge and the Development of the Horror Genre (McFarland, 2008)

"A Hideous Bit of Morbidity"

An Anthology of Horror Criticism from the Enlightenment to World War I

Edited by
JASON COLAVITO

McFarland & Company, Inc., Publishers
Jefferson, North Carolina, and London

The present work is a reprint of the library bound edition of "A Hideous Bit of Morbidity": An Anthology of Horror Criticism from the Enlightenment to World War I, *first published in 2008 by McFarland.*

LIBRARY OF CONGRESS CATALOGUING-IN-PUBLICATION DATA

"A hideous bit of morbidity" : an anthology of horror criticism from the Enlightenment to World War I / edited by Jason Colavito.
    p.   cm.
Includes bibliographical references and index.

ISBN 978-0-7864-6909-3
softcover : acid free paper ∞

1. Horror tales, English—History and criticism.
2. Horror tales, American—History and criticism.
3. Criticism—Great Britain—History.   4. Criticism—United States—History.   I. Colavito, Jason.
PR67.H53   2012
823'.0873809—dc22   2008030516

BRITISH LIBRARY CATALOGUING DATA ARE AVAILABLE

© 2008 Jason Colavito. All rights reserved

No part of this book may be reproduced or transmitted in any form or by any means, electronic or mechanical, including photocopying or recording, or by any information storage and retrieval system, without permission in writing from the publisher.

Front cover: poster titled *Newmann's wonderful spirit mysteries,* Donaldson Lith. Co., Newport, Kentucky, 1911 (McManus-Young Collection, Library of Congress

Manufactured in the United States of America

McFarland & Company, Inc., Publishers
   Box 611, Jefferson, North Carolina 28640
   www.mcfarlandpub.com

Table of Contents

Introduction 1
A Note on the Text 11

1. FEAR, TERROR, AND THE SUPERNATURAL 13

   On the Words for "Fear" in Certain Languages:
   A Study in Linguistic Psychology
      Alex F. Chamberlain 13

   Excerpt from *On the Sublime and Beautiful*
      Edmund Burke 18

   On the Pleasure of Writing Dismal Stories,
   Exciting Surprize and Horror
      Daniel Defoe 22

   Excerpt from "The Prodigal and His Brother"
      Frederick W. Robertson 25

   The Dread of the Supernatural
      The Spectator 27

   Gothic Horror
      Lafcadio Hearn 31

2. THE GOTHICS AND THEIR SUCCESSORS 37

   Excerpt from *The Supernatural in Romantic Fiction*
      Edward Yardley 37

   Excerpt from "On Gothic Superstition"
      Nathan Drake 41

Excerpt from a Review of *Literary Hours*
by Nathan Drake
    The Monthly Review 47

Introductory Dialogue to *Tales of Terror*
    Matthew Lewis (attributed) 50

Excerpt from "The Revival of Romance"
    Walter Raleigh 53

The School of Terror
    Thomas E. Rankin and *Wilford M. Aikin* 58

Fiction in the Romantic Movement
    William Allen Neilson 59

Excerpt from "Mrs. Ann Radcliffe"
    Sir Walter Scott 60

Excerpt from "Fragments of an Unpublished Manuscript"
    Adam Eagle (*Fitz-James O'Brien*) 65

Letter to William Godwin
    Charles Lamb 66

Introduction to *Ghost Stories*
    Rudolph Ackermann 67

A Tale for a Chimney-Corner
    Leigh Hunt 68

Excerpt from "A Letter from Geneva"
    John Polidori 77

Remarks on *Frankenstein, or the Modern Prometheus*
    Sir Walter Scott 79

Excerpt from a Review of *Frankenstein;
or, the Modern Prometheus*
    John Croker 93

Excerpt from a Review of *Frankenstein;
or, the Modern Prometheus*
    The Edinburgh Magazine and Literary Miscellany 94

Review of *Presumption; or the Fate of Frankenstein*
    The London Magazine 97

Excerpt from "Mrs. Shelley"
   R. H. Horne 99
Letter Denying Authorship of *The Vampire*
   Lord Byron 103
Excerpt from "Ellis, Acton, and Currer Bell"
   Peter Bayne 105

3. POE AND HIS SUCCESSORS 108

Excerpt from "Later German Romanticism"
   George H. Danton 108
The Origins of Hawthorne and Poe
   Paul Elmer More 110
Edgar Allan Poe
   Robert Chambers 122
Excerpt from "Edgar Allan Poe"
   James Russell Lowell 126
Review of *The Raven and Other Poems*
   The Knickerbocker 129
Poe: Lack of Substance
   W. C. Brownell 132
Poe's Fixing of the Short-Story Form
   Charles Sears Baldwin 138
Fitz-James O'Brien
   Charles Sears Baldwin 144
Excerpt from "The Mid-Century in America"
   Henry Seidel Canby 145
Maupassant and Poe
   Frederic Rowland Marvin 148
Advertisement for *Tales of Soldiers and Civilians*
   American Publishers 152
Excerpt from "Ambrose Bierce: An Appraisal"
   Frederic Taber Cooper 152
Bierce: Satire, Romance, Philosophy
   Edwin Markham 158

Excerpt from "The Short Story"
Fred Lewis Pattee 160

Excerpt from "Concerning Irvin Cobb"
The Bookman 161

4. MONSTERS OF THE GILDED AGE 164

The Physiology of "Penny Awfuls"
The London Hermit *(Walter Parke)* 164

Review of *The Purcell Papers* by J. Sheridan Le Fanu
The Saturday Review 182

Excerpt from "Concerning Tea"
E. V. Lucas 183

Excerpt from "The New Gallery"
J. Charles Cox 185

The Religion of Robert Louis Stevenson
W. J. Dawson 187

Review of *The Strange Case of Dr. Jekyll and Mr. Hyde*
The Dublin Review 194

Excerpt from "Novelists' Law"
Alfred Bailey 195

The Secret Out
The New York Herald Tribune 196

Excerpt from "Richard Mansfield"
William Henry Frost 199

Excerpt from "R. L. Stevenson"
Richard Le Gallienne 200

Excerpt from "Our Library List"
Murray's Magazine 200

Review of *Dracula*
Baron de Book-Worms 201

Supped Full with Horrors
Charles F. Lummis 202

Review of *Dracula*
The Literary World 204

Excerpt from "Open Questions:
  Talks with Correspondents"
    Current Literature 204

Excerpt from *Human Sexuality*
    J. Richardson Parke 205

Letter to Julian Hawthorne
    Edmund Clarence Stedman 206

Excerpt from *Modern Vampirism*
    A. Osborne Eaves 207

Frankenstein
    The Bookman 208

5. FIN DE SIÈCLE SCIENCE, DETECTION, AND TERROR 209
    Excerpt from "Fictions of the Future"
        The Dublin Review 209

    Review of *The Island of Dr. Moreau*
        The Baron de Book-Worms 211

    Review of *The Invisible Man*
        William Morton Payne 214

    Excerpt from "Love, War and Pseudo-science"
        William Lyon Phelps 215

    Mr. Wells's *War of the Worlds*
        Clement Shorter 215

    Review of *The War of the Worlds*
        William Morton Payne 218

    Excerpt from *The Technique of the Mystery Story*
        Carolyn Wells 219

    Review of *My Friend the Murderer*
        The Literary World 220

    Excerpt from "Conan Doyle's *The Hound of the Baskervilles*"
        Arthur Bartlett Maurice 221

    Curiosity and Horror in the Theatre
        Arthur Bingham Walkley 223

Review of *The Three Imposters*
  The Bookman 227
Review of *The Great God Pan*
  Richard Henry Stoddard 228
The Gospel of Intensity
  Harry Quilter 230
Excerpt from "Oscar Wilde"
  A. Edward Newton 255
Art and Luxury
  Ramiro de Maetzu 257

6. GHOSTS AND KINDRED HORRORS 265
  Excerpt from "A Study of Individual Psychology"
    Caroline Miles 265
  The Value of the Supernatural in Fiction
    Lafcadio Hearn 267
  Some Japanese Bogie-Books
    Andrew Lang 279
  Ghost Stories
    W. F. Dawson 292
  Excerpt from "Books of the Christmas Season"
    Noah Brooks 294
  Two Volumes from Henry James
    Henry Wysham Lanier 295
  Excerpt from "Gillette"
    Amy Leslie 297
  Excerpt from "Chronicle and Comment"
    The Bookman 299
  Review of *The King in Yellow*
    The Literary World 300
  Review of *The Wind in the Rose Bush*
    The Literary World 300
  Mr. Morris's "The Footprint"
    Ward Clark 301

Algernon Blackwood—An Appreciation
   Grace Isabel Colbron 303
Robert Hichens
   Frederic Taber Cooper 307
The Creeps
   H. D. Traill 324
The Decay of the Ghost in Fiction
   Olivia Howard Dunbar 329

7. TOWARD A HORROR GENRE 337
   The Supernatural in Fiction
      Andrew Lang 337
   The Abuse of the Supernatural in Fiction
      Edmund Gosse 342
   Review of *The Supernatural in Modern English Fiction*
      Montague Summers 350
   Excerpt from *The Supernatural in Modern English Fiction*
      Dorothy Scarborough 356

Appendix: Timeline of Major Works of Horror 367
Index 369

Introduction

"The history of the Victorian age," Lytton Strachey said in *Eminent Victorians*, his 1918 examination of the era, "will never be written: we know too much about it."[1] Of course, Strachey came not to praise the Victorians but to bury them. The purpose of this volume is altogether different, but on one thing we must steadfastly agree with the eminent author: The Victorians (and their immediate predecessors) "poured forth and accumulated so great a quantity of information"[2] that it is virtually impossible to gain a hold on the vast torrent of verbiage spilled in the newspapers, magazines, and books of the era, even when we restrict our inquiry to a single subject; in this case, the literature of fear. However, the daunting challenge of sifting through the detritus has too often resulted in a cultural amnesia in which the opinions of past critics sink like forgotten fossils beneath each new layer of intellectual sedimentation. True, a few excavators, mainly in the academy, occasionally raise the bones of an old review or critical essay, selecting few choice words to adorn a new piece, but there is rarely a concerted effort to put together a large-scale collection that preserves the flavor of the era on its own terms.

The present volume serves as a repository of the critical reaction to horror literature from its inception in the eighteenth century through the First World War, the conflict that brought to a close the first great age of terror tales and launched the modern horror genre, from which we have yet to emerge. In order to more fully explain the conception and execution of the text to follow, I will first briefly sketch the major contours of horror literature and the critical reaction to it. (Except when noted, all of the quotations in the sections to follow are from articles reprinted in the present volume.)

A Literature of Fear

Prior to the First World War, there was no "horror genre" in the sense we consider it today. That beast was an outgrowth of a change in how frightening tales were produced and consumed during the early twentieth century, when horror passed from mainstream literature to the pulp fiction ghetto. Instead, what we think of today as "horror literature" was first conceived as wondrous, fantastic, grotesque, or arabesque tales, where the supernatural intruded into domestic melodrama and sensation mixed with romance. Traditionally, scholars assign the genre's inception to the moment when Horace Walpole published *The Castle of Otranto* in 1764, though it is as much a result of the Romantic Movement and its reaction to the rational excesses of the Enlightenment as it is the work of any one man. Walpole's bloody ghost story was set in a medieval fortress, from whose architecture derives the name given to the book and its imitators: the Gothic novel.

In the novel, the sudden and dramatic appearance of the ghost "may be taken as a symbol and type of the suddenness with which supernatural terror was re-introduced into English," the scholar Walter Raleigh wrote in 1894, crediting the novel with originality but not with quality. *Otranto* had taken its coloring from Edmund Burke, the British philosopher who in 1757 had outlined in his treatise *On the Sublime and Beautiful* the manifold ways that terror could produce transcendence: including dark and stormy nights, massive architecture, screams—the entire panoply of Gothic clichés, which of course were then new. In *Otranto* was Burke's philosophy turned to terror. Most Gothic tales thereafter looked back toward the Middle Ages, and a ghost or two were essential to the execution of a properly sensational story. The Gothic writers who followed, including Matthew Lewis and Ann Radcliffe, remained popular through the early nineteenth century, and Gothic novels, stories, and stage plays had become a lucrative and prolific species of literature.

Of course, many critics of the day were gravely concerned that these ghostly goings-on would unduly confound the common man into believing in the reality of the supernatural (an elitist position shared by three centuries of horror critics). The publisher Rudolph Ackermann went so far as to create in 1823 an entire book of faux–Gothic tales which ended in the revelation that each story's ghost was an illusion or a hoax to show "ignorant or credulous persons" that "no ghost is there." More to the point, the essayist Nathan Drake wrote in 1798 that even the "most enlightened mind, the mind free from all taint of superstition, involuntarily acknowledges the power of gothic agency; and the late favourable reception which two or three publications in this style have met with, is a convincing proof of the assertion." But *The Monthly Review* had fewer concerns about the impact of Gothic horror: "Spectres will lose their claim to reverence if they become too common," it wrote in 1799, and surely enough the Gothic school of ghostly terror soon wore out its welcome when its output exceeded demand by too high a quotient.

Though some Enlightenment critics attacked the Gothic, many Romantics rose up to defend it. Sir Walter Scott, himself no stranger to horror writing, argued for its merit in a piece eulogizing Ann Radcliffe:

> Perhaps the perusal of such works may, without injustice, be compared with the use of opiates, baneful, when habitually and constantly resorted to, but of most blessed power in those moments of pain and of languor, when the whole head is sore, and the whole heart sick. If those who rail indiscriminately at this species of composition, were to consider the quantity of actual pleasure which it produces, and, the much greater proportion of real sorrow and distress which it alleviates, their philanthropy ought to moderate their critical pride, or religious intolerance.

At the time that the Gothic was fading in Europe, the American authors Nathaniel Hawthorne and Edgar Allan Poe produced an indigenous literature of the macabre, and in Europe the young Mary Shelley forever changed the direction of horror by marrying the atmosphere of Gothicism to contemporary concerns over the role of science in society in her novel *Frankenstein; or, the Modern Prometheus* (1818). Shelley's work attracted mixed reviews from the same types of critics who argued over the Gothic. Scott thought it a miracle of rare genius, but the more conservative John Croker raged that the foul book "fatigues the feelings without interesting the understanding; it gratuitously harasses the heart, and wantonly adds to the store, already too great, of painful sensations." He also thought Shelley was mentally ill, a frequent *ad hominem* complaint about horror authors.

Poe fared little better. A mid-nineteenth century biographical entry in Robert Chambers' *Book of Days* said that the master storyteller "lived, from the cradle to the grave, on the verge of madness, when he was not absolutely mad," and therefore his works were those of insanity. W. C. Brownell, the literary critic, complained in 1909 that Poe made "exclusive appeal to the nerves" and therefore did not write true literature. Fortunately, such opinions were balanced by critics like Charles Sears Baldwin and Paul Elmer More, who strove to enshrine Poe in the American pantheon of major authors. Poe's successors, Fitz-James O'Brien and Ambrose Bierce, benefited from the passion of their predecessor and experienced a more favorable reception.

Midcentury onward found horror turning away from Gothic ghostliness toward a series of monsters that bridged the gap between human and animal, much the way the contemporary Charles Darwin linked man to beast in his *Origin of Species* (1859). John Polidori, James Malcolm Rhymer, J. Sheridan Le Fanu, and Bram Stoker all penned well-known stories of vampires. H. G. Wells wrote of invaders from another world and mad scientists in this world. Robert Louis Stevenson created the dual life of *Dr. Jekyll and Mr. Hyde* (1886), and Arthur Machen wrote of the fluid line between humankind and monsters from beyond our ken. Such works were popularly successful, but the critics who wrote, analyzed, and safeguarded English literature were less taken with them. "Unrelieved horror is not satisfactory material for fiction," wrote the *Literary World* in a review of one of Conan Doyle's horror collections.

The humorist and critic Walter Parke wrote in 1872 that popular horror stories like Rhymer's *Varney the Vampire* (previously attributed to Thomas Preskett Prest) were "an evil of considerable magnitude, for which a remedy is urgently needed" because inexpensive "penny dreadful" paperback books encouraged impressionable youth to idolize monsters, highwaymen, pirates, and other unsavory characters, whereas true literature was uplifting and imparted morality and virtue. Even in praising J. Sheridan Le Fanu's lesbian vampire tale "Carmilla," a reviewer of 1881 warned parents to "make haste not to place [it] in the hands of the young." On the other hand, Bram Stoker's *Dracula* earned mixed but less outraged reception in London, and generally strong praise in the United States. Stevenson's *Jekyll* was near-universally heralded as a masterpiece of literature, perhaps because it wasn't aimed at *Varney*'s impressionable working-class audience but at intelligent, higher-class readers for whom it was less morally dangerous.

Perhaps no single work of the period was responsible for angrier commentary than Arthur Machen's "The Great God Pan" (1894), a story that received several good reviews from newspapers and a string of negative evaluations from the old guard, who considered it too "intense" and morally unfounded. "Too morbid to be the production of a healthy mind," wrote the elderly critic Richard Henry Stoddard. The art critic Harry Quilter seemed near to a paroxysm of rage upon reading "Pan," resorting to the implication of insanity:

> There is but one point of view from which such writing can be tolerated, and that is the point of view of those who deny that there is any obligation, any responsibility laid upon a writer not to produce unwholesome work.... Why should we tolerate in our fiction that which we could not tolerate in our conversation or our life? Why should we allow a novelist to describe abortions, moral and physical, which in reality would fill us with horror and disgust? ... Why should he be allowed, for the sake of a few miserable pounds, to cast into our midst these monstrous creations of his diseased brain?

But yet it sold, and was praised by those who represented the more libertine future beyond Victoria's reign. However, even the period's visual arts did not escape the critics' ire. J. Charles Cox savaged Philip Burne-Jones's *The Vampire* (1897), a painting depicting a female vampire atop a recumbent male—a subversive inversion of traditional vampire stories—as "uselessly morbid." This, one must remember, came in the context of a culture besotted by death, which preserved *post mortem* photographs of the dead as treasured keepsakes, and whose exemplar, Queen Victoria, spent most of her life in mourning.

Nearer the nineteenth century's end and into the twentieth century, authors produced a volume of ghost stories unparalleled before and largely unmatched since. This was mostly in response to the Spiritualist movement, a belief originating in the United States which held that the souls of the dead could be contacted through "mediums," women (and some men) who had the gift to act as receivers for their energies and could channel them by rapping on tables, talking in trances, or automatic writing. Such beliefs fueled the market for ghostly fiction to compliment the belief in ghostly fact. These stories, more traditional than the monsters and hallowed by more than a century of Gothic tradition, received greater critical praise, if not acceptance.

In 1898 Henry Wysham Lanier commended Henry James's *The Turn of the Screw* (1898), saying it "puts to shame by its penetrating force and quiet ghastliness the commonplace, unreal 'horrors' of the ordinary ghost-story." Ten years later Ward Clark praised Gouverneur Morris's ghostly collection *The Footprint* (1908), but warned that "morbid efforts have no rightful place in our healthy Anglo-Saxon literature" so the author had best write stories "more like those that the great American public is used to reading," that is, sentimental romances. In 1910 Frederic Taber Cooper wrote off Robert Hichens's ghost story "How Love Came to Professor Guildea" (1900) simply as "a hideous bit of morbidity." With such views, it was no wonder then that Olivia Howard Dunbar proclaimed "The Decay of the Ghost in Fiction" in 1905 and hoped for a revitalization of the ghost story at some future date.

On the eve of the First World War, scholars and critics had only just begun to see Gothic novels, monster stories, and ghost tales as part and parcel of a single genre, horror. Before this, the literature of fear had not yet been clearly distinguished from related works in tales of mystery and detection (both Poe and Conan Doyle, for example, were active in both fields), or science fiction and fantasy (which are not wholly separate even today). Dorothy Scarborough offered the era's most thorough exploration of horror in her book *The Supernatural in Modern English Fiction* (1917), though for her the presence of the supernatural was the *sine qua non* of her study—"a significant and vital phase of our literature." As a result, her work did not distinguish between horror, fantasy, mystery, fairy tales, or religious works, as all included elements from a realm beyond the material plane. Any opus that could call *Ben-Hur* and *Dracula* part and parcel of the same species of literature left something to be desired.

That was where horror stood as World War I ground to its unsatisfactory conclusion. In the years that followed, the American horror master H. P. Lovecraft (1890–1937) would finally define the horror genre as such in his miniature masterpiece *Supernatural Horror in Literature* (1927). Unique to Lovecraft, this definition of the genre was that which all critics today take as self-evident: it is literature dealing with the emotion of fear, or as Lovecraft put it: "The one test of the really weird is simply this—whether or not there be excited in the reader a profound sense of dread, and of contact with unknown spheres and powers; a subtle attitude of awed listening, as if for the beating of black wings or the scratching of outside shapes and entities on the known universe's utmost rim."[3] Though Lovecraft scrupulously exempted the non-supernatural tale of gruesomeness, such as some of Poe's studies of morbid psychology, horror would eventually come to embrace forms of earth-bound terror along with the supernatural horror he favored.

But Lovecraft's own fiction—the Cthulhu Mythos—did not receive the same reception as Ambrose Bierce, or even Arthur Machen. Those authors and the others whose work is examined in these pages, along with their critics, published in best-selling books, in well-circulated major magazines and even in big city newspapers. During the nineteenth century horror literature was a division of mainstream discourse, at or near the head of the column of authors marching into battle to compete for readers' and critics' attention. In time, its works became part of the standard literary canon. In Lovecraft's time, though, horror was in retreat. It no longer commanded the best magazines or the attention of the greatest critics. Instead, horror stories moved down-market into the so-called "pulp" magazines, those low-cost publications aimed at a lower-class mass audience, where horror became a genre in the worst sense of the word, competing with (and losing to) such rivals as the detective genre, the Western genre, and the railroad genre. Quality had not diminished—in fact Lovecraft's fiction rivaled that of Poe as horror's finest—but it lost respectability, which it never fully regained, as the vogue for realist and modern fiction led critics to reject any genre tainted with the stench of Victorianism. Forever after horror would remain in a literary ghetto, separate but unequal, bastard cousin to literary fiction, the "true" literature.

But for a glorious century and a half, from *The Castle of Otranto* through the guns of August, horror literature was at the forefront of English letters (if not critical respectability). For this reason, if for no other, the opinions and ideas of those who experienced this literary phenomenon first hand are vital to understanding the development of a genre now too often seen as a bloody mess on the fringes of the respectable. I hope this volume goes some ways toward resurrecting the forgotten history of horror, and the ways contemporaries viewed the developing genre.

About the Book

Those who wrote and published between the 1750s and 1917, the years covered by this volume, produced an impossibly vast collection of texts, so vast in fact that no one could seriously attempt to read all of it. It seems somewhat strange to say this today, given the vastness of our modern output, which each year dwarfs all the written material of the nineteenth century. Nevertheless, it is true, and as a result much of the nineteenth century (if I may abbreviate the period's name somewhat) conversation about horror has understandably faded away as ever more modern critiques and analyses take their place. Much of the material included in this volume has remained out of print since its first publication one or two centuries ago, confined to dusty library shelves or even microfilm, virtually lost. Because there was no defined horror genre in the nineteenth century, these pieces were not indexed as criticism thereof; and Victorian tables of contents being what they were, discovering their very existence was at times a trying task. For this reason, if for no other, this volume returns these critical masterpieces to print in one accessible place.

Because of the quantity of literary criticism the Victorians produced, I tried to follow some rules to govern selection of materials for this book to prevent any one author from monopolizing space and to provide a diversity of opinions on a range of topics, both well known and obscure.

1. I have limited this volume to non-fiction works.
2. I have given the majority of space to pieces covering literature, with occasional forays into drama, the visual arts, and so on.
3. I have restricted the material covered to discussion and criticism of published works. This is not a book about writing horror fiction, so I have excluded horror authors' diary entries, letters, and explications of their own work or the writing process.
4. I have limited each author reprinted in the volume to two pieces to provide a greater range of opinion and have limited the number of pieces dealing primarily with any one horror story or author to cover a greater range of works.
5. Lastly, I have favored out-of-print or rare pieces at the expense of frequently reprinted works. A few exceptional pieces, like Harry Quilter's "The Gospel of Intensity," are reproduced in full even though the specific criticism of horror is limited to a portion of the article because the cumulative effect of the argument and the context in which it is delivered are as important as the specific criticisms themselves.

Of course, no book of literary criticism can be comprehensive either in the scope of literature surveyed or in the range of criticism presented, and this book makes no claim to be definitive, only useful and, I hope, entertaining.

I have divided the book into several categories—by no means definitive—that provide a loose framework for collecting horror criticism. The first section, "Fear, Terror, and Supernatural," provides a background for the development of horror. The next section, which I call "The Gothics and Their Successors," covers the first wave of horror writers. Following that, we turn to "Poe and His Successors" and focus on the American (and one French) writers who produced short fiction in Poe's macabre vein. Next we explore "Monsters of the Gilded Age," which focuses on stories of vampires and other beastly creatures. "Fin de Siècle Science, Detection and Terror" explores the relationship between horror, science fiction, and mystery and detective stories at century's end. "Ghosts and Kindred Horrors" looks at the Spiritualist-inspired ghostly fiction of the late nineteenth and early twentieth centuries. A final section, "Toward a Horror Genre," presents pieces that attempt to define the literature of fear as a distinct literary tradition.

I have headed each article or excerpt with a brief explanation of its context, providing background on the author(s) or work(s) discussed in the piece, a brief biography of the article's author (when information is known—some authors have vanished into the mists of time), and the original place of publication for the article. I have also equipped the articles with a few explanatory notes (superscript lowercase letters) for now-obscure references or un-documented quotations; I have presumed the reader is at least somewhat familiar with horror literature and has an awareness of its major authors and their works so lengthy annotation of these would be unnecessary. For convenience, I have included an appendix with a chronology of the major pieces of horror literature discussed in these pages for ease of reference.

The pieces you are about to read cover the full range of the history of horror, and they represent a diversity of opinions. Here you will find articles from newspapers and magazines, scholarly criticism, excerpts from popular and academic books, and a few personal letters, poems, and advertisements. The writers encountered here loved horror, hated it, thought it high art, or considered it dangerous, vulgar, and unworthy. In other words, the critics of the nineteenth century were every bit the same as the critics of our own day. Their thoughts about the literature of fear are very much with us today, and continue to define the way modern society views horror. Their praise of the genre's imagination helped canonize Victorian horror among the classics of English literature, and their rage at horror's violence, sexuality, and vulgarity echoes our own discomfort with the genre's excesses and hackwork.

To take but one example: When the National Book Foundation awarded current grand master of horror Stephen King a National Book

Award in 2003 for his contribution to American letters, Yale professor and literary critic Harold Bloom exclaimed, "He is a man who writes what used to be called penny dreadfuls. That they could believe that there is any aesthetic accomplishment or signs of an inventive human intelligence is simply a testimony of their own idiocy."[4] How far was this from W. C. Brownell's complaint that Poe lacked substance, or Harry Quilter's claim that the morbid was not true art?

Alternately, though, Victorian horror criticism reminds us how much we lose when we forget the history and traditions that underpin the genre. In this volume sits a 1908 discussion—written by a man of the cloth—of the tradition of the Christmas ghost story, "that strange chill of the blood, that creeping kind of feeling all over you, which is one of the enjoyments of Christmastide." Contrast that with the recent furor of fundamentalist religious groups outraged that horror movies played in theaters on Christmas Day: "It's not enough to ignore and omit Christmas, but now it has to be offended, insulted and desecrated.... Our most sacred holiday, actually a holy day, is being assaulted."[5] Ignorant of history, this vitriol has become an annual event sponsored by the same groups who preach a return to the moral virtue of past centuries.

Therefore, to review the history of horror is to avoid repeating and fighting anew the same battles waged one or two centuries ago. To engage the critics of the nineteenth century is to view horror through a different set of cultural assumptions and a different framework of critical theory—in other words, to find something new and different among the very old and to commune for a moment with a past that, like the best horror monsters, refuses to stay dead.

Notes

1. Lytton Strachey, *Eminent Victorians* (New York: G. Putnam's Sons, 1918), v.
2. Ibid.
3. H. P. Lovecraft, *The Annotated Supernatural Horror in Literature*, edited by S. T. Joshi (New York: Hippocampus Press, 2000), 23.
4. David D. Kirkpatrick, "A Literary Award for Stephen King," *The New York Times*, September 15, 2003, E1, E5.
5. "Black Christmas Not Merry for Religious Groups," *CBC*, December 15, 2006 <http://www.cbc.ca/arts/story/2006/12/15/black-christmas-protest.html>.

A Note on the Text

The following pieces are presented as they were written, with only obvious typographical errors corrected. Otherwise, I have retained the original spelling, syntax, and punctuation of the material presented here except where indicated with square brackets. Therefore, since these pieces were written by many hands over a century and a half, there is considerable variation in mechanics from piece to piece. As a concession to modernity, though, I have removed the spaces originally placed around quotation marks and before semicolons, exclamation points, and question marks. Except where indictated, the period illustrations have been added by me and are not original to the text. My notes are superscript lowercase letters and are collected at the end of each selection under "Notes." Notes that are original to a selection are indicated by asterisks or superscript numbers and appear as footnotes.

1. Fear, Terror, and the Supernatural

The anthropologist Alexander F. Chamberlain (1865–1914) was born in Great Britain but spent much of his life in the United States and Canada. He earned the United States' first Ph.D. in anthropology under the tutelage of Franz Boas. Chamberlain's great interest was the relationship between anthropology and psychology, which he put to some use in discussing the origins of the words humans use to describe various states of fear, a vocabulary of terror that defines that way we view horror. His scholarly analysis "On the Words for 'Fear'" first appeared in January 1899.

On the Words for "Fear" in Certain Languages: A Study in Linguistic Psychology*

ALEX F. CHAMBERLAIN, PH.D.,
CLARK UNIVERSITY, WORCESTER, MASS.

In a previous essay[1] the writer discussed anger-words, and reference to this will be necessary since not a few fear-words are akin to those used to denote anger.

I. *Fear*, if we trust the etymology of its English name, is "*an experience;*" Skeat tells us that the word was "originally used of the *perils* and *experiences*; of a way-*faring.*" The Anglo-Saxon *fáer* meant "a sudden peril, danger, panic, fear;" cognate are Icelandic *fár*, "bale, harm, mischief," Old

---

*Alex F. Chamberlain, "On the Words for 'Fear' in Certain Languages: A Study in Linguistic Psychology," *American Journal of Psychology* X, no. 2 (January 1899): 302–305.

1. *Amer. Jour. Psychol.*, vol. VI, pp. 585–592.

High German *fára*, *vàr*, "treason, danger, fright," Modern German *Gefahr*, "danger, peril, risk." Related also are: Latin *periculum*, "peril, trial, danger" (from *perior*, the root of *peritus*, "experienced, skilled"), *experientia*, "experience, trial, proof;" Greek πειρα, "attempt, stratagem, trick," περάω "I go through." The common radical of all these terms is the Indo-European root Per, "to pass through, to travel, to *fare* (as our own English word from the same stock has it)." In Old Norse *fár* has the additional signification of "plague, pestilence, misfortune," which may go to somewhat explain our expression "a plague of fear." *Fear*, then, emphasizes "what one has *passed* through."

II. "All of a *tremble*" is a popular description of the state of fear or terror, and not a few of our fear-words contain this primitive idea. We say "*trembling, shaking, quaking* with fear," and these expressions find their analogues in many other tongues. George Fox tells us in his "Journal" that "Justice Bennet [in 1650] was the first to call us Quakers, because I bade him quake and tremble at the word of the Lord," and all over the world the "fear of the Lord" has been largely associated with *quaking* and *trembling*.

The English word *terror* (French *terreur*, Latin *terror*), goes back to the same root which gave birth to Latin *terrere* (older form, *tersere*), "to dread, to be afraid," and, originally, "to tremble;" Russian *triasti* (*triasate*), "to shake, to shiver;" Lithuanian *triszëti*, "to tremble;" Sanskrit *tras*, "to tremble, to be afraid," *trása*, "terror"—the radical of all being Indo-European *ters*, "to tremble, to be afraid." Of similar meaning, ultimately are *tremor* and cognate words derived from the Latin, and the derivatives of Greek Τρὲω, "I tremble, quake, fear, dread, am afraid of."

The German *Furcht* (the Middle High German *vorhte* signified "fear, anxiety, apprehension") is the abstract of the verb *fürchten*, cognate with Gothic *faúrhtjan*, "to fear, to be afraid of," to which is related the adjective-participle *faúrhts*, "fearful, timid," *faúrhtei*, "fear." The Teutonic radical *forh*, together, perhaps, with the roots of Latin *querquerus*, "shivering with cold," and Greek χαρχαίρω, "I tremble," goes back to the Indo-European *perk* or *qerk*, "to tremble." Another word embodying the same idea is Gothic *reiro*, "tremble, terror"—*reiran*, "to tremble." To "tremble like an aspen" is a very ancient Indo-European figure of speech. The Latin *pavor*, "quaking, trembling, throbbing with desire, joy, fear," "anxiety, fear, dread,—the god of fear is personified as *Pavor*,—to be afraid, to fear, to tremble," and the Greek Φόβος, with all the *phobias* to which it has given rise in the various civilized languages, have at their base radicals which signify "to tremble." The corresponding verbs in Greek Φόβέω and Φἐβοηαι are related to Sanskrit *bhí*, "fear," *bibhêti*, "he is afraid," Lithuanian *bàimé*, " fear," *bijétis*, "to be afraid," *bajùs*, "terrible," *baisà*, "terror," while the modern German *beben*, "to tremble, quake," goes back to the same Indo-European radical.

We speak in English of "shivering with terror, or fear," and it is interesting to note that in the "Gest Hystoriale of the Destruction of Troy," an English Romance *circa* 1390 A.D., we find "Achilles at the choice men *cheuert* (shivered) for anger."

The French word, *craindre*, "to fear," belongs here also, being derived from the Latin *tremere*.

The radical meaning of the English *shudder* is to "tremble."

III. Another closely related series of words is that in which the basal idea is *agitation, movement, stir*. Here belong the Latin *metus*, "agitation, anxiety, fear, dread, terror," *metuere*, "to fear, to be afraid of,"—allied perhaps to *mōtus*, "moved, affected, disturbed." Trepidation,—the Latin *trepidatio* signified "confused hurry, alarm, consternation, terror, trepidation,"— has a curious etymology. Festus, the ancient grammarian, glosses the old Latin *trepit* by *uertit*, adding the remark "unde *trepidus* et *trepidatio*, quia turbatione mens uertitur." The Latin adjective *trepidus*, "trembling, alarmed, fearful, anxious," etc., would then seem to signify "in a state of disturbance, as if the mind is being continually turned about or agitated (Skeat)." The Old Latin *trepere* is cognate with Greek Τρὲπειυ, "to turn," and also with Latin *torquere* (whence *torture*), the basis of all being the Indo-European radical *t-rk*, "to turn, to twist." So when we speak of being tortured by our fears we are but repeating a very old figure of speech. A coward we often say "*writhes* with fear."

IV. A common expression in English is "to *start* with fear," with which may be compared the colloquial "to almost *jump* out of one's boots;" we have also the derivative "to *startle*." The same idea is at the basis of the modern High German *Schreck*, "terror, fright, fear, horror," the Old High German verb *scrĕckón* signifying, "to start up, to leap, to hop," the Middle High German substantive *schric*, "a sudden start, terror," and the causative verb *schrecken*, "to cause to start, to make afraid." The radical is *skrik*, "to leap, to move suddenly, to start."

A cognate idea resides in the Modern German *sich entsetzen*, "to be startled at, to be terrified, to shudder," and the substantive *Entsetzen*, "terror, dread, horror, fright." The Middle High German *entsetzen*

Hamlet, Prince of Denmark. Chamberlain notes that Shakespeare has the ghost of Hamlet's father describe the symptoms of fear. In this 1796 illustration, we see Hamlet, Horatio, and Marcellus encountering the ghost. The use of the supernatural in Shakespeare is typical of the way horrific elements were deployed before there was a formal horror genre, with ghosts and monsters appearing as an element of the story rather than the focus of the tale (Library of Congress, Prints and Photographs Division, LC-USZ62-115274).

signified, "to cast down, to disconcert, to fear, to be afraid of," the Old High German *intsizzen* (there is also a M. H. G. from *entsitzen*), "to come out of one's seat, to lose one's composure, to fear, to be afraid of." In Gothic we find *andasēts*, "horrible," *andsitan*, "to be terrified." These words are all based upon the Indo-European root *sed*, "to sit," with a privative, or disjunctive prefix (Mod. German *ent*, Gothic *and*). The idea at the root of *Entsetzen*, is "starting from one's seat in terror."

V. The sinking of the heart and of the vital organs generally is a familiar conception of "fear" among primitive peoples, and one which appears very often in picture-writing and sign-language, as Col. Mallery has pointed out. Our own language furnishes cognate expressions, "to have one's heart in one's boots," "to feel one's heart sink," etc. Being "downhearted" is thus a very early form of fear.

Perhaps, here belong also the Yoruba (a West African language) *aí ya fò mi*, "I am afraid," literally, "the heart jumps me," *daiyafo*, "to frighten," etc., although the jumping is here the other way. We say, analogously, in

English "my heart leaped into my mouth," in speaking of certain aspects of fear.

VI. The ghost in "Hamlet" describes several of the known symptoms of fear:

> "I could a tale unfold, whose lightest word
> Would harrow up thy soul, freeze thy young blood,
> Make thy two eyes, like stars, start from their spheres,
> Thy knotted and combined locks to part,
> And each particular hair to stand on end,
> Like quills upon the fretful porpentine."

The last mentioned symptom is illustrated by the etymology of the word *horror*. The Latin horror, "a standing on end, bristling, terror, dread," and *horrere*, "to stand erect, to bristle, to be afraid, astonished, amazed, to startle with fear," etc., as the older form (*horsere*) of the verb (cf. *hirsutus*, "rough, hairy, shaggy") shows, refer to the "bristling of the hair in fear." In Sanskrit *hirsh*, "to bristle," is said of the hair, "especially as a token of anger or pleasure" (Skeat).

Virgil refers to the bristling of the hair in the *Aen.*, II, 774:
Obstupui, steteruntqne comæ, et vox faucibus hæsit.

VII. The "freezing of the blood" finds cognate expression in some of our fear-words, and besides we speak often enough of "the cold shivers" of fear, and "the cold sweat" that accompanies it. Our English *afraid* is the past participle of the verb *affray* "to frighten," which Skeat traces through the Old French *effreier* (effraier, esfreër), "to frighten," to a Low Latin *exfrigidare* (from *frigus*, "cold"), "to freeze with terror,"—in Latin frigidus meant "dead or stiffened with cold or fright," and Horace even uses it in the sense of "fearful." A common phrase in English is *"numbed* with fear."

VIII. Our English *dismay*, "to terrify, to discourage," comes, according to the Skeat, from Old French *dismayer* (cf. Spanish *desmayar*, "to dismay, to dishearten, to be discouraged, to lose heart"), which seems to have been supplanted very early by the verb *esmayer*, "to dismay, to terrify, to strike powerless"—the intransitive sense of which "to lose power, to faint, to be discouraged," would appear to be the older. *Desmayer* and *esmayer*, according to the best authorities, are derived from the Old High German *magan* (Mod. Germ. *mögen*, Mod. Engl. *may*), with the Latin prefixes dis-, ex-. The "loss of power" is the basal idea here. From Old French *esmayer* comes Modern French *émoi*, "fright, terror." Cognate also is the Italian *sma-*

gare, "to lose courage." The English word *misgiving* has somewhat of the idea in *dismay*. With us, in English "to lose heart" is "to give way to fear."

IX. The Latin *consternatio* (whence our consternation), signified "consternation, fright, tumult"; the corresponding verb is *consternare*, "to stretch on the ground, to prostrate, to terrify, to alarm, to dismay"—the participle *consternatus* meaning "cast down, prostrate, frightened." The basal idea is seen in Latin *sternere*, "to throw down, to throw to the ground," from the Indo-European radical *st-r*, "to spread out." We employ a somewhat similar figure when we speak of "*abject* fear."

X. We often speak of persons being "rooted to the ground with fear," "transfixed with fear," etc.; from fright people often stand "stock still." In Gothic we find *usgaisjan*, "to terrify," *usgeisnan*, "to be terrified," cognate with Old Norse *geiska-fullr*, "filled with terror," and Lithuanian *gaïszti*, "to swoon." Related also is the Latin *hærere* (older form *hæsere*), "to cling to, to stick, to be unable to move away"—the radical of the whole series being Indo-European *ghais*, "to stick." We still say of a valiant man that "he will not *stick* at anything."

The Irish parliamentarian and philosopher Edmund Burke (C. 1729–1797) is today remembered for his defense of the American colonies' claims in the House of Commons during the Revolutionary War. However, Burke was also a keen philosopher with a well-developed theory of aesthetics. In *On the Sublime and Beautiful* (1757), the young Burke laid out a theory of the sublime that found in terror a source of the awe that transcends mundane experience. This work was, in essence, the birth certificate of the horror genre, influencing Horace Walpole and the later Gothic writers who adopted his set-pieces of terror (darkness, dungeons, and so on) in their novels.

Below are a few relevant passages from the sections on "Terrour" and "Pain" to give a sample of this work. I have omitted a few footnotes that refer to other parts of the opus not here reproduced. The interested reader should, of course, consult the whole of this fascinating treatise.

Excerpt from On the Sublime and Beautiful*
EDMUND BURKE

No passion so effectually robs the mind of all its powers of acting and reasoning as *fear*. For fear being an apprehension of pain or death, it

---

*Edmund Burke, "On the Sublime and Beautiful," in *The Works of the Right Hon. Edmund Burke*, vol. 1 (London: Holdsworth and Ball, 1834), 38, 60–61.

Excerpt from On the Sublime and Beautiful (Burke) 19

EDW.D KELLY, A MAGICIAN.
in the Act of invoking the Spirit of a Deceased Person

Edward Kelly, A Magician. Edmund Burke's theory of terror's relationship to the sublime inspired many writers of Gothic fiction. In this 1806 depiction of the Elizabethan sorcerer-alchemist Edward Kelly (or Kelley) (1555–1597) raising the dead, we see a number of typically Gothic elements of terror at work: a dark and stormy night, Gothic architecture, a graveyard, the occult, and a shrouded corpse. These Burkean set-pieces continue to delineate the territory of horror, even after becoming clichés through overuse.

operates in a manner that resembles actual pain. Whatever therefore is terrible, with regard to sight, is sublime too, whether this cause of terrour be endued with greatness of dimensions or not; for it is impossible to look on anything as trifling, or contemptible, that may be, dangerous. There are many animals, who though far from being large, are yet capable of raising ideas of the sublime, because they are considered as objects of terrour. As serpents and poisonous animals of almost all kinds. And to things of great dimensions, if we annex an adventitious idea of terrour, they become without comparison greater. A level plain of a vast extent on land, is certainly no mean idea; the prospect of such a plain may be as extensive as a prospect of the ocean: but can it ever fill the mind with anything so great as the ocean itself? This is owing to several causes but it is owing to none more than this, that the ocean is an object of no small terrour. Indeed, terrour is in all cases whatsoever, either more openly or latently, the ruling principle of the sublime.[...]

I have before observed, that whatever is qualified to cause terrour is a foundation capable of the sublime; to which I add, that not only these, but many things from which we cannot probably apprehend any danger, have a similar effect, because they operate in a similar manner. I observed too, that whatever produces pleasure, positive and original pleasure, is fit to have beauty ingrafted on it. Therefore, to clear up the nature of these qualities, it may be necessary to explain the nature of pain and pleasure on which they depend. A man who suffers under violent bodily pain, (I suppose the most violent, because the effect may be the more obvious), I say a man in great pain has his teeth set, his eyebrows are violently contracted, his forehead is wrinkled, his eyes are dragged inwards, and rolled with great vehemence, his hair stands on end, the voice is forced out in short shrieks and groans, and the whole fabric totters. Fear, or terrour, which is an apprehension of pain or death, exhibits exactly the same effects, approaching in violence to those just mentioned, in proportion to the nearness of the cause, and the weakness of the subject. This is not only so in the human species; but I have more than once observed in dogs, under an apprehension of punishment, that they have writhed their bodies, and yelped, and howled, as if they had actually felt the blows. From hence I conclude, that pain and fear act upon the same parts of the body, and in the same manner, though somewhat differing in degree; that pain and fear consist in an unnatural tension of the nerves; that this is sometimes accompanied with an unnatural strength, which sometimes suddenly changes into an extraordinary weakness; that these effects often come on alternately, and are sometimes mixed with each other. This is the nature of all convulsive agitations, especially in weaker subjects, which are the most liable to the severest impressions of pain and fear. The only difference between pain and terrour is, that things which cause pain operate on the mind by the intervention of the body; whereas things that cause terrour generally affect the bodily organs by the operation of the mind suggesting the danger; but both agreeing, either primarily or secondarily, in producing a tension, contraction, or violent emotion of the nerves, they agree likewise in everything else. For it appears very clearly to me, from this, as well as from many other examples, that when the body is disposed, by any means whatsoever, to such emotions as it would acquire by the means of a certain passion; it will of itself excite something very like that passion in the mind.[...]

Having considered terrour as producing an unnatural tension and certain violent emotions of the nerves; it easily follows, from what we have just said, that whatever is fitted to produce such a tension must be productive of a passion similar to terrour, and consequently must be a source of the sublime, though it should have no idea of danger connected with it. So that little remains towards showing the cause of the sublime, but to show that the instances we have given of it in the second part relate to such things as are fitted by nature to produce this sort of tension, either by the primary operation of the mind or the body. With regard to such things as effect by the associated idea of danger, there can be no doubt but that they produce terrour, and act by some modification of that passion; and that terrour, when sufficiently violent, raises the emotions of the body just mentioned, can as little be doubted. But if the sublime is built on terrour, or some passion like it, which has pain for its object, it is previously proper to inquire how any species of delight can be derived from a cause so apparently contrary to it. I say *delight*, because, as I have often remarked, it is very evidently different in its cause, and in its own nature, from actual and positive pleasure.

Providence has so ordered it, that a state of rest and inaction, however it may flatter our indolence, should be productive of many inconveniences; that it should generate such disorders, as may force us to have recourse to some labour, as a thing absolutely requisite to make us pass our lives with tolerable satisfaction; for the nature of rest is to suffer all the parts of our bodies to fall into a relaxation, that not only disables the members from performing their functions, but takes away the vigorous tone of fibre which is requisite for carrying on the natural and necessary secretions. At the same time, that in this languid inactive state, the nerves are more liable to the most horrid convulsions, that when they are sufficiently braced and strengthened. Melancholy, dejection, despair, and often self-murder, is the consequence of the gloomy view we take of things in this relaxed state of body. The best remedy for all these evils is exercise or *labour;* and labour is a surmounting of *difficulties,* an exertion of the contracting power of the muscles; and as such resembles pain, which consists in tension or contraction, in everything but degree. Labour is not only requisite to preserve the coarser organs in a state fit for their functions; but it is equally necessary to those finer and more delicate organs, on which, and by which, the imagination, and perhaps the other mental powers, act. Since it is probable, that not only the inferior parts of the soul, as the passions are called, but the understanding itself, makes use of some fine corporeal instruments in its operation; though what they are, and where they are, may be somewhat hard to settle; but that it does make use of such, appears from hence; that a long exercise of the mental powers induces a remarkable lassitude of the whole body; and, on the other hand, that great bodily labour, or pain, weakens, and sometimes actually destroys, the mental faculties. Now, as a due exercise is essential to the coarse muscular parts of the constitution, and that without this rousing they would become languid and diseased, the very same rule holds with regard to those finer parts we have mentioned; to have them in proper order, they must be shaken and worked to a proper degree.

Daniel Defoe (C. 1660–1731) is best known as the author of *Robinson Crusoe* and *Moll Flanders*, but among his lesser known works is the early ghost story "The Apparition of Mrs. Veal." In this 1723 letter to publisher John Applebee ("Mr. App") Defoe explains the peculiar pleasures of telling "dismal stories." Though his comments refer to real-life horrors lately in the news, especially the fear that the plague that felled tens of thousands in France (1720) would spread to England, his views apply equally to fictional terrors.

On the Pleasure of Writing Dismal Stories, Exciting Surprize and Horror*

DANIEL DEFOE

A. J., Nov. 23.—Sir, I find it very much for my Diversion, and sometimes for my Instruction, to converse with the *Men-Gossips* of the Town. They are very useful People in their Generation I assure you; and, to my particular Satisfaction, we have a tolerable Number, (I was going to say an Intolerable Number,) of them in our Neighbourhood.

Among the many useful Observations which I have made in my long Conversation among these People, this is one, and none of the least improving; Namely, that tho' they love to have a Story of any Kind to tell, and rather than quite Starve their Friends, or make their Society barren and Empty, they will carefully coin every now and then a Tale for them; or, in good Husbandry, and for the Exercise of their Wit make the same Story serve two or three Times by telling it several Ways. I say, tho' they love to have a Story of any kind to tell, yet their principal Gust is to tell bad News. As many Gentlemen will strain a Tale to its utmost Extent, nay, add a little to it to make People laugh; nay, but to obtain the Favour of a Grin; so these will go five Times as far to make them cry.

If they can but make your Blood run chill, or give suitable Horror to their Friends, then their Taste is gratified to the full; nay, I find, nothing relishes with them like it. They take the most complete Pleasure when their Friends find the greatest Surprize; and therefore you find every Story they tell grows worse and worse every Time they tell it. If they give you an Account of a Robbery anywhere, but especially if it be out of the reach of present Enquiry; they fail not to add some Murther to it, or at least something very barbarous. If a Fire, they make it burn more Houses than perhaps were in the Town, or Stacks of Corn than were in the Parish; and Ten to one, but they burn some of the poor People alive for you, or at least half roast them, for the particular Diversion, that is to say, Horror of their Readers.

Now the Fact of this is not so strange, (the frequency of it indeed makes

---

*Daniel Defoe, "On the Pleasure of Writing Dismal Stories, Exciting Surprize and Horror," in *Daniel Defoe: His Life, and Recently Discovered Writings: Extending from 1716 to 1729, vol. III: The Second Volume of His Writings* by William Lee (London: John Camden Hotten, 1869), 207–209.

it familiar,) but the Fountain of it, the Principle from whence it proceeds is very occult, and hard to be accounted for in Nature; and I send it to you Mr. *App*, that the World may judge of it a little, when perhaps some Friendly Reader skilled in the Sympathetick Powers of Nature, may bestow a Line of good Teaching upon us, and tell us from what strange thwart Lines in Nature, this unnatural Disposition can proceed.

 I hope no body that Converses with the polite World will question the Fact; I mean, that the Truth of the Thing is really so. Alas! I can send them to so many of my Neighbours; nay, and perhaps of your Neighbours too, for Examples of the Practice,—nay, to your Brother Journal Men too,—that I can soon give Demonstration of the Thing to general Satisfaction. I'll give you but one Example for the present, and refer you to further Testimonies hereafter; and this is about writing dismal News from Foreign Parts. How diligent were our News-Writers, and indeed, some who carried on the same Thing by the Mouth, to make us believe the Plague in *France*[a] spread this way! How often did they tell us it was come to this Place, and t'other Place, many a Score, nay, Hundred Mile nearer than ever it was found to have been! What Desolation did they tell of! And how many hundred, nay hundred Thousand People did they bury of it, more than ever died! Nay, more sometimes than the Towns mentioned had in them to Bury, tho' they should have buried all the People alive that Inhabited them.

 To bring it nearer home, our present Case gives a Taste of the same Temper. With what Diligence do they labour even just now, to have us believe that the Plague is broken out in *Portugal*, and that at *Lisbon* 25,000 People have died in two Months, which, in a Word, were it true, would soon leave *Lisbon* as Desolate of People almost as old *Carthage*! Nor do these Messengers of evil Tidings consider at all the mischievous Consequences, which such an Alarm would have upon us in our foreign Commerce; and the Confusion, which the fright of it would put us all into at Home. The Consequence, more particularly to us, must be, that Immediately, if the Fact was true, and the Plague was actually broken out at *Lisbon*, we should prohibit Trade with the whole kingdom of *Portugal*, and all Intercourse, of Shipping at least; and they who are ignorant of what would be the Consequence of such a Prohibition, must be ignorant of this known Truth, (viz.) that *Portugal* is next to *Holland*, the Place to which the greatest Trade—for the Exportation of our Wool Manufactures—is carried on, and perhaps there is not a greater Branch of Trade in the World,—or where there is a greater return,—than to that small Kingdom for the Woollen Manufacture. This would immediately stop, the Want of it would be felt by the Poor throughout England, and especially by the Drugget and Cloth Trade of the West, the Shalloon Trade of the North, and above all by the Bay-Makers of *Colchester*.

But what is all this, to the Pleasure of telling a dismal Story? What do the People I am speaking of care who they Injure, or what sudden Damp they bring upon Trade, or what Disadvantages they put upon our Commerce, if they can gratify the Itch of a Talc? Were it a true Story indeed, the alarm would reach other Countries, as well as ours, and we should injure our Trade less; but to make us believe the Plague has begun there, when it is not, is but shutting the Door of Trade against us, and leaving it open to the *French* and *Dutch*, who being rightly informed, would be under no Alarm.

If it is Criminal to cry Fire in the City, when there is no Fire, because of the Hurry and Fright it puts the Neighbourhood into; if it be Criminal in the Camp for a Centinel upon Duty to fire his Musket when he is not Attacked, or sees no Enemy; what do these Men deserve, who give a false Alarm to a whole Nation, and for every Fever, or Sickly Season, which may happen Abroad, cry Fire? That is to say, Plague, which is worse; when upon a full Enquiry into it, they know nothing of the Matter.

Notes

a. An outbreak of plague felled nearly one hundred thousand in Marseilles and the surrounding area between 1720 and 1722. Marseilles authorities lifted the quarantine on a Syrian trading vessel under pressure from merchants, bringing the sickness into the city. The English, the government imposed strict controls to prevent the plague from reaching England, in what Charles F. Mullett has called "The Great English Plague Scare" of 1720–1723.

The Rev. Frederick W. Robertson (1816–1853) was among the most famous preachers in nineteenth century Britain. His well-known sermons at Trinity Chapel in Brighton attracted large and diverse audiences. In his sermon "The Prodigal and His Brother," preached at Trinity Chapel on February 21, 1853, Robertson relates the parable of the Prodigal Son (Luke 15: 11–32), the story of a wayward son who is welcomed home when he seeks his father's mercy, to the dismay of his brother who wishes to be rewarded for his loyalty. After describing the father's admonition that they should rejoice at the wayward youth's return to grace, as we see in this excerpt, Robertson explains how in his view a belief in the supernatural and the human capacity to feel terror are springboards to faith, and proof of God's manifest presence.

Excerpt from "The Prodigal and His Brother"*
FREDERICK W. ROBERTSON

The first truth exhibited in this parable is the alienation of man's heart from God. Homelessness, distance from our Father—that is man's state by nature in this world. The youngest son gathered all together and took his journey into a *far* country. Brethren, this is the history of worldliness. It is a state far from God; in other words, it is a state of homelessness. And now let us ask what that means. To English hearts it is not necessary to expound elaborately the infinite meanings which cluster round that blessed expression "home." Home is the one place in all this world where hearts are sure of each other. It is the place of confidence. It is the place where we tear off that mask of guarded and suspicious coldness which the world forces us to wear in self-defence, and where we pour out the unreserved communications of full and confiding hearts. It is the spot where expressions of tenderness gush out without any sensation of awkwardness and without any dread of ridicule. Let a man travel where he will, home is the place to which "his heart untravelled fondly turns." He is to double all pleasure there. He is there to divide all pain. A *happy home* is the single spot of rest which a man has upon this earth for the cultivation of his noblest sensibilities.

And now my brethren, if that be the description of home, is God's place of rest your home? Walk abroad and alone by night. That awful other world in the stillness and the solemn deep of the eternities above, is it your home? Those graves that lie beneath you, holding in them the infinite secret, and stamping upon all earthly loveliness the mark of frailty and change and fleetingness—are those graves the prospect to which in bright days and dark days you can turn without dismay? God in his splendours,—dare we feel with Him affectionate and familiar, so that trial comes softened by this feeling—it is my Father, and enjoyment can be taken with a frank feeling; my Father has given it me, without grudging, to make me happy? All that is having a home in God. Are we at home there? Why there is demonstration in our very childhood that we are not at home with that other world of God's. An infant fears to be alone, because he feels he is not alone. He trembles in the dark, because he is conscious of the presence of the world of spirits. Long before

---

*Frederick W. Robertson, "The Prodigal and His Brother," in *Sermons Preached at Trinity Chapel, Brighton*, vol. 1 (Leipzig: Bernhard Tauchnitz, 1861), 263–265.

he has been told tales of terror, there is an instinctive dread of the supernatural in the infant mind. It is the instinct which we have from childhood that gives us the feeling of another world. And mark, brethren, if the child is not at home in the thought of that world of God's, the deep of darkness and eternity is, around him—God's home, but not his home, for his flesh creeps. And that feeling grows through life; not the fear—when the child becomes a man he gets over fear—but the dislike. The man feels as much aversion as the child for the world of spirits.

Sunday comes. It breaks across the current of his worldliness. It suggests thoughts of death and judgment and everlasting existence. Is that home? Can the worldly man feel Sunday like a foretaste of his Father's mansion? If we could but know how many have come here to-day, not to have their souls lifted up heavenwards, but from curiosity, or idleness, or criticism, it would give us an appalling estimate of the number who are living in a far country, "having no hope and without God in the world."[a]

Notes

a. Ephesians 2:12.

The supernatural was the subject of great controversy in the nineteenth century, with scientific skeptics casting doubt on its existence and believers in Spiritualism proclaiming its manifest entry into the world of men. This anonymous 1897 article from *The Spectator*, as reprinted in the November 1897 *Current Literature*, the *Reader's Digest* of its day, explores late Victorian ideas about the supernatural and the literature of horror derived from it.

The Dread of the Supernatural*

THE SPECTATOR

Both those who believe and those who disbelieve in the notion that the veil between this world and the other is capable of being lifted agree in one thing. They all recognize the fact that most people feel fear, or something

*"The Dread of the Supernatural," *Current Literature: A Magazine of Contemporary Record* XXII, no. 5 (November 1897): 462–463.

Newmann's Wonderful Spirit Mysteries. Though the supernatural could be seen as a source of terror and dread, it was also the realm of mystery and awe. By the early twentieth century, stage magicians offered "spirit mysteries" as a lucrative part of their acts, imitating with illusions the supposedly real-life supernatural experiences of Spiritualist mediums, as this ad from around 1911 shows (Library of Congress, Prints and Photographs Division, LC-USZC4-13484).

akin to fear, at what they believe to be the occurrence of supernatural phenomena. There is here, therefore, a piece of ground which may be explored without any begging of the question as to whether the fear is caused by real ghosts or by trickery, by rats and water-pipes, or by genuine glimpses of the people of another world. One would like to know whether the fear felt is akin to that experienced when a man is frightened by a runaway horse or a fire or any other imminent risk of life, or whether it is something different in kind. Speaking broadly and without any minute consideration of the facts, one would say that ghost-fright did differ in kind from the fright that comes from active danger. Most people have, we imagine, at some time or other in their lives experienced that eerie, uncanny, creepy feeling which is associated with the possibility of contact with the supernatural. Yet few would declare that it was in any sense connected with the dread of loss of life or limb. The man or woman who wakes up in the middle of the night and hears strange noises—thumps, raps, clangs, and creakings—or sees lights or feels the touch of unseen hands, is probably very frightened, but the sense of bodily fear is not present. There is no dread of being killed. People in the agony of terror caused by dangerous accidents constantly call out that they are going to be killed, but we doubt if that is ever the case in the fright caused by haunted houses.... The fear caused by what is supposed to be a supernatural agency seems, then, to have in it some element not found in ordinary fear. If and when the haunting phenomena cause fear they seem to give a shock of quite special keenness.

Another strange thing about the dread of the supernatural is its greater power of transmission. One may, no doubt, read about hairbreadth escapes with a pleasing thrill of danger, and very sensitive people may even find it "trying" to hear how the hero of a mountain climb crawled along a ledge of rotten rock with a two thousand feet drop below and a sheer wall of cliff above, but no one is really terrified by this in the way that sensitive people are terrified by reading or hearing ghost-stories. People susceptible to such impressions not unfrequently find themselves in the position of Sir Walter Scott and Hannah More, who sat up telling ghost-stories till they were both afraid to go to bed. Unquestionably the fear which we call "creepiness" is much more easily kindled at second hand than the good honest dread of having one's skull split. Yet another curious fact about the form of fear we are discussing is its admitted unreasonableness and want of sufficient cause apparent to account for it. If a man is asked why he is afraid of standing in the line of fire when soldiers are shooting, or of doing any other dangerous thing, there is no sort of mystery about his answer. He tells you at once, "I am afraid of doing this or that because I don't want to be killed." If you ask him why he is afraid of sleeping in a haunted room, as in many cases he undoubtedly will be, even though perfectly sane and sufficiently brave, he will be unable to tell you. He will probably declare that he does not believe in ghosts, and does not believe, indeed, in any supernatural phenomena being permitted. Yet he will, if he is honest, add that there is no sort of uncertainty about his objection to sleeping in a room believed to be haunted. He may say, of course, that he could force himself on good grounds to submit to being frightened, but he will not deny the fright. If you ask him, further, what are the consequences of which he is afraid, he will, as we have said, be unable to tell you. He will admit that there is no fear of the figure said to haunt the room injuring him in any possible way, and he will laugh at the notion of low voices, or loud explosive raps, or touches from cold fingers doing him bodily damage. In the end, indeed, he will be forced to admit that what he is really afraid of is being frightened. "Experience tells us that these things, whatever they are, cause a very unpleasant form of terror in the human mind, and experience is backed up by a strong instinctive feeling in most men's minds. I don't know in the least why these things should cause alarm, but as they do I intend to avoid them." ... When a normally constituted man is made subject to an illusion either by being influenced beforehand by thrilling accounts of what he is likely to see, or else by some curious set of accidents and coincidences, it is only natural that he should be much disturbed in body and mind. The perfectly healthy organization abhors and resists illusions, and therefore when it is subject to them by some accident the reaction is very strongly marked....

There is yet another explanation of the mystery surrounding this dread of the supernatural which may be worth considering. It may be that man has been endowed with this almost universal horror of the supernatural because he was not meant to peep behind the veil. It can hardly be doubted that mankind in general would not be doing their true work if they were perpetually engaged in efforts to lift that veil. For what purpose was the veil interposed if not to prevent such prying? But granted that it would be a hindrance to man's development to traffic with the other world, or to learn too much about it at first hand, would not man be very likely to have developed a keen instinctive horror of any contact with the unseen world, just as many animals have an instinctive horror of plants that will injure them? Be that as it may, ... why so many of us should be afraid of things which we know will, under no circumstances, do us bodily harm, and which most of us sincerely believe have no existence whatever, is in any case a very curious problem.

Lafcadio Hearn (Koizumi Yakumo) (1850–1904) was a lecturer of English literature at the Imperial University in Tokyo. Born in Greece to Irish parents, Hearn eventually moved to Japan, where he gained citizenship in that Empire. A scholar of the supernatural, Hearn collected a number of Japanese ghost stories and legends; but in the following piece, first published in *Shadowings* (1900), he reflects on the strangeness and terror of Gothic architecture, something he found much more horrible than the exotic Orient he presented to the West in his books.

*Gothic Horror**

LAFCADIO HEARN

I

Long before I had arrived at what catechisms call the age of reason, I was frequently taken, much against my will, to church. The church was very old; and I can see the interior of it at this moment just as plainly as I saw it forty years ago, when it appeared to me like an evil dream. There I first learned to know the peculiar horror that certain forms of Gothic architecture can inspire.... I am using word "horror" in a classic sense,—in its antique meaning of ghostly fear.

On the very first day of this experience, my child-fancy could place the source of the horror. The wizened and pointed shapes of the windows immediately terrified me. In their outline I found the form of apparitions that tormented me in sleep;—and at once I began to imagine some dreadful affinity between goblins and Gothic churches. Presently, in the tall doorways, in the archings of the aisles, in the ribbings and groinings of the roof, I discovered other and wilder suggestions of fear. Even the façade of the organ, peaking high into the shadow above its gallery, seemed to me a frightful thing.... Had I been then suddenly obliged to answer the

---

*Lafcadio Hearn, "Gothic Horror," in Shadowings (Boston: Little, Brown, and Company, 1905), 213–222.

question, "What are you afraid of?" I should have whispered, "*Those points!*" I could not have otherwise explained the matter: I only knew that I was afraid of the "points."

Of course the real enigma of what I felt in that church could not present itself to my mind while I continued to believe in goblins. But long after the age of superstitious terrors, other Gothic experiences severally revived the childish emotion in so startling a way as to convince me that childish fancy could not account for the feeling. Then my curiosity was aroused; and I tried to discover some rational cause for the horror. I read many books, and asked many questions; but the mystery seemed only to deepen.

Books about architecture were very disappointing. I was much less impressed by what I could find in them than by references in pure fiction to the awfulness of Gothic art,—particularly by one writer's confession that the interior of a Gothic church, seen at night, gave him the idea of being inside the skeleton of some monstrous animal; and by a far-famed comparison of the windows of a cathedral to eyes, and of its door to a great mouth, "devouring the people." These imaginations explained little; they could not be developed beyond the phase of vague intimation: yet they

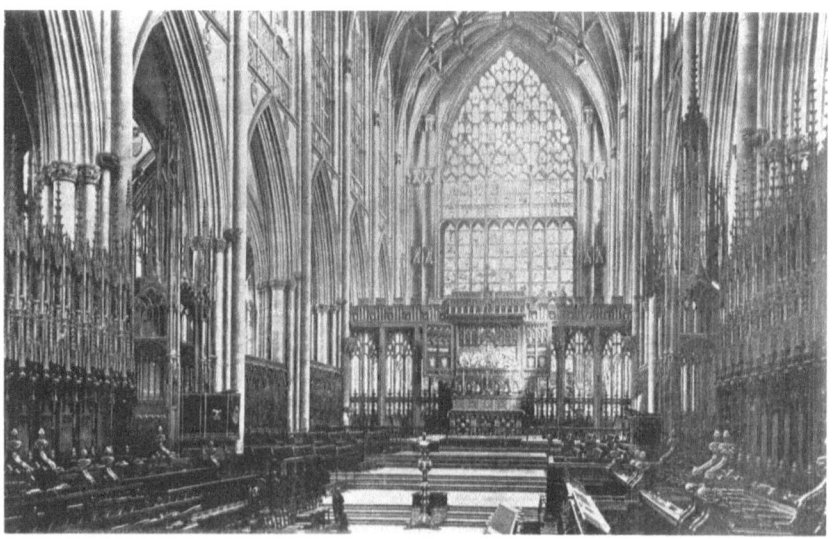

The Cathedral of York. Gothic architecture is distinguished by its pointed arches and graceful interplay of light and shadow. Gothic buildings, like the Cathedral of York seen here as it appeared in 1919, have been variously compared to stone forests and the skeletons of dead monsters. When Horace Walpole wedded Gothic architecture to ghostly fiction in The Castle of Otranto, *creating the Gothic novel, the style became forever associated with horror.*

stirred such emotional response that I felt sure they had touched some truth. Certainly the architecture of a Gothic cathedral offers strange resemblances to the architecture of bone; and the general impression that it makes upon the mind is an impression of life. But this impression or sense of life I found to be indefinable,—not a sense of any life organic, but of a life latent and dæmonic. And the manifestation of that life I felt to be in the *pointing* of the structure.

Attempts to interpret the emotion by effects of altitude and gloom and vastness appeared to me of no worth; for buildings loftier and larger and darker than any Gothic cathedral, but of a different order of architecture,—Egyptian, for instance,—could not produce a like impression. I felt certain that the horror was made by something altogether peculiar to Gothic construction, and that this something haunted the tops of the arches.

"Yes, Gothic architecture is awful," said a religious friend, "because it is the visible expression of Christian faith. No other religious architecture symbolizes spiritual longing; but the Gothic embodies it. Every part climbs or leaps; every supreme detail soars and points like fire...." "There may be considerable truth in what you say," I replied;—"but it does not relate to the riddle that baffles me. Why should shapes that symbolize spiritual longing create horror? Why should any expression of Christian ecstasy inspire alarm?..."

Other hypotheses in multitude I tested without avail; and I returned to the simple and savage conviction that the secret of the horror somehow belonged to the points of the archings. But for years I could not find it. At last, at last, in the early hours of a certain tropical morning, it revealed itself quite unexpectedly, while I was looking at a glorious group of palms.

Then I wondered at my stupidity in not having guessed the riddle before.

II

The characteristics of many kinds of palm have been made familiar by pictures and photographs. But the giant palms of the American tropics cannot be adequately represented by the modern methods of pictorial illustration: they must be seen. You cannot draw or photograph a palm two hundred feet high.

The first sight of a group of such forms, in their natural environment of tropical forest, is a magnificent surprise,—a surprise that strikes you dumb. Nothing seen in temperate zones,—not even the huger growths of the Californian slope,—could have prepared your imagination for the weird solemnity of that mighty colonnade. Each stone-grey trunk is a perfect pillar, but a pillar of which the stupendous grace has no counterpart in the works of man. You must strain your head well back to follow the soaring of the prodigious column, up, up, up through abysses of green twilight, till at last—far beyond a break in that infinite interweaving of limbs and lianas which is the roof of the forest—you catch one dizzy glimpse of the capital: a parasol of emerald feathers outspread in a sky so blinding as to suggest the notion of azure electricity.

Now what is the emotion that such a vision excites,—an emotion too powerful to be called wonder, too weird to be called delight? Only when the first shock of it has passed,—when the several elements that were combined in it have begun to set in motion widely different groups of ideas,—can you comprehend how very complex it must have been. Many impressions belonging to personal experience were doubtless revived in it, but also with them a multitude of sensations more shadowy,—accumulations of organic memory; possibly even vague feelings older than man,—for the tropical shapes that aroused the emotion have a history more ancient than our race.

One of the first elements of the emotion to become clearly distinguishable is the æsthetic; and this, in its general mass, might be termed the sense of terrible beauty. Certainly the spectacle of that unfamiliar life,—silent, tremendous, springing to the sun in colossal aspiration, striving for light against Titans, and heedless of man in the gloom beneath as of a groping beetle,—thrills like the rhythm of some single marvellous verse that is learned in a glance and remembered forever. Yet the delight, even at its vividest, is shadowed by a queer disquiet. The aspect of that monstrous, pale, naked, smooth-stretching column suggests a life as conscious as the serpent's. You stare at the towering lines of the shape,—vaguely fearing to discern some sign of stealthy movement, some beginning of undulation. Then sight and reason combine to correct the suspicion. Yes, motion is there, and life enormous—but a life seeking only sun,—life, rushing like the jet of a geyser, straight to the giant day.

III

During my own experience I could perceive that certain feelings commingled in the wave of delight,—feelings related to ideas of power and splendor and triumph,—were accompanied by a faint sense of religious awe. Perhaps our modern æsthetic sentiments are so interwoven with various inherited elements of religious emotionalism that the recognition of beauty cannot arise independently of reverential feeling. Be this as it may, such a feeling defined itself while I gazed;—and at once the great grey trunks were changed to the pillars of a mighty aisle; and from altitudes of dream there suddenly descended upon me the old dark thrill of Gothic horror.

Even before it died away, I recognized that it must have been due to some old cathedral-memory revived by the vision of those giant trunks uprising into gloom. But neither the height nor the gloom could account for anything beyond the memory. Columns tall as those palms, but supporting a classic entablature, could evoke no sense of disquiet resembling the Gothic horror. I felt sure of this,—because I was able, without any difficulty, to shape immediately the imagination of such a façade. But presently the mental picture distorted. I saw the architrave elbow upward in each of the spaces between the pillars, and curve and point itself into a range of prodigious arches;—and again the sombre thrill descended upon me. Simultaneously there flashed to me the solution of the mystery. I understood that the Gothic horror was *a horror of monstrous motion*,—and that it had seemed to belong to the points of the arches because the idea of such motion was chiefly suggested by the extraordinary angle at which the curves of the arching touched.

To any experienced eye, the curves of Gothic arching offer a striking resemblance to certain curves of vegetal growth;—the curves of the palm-branch being, perhaps, especially suggested. But observe that the architectural form suggests more than any vegetal comparison could illustrate! The meeting of two palm-crests would indeed form a kind of Gothic arch; yet the effect of so short an arch would be insignificant. For nature to repeat the strange impression of the real Gothic arch, it were necessary that the branches of the touching crests should vastly exceed, both in length of curve and strength of spring, anything of their kind existing in the vegetable world. The effect of the Gothic arch depends altogether upon the intimation of energy. An arch formed by the intersection of two short sprouting lines could suggest only a feeble power of growth; but the lines of the tall mediæval arch seem to express a crescent force immensely surpassing that of nature. And the horror of Gothic architecture is not in the mere suggestion of a growing life, but in the suggestion of an energy supernatural and tremendous.

Of course the child, oppressed by the strangeness of Gothic forms, is yet incapable of analyzing the impression received: he is frightened without comprehending. He cannot divine that the points and the curves are terrible to him because they represent the prodigious exaggeration of a real law of vegetal growth. He dreads the shapes because they seem alive; yet he does not know how to express this dread. Without suspecting why, he feels that this silent manifestation of power, everywhere pointing and piercing upward, is not natural. To his startled imagination, the building stretches itself like a phantasm of sleep,—makes itself tall and taller with intent to frighten. Even though built by hands of men, it has ceased to be a mass of dead stone: it is infused with Something that thinks and threatens;—it has become a shadowing malevolence, a multiple goblinry, a monstrous fetish!

2. The Gothics and Their Successors

Edward Yardley, Jr. was a mid–Victorian writer of stories and poems, perhaps best remembered for his book of fantasies, *Fantastic Stories* (1865), and his scholarly study of the supernatural in literature. Arranged by topic, Yardley's *The Supernatural in Romantic Fiction* (1880) provides an encyclopedia of supernatural occurrences in literature up to the early nineteenth century, though he does not distinguish between fantasy, romance, and horror, as we would today. Most of the entries deal primarily with the appearance of sprites and fairies and the white and black magic of fantasy. In the following few entries we see Mr. Yardley discuss a few topics that more properly verge upon the territory of Gothic horror.

Excerpt from The Supernatural in Romantic Fiction*

Edward Yardley

VAMPIRES, AND ANIMATED CORPSES.

When a vampire dies, he rises from his grave at night, and supports a fresh existence by sucking the blood of other persons whilst they are asleep. These other persons soon die, and themselves become vampires. A body suspected of Vampirism is disinterred, and is generally recognised by the freshness of the face. A stake is driven through the heart of the vampire, who then utters a loud scream. The body is burnt to ashes. This is supposed to be the only way of finally getting rid of the nuisance. Lord

---

*Edward Yardley, *The Supernatural in Romantic Fiction* (London: Longmans, Green, and Co., 1880), 89–96.

Byron's lines in the 'Giaour' will be remembered.[a] A story is to be found in Phlegon's treatise on wonderful things concerning a girl of the name of Philinnium, a native of Tralles, in Asia Minor, who not only after her death visited her lover, but ate, drank, and even cohabited with him. This event, which happened in the time of the Emperor Hadrian, is the subject of Goethe's poem, 'The Bride of Corinth.' Similar stories have been told by Alexandre Dumas, Washington Irving, and perhaps by others. Hauff has a story concerning a vessel, which a couple of shipwrecked sailors boarded. They found only corpses in the vessel, but at nighttime these corpses were animated, and worked the ship. In Coleridge's 'Ancient Mariner' dead seamen are reanimated. In a story by Marryat, half the crew of a vessel murdered the other half, including the boatswain, and threw their bodies overboard. At night the guilty survivors hear the boatswain's whistle, accompanied by the summons for all hands to go on deck. They go, and find the corpses, of which they thought they had rid themselves, still on deck. They try to throw them into the sea again, but the corpses cling to the murderers, and roll with them overboard.

GHOSTS.

Apparitions are generally ghosts, but there may be apparitions, raised by magic or witchcraft, which are not ghosts. Such are the apparitions of the armed head, bloody child, and eight kings in 'Macbeth.' The apparitions of the dead have always been an important element in the supernatural. Amongst others, the spirit of Caligula is said to have walked very much in the manner of a modern ghost. It will be quite impossible to deal completely with the ghosts that belong to romantic fiction. Some, like the spirits of Hamlet and Guido Cavalcanti, are too celebrated to require mention; others are too numerous and too insignificant. A few, however, will be specified. The Wild Huntsman, if not himself a ghost, is always in ghostly company. He is supposed by some to be Odin, by others to be one of the classic gods. He issues from the Venusberg, the refuge of the classic gods of antiquity, who fled thither on the prevalence of Christianity. He rides on stormy nights, followed by a train both of the living and the dead. The ghost of the Trusty Eckart, who died contending with the demons of the Venusberg, and who in vain warned Tannenhauser not to enter it, precedes the hellish crew, and warns men of their approach. For it is dangerous to meet them; and if any person is so unfortunate as to come across them, he is generally smitten with paralysis or insanity. Those who have met nymphs, peris,[b] and fairies seem to have been liable to a similar mischief. Herne the Hunter, described by Shakespeare, is a ghost who bears some resemblance to the Wild Huntsman. The Willis, or Wilis (for the name seems to be spelt either way), exist chiefly in Hungary. They are the spirits of brides, who die on their wedding-day before consummation of marriage. They are to be seen by moonlight, where cross-roads meet; and they dance to death any unlucky man who encounters them. The story of Burger's 'Lenore' is this: Lenore's lover, William, had fought on King Frederick's side at the battle of Prague. The army returns, but no news is heard of William; and Lenore, in spite of her mother's supplications, curses God. At midnight she hears the tramp of a horse's hoofs beneath the window, and the voice of her lover calling her to ride with him to their wedding-bed. She descends and mounts behind him, learning too late that she is carried off by the spectre of her lover, who is bearing her to the grave, to punish her for her blasphemy. This, however, may perhaps be more properly considered a devil in the form of a lover than a ghost. Another German ghost is the Bleeding Nun. This was a nun who, after committing many crimes and debaucheries, was assassinated by one of her paramours, and denied the rites of burial. After this she used to haunt the castle, where she was murdered, in her nun's dress, with her bleeding wounds. On one occasion, a young lady of the castle, wishing to elope with her lover, in order to make her flight easier, personated the bleeding nun. Unfortunately the lover, whilst expecting his lady under this disguise, eloped with the spectre herself, who presented herself to him and haunted him afterwards. This story is told by Lewis in his 'Monk,' and also by Musaeus. The Belludo is a Spanish ghost, mentioned by Washington Irving in his 'Tales of the Alhambra.' It issues forth in the dead of night, and scours the avenues of the Alhambra and the streets of Granada, in the shape of a headless horse, pursued by six hounds, with terrible yells and howlings. It is said to be the spirit of a Moorish king, who killed his six sons. And these sons hunt him in the shape of hounds at night-time in revenge. Besides the apparitions of the dead, there are apparitions of the living. It is mentioned, in one of the notes to 'Monsieur Oufle,' by the Abbé Bordelon, that monks and nuns, a short time before their death, have seen the images of themselves seated in their chairs or stalls. Another example may be given. Catherine of Russia, after retiring to her bedroom, was told that she had been seen just before to enter the state chamber. On hearing this she went thither, and saw the exact similitude of herself seated upon the throne. She ordered her guards to fire upon it. Another sort of ghost of the living is mentioned in an Eastern story. A soldier of the guard of a certain king met a spirit in the form of a beautiful woman, who was wailing bitterly; and she told him that she was the soul of the king, his master, who was fated to die within three days. Ghosts sometimes leave behind them substantial marks of their visits. In Scott's well-known ballad[c] the phantom knight impresses an indelible mark on the lady who has been his paramour. In the Tartar stories, written by a Frenchman, a series of stories neither original nor well constructed, a ghost appears to Prince Faruk in a dream, and touches him on the arm. The prince finds the mark of the burn when he awakes.[...]

HAUNTED HOUSES.

Ali of Cairo, in the 'Arabian Nights,' was taken to a deserted house, but was advised not to lodge there, being told that the house was haunted, and that every one who had passed the night in it had become a corpse before morning. Ali, being in a desperate condition, determined to pass the night in the house, thinking that to do so would be a very convenient way of committing suicide. He supped in a magnificent saloon of the house, and was about to retire to bed, when a voice said: 'Ali, shall I send thee down gold?' Thereupon a shower of gold fell into the apartment. It was a Jinnee that haunted the place. Ali was the person for whom the gold was destined. The Jinnee had killed all the wrong persons who had lodged in the house; and now benefited the right person. Stories of haunted houses are very common in the literature of modern Europe. For instance, the apparition of a bleeding child always presented itself to anybody, staying in a particular house, who was destined to die a violent death. In another house the sound of some one, drumming through all the passages, was always heard just before the death of any of the family to whom the house belonged. The child and the drummer had originally been murdered in these houses; and their ghosts in consequence made themselves disagreeable. In Scott's 'Tapestried Chamber' the ghost that haunts the chamber is an old woman. It may be seen in the 'Mostellaria' of Plautus that haunted houses were not unknown to the Greeks and Romans.

Notes

a. From "Giaour" (1813):
> Wet with thine own best blood shall drip,
> Thy gnashing tooth and haggard lip;
> Then stalking to thy sullen grave—
> Go—and with Gouls and Afrits rave;
> Till these in horror shrink away
> From spectre more accursed than they!

b. Persian spirits descended from fallen angels.
c. *The Last Lay of the Minstrel* (1805).

Nathan Drake (1766–1836) was an English doctor and essayist, known for his collections of literary essays and criticism and a work on Shakespeare which gathered together all of the known material on the author then extant, including a chronology of his works. The following excerpt from *Literary Hours* (1798), a collection of literary essays and stories (including the Gothic novella *Henry Fitzowen*), gives Dr. Drake's position on the use of supernatural in literature, especially in the emerging Gothic school, and its importance and utility in the face of Enlightenment thinkers who believed the supernatural was a dangerous indulgence that too frequently led malleable minds into superstitious folly. Drake, though, cautioned that the supernatural should be employed for more than just horror and could be used for "sport" as Shakespeare had done.

The following is most of Hour No. VIII, "On Gothic Superstition." I have omitted a lengthy poem of Dr. Drake's that followed the essay, which essay Dr. Drake maintained was necessary to allow the reader to decide whether to proceed on to the poem or avoid its Gothic horrors.

*Excerpt from "On Gothic Superstition"**

NATHAN DRAKE

NUMBER VIII.

> There would he dream of graves, and corses pale;
> And ghosts, that to the charnel-dungeon throng,
> And drag a length of clanking chain, and wail,
> Till silenc'd by the owl's terrific song,
> Or blasts that shriek by fits the shuddering isles along.
>
> Anon in view a portal's blazon'd arch
> Arose; the trumpet bids the valves unfold;

---

*Nathan Drake, *Literary Hours, or, Sketches Critical and Narrative*, vol. 1, 2d ed. (London: J. Burkitt for T. Cadell, Jr., and W. Davies, 1800), 137–154.

> And forth an host of little warriors march,
> Grasping the diamond lance, and targe of gold:
> Their look was gentle, their demeanour bold,
> And green their helms, and green their silk attire;
> And here and there, right venerably old,
> The long rob'd minstrels wake the warbling wire,
> And some with mellow breath the martial pipe inspire.
>
> BEATTIE.[a]

Of the various kinds of superstition which have in any age influenced the human mind, none appear to have operated with so much effect as what has been termed the Gothic. Even in the present polished period of society, there are thousands who are yet alive to ail the horrors of witchcraft, to all the solemn and terrible graces of the appalling spectre. The most enlightened mind, the mind free from all taint of superstition, involuntarily acknowledges the power of gothic agency; and the late favourable reception which two or three publications in this style have met with, is a convincing proof of the assertion. The enchanted forest of Tasso, the spectre of Camoens, and the apparitions of Shakspeare [sic], are to this day highly pleasing, striking, and sublime features in these delightful compositions.—

And although this kind of superstition be able to arrest every faculty of the human mind, and to shake, as it were, all nature with horror, yet does it also delight in the most sportive and elegant imagery. The traditionary tales of elves and fairies still convey to a warm imagination an inexhausted source of invention, supplying all those wild, romantic, and varied ideas with which a wayward fancy loves to sport. The Provençal bards, and the neglected Chaucer and Spenser, are the originals from whence this exquisite species of fabling has been drawn, improved, and applied with so much inventive elegance by Shakspeare. The flower and the leaf of Chaucer is replete with the most luxuriant description of these preternatural beings.—

The vulgar gothic therefore, an epithet here adopted to distinguish it from the regular mythology of the Edda,[b] turns chiefly on the awful ministration of the Spectre, or the innocent gambols of the Fairy, the former, perhaps, partly derived from Platonic Christianity, the latter from the fictions of the East, as imported into Europe during the period of the Crusades; but whatever be its derivation, it is certainly a mode of superstition so assimilated with the universal apprehension of superior agency, that few minds have been altogether able to shake it off. Even to Philosophy admitting of the doctrine of immaterialism, it becomes no easy task consistently to deny the possibility of such an interference. Whilst it therefore gives considerable latitude to the imagination, it seems to possess more rationality than almost any other species of fabling; for confined by no adherence to any regular mythological system, but depending merely upon the possible, and to some highly probable, visitation of immaterial agents, it has even in the present metaphysical period still retained such a degree of credit as yet to render it an important and impressive machine beneath the guidance of genuine poesy. If to those who have paid the most subtile attention to the existence and relative action of matter and spirit, it becomes a subject of doubt to deny the viable operation of spirit, surely in the bosom of the million it must still preserve some portion of influence, and as, if such an agency exist, its laws and direction must be to us altogether unknown, it furnishes, if not the probable, at least the possible, at all times a sufficient basis, for the airy structure of the poet.—

It is remote from every wish of the Author to encourage any superstition that may render his fellow creatures alive to unnecessary and puerile terror, but allowing the existence and occasionally the visible exertion of spirit upon matter, with the wise and with the good no painful emotion can arise, and if one more pang be added to the struggles of conscious guilt, the world, he should imagine, would be no sufferer; but it is here only as furnish fit materials for poetical composition that a wish for preserving such a source of imagery is expressed. When well conducted, a grateful astonishment, a welcome sensation of fear, will alike creep through the bosom of the Sage and of the Savage, and it is, perhaps, to the introduction of such well-imagined agency, or when not introduced upon the scene, to a very frequent allusion to it, that Shakspeare, beyond any other poet, owes the capability of raising the most awful, yet the most delightful species of terror. No poet, adopting a machinery of a similar kind, has wielded it with equal effect. Among the Italians it is too frequently addressed solely to the imagination, Ariosto in general, and Tasso sometimes, descending to all the extravaganza of oriental fiction; conducted, as by Shakspeare, it powerfully moves the strongest passions of the heart.—

Next to the Gothic in point of sublimity and imagination comes the Celtic, which, if the superstition of the Lowlands be esteemed a part of it, may with equal propriety, be divided into the terrible and the sportive; the former, as displayed in the poems of Ossian;[c] the latter, in the songs and ballads of the Low Country. This superstition, like the gothic, has the same happy facility of blending its ideas with the common apprehensions of mankind; it does not, like most mythological systems, involve every species of absurdity, but, floating loose upon the mind, founds its imagery upon a metaphysical possibility, upon the appearance of superior, or departed beings. Ossian has, however, opened a new field for invention, he has given fresh colouring to his supernatural agents, he has given them employments new to gothic fiction: his ghosts are not the ghosts of Shakspeare, yet are they equally solemn and striking. The abrupt and rapid fervour of imagination, the vivid touches of enthusiasm, mark his composition, and his spectres rush upon the eye with all the stupendous vigour of wild and momentary creation. So deep and uniform a melancholy pervades the poetry of this author, that, whether from natural disposition, or the pressure of misfortune, from the face of the country which he inhabited, or the insulated state of society, he us ever to have avoided imagery of a light and airy kind; otherwise, from the originality of his genius, much in this way might have been expected. As to the superstition of the Lowlands, it differs so little from the lighter gothic, that I am not warranted in drawing any distinction between them. It is not, however, peculiar to this district of Scotland, the Highlanders in many parts, especially in their beautiful little vales, being still enthusiastic in their belief of it.—

And here may I be pardoned if I offer a few strictures upon the dress which the British Ossian has assumed. Greatly as I admire the pathos and sublime imagery of this Bard of other times, I cannot but regret the style in which Mr. Macpherson has chosen to clothe him. A stiffness the most rigid, a monotony the most tedious, are its general characteristics, and were it not for the very powerful appeals to the heart and imagination few readers would be tempted to a second perusal. That Dr. Blair, however, a Critic of acknowledged taste and judgement, that he should approve of this mode of composition, nay, should prefer it to any species of versification, is, to me, still more extraordinary; nor can I any way account for such a remarkable, and as I should hope almost insulated, opinion, for in other instances, the perfect judge of melody and rhythm in English poetry, is apparent. How had the pathos and sublimity of Ossian been heightened, how mingled with every variety of harmony and rhythmical cadence, had the versification of Cowper and Milton been adopted. Mr. Macpherson has termed his translation a literal one, but if really built upon oral tradition, upon a species of legendary poesy sang and set to music in a manner calculated to assist the memory, how monstrously must it have deviated from the originals; had it been his wish to have given us a faithful copy of these interesting fictions, the ballad stanza would, perhaps have afforded the choicest vehicle, but if ambitious of founding a structure of his own on these tales, the boundless variety of blank verse would surely have done more justice to his conceptions; they certainly merit a better style, and when this desideratum is obtained I shall not hesitate in placing Ossian (whether of ancient or modern production is to me perfectly indifferent) on the same shelf with Homer, Shakspeare, and Milton.—

But to return.—These are then (the vulgar gothic and the Celtic) the only two species of superstition which are still likely to retain their ground; founded chiefly on the casual interference of immaterial beings, and therefore easily combining with the common feelings of humanity, they may yet with propriety d[e]corate the pages of the poet, when the full-formed system of mythology, will be rejected as involving too much fiction. Some attempts, however, have been lately made to revive the Scandinavian or Islandic [sic] mythology, and the sublime effusions of Gray and Sayers have thrown a magic lustre round the daring creations of the Edda. That they will ever become popular must, I should imagine, be a matter of considerable doubt, but these authors have written for the few, for the lovers of genuine poetry, and with their suffrage they will certainly be contented.

It has been however too much the fashion among critical writers to condemn the introduction of any kind of supernatural agency although perfectly consonant with the common feelings of mankind; and the simple, yet powerful superstitions recommended to the poet in this paper, seem to bid fair for sharing the fate of more complex systems: but whilst they are thus formed to influence the people, to surprise, elevate, and delight, with a willing admiration, every faculty of the human mind, how shall criticism with impunity dare to expunge them? Genius has ever had a predilection for such imagery, and I may venture, I think, to predict, that if at any time these romantic legends be totally laid aside, our national poetry will degenerate into mere morality, criticism, and satire; and that the sublime, the terrible, and the fanciful in poetry, will no longer exist. The recent publication of Mr. Hole's Arthur[d] has, indeed, called the attention of the public to many of these fertile sources of invention, but although the work has great merit, it is confessedly built too much upon the Italian mode of fabling; the machinery is not sufficiently awful to excite eager attention, and throughout the whole poem, perhaps, the heart is too little engaged. Imagery of this kind should not only awaken surprise, but, to leave a lasting impression, both pity and terror. Should Arthur, however, in a future edition be enlarged, and what enlargement may not a work of pure imagination admit of, a more frequent introduction of the pathetic would, most probably, seal it for immortality, for it is nevertheless

> In scenes like these, which daring to depart
>   From sober truth, are still to nature true,
> And call forth fresh delight to Fancy's view,
>   Th' heroic muse employ'd her Tasso's art!
> How have I sat, when pip'd the pensive wind,
>   To hear his harp, by British Fairfax strung,
> Prevailing poet, whose undoubting mind
>   Believ'd the magic wonders which he sung!
> Hence at each sound imagination glows;
> Hence his warm lay with softest sweetness flows;
> Melting, it flows, pure, num'rous, strong and clear,
> And fills th' impassion'd heart, and wins th' harmonious ear.
> COLLINS.[e]

Although so great a disparity evidently obtains between the two species of Gothic superstition, the terrible and the sportive; yet no author, that I am acquainted with, has, for narrative machinery, availed himself of this circumstance, and thrown them into immediate contrast. In a beautiful fragment lately published by Mrs. Barbauld, under the title of Sir Bertrand,[f] the transition is immediately from the deep Gothic to the Arabic or Saracenic superstition; which, although calculated to surprise, would have given more pleasure, perhaps, and would have rendered the preceding scenes of horror more striking, had it been of a light and contrasted kind.

Notes

    a. From James Beattie's (1735–1803) "The Minstrel" (1771/2).
    b. The Elder and Younger Eddas, the books of Scandinavian mythology which by virtue of their age were associated with the prose of the "Gothic" or medieval period in the eighteenth century.
    c. Ossian is the ostensible narrator and author of supposedly ancient Celtic poems fabricated by James Macpherson (1736–1796) in 1760.
    d. *Arthur*, by Richard Hole (1798).
    e. From William Collins (1721–1759), "An Ode on the Popular Superstitions of the Highlands of Scotland, Considered as the Subject of Poetry" (1749).
    f. Oddly enough, known as "Sir Bertrand: A Fragment" (1773) by Anna Barbauld.

In the eighteenth century, Gothic literature was still new, and the literary journals of the age spilled not an inconsiderable amount of ink delineating the borders of this strange new development in literature. This anonymous article from the *Monthly Review* for July 1799 surveys our last selection, Drake's *Literary Hours*, and offers the *Review*'s ideas about the Gothic. I have here excerpted the passages directly relevant to Gothic literature. The passage labeled "No. 6" here corresponds with our previous passage, which was Hour VIII in the second edition.

Excerpt from a Review of Literary Hours *by Nathan Drake**

THE MONTHLY REVIEW

ART. V. *Literary Hours, or Sketches critical and narrative.* By Nathan Drake, M. D. 8vo. pp. 530. 12s. Boards. Cadell jun. and Davies. 1798.

This miscellaneous volume is evidently the production of an accomplished critic. Dr. Drake has perused the works, and appreciated the merits, of most of the celebrated poets of antient and modern Europe; and could he divest himself of too exclusive an admiration for the terrible and gigantic, we should seldom be induced to dissent from his conclusions. The mouldering cloyster, the gloomy cell, the awe-stricken votary of superstition, and the midnight-spectre, are the objects which his imagination delights to contemplate[...].

No. 6. On Gothic Superstition.

In order to obviate the pre-disposition of modern critics to censure the introduction of supernatural Beings in works of imagination, the author remarks that 'genius has ever had a predilection for such imagery, and may venture, I think, to predict, that, if at any time these romantic legends be laid aside, our national poetry will degenerate into mere morality, criticism, and satire; and that the sublime, the terrible, and the fanciful in poetry, will no longer exist.' In this observation, we think, there is some truth, with some exaggeration. In works addressed chiefly to the imagination, the rare introduction of supernatural agency, for an object manifestly beyond the sphere of human operation, is doubtless admissible: but, the more frequent

*Review of *Literary Hours* by Nathan Drake, *The Monthly Review* (July 1799): 282, 284–285, 287, 292.

Midnight Revels. Early horror critics frequently felt that the supernatural was an inappropriate topic for fiction on the grounds that depictions of ghosts and ghouls would encourage superstition. Where Gothic horror writers imagined supernatural monsters, critics acted like the couple in this 1795 cartoon, chasing cats from the roof with pots and brooms, dispelling the supernatural (Library of Congress, Prints and Photographs Division, LC-USZ62-86570).

is the poet's recourse to such auxiliaries, the less will be their effect; and he should never forget that, in such aerial excursions, lie treads on the very confines of the burlesque. Dr. Drake informs us that the vulgar Gothic is an epithet adopted to distinguish it from the regular mythology of the Edda; and this he considers as affording the most convenient machinery, being confined by no adherence to any regular system, but depending merely on the possible visitation of immaterial agents. It appears to turn chiefly on the power of incantations, the appearance of spectres, and the gambols of fairies. We are at a loss to discern the propriety of terming the popular belief in these fables, 'Gothic superstition.' The first two claim a higher origin than the Edda, and may undoubtedly be traced to a real transaction; that of the witch of Endor, and the apparition of Samuel. Fairies, who (as Mr. Addison observes) are capable of becoming very entertaining persons when properly managed, are the unquestionable productions of Persian romance, and were probably imported into Europe by our first crusaders. In all this we perceive no connection with the Goths. Our author resolves what he terms Gothic superstition into the terrible and the sportive; and, attracted by the exquisite beauty which (he thinks) would result from an opposition of such imagery, he has availed himself of both in the following numbers; viz.

No. 7, 8, and 9. Henry Fitzowen, a Gothic Tale,

The principal fiend-like character of this tale bears too great a resemblance to the lord of Conway-castle. Will not Horace's maxim, not to trouble the gods on trivial occasions, equally apply to phantoms? Spectres will lose their claim to reverence if they become too common, and here they are marshalled in legions. Were it worth while to prescribe rules for this grotesque species of composition, we should require an air of antiquity in the style; brevity, general simplicity, but occasional quaintness, should constitute its characteristics. Dr. Drake's obsolete fictions comport but ill with the elegance of his periods.

No. 15. On Objects of Terror; Montmorenci, a Fragment.

In works of imagination, terror is excited either by the agency of superhuman beings, or depends on natural causes and events for its production. Of the latter description, the subjects are seldom susceptible of being rendered pleasing by all the art of the writer, or the artist. The perpetration of shocking crimes can excite no sensation but horror; and we do not applaud the taste of Sir Joshua Reynolds,[a] when he selected the disgusting story of Ugolino for the exercise of his uncommon powers. — The fragment of Montmorenci[b] is a specimen of that style in which our author awards the palm to Dante, Collins, and Mrs. Radcliffe.

[...]

We have now analysed the contents of a volume which has afforded us much pleasure in the perusal, and which will probably become a favourite with the public, as containing an ample fund of valuable, amusing, and generally candid criticism.

Notes

a. Sir Joshua Reynolds (1723–1792) was a painter and the first president of the Royal Academy. His *Ugolino and His Children* (1773) illustrates a passage from Dante's *Inferno* (canto 33), which Reynolds was credited for having popularized.

b. This refers to a Gothic fragment Drake wrote to accompany his essay on terror in the style of Ann Radcliffe, published elsewhere as "Captive of the Banditti."

One of the masters of Gothic horror, Matthew Gregory "Monk" Lewis (1775–1818) was responsible for the horrific novel *The Monk* (1794) and the wildly successful stage play *The Castle Spectre* (1796). Lewis's fame was such that two anthologies of comedic and horrific Gothic tales, *Tales of Wonder* (1801) and *Tales of Terror* (1801) were ascribed to him, though the latter was an anonymous satire of the former. In 1887 the literature professor Henry Morely merged the two into a single volume under Lewis's name, to whom he (mis)attributed the following introduction from the anonymous *Terror*.

Introductory Dialogue to Tales of Terror[*]

MATTHEW LEWIS (Attributed)

Si erro, libenter erro, nee mihi hunc errorem,
dum vivo, extorqueri volo. — *CICERO.*[a]

    FRIEND.
What, scribble tales? Oh, cease to play the fool!
Christmas is past, and children gone to school;
E'en active Harlequin abashed retires,

[*]"Introductory Dialogue," in *Tales of Terror and Wonder*, collected by Matthew Gregory Lewis, introduction by Henry Morley (London: George Routledge and Sons, 1887), 9–13.

Neglected witches quench the cauldron's fires,
Whilst fairy phantoms vanish swift away,
And sense and nature reassume their sway.
    What gain, what pleasure, can your labours crown?
A nursery's praise shall be your best renown;
Each feeble tale ingloriously expire,
A gossip's story at a winter's fire!

    AUTHOR.

    Oh! cease this rage, this misapplied abuse,
Satire gives weapons for a nobler use;
Why draw your sword against my harmless quill,
And strive, in vain, a *ghostly muse* to kill?
That task is *ours*: if I can augur well,
Each day grows weaker her unheeded spell,
Her eager votaries shall fix her doom,
And lay her spirit in Oblivion's tomb.

    FRIEND.

    Yes! thus I oft my drooping hopes revive,
Prepost'rous births are seldom known to thrive;
These scribblers soon shall mourn their useless pains,
And weep the short-lived product of their brains,
These active panders to perverted taste
Shall mar their purpose by too anxious haste.
    As earthquakes Nature's harmony restore,
And air grows purer in the tempest's roar,
So the strange workings of a monstrous mind
Will quickly fade, and leave no trace behind;
Like brilliant bubbles, glitter for a day,
Till, swoln too big, they burst, and pass away.
We need not call ethereal spirits down
To rouse the torpid feelings of the town;
Or bid the dead their ghastly forms uprear,
To freeze some silly female breast with fear;
No—I have hopes you'll find this rage decreased,
And send a dish too much to Terror's feast;
The vicious taste, with such a rich supply
Quite surfeited, "will sicken, and so die."

    AUTHOR.

    My friend, believe me, with indifferent view
I mark opinion's every-varying hue,
Let tasteless fashion guide the public heart,
And, without feeling, scan the poet's art.
Fashion! dread name in criticism's field.
Before whose sway both sense and judgment yield,

Whether she loves to hear, 'midst deserts bleak,
The untaught savage moral axioms speak;
O'er modern, six weeks, epic strains to doze,
To sigh in sonnets, or give wings to prose;
Or bids the bard, by leaden rules confined,
To freeze the bosom and confuse the mind,
While feeling stagnates in the drawler's veins,
And Fancy's fettered in didactic chains;—
Or rouses the dull German's gloomy soul,
And Pity leaves for Horror's wild control,
Pouring warm tears for *visionary* crimes,
And softening sins to mend these *moral* times;
It boots not *me—my* taste is still my own,
Nor heeds the gale by wavering fashion blown.
My mind unaltered views, with fixed delight,
The wreck of learning snatched from Gothic night;
Changed by no time, unsettled by no place,
It feels the Grecian fire, the Roman grace;
Exulting marks the flame of ancient days,
In Britain with triumphant brightness blaze!

    Yet still the soul for *various* pleasure formed,
By Pity melted, and by Terror stormed,
Loves to roam largely through each distant clime.
And "leap the flaming bounds of space and time!"
The mental eye, by constant lustre tires.
Forsakes, fatigued, the object it admires,
And, as it scans each various nation's doom,
From classic brightness turns to Gothic gloom.
Oh! it breathes awe and rapture o'er the soul
To mark the surge in wild confusion roll,
And when the forest groans, and tempest lours,
To wake Imagination's darkest powers!
How throbs the breast with terror and delight,
Filled with rude scenes of Europe's barbarous night!
When restless war with papal craft combined,
To shut each softening ray from lost mankind;
When nought but Error's fatal light was shown,
And taste and science were alike unknown;
To mark the soul, benumbed its active powers,
Chained at the foot of Superstition's towers;
To view the pale-eyed maid in penance pine,
To watch the votary at the sainted shrine;
And, while o'er blasted heaths the night-storm raves,
To hear the wizard wake the slumb'ring graves;
To view war's glitt'ring front, the trophied field,
The hallowed banner, and the red-cross shield;

The tourney's knights, the tyrant baron's crimes,
"Pomp, pride, and circumstance," of feudal times!

    The enraptured mind with fancy loves to toil
O'er rugged Scandinavia's martial soil;
With eager joy the 'venturous spirit goes
O'er Morven's mountains, and through Lapland's snows;
Sees barbarous chiefs in fierce contention fall,
And views the blood-stained feasts of Odin's hall;
Hears Ossian's harp resound the deeds of war,
While each grey soldier glories in his scar;
Now marks the wand'ring ghost, at night's dull noon,
Howl out its woes beneath the silent moon;
Sees Danish pirates plough th' insulted main,
Whilst Rapine's outcry shakes the sacred fane!
Observes the Saxon baron's sullen state,
Where rival pride enkindles savage hate;
Each sound, each sight, the spell-bound sense appals
Amid some lonely abbey's ivied walls!
The night-shriek loud, wan ghost, and dungeon damp,
The midnight cloister, and the glimm'ring lamp,
The pale procession fading on the sight,
The flaming tapers, and the chanted rite,
Rouse, in the trembling breast, delightful dreams,
And steep each feeling in romance's streams!
Streams, which afar in restless grandeur roll,
And burst tremendous on the wond'ring soul!
Now gliding smooth, now lashed by magic storms,
Lifting to light a thousand shapeless forms;
A vaporous glory floats each wave around,
The dashing waters breathe a mournful sound,
Pale Terror trembling guards the fountain's head,
And rouses Fancy on her wakeful bed;
"From realms of viewless spirits tears the veil,
And half reveals the unutterable tale!"

    March 1, 1801.

Notes

  a. If I err ... I err gladly; nor will I let my error be taken from me so long as I live. (Paraphrased from chapter 23 of "On Old Age" in which Cicero defends his belief in immortality.)

Sir Walter Alexander Raleigh (1861–1922) was a professor of Modern Literature at University College, Liverpool at the time he wrote *The English Novel* (1894), a study

2. The Gothics and Their Successors

of the same from *Beowulf* to Sir Walter Scott's *Waverley* (1822). He was also his era's foremost defender of the Gothic novelist Ann Radcliffe. In this excerpt from the chapter "The Revival of Romance," the professor surveys early Gothic literature and gives his opinion on the relative merits (or, more accurately, demerits) of Horace Walpole's *The Castle of Otranto* (1764), the first Gothic novel and progenitor of modern horror fiction.

Excerpt from "The Revival of Romance"*
WALTER RALEIGH

"*We are affected only as we believe.*" The sentence gives a terse and final statement of the chief eighteenth-century heresy. It is the key to the religious controversies of the century, reaching an abyss of bathos in the apologetics of Paley; it is the key likewise to the dominant methods in the art

The Castle of Otranto. This illustration to the 1791 edition of The Castle of Otranto *depicts the actual Castle of Otranto (Taranto) as rebuilt for Alfonso I of Aragon in the fifteenth century. However, despite Walpole's claims that the novel was a translation of a genuinely ancient Italian manuscript, the book was his own invention, and the castle in it was modeled on Walpole's own home of Strawberry Hill rather than its Italian namesake (Beinecke Rare Book and Manuscript Library, Yale University).*

*Walter Raleigh, *The English Novel: Being a Short Sketch of Its History from the Earliest Times to the Appearance of* Waverley (New York: Charles Scribner's Sons, 1895), 221–226.

of fiction. But the statement is not true, for we are affected also as we imagine. And his recognition of this long-forgotten truth entitles Horace Walpole, who hit upon it in blundering dilettante fashion, and illustrated it by his *Castle of Otranto*, to a high place among the founders of modern Romanticism. *The Castle of Otranto, a Gothic Story; translated by William Marshal, Gent., from the original Italian of Onuphrio Muralto, Canon of the Church of St. Nicholas at Otranto* (1764), is the title of the brief story that founded a school of romance. After the assured success of the book, Walpole discarded these solemn pretences, and came forward, in his preface to the second edition, with an acknowledgment of authorship and an interesting account of the inspirations and aims of his book. This preface is enough to show that the *Castle of Otranto* was a more serious and deliberate experiment than its prototype of Strawberry Hill;[a] its author meant it to last longer than the lath and plaster battlements with which he decorated his toy Gothic mansion.

Fifty years before the success of Scott, the attempt was here made "to blend the two kinds of romance, the I ancient and the modern," to reintroduce, that is, the greatest possible freedom of invention, and to give full rein to fancy by the admission of the supernatural element of the old romances, at the same time borrowing from the newly developed novel its close adherence to nature and life in the matter of character and conversation. "The old romances" that Walpole had in mind were probably most of them no older than the pastoral and heroic schools, and a precedent that swayed him more is supplied by the later part of the preface, where Shakespeare is proclaimed as the great model for the heightening of the sublime by contrast with the commonplace or the ridiculous. The defence of Shakespeare that Walpole interpolates in his preface is highly significant. A revival of romance in England must have meant a revival of Shakespeare, but here he is definitely and closely associated with the first stirring of the new spirit. He is made responsible for "the deportment of the domestics" in the *Castle of Otranto* years before he taught Mrs. Radcliffe and Maturin, who were both steeped in Shakespeare, their best artistic effects. "I might have pleaded," says Walpole, "that having created a new species of romance, I was at liberty to lay down what rules I thought fit for the conduct of it: but I should be more proud of having imitated, however faintly, weakly, and at a distance, so masterly a pattern, than to enjoy the entire merit of invention, unless I could have marked my work with genius as well as with originality."

Originality the work may safely claim. The mountainous helmet, with its waving sable plumes, which crashes down into the courtyard of the Castle of Otranto at the very beginning of the narrative, unheralded and unexplained, may be taken as a symbol and type of the suddenness with which supernatural terror was re-introduced into English fiction by Horace Walpole. Here, with a decisive hand, was struck the keynote of all those later romances which gave only too much ground for Goethe's pithy maxim, "The classical is health; and the romantic, disease." The very violence and crudity of Walpole's originality proved an invitation to his imitators to better the instruction he gave them. But romantic after the manner of Shakespeare the work is not. For nothing is more characteristic of the great masters of romance than the subtlety and guardedness of their use of the supernatural. Their ghosts do not come uncalled for. Macbeth is startled when the witches speak to him, because what they have to tell him is familiar to his thoughts. The tricks and fantasies of supernaturalism are meaningless and powerless save in alliance with the mysterious powers of human nature, and, failing this, not all the realistic circumstance in the world can give them life or meaning. And where this alliance between the evil within and the unknown powers without is less marked, the care wherewith a great romancer prepares the way for the supernatural, so that it comes as the bodily fulfilment of an unbodied fear, is well seen in the palmary instance of *The Ancient Mariner*. The skeleton ship, with the spectre-woman and her death-mate, is ushered in by all the silences and wonders of a tropical sea, by loneliness and dreams.

But Walpole was no poet, and the gaiety and inconsequence of his excursions into the supernatural can hardly avoid the suspicion of latent humour. Huge hands and legs clad in armour obtrude themselves at odd moments on the attention of alarmed domestics, whose account of their experiences furnishes the comedy of the book. When Manfred offers marriage to the Lady Isabella, "at that instant the portrait of his grandfather, which hung over the bench where they had been sitting, uttered a deep sigh, and heaved its breast." On another occasion "three drops of blood fell from the nose of Alfonso's statue." And portent follows portent, each more surprising and unintelligible than the last; the surmises of the reader as to the cause and meaning of the whole incongruous dance are like the conjectures offered by the spectators of the descent of the helmet, "as absurd and improbable as the catastrophe itself was unprecedented." Moreover, *The Castle of Otranto*, as a story, is raised on the structural scheme of the modern detective novel; the puzzle which every page complicates finds its solution only in the last few pages. But this particular structure is perfectly unwarrantable and ineffective where the solution itself contains free use of the supernatural. Even in so fine a story as *Dr. Jekyll and Mr. Hyde*, the reader is unjustifiably cheated into attempting a natural solution of apparently inexplicable phenomena. The supernatural solution, when it comes, is no solution; there are a hundred ways of explaining the impossible by the impossible. In its fit artistic place the supernatural explains the natural, and itself needs no explanation. The secret of such an employment of the supernatural is given by Coleridge in his account of the inception of that monument of the Romantic revival in England, the *Lyrical Ballads*. "It was agreed that my endeavours should be directed to persons and characters supernatural, or at least romantic; yet, so as to transfer from our inward nature a human interest and a semblance of truth sufficient to procure for these shadows of imagination that willing suspension of disbelief for the moment, which constitutes poetic faith. Mr. Wordsworth, on the other hand, was to propose to himself, as his object, to give the charm of novelty to things of every day, and to excite a feeling analogous to the supernatural, by awakening the mind's attention from the lethargy of custom, and directing it to the loveliness and the wonder of the world before us."

That these "two sorts" of poems were part of one series and of one scheme gives its chief importance to the poetic confession of faith contained in the *Lyrical Ballads*. For, indeed, the two processes described by Coleridge are mutually indispensable. The man to whom the natural has never seemed supernatural can by no device make the supernatural appear natural. And Wordsworth himself, who was confined to one half of the task, is seen in his finest poems constantly on the verge of passing from the disembodied marvels of the mind to authentic and embodied powers more than human. In such lines as these—

> "There's not a breathing of the common wind
> That will forget thee; thou hast great allies;
> Thy friends are exultations, agonies,
> And love, and Man's unconquerable mind,"

he approaches the mythopœic, while he expresses one; of the simplest and intensest of human feelings.

But Walpole, writing not only thirty-five years before Coleridge and Wordsworth, but also long before Burns and Cowper, and long before the French Revolution, was both in the eighteenth century and of it. To have awakened the hidden springs of supernatural terror is a sufficiently notable achievement. To transfer to supernatural characters "a human interest and a semblance of truth" from his inward nature was beyond his power, for in that inward nature he recognized nothing akin to the supernatural.

Thus Walpole remains one of those paradoxes with which the history of literature abounds. The inaugurator and, in some sense, the founder of a literary movement that took Europe by storm, his temper and character would have qualified him better to be its critic, or even its parodist. With no intention of criticism or parody, but in mere playfulness, he made a wooden jack-in-the box. Wooden though it was, it served as a decoy for the multitude of ghosts that squeaked and gibbered in the highways of literature for half a century and more, until, in *Frankenstein* and *Melmoth the Wanderer*, the romantic orgy reached its height.

Notes

a. Walpole built a faux–Gothic castle at Strawberry Hill, setting off the craze for neo-Gothic architecture. Its design directly inspired him to write *Otranto*, which castle he modeled on his own.

Thomas E. Rankin (1872–1953) was a professor of rhetoric at the University of Michigan, and Wilford M. Aikin (1882–1965) was a professor of education at Ohio State. Together they wrote a survey of English literature meant to teach students how to think about books because "it is not of so much importance that a reader shall be pleased with what he pursues as that he shall be 'right' in being pleased." According to the authors, no reader would be right to be pleased with the horror stories produced by the Gothic writers, and so they passed over the period with only a few sentences. "The School of Terror" comes from the chapter "The Eighteenth Century" in their *English Literature* (1917).

*The School of Terror**

THOMAS E. RANKIN *and* WILFORD M. AIKIN

Of Horace Walpole's *Castle of Otranto*, William Beckford's *History of the Caliph Vathek*, Matthew Gregory Lewis's *Monk*, and Mrs. Anne [*sic*] Radcliffe's *Mysteries of Udolpho*, we need only say here that they were foundation stones for the rather hideous pseudo-supernatural structure known as the "school of terror." The first of these books was printed in 1764 and

*Thomas E. Rankin and Wilford M. Aikin, *English Literature* (New York: Macmillan, 1917), 180.

the last in 1794; the other two, between these dates. These works were early called gothic, in the somewhat distorted sense of grotesque and barbarous. Into this grotesquely barbarous work came elements of the pseudo-supernatural and of the eighteenth-century German handling of the medieval; but it takes a twentieth-century reader's hardest endeavors to induce an attitude of anything else than amusement at what the late years of the eighteenth century and the early years of the nineteenth century shuddered at as unspeakably terrible.

William Allen Neilson (1869–1946) was a writer, professor, and editor of the second edition of *Webster's New International Dictionary* (1934). He also served as editor of *Lectures on the Harvard Classics*. Here he describes the development of the Gothic, which Neilson, like most critics of the age, considered "rather worthless" and important only for its more legitimate progeny, the historical novel, like Sir Walter Scott's *Ivanhoe* (1819). "Fiction in the Romantic Movement" comes from his "General Introduction" to the *Lectures on the Harvard Classics* (1914) section on prose fiction.

Fiction in the Romantic Movement[*]
WILLIAM ALLEN NEILSON

[T]here had begun in England, as elsewhere, that complex reaction against the intellectualism of the eighteenth century known as the Romantic Movement. Among its more obvious phases was the revival of interest in remote places and periods, and especially in the Middle Ages. The extent to which this interest was ill-informed and merely sentimental is nowhere better illustrated than in the rise of the so-called "Gothic Romance." This variety of fiction is usually regarded as beginning with "The Castle of Otranto" of Horace Walpole, the son of the great Whig minister, Sir Robert Walpole, and the type of the fashionable dilettante of the London of his day. Walpole had no real understanding or sympathy for the spirit of the Middle Ages, but one of his fads was mediæval armor, furniture, and architecture, and out of this arose his curious half-sincere experiment in fiction. The real leader in the production of this sort of

[*]William Allen Neilson, "General Introduction," in *Lectures on the Harvard Classics*, edited by William Allen Neilson, *The Harvard Classics*, ed. Charles W. Elliot (New York: P. F. Collier & Son, 1914), 212–214.

"thriller," however, was Mrs. Radcliffe, who was followed by Clara Reeves and scores of minor imitators. The novels of these ladies were set in a vaguely remote period of chivalry, their scenes were ancient castles, with concealed panels, subterranean passages, and family ghosts; their plots turned upon the usurpation of family estates by wicked uncles or villainous neighbors, and on the reparations and sufferings of missing heirs and heroines of "sensibility"; and their characters were the stereotyped figures of ordinary melodrama. A special development of this type appeared in the "School of Terror" headed by M. G. Lewis, whose nickname of "Monk" Lewis was derived from his novel of "Ambrosio, or the Monk," in which the terrifying and, it must be said, the licentious possibilities of the Gothic romance were carried to a high pitch. This, on the whole, rather worthless species, which had been accompanied by many feeble attempts at a more definitely historical type of novel, culminated surprisingly in the romances of Sir Walter Scott. Scott, however, had in his training and in his vast reading a basis for historical and romantic fiction all his own. He stripped the Gothic type of romance of its sentimentality and absurdity, strengthened it with his great fund of historical and legendary information, gave it stability with his sanity and humor, and interest by his creation of a great series of vigorous and picturesque creations. The art of fiction has gained in technical dexterity since Scott's day, stories now begin sooner and move more rapidly, conversation is reported with a greater lifelikeness, the tragedy in human life is more often given its due place; but the entrancing narratives of Scott, with all their deliberation, are likely to retain their charm, and his men and women still have blood in their veins. He created the historical novel, not only for Britain but for Europe, and all its writers since have been proud to sit at his feet.

Sir Walter Scott's (1771–1832) name is virtually synonymous with the Romantic Movement in which he worked. Though best remembered today for his historical novels, Scott was also proficient in the tale of terror. His ghost story "The Tapestried Chamber" created the template that nearly all Victorian ghost tales would follow, and his lengthy 1827 essay "On the Supernatural in Fictitious Composition" discussed the supernatural in tragedy, fantasy, and romance and berated the German fantasist Ernst Theodor Wilhelm Hoffmann (1776–1822), who wrote under the pen name E. T. A. Hoffmann, for overly grotesque and absurd use of the same.

As part of a series of biographies written in 1821 as prefaces for new editions of the works of prominent authors, Scott surveyed the life of Ann Radcliffe (1764–1823), the Gothic novelist whose *The Mysteries of Udolpho* (1794) reigned for years as the greatest of the Gothic horrors. In this excerpt from "Mrs. Ann Radcliffe," Scott discusses *Udolpho* and its predecessor, *The Romance of the Forest* (1791), and defends tales of terror as a legitimate literary art form.

*Excerpt from "Mrs. Ann Radcliffe"**
SIR WALTER SCOTT

The Romance of the Forest, which appeared in 1791, placed the author at once in that rank and preeminence in her own particular style of composition, which her works have ever since maintained. Her fancy, in this new effort, was more regulated, and subjected to the fetters of a regular story. The persons, too, although perhaps there is nothing very original in the conception, were depicted with skill far superior to that which the author had hitherto displayed, and the work attracted the public attention in proportion. That of La Motte, indeed, is sketched with particular talent, and most part of the interest of the piece depends upon the vacillations of a character, who, though upon the whole we may rather term him weak and vicious, than villanous, is, nevertheless, at every moment on the point of becoming an agent in atrocities which his heart disapproves of. He is the exact picture "of the needy man who has known better days;" one who, spited at the world, from which he has been expelled with contempt, and condemned by circumstances to seek an asylum in a desolate mansion full of mysteries and horrors, avenges himself, by playing the gloomy despot within his own family, and tyrannizing over those who were subjected to him only by their strong sense of duty. A more powerful agent appears on the scene—obtains the mastery over this dark but irresolute spirit, and, by alternate exertion of seduction and terror, compels him to be his agent in schemes against the virtue, and even the life of an orphan, whom he was hound in gratitude, as well as in honour and hospitality, to cherish and protect.

The heroine, too, wearing the usual costume of innocence, purity, and simplicity, as proper to heroines as white gowns are to the sex in general, has some pleasant touches of originality. Her grateful affection for the La Motte family—her reliance on their truth and honour, when the wife had

*Sir Walter Scott, "Mrs. Ann Radcliffe," in *Biographical Memoirs of Eminent Novelists and Other Distinguished Persons*, vol. I, in *The Miscellaneous Prose Works of Sir Walter Scott, Bart.*, vol. III (Edinburgh: Robert Cadell, 1834), 342–347.

become unkind, and the father treacherous towards her, is an interesting and individual trait in her character.

But although, undoubtedly, the talents of Mrs. Radcliffe, in the important point of drawing and finishing the characters of her narrative, were greatly improved since her earlier attempts, and manifested sufficient power to raise her far above the common crowd of novelists, this was not the department of art on which her popularity rested. The public were chiefly aroused, or rather fascinated, by the wonderful conduct of a story, in which the author so successfully called out the feelings of mystery and of awe, while chapter after chapter, and incident after incident, maintained the thrilling-attraction of awakened curiosity and suspended interest. Of these, every reader felt the force, from the sage in his study, to the family group in middle life, which assembles round the evening taper, to seek a solace from the toils of ordinary existence by an excursion into the regions of imagination. The tale was the more striking, because varied and relieved by descriptions of the ruined mansion, and the forest with which it is surrounded, under so many different points of view, now pleasing and serene, now gloomy, now terrible—scenes which could only have been drawn by one to whom nature had given the eye of a painter, with the spirit of a poet.

In 1793, Mrs Radcliffe had the advantage of visiting the scenery of the Rhine, and, although we are not positive of the fact, we are strongly inclined to suppose, that *The Mysteries of Udolpho* were written, or at least corrected, after the date of this journey; for the mouldering castles of the robber-chivalry of Germany, situated on the wild and romantic banks of that celebrated stream, seem to have given a bolder flight to her imagination, and a more glowing character to her colouring, than are exhibited in *The Romance of the Forest*. The scenery on the Lakes of Westmoreland, which Mrs Radcliffe visited about the same time, was also highly calculated to awaken her fancy, as nature has in these wild but beautiful regions realized the descriptions in which this authoress loved to indulge. Her remarks upon these countries were given to the public in 1794, in a very well-written work, entitled, *A Journey through Holland, &c.*

Much was of course expected from Mrs Radcliffe's next effort, and the booksellers felt themselves authorized in offering what was then considered as an unprecedented sum, L.500, for *The Mysteries of Udolpho*. It often happens, that a writer's previous reputation proves the greatest enemy which, in a second attempt upon public favour, he has to encounter. Exaggerated expectations are excited and circulated, and criticism which had been seduced into

The Mysteries of Udolpho. The Mysteries of Udolpho *was Ann Radcliffe's most successful book and, arguably, the most famous Gothic novel of the age. Unlike many of her contemporaries, Radcliffe undercut the supernatural horror of the Gothic by providing naturalistic explanations for the otherworldly phenomena in her books. The scene depicted here, from the frontispiece of the 1809 edition, shows the heroine, Emily, begging the evil Count Montoni not to lock up his wife, seated at right, in the castle turret (Beinecke Rare Book and Manuscript Library, Yale University).*

former approbation by the pleasure of surprise, now stands awakened and alert to pounce upon every failing. Mrs Radcliffe's popularity, however, stood the test, and was heightened rather than diminished by *The Mysteries of Udolpho*. The very name was fascinating; and the public, who rushed upon it with all lie eagerness of curiosity, rose from it with unsated appetite. When a family was numerous, the volumes always flew, and were sometimes torn, from hand to hand; and the complaints of those whose studies were thus interrupted, were a general tribute to the genius of the author. Another might be found of a different and higher description, in the dwelling of the lonely invalid, or unregarded votary of celibacy, who was bewitched away from a sense of solitude, of indisposition, of the neglect of the world, or of secret sorrow, by the potent charm of this mighty enchantress. Perhaps the perusal of such works may, without injustice, be compared with the use of opiates, baneful, when habitually and constantly resorted to, but of most blessed power in those moments of pain and of languor, when the whole head is sore, and the whole heart sick. If those who rail indiscriminately at this species of composition, were to consider the quantity of actual pleasure which it produces, and, the much greater proportion of real sorrow and distress which it alleviates, their philanthropy ought to moderate their critical pride, or religious intolerance.

To return to *The Mysteries of Udolpho*. The author, pursuing her own favourite bent of composition, and again waving her wand over the world of wonder and imagination, had judiciously used a spell of broader and more potent command. The situation and distresses of the heroines, have here, and in *The Romance of the Forest*, a general aspect of similarity. Both are divided from the object of their attachment by the gloomy influence of unfaithful and oppressive guardians, and both become inhabitants of time-stricken towers, and witnesses of scenes now bordering on the supernatural, and now upon the horrible. But this general resemblance is only such as we love to recognise in pictures which have been painted by the same hand, and as companions for each other. Every thing in *The Mysteries of Udolpho* is on a larger and more sublime scale, than in *The Romance of the Forest*; the interest is of a more agitating and tremendous nature; the scenery of a wilder and more terrific description; the characters distinguished by fiercer and more gigantic features. Montoni, a lofty-souled desperado, and Captain of Condottieri, stands beside La Motte and his Marquis, like one of Milton's fiends beside a witch's familiar. Adeline is confined within a ruined manor-house, but her sister heroine, Emily, is imprisoned in a huge castle, like those of feudal times; the one is attacked and defended by bands of armed banditti, the other only threatened by a visit from constables and thief-takers. The scale of the landscape is equally different; the quiet and limited woodland scenery of the one work forming a contrast with the splendid and high-wrought descriptions of Italian mountain grandeur which occur in the other.

In general, *The Mysteries of Udolpho* was, at its first appearance, considered as a step beyond Mrs Radcliffe's former work, high as that had justly advanced her. We entertain the same opinion in again reading them both, even after some years' interval. Yet there were persons of no mean judgment, to whom the simplicity of *The Romance of the Forest* seemed preferable to the more highly coloured and broader style of *The Mysteries of Udolpho*; and it must remain matter of opinion, whether their preference be better founded than in the partialities of a first love, which in literature, as in life, are often unduly predominant. With the majority of readers, the superior magnificence of landscape, and dignity of conception of character, secured the palm for the more recent work.

The "Fragments of an Unpublished Magazine" were supposedly the work of "Adam Eagle," an editor who used correspondents to create a private magazine never published. According to the *American Whig Review*, these fell into their possession, and from them they copied portions. In fact, in the October 1852 *Whig* publication, it is unclear whether the following passage is Eagle's work, his correspondents', or the *Whig*'s own comment, though this was how its real author wanted it. The "Fragments" are entirely the work of Fitz-James O'Brien (1828–1862), the author of a number of horror masterpieces, such as "What Was It?" At the risk of being reductive, here is an ironic fragment of the "Fragments," covering tales of terror and discussing the work of the poet "Heremon," another of O'Brien's aliases.

*Excerpt from "Fragments of an Unpublished Magazine"**

ADAM EAGLE (FITZ-JAMES O'BRIEN)

A deeper hand now strikes the lyre. The murmur of the ocean shell dies off into silence, and a strain laden with ghostliness and death rises from the harp of the weird contributor. Well may he have chosen the darkened face for his crest. A veil seems to shroud his nature, and his soul

---

*Adam Eagle (Fitz-James O'Brien), "Fragments of an Unpublished Magazine," *The American Whig Review*, October 1852, 364.

revels in mystery. Terror is the monotone which his heart utters when the wind of inspiration sweeps across its chords. His dwelling should be in some dark, German castle, with long corridors, deserted chambers, and pictures that occasionally come down from the wall of their own accord. A clanking spectre should stand every night at his bedside, and he should wear a "death-watch" in his fob. With such adjuncts as these, he of the darkened face might be qualified to fill the niche left vacant by Mrs. Radcliffe, or edit some ghastly magazine, which might perhaps be entitled "The Pyramid of Horrors."

We decidedly object as a rule to these tales of terror. They neither benefit society nor the author. We recollect the time when we could not ourselves write a tale without three murders in it, interspersed with a ghost or two. But these days are gone by with us; and henceforward we will stick to nature.

The British essayist Charles Lamb (1775–1834) composed the *Essays of Elia* and a children's book retelling the plays of William Shakespeare. In this letter, he shares with his editor, William Godwin, the journalist and father of *Frankenstein* author Mary Shelly, his views on the difference between terror and disgust as it pertains to Lamb's *The Adventures of Ulysses* (1808), a retelling of Homer's *Odyssey*, that Godwin wanted to strip of its intimations of horror, which he saw as unsuitable for young readers.

*Letter to William Godwin**
CHARLES LAMB

March 11, 1808.

Dear Godwin—The giant's vomit was perfectly nauseous, and I am glad you pointed it out. I have removed the objection. To the other passages I can find no other objection but what you may bring to numberless passages besides, such as of Scylla snatching up the six men, etc.,—that is to say, they are lively images of *shocking* things. If you want a book, which is not occasionally to *shock*, you should not have thought of a tale which was so full of anthropophagi and wonders. I cannot alter these things without enervating the Book, and I will not alter them if the penalty should be that you and all the London booksellers should refuse it. But speaking as author to author, I must say that I think *the terrible* in those two passages

---

*Charles Lamb, *The Letters of Charles Lamb Newly Arranged, with Additions*, vol. 1, ed. Alfred Ainger (London: Macmillan and Company, 1888), 247–248.

seems to me so much to preponderate over the nauseous, as to make them rather fine than disgusting. Who is to read them, I don't know: who is it that reads "Tales of Terror" and "Mysteries of Udolpho"? Such things sell. I only say that I will not consent to alter such passages, which I know to be some of the best in the book. As an author, I say to you an author: touch not my work. As to a bookseller I say, Take the work such as it is, or refuse it. You are as free to refuse it as when we first talked of it. As to a friend I say, Don't plague yourself and me with nonsensical objections. I assure you I will not alter one more word.

Rudolph Ackermann (1764–1823), a German expatriate inventor (in part responsible for gaslight) and publisher in London, took a dim view of Gothic literary excess, and he created an anthology of ghostly tales for the purpose of demonstrating that the supernatural is a misunderstanding of natural processes. The tales in his *Ghost Stories: Collected with Particular View to Counteract the Vulgar Belief in Ghosts and Apparitions, and to Promote a Rational Estimate of the Nature of Phenomena Commonly Considered as Supernatural* (1823) all ended with an Radcliffe-like revelation of the materialist origins of the tale's otherworldly phenomena. Here, in the introduction, the author explains why he finds ghosts such a silly belief.

Introduction to Ghost Stories[*]

RUDOLPH ACKERMANN

What is a ghost? In the popular acceptation of the term, it is a visible appearance of a deceased person. It is called also a spirit; but, if visible, it must be matter; consequently not a spirit. If it is not matter, it can only exist in the imagination of the beholder; and must therefore be classed with the multifarious phantoms which haunt the sick man's couch in delirium.

But ghosts have appeared to more than one person at a time;—how then? Can he exist in the imagination of two persons at once? That is not probable, and we doubt the "authentic" accounts of ghosts appearing to more than one at a time. The stories we are about to tell will show, however, that in a great many instances several persons have thought that they saw ghosts at the same time, when, in fact, there was no ghost in the case; but substantial flesh and blood and bones.

[*]Rudolph Ackermann, "Introduction," in *Ghost Stories; Collected with a Particular View to Counteract the Vulgar Belief in Ghosts and Apparitions* (Philadelphia: Henry Carey Baird, 1854), 5–6.

But what does a ghost represent? What is it the ghost of? Of a man or woman, to be sure. But does it appear as a man or woman only? Is it nude? Oh no! Oh shocking! This is contrary to all the rules. It always appears dressed? If the man has been murdered, it appears in the very clothes he was murdered in, all bloody, with a pale, murdered-looking face, and a ghastly wound in the breast, head, stomach, back or abdominal region, as the case may be; but always in decent clothes. If the person died quietly a natural death, in bed; then the ghost is generally clad in long white robes, or a shroud; but still properly dressed. So then, we have the ghost of the clothes also—the ghost of the coat and unmentionables—the ghost of the cocked hat and wig. How is this?

But to cut the matter short—the whole theory of ghosts is too flimsy to bear the rough handling of either reason or ridicule. The best way to dissipate the inbred horror of supernatural phantoms, which almost all persons derive from nursery tales or other sources of causeless terror in early life, is to show by example how possible it is to impress upon ignorant or credulous persons the firm belief that they behold a ghost, when in point of fact no ghost is there. We proceed at once to our stories.

The poet and author Leigh Hunt (1784–1859), contemporary and acquaintance of William Hazlitt, Charles Lamb, Percy and Mary Shelly, and Lord Byron, had served time in prison for insulting the Prince Regent in his journal *The Examiner*, and issued a warts-and-all portrait of Byron after his death. As one of that generation of Romantics, he was given to the occasional telling of tales of terror. Here he appends a brief horror story to an essay probing into the popularity of the Gothic school. The piece first ran in *The Indicator* on December 15, 1819, just in time for the popular British tradition of telling yuletide ghost stories (see page 292).

A Tale for a Chimney Corner[*]
Leigh Hunt

A man who does not contribute his quota of grim story now-a-days, seems hardly to be free of the republic of letters. He is bound to wear a death's head as part of his insignia. If he does not frighten everybody,

---

[*]Leigh Hunt, "A Tale for a Chimney Corner," in *The Indicator: A Miscellany for the Fields and the Fire Side* (New York: Wiley and Putnam, 1845), 76–85.

he is nobody. If he does not shock the ladies, what can be expected of him?

We confess we think very cheaply of these stories in general. A story, merely horrible or even awful, which contains no sentiment elevating to the human heart and its hopes, is a mere appeal to the least judicious, least healthy, and least masculine of our passions—fear. They whose attention can be gravely arrested by it, are in a fit state to receive any absurdity with respect; and, this is the reason why less talents are required to enforce it, than in any other species of composition. With this opinion of such things, we may be allowed to say, that we would undertake to write a dozen horrible stories in a day, all of which should make the common worshippers of power, who were not in the very healthiest condition, turn pale. We would tell of Haunting Old Women, and Knocking Ghosts, and Solitary Lean Hands, and Empusas on One Leg, and Ladies growing Longer and Longer, and Horrid Eyes meeting us through Keyholes, and Plaintive Heads, and Shrieking Statues, and shocking Anomalies of Shape, and Things which when seen drove people mad; and Indigestion knows what besides. But who would measure talents with a leg of veal or a German sausage?

Mere grimness is as easy as grinning; but it requires something to put a handsome face on a story. Narratives become of suspicious merit in proportion as they lean to Newgate-like offences, particularly of blood and wounds. A child has a reasonable respect for a Raw-head-and-bloody-bones, because all images whatsoever of pain and terror are new and fearful to his inexperienced age; but sufferings merely physical (unless sublimated like those of Philoctetes) are commonplace to a grown man. Images, to become awful to him, must be removed from the grossness of the shambles. A death's-head was a respectable thing in the hands of a poring monk, or of a nun compelled to avoid the idea of life and society, or of a hermit already buried in the desert. Holbein's Dance of Death, in which every grinning skeleton leads along a man of rank, from the Pope to the gentleman, is a good Memento Mori; but there the skeletons have an air of the ludicrous and satirical. If we were threatened with them in a grave way, as spectres, we should have a right to ask how they could walk about without muscles. Thus many of the tales written by such authors as the late Mr. Lewis, who wanted sentiment to give him the heart of truth, are quite puerile. When his spectral nuns go about bleeding, we think they ought in decency to have applied to some ghost of a surgeon. His little

Grey Men, who sit munching hearts, are of a piece with fellows that eat cats for a wager.

Stories that give mental pain to no purpose, or to very little purpose compared with the unpleasant ideas they excite of human nature, are as gross mistakes, in their way, as these, and twenty times as pernicious; for the latter becomes ludicrous to grown people. They originate also in the same extremes, of callousness, or of morbid want of excitement, as the others. But more of these hereafter. Our business at present is with things ghastly and ghostly.

A ghost story, to be a good one, should unite, as much as possible, objects such as they are in life with a preternatural spirit. And to be a perfect one,—at least, to add to the other utility of excitement a moral utility,—they should imply some great sentiment,—something that comes out of the next world to remind us of our duties in this; or something that helps to carry on the idea of our humanity into afterlife, even when we least think we shall take it with us. When "the buried majesty of Denmark" revisits earth to speak to his son Hamlet, he comes armed, as he used to be, in his complete steel. His visor is raised; and the same fine face is there; only, in spite of his punishing errand and his own sufferings, with

> A countenance more in sorrow than in anger.

When Donne the poet, in his thoughtful eagerness to reconcile life and death, had a figure of himself painted in a shroud, and laid by his bedside in a coffin, he did a higher thing than the monks and hermits with their skulls. It was taking his humanity with him into the other world, not affecting to lower the sense of it by regarding it piecemeal or in the framework. Burns, in his *Tam O'Shanter*, shows the dead in their coffins after the same fashion. He does not lay bare to us their skeletons or refuse, things with which we can connect no sympathy or spiritual wonder. They still are flesh and body to retain the one; yet so look and behave, inconsistent in their very consistency, as to excite the other.

> Coffins stood round like open presses,
> Which showed the dead in their last dresses:
> And by some devilish cantrip sleight,
> Each, in his cauld hand, held a light.

Re-animation is perhaps the most ghastly of all ghastly things, uniting as it does an appearance of natural interdiction from the next world, with a

A Galvanized Corpse. This 1838 cartoon from the era of Andrew Jackson makes use of the phenomenon of galvanization to mock newspaper editor and Jackson advisor Francis Preston Blair as a corpse brought to life for Jackson. In 1803 Giovanni Aldini galvanized a corpse into convulsions, and in 1818 Andrew Ure induced facial expressions through the application of electricity to the dead. Such experiments led scientists to wonder if electricity could bring the dead to life, and influenced Mary Shelley's Frankenstein *(Library of Congress, Prints and Photographs Division, LC-USZ62-119166).*

supernatural experience of it. Our human consciousness is jarred out of its self-possession. The extremes of habit and newness, of commonplace and astonishment, meet suddenly, without the kindly introduction of death and change; and the stranger appals us in proportion. When the account appeared the other day in the newspapers of the galvanized dead body,[a] whose features as well as limbs underwent such contortions, that it seemed as if it were about to rise up, one almost expected to hear, for the first time, news of the other world. Perhaps the most appalling figure in Spenser is that of Maleger: (*Faerie Queene*, b. ii. c. xi)

> Upon a tygre swift and fierce he rode,
> That as the winde ran underneath his lode,
> Whiles his long legs nigh raught unto the ground:
> Full large he was of limbe, and shoulders brode,
> But of such subtile substance and unsound,
> That like a ghost he seemed, whose grave-clothes were unbound.

Mr. Coleridge, in that voyage of his to the brink of all unutterable things, the *Ancient Mariner* (which works out, however, a fine sentiment), does not set mere ghosts or hobgoblins to man the ship again, when its crew are dead; but reanimates, for awhile, the crew themselves. There is a striking fiction of this sort in Sale's notes upon the Koran. Solomon dies during the building of the temple, but his body remains leaning on a staff and overlooking the workmen, as if it were alive; till a worm gnawing through the prop, he falls down.—The contrast of the appearance of humanity with something mortal or supernatural, is always the more terrible in proportion as it is complete. In the pictures of the temptations of saints and hermits, where the holy person is surrounded, teased, and enticed, with devils and fantastic shapes, the most shocking phantasm is that of the beautiful woman. To return also to the poem above-mentioned. The most appalling personage in Mr. Coleridge's *Ancient Mariner* is the Spectre-woman, who is called Life-in-Death. He renders the most hideous abstraction more terrible than it could otherwise have been, by embodying it in its own reverse. "Death" not only "lives" in it, but the "unutterable" becomes uttered. To see such an unearthly passage end in such earthliness, seems to turn commonplace itself into a sort of spectral doubt. The Mariner, after describing the horrible calm, and the rotting sea in which the ship was stuck, is speaking of a strange sail which he descried in the distance:

> The western wave was all a-flame,
> The day was well nigh done!
> Almost upon the western wave
> Rested the broad bright sun;
> When that strange ship drove suddenly
> Betwixt us and the sun.
>
> And straight the sun was flecked with bars,
> (Heaven's Mother send us grace!)
> As if through a dungeon-grate he peer'd,
> With broad and burning face.
>
> Alas! (thought I, and my heart beat loud)
> How fast she nears and nears!
> Are those *her* sails that glance in the sun
> Like restless gossamers?
>
> Are those *her* ribs, through which the sun
> Did peer as through a grate?

> And is that Woman all her crew?
> Is that a death? and are there two?
> Is Death that Woman's mate?
>
> Her lips were red, her looks were free,
> Her locks were yellow as gold,
> Her skin was as white as leprosy,
> The Night-Mare Life-in-Death was she,
> Who thicks man's blood with cold.

But we must come to Mr. Coleridge's story with our subtlest imaginations upon us. Now let us put our knees a little nearer the fire, and tell a homelier one about Life in Death, the ground work of it is in Sandys' Commentary upon Ovid, and quoted from Sabinus.*

A gentleman of Bavaria, of a noble family, was so afflicted at the death of his wife, that, unable to bear the company of any other person, gave himself up to a solitary way of living. This was the more remarkable in him, as he had been a man of jovial habits, fond of his wine and visitors, and impatient of having his numerous indulgences contradicted. But in the same temper, perhaps, might be found the cause of his sorrow; for though he would be impatient with his wife, as with others, yet his love for her was one of the gentlest wills he had; and the sweet and unaffected face which she always turned upon his anger, might have been a thing more easy for him to trespass upon, while living, than to forget when dead and gone. His very angry towards her, compared with that towards others, was a relief to him. It was rather a wish to refresh himself in the balmy feeling of her patience, than to make her unhappy herself, or to punish her, as some would have done, for that virtuous contrast to his own vice.

But whether he bethought himself, after her death, that this was a very selfish mode of loving; or whether, as some thought, he had wearied out her life with habits so contrary to her own; or whether, as others reported, he had put it to a fatal risk by some lordly piece of self-will, in consequence of which she had caught a fever on the cold river during a night of festivity; he surprised even those who thought that he loved her by the extreme bitterness of his grief. The very mention of festivity, though he was patient for the first day or two, afterwards threw him into a passion or rage; but by degrees even his rage followed his other old habits. He was gentle, but ever silent. He ate and drank but sufficient to keep him

---

*The Saxon Latin poet, we presume, professor of belles-lettres at Frankfurt. We know nothing of him, except from a biographical dictionary.

alive; and used to spend the greater part of the day in the spot where his wife was buried.

He was going there one evening, in a very melancholy manner, with his eyes turned towards the earth, and had just entered the rails of the burial-ground, when he was accosted by the mild voice of somebody coming to meet him. "It is a blessed evening, sir," said the voice. The gentleman looked up. Nobody but himself was allowed to be in the place at that hour, and yet he saw with astonishment a young chorister approached him. He was going to express some wonder, when, he said, the modest though assured look of the boy, and the extreme beauty of his countenance, which glowed in the setting sun before him, made an irresistible addition to the singular sweetness of his voice; and he asked him with an involuntary calmness, and a gesture of respect, not what he did there, but what he wished. "Only to wish you all good things," answered the stranger, who had now come up, "and to give you this letter." The gentleman took the letter, and saw upon it, with a beating yet scarcely bewildered heart, the handwriting of his wife. He raised his eyes again to speak to the boy, but he was gone. He cast them far and near round the place, but there were no traces of a passenger. He then opened the letter, and by the divine light of the setting sun, read these words:

"To my dear husband, who sorrows for his wife:
"Otto, my husband, the soul you regret so is returned. You will know the truth of this, and be prepared with calmness to see it, by the divineness of the messenger who has passed you. You will find me sitting in the public walk, praying for you, praying that you may never more give way to those gusts of passion and those curses against others, which divided us.
"This, with a warm hand, from the living Bertha."

Otto (for such, it seems, was the gentleman's name) went instantly, calmly, quickly, yet with a sort of benumbed being, to the public walk. He felt, but with only a half-consciousness, as if he glided without a body, but all his spirit was awake, eager, intensely conscious. It seemed to him as if there had been but two things in the world—Life and Death; and that Death was dead. All else appeared to have been a dream. He had awaked from a waking state, and found himself all eye, and spirit, and locomotion. He said to himself, once, as he went: "This is not a dream. I will ask my great ancestors tomorrow to my new bridal feast, for they are alive." Otto had been calm at first, but something of old and triumphant feelings seemed again to come over him. Was he again too proud and confident? Did his earthly humors prevail again, when he thought them least upon him? We shall see.

The Bavarian arrived at the public walk. It was full of people with their wives and children, enjoying the beauty of the evening. Something like common fear came over him as he went in and out among them, looking at the beaches on each side. It happened that there was only one person, a lady, sitting upon them. She had her veil down, and his being underwent a fierce but short convulsion as he went near her. Something had a little baffled the calmer inspiration of the angel that had accosted him, for fear prevailed at the instant, and Otto passed on. He returned before he had reached the end of the walk, and approached the lady again. She was still sitting in the same quiet posture, only he thought she looked at him. Again he passed her. On his second return, a grave and sweet courage came upon him, and in a quiet but firm tone of inquiry, he said, "Bertha?"—"I thought you had forgotten me," said that well-known and mellow voice, which he had seemed as far from ever hearing again as earth is from heaven. He took her hand, which grasped his in turn; and they walked home in silence together, the arm, which was wound within his, giving warmth for warmth.

The neighbors seemed to have a miraculous want of wonder at the lady's re-appearance. Something was said about a mock funeral, and her having withdrawn from his company for awhile; but visitors came as before, and his wife returned to her household affairs. It was only remarked that she always looked pale and pensive. But she was more kind to all, even than before; and her pensiveness seemed rather the result of some great internal thought, than of unhappiness.

For a year or two the Bavarian retained the better temper which he acquired. His fortunes flourished beyond his earliest ambition; the most amiable as well as noble persons of the district were frequent visitors; and people said that to be at Otto's house must be the next thing to being in heaven. But by degrees his self-will returned with his prosperity. He never vented impatience on his wife, but he again began to show that the disquietude it gave her to see it vented on others was a secondary thing, in his mind, to the indulgence of it. Whether it was that his grief for her loss had been rather remorse than affection, and so he held himself secure if he treated her well, or whether he was at all times rather proud of her than fond, or whatever was the cause which again set his antipathies above his sympathies, certain it was that his old habits returned upon him; not so often, indeed, but with greater violence and pride when they did. These were the only times at which his wife was observed to show any ordinary symptoms of uneasiness.

At length, one day, some strong rebuff which he had received from an alienated neighbor threw him into such a transport of rage that he gave way to the most bitter imprecations, crying with a loud voice, "This treatment to *me* too! To *me!* To me, who if the world knew all"—At these words, his wife, who had in vain laid her hand upon his, and looked him with dreary earnestness in the face, suddenly glided from the room. He and two or three who were present were struck with a dumb horror. They said she did not walk out, nor vanish suddenly, but glided as one who could dispense with the use of feet. After a moment's pause, the others proposed to him to follow her. He made a movement of despair, but they went. There was a short passage which turned to the right into her favourite room. They knocked at the door twice or three times, and received no answer. At last one of them gently opened it, and, looking in, they saw her, as they thought, standing before a fire, which was the only light in the room. Yet she stood so far from it as rather to be in the middle of the room; only the face was towards the fire, and she seemed looking upon it. They addressed her, but received no answer. They stepped gently towards her, and still received none. The figure stood dumb and unmoved. At last, one of them went round in front, and instantly fell on the floor. The figure was without body. A hollow hood was left instead of a face. The clothes were standing upright by themselves.

That room was blocked up for ever, for the clothes, if it might be so, to moulder away. It was called the Room of the Lady's Figure. The house after the gentleman's death was long uninhabited, and at length burnt by the peasants in an insurrection. As for himself, he died about nine months after, a gentle and childlike penitent. He had never stirred from the house since, and nobody would venture to go near him but a man who had the reputation of being a reprobate. It was from this man that the particulars of the story came first. He would distribute the gentleman's alms in great abundance to any poor stranger who would accept them, for most of the neighbors held them in horror. He tried all he could to get the parents among them to let some of their little children, or a single one of them, go to see his employer. They said he even asked it one day with tears in his eyes. But they shuddered to think of it; and the matter was not mended when this profane person, in a fit of impatience, said one day that he would have a child of his own on purpose. His employer, however, died in a day or two. They did not believe a word he told them of all the Bavarian's gentleness, looking upon the latter as a sort of ogre, and upon his agent as little better, though a good-natured-looking, earnest kind of person. It was said many years after, that this man had been a friend of the Bavarian's when young, and had been deserted by him. And the young believed it, whatever the old might do.

Notes

a. Galvanism was the name given to the application of electricity in honor of Luigi Galvani, who caused frog's legs to twitch when hooked up to an early form of a battery. In 1803 Giovanni Aldini galvanized the corpses of murderers to induce life-like convulsions. In 1818, Dr. Andrew Ure galvanized the corpse of a hanged murderer, producing convulsions and a range of facial expressions. Audiences were horrified, but scientists wondered if the process might restore the dead to life. These experiments influenced Mary Shelley's development of *Frankenstein* and also formed the basis of modern-day defibrillation, in which electric paddles shock stopped hearts back to life.

On a suitably Gothic stormy night in 1816, Lord Byron, John Polidori, Mary Godwin (later Shelley), and Percy Bysshe Shelley decided to write ghost stories in imitation of the German tales they encountered while on vacation in Geneva. Mary Shelley's version of the event is well known from her preface to *Frankenstein*, one of the tales that grew out of that night. Here, Byron's personal physician, John Polidori (1795–1821), writing as an anonymous observer, relates another version of the now-famous night at the Villa Diadoti, which also gave rise to his own novel, *The Vampyre* (1819), from a fragment by Byron. Here Polidori conflates the night in June when the story competition began with a July evening in which the trio and Matthew "Monk" Lewis listened to a reading of Coleridge's vampire poem *Christabel* (1816).

Polidori, dismissed from Byron's service, battled depression and likely committed suicide, though officially his death at age 26 was attributed to natural causes. This excerpt from his "Extract of a Letter from Geneva" ran as an anonymous preface to the first edition of *The Vampyre* (see page 103). It begins by describing Byron.

*Excerpt from "A Letter from Geneva"**
John Polidori

As he became intimate, from long acquaintance, with several of the families in this neighbourhood, I have gathered from their accounts some

---

*"Extract of a Letter from Geneva," in *The Vampyre; A Tale* (London: Sherwood, Neely, and Jones, 1819), xiv–xvi.

excellent traits of his lordship's character, which I will relate to you at some future opportunity. I must, however, free him from one imputation attached to him—of having in his house two sisters as the partakers of his revels. This is, like many other charges which have been brought against his lordship, entirely destitute of truth. His only companion was the physician I have already mentioned. The report originated from the following circumstance: Mr. Percy Bysshe Shelly [sic], a gentleman well known for extravagance of doctrine, and for his daring, in their profession, even to sign himself with the title of Αθεος in the Album at Chamouny, having taken a house below, in which he resided with Miss M. W. Godwin and Miss Clermont, (the daughters of the celebrated Mr. Godwin) they were frequently visitors at Diodati, and were often seen upon the lake with his Lordship, which gave rise to the report, the truth of which is here positively denied.

Among other things which the lady, from whom I procured these anecdotes, related to me, she mentioned the outline of a ghost story by Lord Byron. It appears, that one evening Lord B., Mr. P. B. Shelly, the two ladies and the gentleman before alluded to, after having perused a German work, which was entitled Phantasmagoriana,[a] began relating ghost stories; when his lordship having recited the beginning of Christabel, then unpublished, the whole took so strong a hold of Mr. Shelly's mind, that he suddenly started up and ran out of the room. The physician and Lord Byron followed, and discovered him leaning against a mantle-piece, with cold drops of perspiration trickling down his face. After having given him something to refresh him, upon enquiring into the cause of his alarm, they found that his wild imagination having pictured to him the bosom of one of the ladies with eyes (which was reported of a lady in the neighbourhood where he lived) he was obliged to leave the room in order to destroy the impression. It was afterwards proposed, in the course of conversation, that each of the company present should write a tale depending upon some supernatural agency, which was undertaken by Lord B., the physician, and Miss M. W. Godwin.* My friend, the lady above referred to, had in her possession the outline of each of these stories; I obtained them as a great favour, and herewith forward them to you, as I was assured you would feel as much curiosity as myself, to peruse the *ebauches* of so great a genius, and those immediately under his influence.

*Since published under the title of "Frankenstein; or, The Modern Prometheus."

Notes

a. Polidori refers here to the French translation of parts of the first two volumes of the German *Das Gespensterbuch* ("The Ghost Book") (1811–1815) by Friedrich Laun (Friedrich August Schultz) and Johann August Apel. The French version was called *Fantasmagoriana, ou Recueil d'Histoires d'Apparitions de Spectres, Revenans, Fantomes, etc.; traduit de l'allemand, par un Amateur*, and was published Jean Baptiste Benoit Eyries in 1812. Sarah Elizabeth Utterson translated parts of the French book into English as *Tales of the Dead* (1813), to which she added a story of her own. Both *Tales* and *Fantasmagoriana* had only one edition and remained out of print until the 1990s.

We have already seen Sir Walter Scott's evaluation of Ann Radcliffe, but Scott was equally familiar with other manifestations of the Gothic. In March 1818 Scott reviewed the newly-released *Frankenstein* by Mary Shelly (1797–1851), publishing the following remarks in an unsigned article in *Blackwood's Edinburgh Magazine*, a favored journal for writers of Gothic horror. Scott's review was largely positive, one of the few to approve of Shelley's novel. As such it is frequently excerpted, but here it is given in full, including the lengthy excerpts from the novel under review which early critics believed were essential for readers to "taste" the text before making a purchase. Note, though, that since *Frankenstein* was published anonymously, Scott refers to its author as a man, assuming it to be the work of Mary's husband, Percy Bysshe Shelley.

Remarks on Frankenstein, or the Modern Prometheus[*]
SIR WALTER SCOTT

> Did I request thee, Maker, from my clay,
> To mould me man? Did I solicit thee
> From darkness to promote me?—
> > Paradise Lost.

This is a novel, or more properly a romantic fiction, of a nature so peculiar, that we ought to describe the species before attempting any account of the individual production.

The first general division of works of fiction, into such as bound the events they narrate by the actual laws of nature, and such as, passing these

---

[*]"Remarks on Frankenstein, or the Modern Prometheus; A Novel," *Blackwood's Edinburgh Magazine*, March 1818, 613–620.
Frankenstein; or, the Modern Prometheus. 3 vols 12 mo. 16s. 6d. Lackington and Co. London. 1818.

limits, are managed by marvellous and supernatural machinery, is sufficiently obvious and decided. But the class of marvellous romances admits of several subdivisions. In the earlier productions of imagination, the poet, or tale-teller does not, in his own opinion, transgress the laws of credibility, when he introduces into his narration the witches, goblins, and magicians, in the existence of which he himself, as well as his hearers, is a firm believer. This good faith, however, passes away, and works turning upon the marvellous are written and read merely on account of the exercise which they afford to the imagination of those who, like the poet Collins, love to riot in the luxuriance of oriental fiction, to rove through the meanders of enchantment, to gaze on the magnificence of golden palaces, and to repose by the water-falls of Elysian gardens. In this species of composition, the marvellous is itself the principal and most important object both to the author and reader. To describe its effect upon the mind of the human personages engaged in its wonders, and dragged along by its machinery, is comparatively an inferior object. The hero and heroine, partakers of the supernatural character which belongs to their adventures, walk the maze of enchantment with a firm and undaunted step, and appear as much at their ease, amid the wonders around them, as the young fellow described by the Spectator, who was discovered taking a snuff with great composure in the midst of a stormy ocean, represented on the stage of the Opera.

A more philosophical and refined use of the supernatural in works of fiction, is proper to that class in which the laws of nature are represented as altered, not for the purpose of pampering the imagination with wonders, but in order to shew the probable effect which the supposed miracles would produce on those who witnessed them. In this case, the pleasure ordinarily derived from the marvellous incidents is secondary to that which we extract from observing how mortals like ourselves would be affected,

> By scenes like these which, daring to depart
> From sober truth, are still to nature true.

Even in the description of his marvels, however, the author who manages the style of composition with address, gives them an indirect importance with the reader, when he is able to describe with nature, and with truth, the effects which they are calculated to produce upon his dramatis personæ. It will be remembered, that the sapient Partridge was too wise to be terrified at the mere appearance of the ghost of Hamlet, whom he knew to be a man dressed up in pasteboard armour for the nonce—it was when he saw the "little man," as he called Garrick, so frightened, that a sympathetic horror took hold of him. Of this we shall presently produce some examples from the narrative before us. But success in this point is still subordinate to the author's principal object, which is less to produce an effect by means of the marvels of the narrations, than to open new trains and channels of thought, by placing men in supposed situations of an extraordinary and preternatural character, and then describing the mode of feeling and conduct which they are most likely to adopt.

To make more clear the distinction we have endeavoured to draw between the marvellous and the effects of the marvellous, considered as separate objects, we may briefly invite our readers to compare the common tale of Tom Thumb with Gulliver's Voyage to Brobdingnag; one of the most childish fictions, with one which is pregnant with wit and satire, yet both turning upon the same assumed possibility of the existence of a pigmy among a race of giants. In the former case, when the imagination of the story-teller has exhausted itself in every species of hyperbole, in order to describe the diminutive size of his hero, the interest of the tale is at an end; but in the romance of the Dean of St Patrick's, the exquisite humour with which the natural consequences of so strange and unusual a situation is detailed, has a canvass on which to expand itself, as broad as the luxuriance even of the author's talents could desire. Gulliver stuck into a marrow bone, and Master Thomas Thumb's disastrous fall into the bowl of hasty-pudding, are, in the general outlines, kindred incidents; but the jest is exhausted in the latter case, when the accident is told; whereas in the former, it lies not so much in the comparatively pigmy size which subjected Gulliver to such a ludicrous misfortune, as in the tone of grave and dignified feeling with which he resents the disgrace of the incident.

In the class of fictitious narrations to which we allude, the author opens a sort of account-current with the reader; drawing upon him, in the first place, for credit to that degree of the marvellous which he proposes to employ; and becoming virtually bound, in consequence of this indulgence, that his personages shall conduct themselves, in the extraordinary circumstances in which they are placed, according to the rules of probability, and the nature of the human heart. In this view, the *probable* is far from being laid out of sight even amid the wildest freaks of imagination; on the contrary, we grant the extraordinary postulates which the author demands as the foundation of his narrative, only on condition of his deducing the consequences with logical precision.

We have only to add, that this class of fiction has been sometimes applied to the purposes of political satire, and sometimes to the general illustration of the powers and workings of the human mind. Swift, Bergerac, and others, have employed it for the former purpose, and a good illustration of the latter is the well known Saint Leon of William Godwin. In this latter work, assuming the possibility of the transmutation of metals, and of the *elixir vitæ*, the author has deduced, in the course of his narrative, the probable consequences of the possession of such secrets upon the fortunes and mind of him who might enjoy them. Frankenstein is a novel upon the same plan with Saint Leon; it is said to be written by Mr Percy Bysshe Shelley, who, if we are rightly informed, is son-in-law to Mr Godwin; and it is inscribed to that ingenious author.

In the preface, the author lays claim to rank his work among the class which we have endeavoured to describe.

> "The event on which this fiction is founded has been supposed by Dr. Darwin,[a] and some of the physiological writers of Germany, as not of impossible occurrence. I shall not be supposed as according the remotest degree of serious faith to such an imagination; yet, in assuming it as the basis of a work of fancy, I have not considered myself as merely weaving a series of supernatural terrors. The event on which the interest of the story depends is exempt from the disadvantages of a mere tale of spectres or enchantment. It was recommended by the novelty of the situations which it developes; and, however impossible as a physical fact, affords a point of view to the imagination for the delineating of human passions more comprehensive and commanding than any which the ordinary relations of existing events can yield.
>
> "I have thus endeavoured to preserve the truth of the elementary principles of human nature, while I have not scrupled to innovate upon their combinations. The *Iliad*, the tragic poetry of Greece—Shakespeare, in the *Tempest* and *Midsummer Night's Dream*—and most especially Milton, in *Paradise Lost*, conform to this rule; and the most humble novellist, who seeks to confer or receive amusement from his labours, may, without presumption, apply to prose fiction a license, or rather a rule, from the adoption of which so many exquisite combinations of high feeling have resulted in the highest specimens of poetry."

We shall, without farther preface, detail the particulars of the singular story, which is thus introduced.

A vessel, engaged in a voyage of discovery to the North Pole, having become come embayed among the ice at a very high latitude, the crew, and particularly the captain or owner of the ship, are surprised at perceiving a gigantic form pass at some distance from them, on a car drawn by dogs, in a place where they conceived no mortal could exist. While they are speculating on this singular apparition, a thaw commences, and disengages them from their precarious situation. On the next morning they pick up, upon a floating fragment of the broken ice, a sledge like that they had before seen, with a human being in the act of perishing. He is with

An Anatomy Lesson. In this scene from an Italian text on the application of anatomy to the depiction of the human body in the arts, medical students gather around to watch a dissection. In the eighteenth and nineteenth centuries, bodies for dissection were in short supply, leading grave-robbers to supply medical schools with stolen corpses, a practice that inspired Victor Frankenstein's charnel activities (National Library of Medicine).

difficulty recalled to life, and proves to be a young man of the most amiable manners and extended acquirements, but, extenuated by fatigue, wrapped in dejection and gloom of the darkest kind. The captain of the ship, a gentleman whose ardent love of science had engaged him on an expedition so dangerous, becomes attached to the stranger, and at length extorts from him the wonderful tale of his misery, which he thus attains the means of preserving from oblivion.

Frankenstein describes himself as a native of Geneva, born and bred up in the bosom of domestic love and affection. His father—his friend Henry Clerval—Elizabeth, an orphan of extreme beauty and talent, bred up in the same house with him, are possessed of all the qualifications which could render him happy as a son, a friend, and a lover. In the course of his studies he becomes acquainted with the works of Cornelius Agrippa, and other authors treating of occult philosophy, on whose venerable tomes modern neglect has scattered no slight portion of dust. Frankenstein remains ignorant of the contempt in which his favourites are held, until he is separated from his family to pursue his studies at the university of Ingolstadt. Here he is introduced to the wonders of modern chemistry, as well as of natural philosophy in all its branches. Prosecuting these sciences into their innermost and most abstruse recesses, with unusual talent and unexampled success, he at length makes that discovery on which the marvellous part of the work is grounded. His attention had been especially bound to the structure of the human frame and of the principle of life. He engaged in physiological researches of the most recondite and abstruse nature, searching among charnel vaults and in dissection rooms, and the objects most insupportable to the delicacy of human feelings, in order to trace the minute chain of causation which takes place in the change from life to death, and from death to life. In the midst of this darkness a light broke in upon him.

> "Remember," says his narrative, "I am not recording the vision of a madman. The sun does not more certainly shine in the heavens than that which I now affirm is true. Some miracle might have produced it, yet the stages of the discovery were distinct and probable. After days and nights of incredible labour and fatigue, I succeeded in discovering the cause of generation and life; nay, more, I became myself capable of bestowing animation upon lifeless matter."

This wonderful discovery impelled Frankenstein to avail himself of his art by the creation (if we dare to call it so), or formation of a living and sentient being. As the minuteness of the parts formed a great difficulty, he constructed the figure which he proposed to animate of a gigantic size, that is, about eight feet high, and strong and large in proportion. The feverish anxiety with which the young philosopher toils through the horrors of his secret task, now dabbling among the unhallowed reliques of the grave, and now torturing the living animal to animate the lifeless clay, are described generally, but with great vigour of language. Although supported by the hope of producing a new species that should bless him as his creator and source, he nearly sinks under the protracted labour, and loathsome details, of the work he had undertaken, and scarcely is his fatal enthusiasm sufficient to support his nerves, or animate his resolution. The result of this extraordinary discovery it would be unjust to give in any words save those of the author. We shall give it at length, as an excellent specimen of modern chemistry, as well as of the style and manner of the work.

> "It was on a dreary night of November that I beheld the accomplishment of my toils. With an anxiety that almost amounted to agony, I collected the instruments of life around me, that I might infuse a spark of being into the lifeless thing that lay at my feet. It was already one in the morning; the rain pattered dismally against the panes, and my candle was nearly burnt out, when, by the glimmer of the half-extinguished light, I saw the dull yellow eye of the creature open; it breathed hard, and a convulsive motion agitated its limbs.
> "How can I describe my emotions at this catastrophe, or how delineate the wretch whom with such infinite pains and care I had endeavoured to form? His limbs were in proportion, and I had selected his features as beautiful. Beautiful!—Great God! His yellow skin scarcely covered the work of muscles and arteries beneath; his hair was of a lustrous black, and flowing; his teeth of a pearly whiteness; but these luxuriances only formed a more horrid contrast with his watery eyes, that seemed almost of the same colour as the dun white sockets in which they were set, his shrivelled complexion and straight black lips.
> "The different accidents of life are not so changeable as the feelings of human nature. I had worked hard for nearly two years, for the sole purpose of infusing life into an inanimate body. For this I had deprived myself of rest and health. I had desired it with an ardour that far exceeded moderation; but now that I had finished, the beauty of the dream vanished, and breathless horror and disgust filled my heart. Unable to endure the aspect of the being I had created, I rushed out of the room, and continued a long time traversing my bedchamber, unable to compose my mind to sleep. At length lassitude succeeded to the tumult I had before endured; and I threw myself on the bed in my clothes, endeavouring to seek a few moments of forgetfulness. But it was in vain: I slept, indeed, but I was disturbed by the wildest dreams. I thought I saw Elizabeth, in

the bloom of health, walking in the streets of Ingolstadt. Delighted and surprised, I embraced her; but as I imprinted the first kiss on her lips, they became livid with the hue of death; her features appeared to change, and I thought that I held the corpse of my dead mother in my arms; a shroud enveloped her form, and I saw the grave-worms crawling in the folds of the flannel. I started from my sleep with horror; a cold dew covered my forehead, my teeth chattered, and every limb became convulsed; when, by the dim and yellow light of the moon, as it forced its way through the window shutters, I beheld the wretch—the miserable monster whom I had created. He held up the curtain of the bed and his eyes, if eyes they may be called, were fixed on me. His jaws opened, and he muttered some inarticulate sounds, while a grin wrinkled his cheeks. He might have spoken, but I did not hear; one hand was stretched out, seemingly to detain me, but I escaped, and rushed down stairs. I took refuge in the court-yard belonging to the house which I inhabited; where I remained during the rest of the night, walking up and down in the greatest agitation, listening attentively, catching and fearing each sound as if it were to announce the approach of the demoniacal corpse to which I had so miserably given life.

"Oh! no mortal could support the horror of that countenance. A mummy again endued with animation could not be so hideous as that wretch. I had gazed on him while unfinished; he was ugly then; but when those muscles and joints were rendered capable of motion, it became a thing such as even Dante could not have conceived.

"I passed the night wretchedly. Sometimes my pulse beat so quickly and hardly, that I felt the palpitation of every artery; at others, I nearly sank to the ground through languor and extreme weakness. Mingled with this horror, I felt the bitterness of disappointment: dreams, that had been my food and pleasant rest for so long a space, were now become a hell to me; and the change was so rapid, the overthrow so complete!

"Morning, dismal and wet, at length dawned, and discovered to my sleepless and aching eyes the church of Ingolstadt, its white steeple and clock, which indicated the sixth hour. The porter opened the gates of the court, which had that night been my asylum, and I issued into the streets, pacing them with quick steps, as if I sought to avoid the wretch whom I feared every turning of the street would present to my view. I did not dare return to the apartment which I inhabited, but felt impelled to hurry on, although wetted by the rain which poured from a black and comfortless sky.

"I continued walking in this manner for some time, endeavouring, by bodily exercise, to ease the load that weighed upon my mind. I traversed the streets without any clear conception of where I was or what I was doing. My heart palpitated in the sickness of fear; and I hurried on with irregular steps, not daring to look about me:

> 'Like one who, on a lonely road,
> Doth walk in fear and dread,

> And, having once turned round, walks on,
> And turns no more his head;
> Because he knows a frightful fiend
> Doth close behind him tread*.'"

He is relieved by the arrival of the diligence from Geneva, out of which jumps his friend Henry Clerval, who had come to spend a season at the college. Compelled to carry Clerval to his lodgings, which, he supposed, must still contain the prodigious and hideous specimen of his Promethean art, his feelings are again admirably described, allowing always for the extraordinary cause supposed to give them birth.

> "I trembled excessively; I could not endure to think of, and far less to allude to, the occurrences of the preceding night. I walked with a quick pace, and we soon arrived at my college. I then reflected, and the thought made me shiver, that the creature whom I had left in my apartment might still be there, alive, and walking about. I dreaded to behold this monster; but I feared still more that Henry should see him. Entreating him, therefore, to remain a few minutes at the bottom of the stairs, I darted up towards my own room. My hand was already on the lock of the door before I recollected myself. I then paused; and a cold shivering came over me. I threw the door forcibly open, as children are accustomed to do when they expect a spectre to stand in waiting for them on the other side; but nothing appeared. I stepped fearfully in: the apartment was empty; and my bed-room was also freed from its hideous guest. I could hardly believe that so great a good fortune could have befallen me; but when I became assured that my enemy had indeed fled, I clapped my hands for joy, and ran down to Clerval."

The animated monster is heard of no more for a season. Frankenstein pays the penalty of his rash researches into the *arcana* of human nature, in a long illness, after which the two friends prosecute their studies for two years in uninterrupted quiet. Frankenstein, as may be supposed, abstaining, with a sort of abhorrence, from those in which he had once so greatly delighted. At the lapse of this period, he is made acquainted with a dreadful misfortune which has befallen his family, by the violent death of his youngest brother, an interesting child, who, while straying from his keeper, had been murdered by some villain in the walks of Plainpalais. The marks of strangling were distinct on the neck of the unfortunate infant, and a gold ornament which it wore, and which was amissing, was supposed to have been the murderer's motive for perpetrating the crime.

At this dismal intelligence Frankenstein flies to Geneva, and impelled

---

*Coleridge's "Ancient Mariner"

by fraternal affection, visits the spot where this horrid accident had happened. In the midst of a thunder-storm, with which the evening had closed, and just as he had attained the fatal spot on which Victor had been murdered, a flash of lightning displays to him the hideous demon to which he had given life, gliding towards a neighbouring precipice. Another flash shews him hanging among the cliffs, up which he scrambles with far more mortal agility, and is seen no more. The inference, that this being was the murderer of his brother, flashed on Frankenstein's mind as irresistibly as the lightning itself, and he was tempted to consider the creature whom he had cast among mankind to work, it would seem, acts of horror and depravity, nearly in the light of his own vampire let loose from the grave, and destined to destroy all that was dear to him.

Frankenstein was right in his apprehensions. Justine, the maid to whom the youthful Victor had been intrusted, is found to be in possession of the golden trinket which had been taken from the child's person; and by a variety of combining circumstances of combined evidence, she is concluded to be the murderess, and, as such, condemned to death and executed. It does not appear that Frankenstein attempted to avert her fate, by communicating his horrible secret; but, indeed, who would have given him credit, or in what manner could he have supported his tale?

In a solitary expedition to the top of Mount Aveyron, undertaken to dispel the melancholy which clouded his mind, Frankenstein unexpectedly meets with the monster he had animated, who compels him to a conference and a parley. The material demon gives an account, at great length, of his history since his animation, of the mode in which he acquired various points of knowledge, and of the disasters which befell him, when, full of benevolence and philanthropy, he endeavoured to introduce himself into human society. The most material part of his education was acquired in a ruinous pig-stye—a Lyceum which this strange student occupied, he assures us, for a good many months undiscovered, and in constant observance of the motions of an amiable family, from imitating whom he learns the use of language, and other accomplishments, much more successfully than Caliban, though the latter had a conjuror to his tutor. This detail is not only highly improbable, but it is injudicious, as its unnecessary minuteness tends rather too much to familiarize us with the being whom it regards, and who loses, by this *lengthy* oration, some part of the mysterious sublimity annexed to his first appearance. The result is, this monster, who was at first, according to his own account, but a harmless monster, becomes ferocious and malignant, in consequence of finding all his approaches to human society repelled with injurious violence and offensive marks of disgust. Some papers concealed in his dress acquainted him with the circumstances and person to whom he owed his origin; and the hate which he felt towards the whole human race was now concentrated in resentment against Frankenstein. In his humour he murdered the child, and disposed the picture so as to induce a belief of Justine's guilt. The last is an inartificial circumstance: this indirect mode of mischief was not likely to occur to the being the narrative presents to us. The conclusion of this strange narrative is a peremptory demand on the part of the demon, as he is usually termed, that Frankenstein should renew his fearful experiment, and create for him an helpmate hideous as himself, who should have no pretense for shunning his society. On this condition he promises to withdraw to some distant desert, and shun the human race for ever. If his creator shall refuse him this consolation, he vows the prosecution of the most frightful vengeance. Frankenstein, after a long pause of reflection, imagines he sees that the justice due to the miserable being, as well as to mankind, who might be exposed to so much misery, from the power and evil dispositions of a creature who could climb perpendicular cliffs and exist among glaciers, demanded that he should comply with the request; and granted his promise accordingly.

Frankenstein retreats to one of the distant islands of the Orcades, that in secrecy and solitude he might resume his detestable and ill-omened labours, which now were doubly hideous, since he was deprived of the enthusiasm with which he formerly prosecuted them. As he is sitting one night in his laboratory, and recollecting the consequences of his first essay in the Promethean art, he begins to hesitate concerning the right he had to form another being as malignant and bloodthirsty as that he had unfortunately already animated. It is evident that he would thereby give the demon the means of propagating a hideous race, superior to mankind in strength and hardihood, who might render the very existence of the present human race a condition precarious and full of terror. Just as these reflections lead him to the conclusion that his promise was criminal, and ought not to be kept, he looks up, and sees, by the light of the moon, the demon at the casement.

> "A ghastly grin wrinkled his lips as he gazed on me, where I sat fulfilling the task which he had allotted to me. Yes, he had followed me in my travels; he had loitered in forests, hid himself in caves, or taken refuge in wide

and desert heaths; and he now came to mark my progress, and claim the fulfillment of my promise.

"As I looked on him, his countenance expressed the utmost extent of malice and treachery. I thought with a sensation of madness on my promise to create another like him, and trembling with passion, tore to pieces the thing on which I was engaged. The wretch saw me destroy the creature on whose future existence he depended for happiness, and, with a howl of devilish despair and revenge, withdrew."

At a subsequent interview, described with the same wild energy, all treaty is broken off betwixt Frankenstein and the work of his hands, and they part on terms of open and declared hatred and defiance. Our limits do not allow us to trace in detail the progress of the demon's vengeance. Clerval falls its first victim, and under circumstances which had very nearly conducted the new Prometheus to the gallows as his supposed murderer. Elizabeth, his bride, is next strangled on her wedding night; his father dies of grief; and at length Frankenstein, driven to despair and distraction, sees nothing left for him in life but vengeance on the singular cause of his misery. With this purpose he pursues the monster from clime to clime, receiving only such intimations of his being on the right scent, as served to shew that the demon delighted in thus protracting his fury and his sufferings. At length, after the flight and pursuit had terminated among the frost-fogs, and icy islands of the northern oceans, and just when he had a glimpse of his adversary, the ground sea was heard, the ice gave way, and Frankenstein was placed in the perilous situation in which he is first introduced to the reader.

Exhausted by his sufferings, but still breathing vengeance against the being which was at once his creature and his persecutor, this unhappy victim to physiological discovery expires just as the clearing away of the ice permits Captain Walton's vessel to hoist sail for the return to Britain. At midnight, the daemon, who had been his destroyer, is discovered in the cabin, lamenting over the corpse of the person who gave him being. To Walton he attempts to justify his resentment towards the human race, while, at the same time, he acknowledges himself a wretch who had murdered the lovely and the helpless, and pursued to irremediably ruin his creator, the select specimen of all that was worthy of love and admiration.

"Fear not," he continues, addressing the astonished Walton, "that I shall be the instrument of future mischief. My work is nearly complete. Neither yours nor any man's death is needed to consummate the series of my being, and accomplish that which must be done; but it requires my own. Do not think that I shall be slow to perform this sacrifice. I shall quit your vessel on the ice-raft which brought me hither, and shall seek the most northern extremity of the globe; I shall collect my funeral pile and consume to ashes this miserable frame, that its remains may afford no light to any curious and unhallowed wretch, who would create such another as I have been.—"

"He sprung from the cabin-window, as he said this, upon the ice-raft which lay close to the vessel. He was soon borne away by the waves, and lost in darkness and distance."

Whether this singular being executed his purpose or not must necessarily remain an uncertainty, unless the voyage of discovery to the north pole should throw any light on the subject.

So concludes this extraordinary tale, in which the author seems to us to disclose uncommon powers of poetic imagination. The feeling with which we perused the unexpected and fearful, yet, allowing the possibility of the event, very natural conclusion of Frankenstein's experiment, shook a little even our firm nerves; although such and so numerous have been the expedients for exciting terror employed by the romantic writers of the age, that the reader may adopt Macbeth's words with a slight alteration:

"We have supp'd full with horrors
Direness, familiar to our "callous" thoughts,
Cannot once startle us."

It is no slight merit in our eyes, that the tale, though wild in incident, is written in plain and forcible English, without exhibiting that mixture of hyperbolical Germanisms with which tales of wonder are usually told, as if it were necessary that the language should be as extravagant as the fiction. The ideas of the author are always clearly as well as forcibly expressed; and his descriptions of landscape have in them the choice requisites of truth, freshness, precision, and beauty. The self-education of the monster, considering the slender opportunities of acquiring knowledge that he possessed, we have already noticed as improbable and overstrained. That he should have not only learned to speak, but to read, and, for aught we know, to write—that he should have become acquainted with Werter, with Plutarch's Lives, and with Paradise Lost, by listening through a hole in a wall, seems as unlikely as that he should have acquired, in the same way, the problems of Euclid, or the art of book-keeping by single and double entry. The author has however two apologies—the first, the necessity that his monster should acquire those endowments, and the other, that his neighbours were engaged in teaching the language of the country to a young foreigner. His progress in self-knowledge, and the acquisition of information, is, after all, more wonderful than that of Hai Eben Yokhdan, or Automathes, or the hero of the little romance called The Child of Nature, one of which works might perhaps suggest the train of ideas followed by the author of Frankenstein. We should also be disposed, in support of the principles with which we set out, to question whether the monster, how tall, agile, and strong however, could have perpetrated so much mischief undiscovered, or passed through so many countries without being secured, either on account of his crimes, or for the benefit of some such speculator as Mr. Polito, who would have been happy to have added to his museum so curious a specimen of natural history. But as we have consented to admit the leading incident of the work, perhaps some of our readers may be of opinion, that to stickle upon lesser improbabilities, is to incur the censure bestowed by the Scottish proverb on those who start at straws after swallowing *windlings*.

The following lines, which occur in the second volume, mark, we think, that the author possesses the same facility in expressing himself in verse as in prose.

> We rest; a dream has power to poison sleep.
> We rise; one wand'ring thought pollutes the day.
> We feel, conceive, or reason; laugh and weep,
> Embrace fond woe, or cast our cares away;
> It is the same: for, be it joy or sorrow,
> The path of its departure still is free.
> Man's yesterday may ne'er be like his morrow;
> Nought may endure but mutability!

Upon the whole, the work impresses us with a high idea of the author's original genius and happy power of expression. We shall be delighted to hear that he has aspired to the *paullo majora*;[b] and, in the meantime, congratulate our readers upon a novel which excites new reflections and untried sources of emotion. If Gray's definition of Paradise, to lie on a couch, namely, and read new novels, come any thing near truth, no small praise is due to him, who, like the author of Frankenstein, has enlarged the sphere of that fascinating enjoyment.

Notes

a. Erasmus Darwin (1731–1802), grandfather to Charles, who preceded his more famous grandson in speculating about the evolution of species.

b. "A loftier strain" (Vergil, *Eclogue* IV); i.e., Scott would like the author to rise above mere Gothic romance and write respectable literature.

The British politician John Croker (1780–1857), alleged coiner of the term "conservative," has been identified as the author of an anonymous review of *Frankenstein* (which itself had been published anonymously) appearing in the *Quarterly Review* in January 1818. In this review, which consists primarily of a detailed plot summary, Croker takes great outrage at the novel being dedicated to the politically radical William Godwin (Mary Shelley's father), and he berates the novel's author for "his" political sensibility. This excerpt picks up after the long summary of the book's plot and omits further copying of passages from the novel.

Excerpt from a Review of Frankenstein; or, the Modern Prometheus*

JOHN CROKER

Our readers will guess from this summary, what a tissue of horrible and disgusting absurdity this work presents.—It is piously dedicated to Mr. Godwin, and is written in the spirit of his school. The dreams of insanity are embodied in the strong and striking language of the insane, and the author, notwithstanding the rationality of his preface, often leaves us in doubt whether he is not as mad as his hero. Mr. Godwin is the patriarch of a literary family, whose chief skill is in delineating the wanderings of the intellect, and which strangely delights in the most afflicting and humiliating of human miseries. His disciples are a kind of *out-pensioners of Bedlam*, and, like 'Mad Bess' or 'Mad Tom,' are occasionally visited with paroxysms of genius and fits of expression, which make sober-minded people wonder and shudder.[...]

It cannot be denied that this [book] is nonsense—but it is nonsense decked out with circumstances and clothed in language highly terrific: it is, indeed,

————————— 'a tale
Told by an idiot, full of sound and fury,
Signifying nothing—'

but still there is something tremendous in the unmeaning hollowness of its sound, and the vague obscurity of its images.

But when we have thus admitted that Frankenstein has passages which appal the mind and make the flesh creep, we have given it all the praise

*Review of *Frankenstein; or, the Modern Prometheus*, *The Quarterly Review*, January 1818, 382, 385.

(if praise it can be called) which we dare to bestow. Our taste and our judgment alike revolt at this kind of writing, and the greater the ability with which it may be executed the worse it is—it inculcates no lesson of conduct, manners, or morality; it cannot mend, and will not even amuse its readers, unless their taste have been deplorably vitiated—it fatigues the feelings without interesting the understanding; it gratuitously harasses the heart, and wantonly adds to the store, already too great, of painful sensations. The author has powers, both of conception and language, which employed in a happier direction might, perhaps, (we speak dubiously,) give him a name among those whose writings amuse or amend their fellow-creatures; but we take the liberty of assuring him, and hope that he may be in a temper to listen to us, that the style which he has adopted in the present publication merely tends to defeat his own purpose, if he really had any other object in view than that of leaving the wearied reader, after a struggle between laughter and loathing, in doubt whether the head or the heart of the author be the most diseased.

Splitting the difference between praise and condemnation, this anonymous review from *The Edinburgh Magazine and Literary Miscellany* for March 1818 falls halfway between those of Croker and Scott, to whom the review has sometimes been erroneously attributed due to confusion between *The Edinburgh Magazine* and *Blackwood's Edinburgh Magazine*, in which Scott's review appeared. I have omitted the exhaustive plot summary to focus on the critical commentary, which compares the incredible events of the novel with the unprecedented events of the Napoleonic era, from which Europe had just emerged.

Excerpt from a Review of Frankenstein; or, the Modern Prometheus[*]

THE EDINBURGH MAGAZINE AND LITERARY MISCELLANY

Here is one of the productions of the modern school in its highest style of caricature and exaggeration. It is formed on the Godwinian manner, and has all the faults, but many likewise of the beauties of that model. In dark and gloomy views of nature and of man, bordering too closely on

[*]Review of *Frankenstein; or, the Modern Prometheus*, The Edinburgh Magazine and Literary Miscellany, March 1818, 249, 252-253.

impiety,—in the most outrageous improbability,—in sacrificing every thing to effect,—it even goes beyond its great prototype; but in return, it possesses a similar power of fascination, something of the same mastery in harsh and savage delineations of passion, relieved in like manner by the gentler features of domestic and simple feelings. There never was a wilder story imagined, yet, like most of the fictions of this age, it has an air of reality attached to it, by being connected with the favourite projects and passions of the times. The real events of the world have, in our day, too, been of so wondrous and gigantic a kind,—the shiftings of the scenes in our stupendous drama have been so rapid and various, that Shakespeare himself, in his wildest flights, has been completely distanced by the eccentricities of actual existence.[...] Our appetite, we say, for every sort of wonder and vehement interest, has in this way become so desperately inflamed, that especially as the world around us has again settled into its old dull state of happiness and legitimacy, we can be satisfied with nothing in fiction that is not highly coloured and exaggerated; we even like a story the better that it is disjointed and irregular, and our greatest inventors, accordingly, have been obliged to accommodate themselves to the taste of the age, more, we believe, than their own judgment can, at all times, have approved of. The very extravagance of the present production will now, therefore, be, perhaps, in its favour, since the events which have actually passed before our eyes have made the atmosphere of miracles that in which we most readily breathe.[...]

It is one of those works, however, which, when we have read, we do not well see why it should have been written;—for a *jeu d'esprit* it is somewhat too long, grave, and laborious,—and some of our highest and met reverential feelings receive a shock from the conception on which it turns, so as to produce a painful and bewildered state of mind while we peruse it. We are accustomed, happily, to look upon the creation of a living and intelligent being as a work that is fitted only to inspire a religious emotion, and there is an impropriety, to say no worse, in placing it in any other light. It might, indeed, be the author's view to shew that the powers of man have been wisely limited, and that misery would follow their extension,—but still the expression "Creator," applied to a mere human being, gives us the same sort of shock with the phrase, "the Man Almighty," and others of the same kind, in Mr Southey's "Curse of Kehama." All these monstrous conceptions are the consequences of the wild and irregular theories of the age; though we do not at all mean to infer that the authors who give into such freedoms have done so with any bad intentions. This incongruity, however, with our established and most sacred notions, is the chief fault in such fictions, regarding them merely in a critical point of view. Shakespeare's Caliban (though his simplicity and suitableness to the place where he is found are very delightful) is, perhaps, a more *hateful* being than our good friend in this book. But Caliban comes into existence in the received way which common superstition had pointed out; we should not have endured him if Prospero had created him. Getting over this original absurdity, the character of our monster is in good keeping;—there is a grandeur, too, in the scenery in which he makes his appearances,—the ice-mountains of the Pole, or the glaciers of the Alps; his natural tendency to kind feelings, and the manner in which they were blighted,—and all the domestic picture of the cottage, are very interesting and beautiful. We hope yet to have more productions, both from this author and his great model, Mr Godwin; but they would make a great improvement in their writings, if they would rather study the established order of nature as it

The Devil's Thumb. The story of Frankenstein *begins with a ship seeking the North Pole discovering Victor Frankenstein in the Arctic wastes like this 1850 illustrations shows. As a place of cold, ice, and void, the Arctic serves as a landscape of horror in opposition to the warm, healthy landscape of human society. It is here that the Frankenstein Monster seeks solace and freedom from humanity. As the nineteenth century progressed, the largely uncharted polar climes (both north and south) would become scenes of terror in works by authors like Edgar Allan Poe and Arthur Conan Doyle (Library of Congress, Prints and Photographs Division, LC-USZC4-11150).*

appears, both in the world of matter and of mind, than continue to revolt our feelings by hazardous innovations in either of these departments.

Mary Shelly's *Frankenstein* was adapted for the stage many times, and the first of these interpretations was Richard Brinsley Peake's *Presumption; or, the Fate of Frankenstein* (1823), which dramatized key scenes from the novel and added Frankenstein's assistant, Fritz, to the mix. The play was first performed at the English Opera House on July 28, 1823, and Mary Shelly herself watched a performance. Though she had mixed feelings about the show, she later incorporated the idea of "presumption" into her 1831 revision of *Frankenstein*. Arguably, the play made the book an icon of horror. Here an anonymous reviewer for *The London Magazine* of September 1823 discusses *Presumption* and the controversy over its "impiety." The review originally ran in a column on new dramas.

Review of Presumption; or the Fate of Frankenstein*
THE LONDON MAGAZINE

The exertions at this theatre to give amusement to the public have been manifold and unceasing during the month; and we are happy to be able to record a disposition on the part of the public to reward those exertions:—indeed the comfort of the house is now so increased, that untenanted boxes are not to be looked for.

A new Melodrama, founded on Mrs. Shelley's grand incoherence of a novel, called Presumption, or the Fate of Frankenstein, has been brought out with a success as strange and mysterious as the being which it brings before us. The audience crowd to it, hiss it, hail it, shudder at it, loath it, dream of it, and come again to it. The piece has been damned by full houses night after night, but the moment it is withdrawn, the public call it up again—and yearn to tremble once more before it. There are very few of our readers, we conjecture, who have not read the novel of Frankenstein,—by stealth, at night, or in some misshapen hour. To them, therefore, the image of the young Frankenstein, with his mad aspirations after knowledge, must be familiar;—to them, his long and dangerous studies, his fearful labours,—his work of creation must be known. To them also, at a thought, must rise

*"The Drama," *The London Magazine*, September 1823, 322–323.

that hideous jumbled being, which Frankenstein gives life to, and which starts at all hours and at all places upon the two terrified victims—Frankenstein and the reader. The description of the first dawn—the first tremulous motion of life, is in the novel frightfully given:—and on recurring to it, we are only surprized that any Melo-dramatist (the wildest going) should ever have thought of bringing it out of the charmed book to the stage—and we are astounded that such an attempt should have been attended with success. The management of this part of the novel in the drama is really the most perfect masterpiece of Melo-dramatic ingenuity that we ever in any piece or on any stage witnessed. We say this unreservedly and decidedly.

We do not think it necessary to give the plot of the drama, since we are sure we should be merely harassing the reader with a twice-told tale:—some alterations were necessarily made—but the leading features of the original work (*features* which, once seen, can never be forgotten) are faithfully preserved. Frankenstein makes his man,—huge, formidable, and grand,—and the creature follows him throughout the world. He is at first disposed to be gentle; but the disgust which his appearance provokes, whets his dislike to man—and he becomes a demon to all connected with Frankenstein. After destroying the betrothed of his *father*,—and running away with a little uncle,—the creature meets Frankenstein in the Alps, and, in a conflict, is buried with the author (not Mr. Peake) under an avalanche. The frightful, awful interest of the novel is wonderfully kept up,—and we will defy any person "to keep the natural ruby of his cheeks" at that period when the red workings of the furnace are seen through a sort of window, and the labours of Frankenstein are evidenced by the intense horror of a foolish domestic who has ventured to peep at what his master is doing. Then the rush of the pale scholar from his laboratory,—astounded at the work he has achieved—and the slaty—supernatural coming of the figure itself—alive—gigantic—without a purpose! fill up the work of terror!—the appearance of this creature at all times is mysterious and terrific!—and though we feel the extravagance of the creation throughout, we cannot but acknowledge that die author has, in our love for the marvellous, "fooled us to the top of our bent."

Something has been said of the impropriety of the production;—and one paper has hinted, with a singular critical sagacity, at the *impiety* of the drama and novel:—surely, nothing can be more idle than such a strain of objection! The moral, if it be needful to require it in this case, is so glaring, as almost to disturb the mystery and interest of the work:—we trust, *we* shall not be thought *impious* for so expressing ourselves. A man, by study, creates a being and gives it life:—he is unable to give it sense, understanding, purpose, or any of those harmonizing qualities which fit it for existence—and the creator falls a victim to his imperfect creature!— Putting the improbability out of the question—where is the vice of all this?—We own we are unable to detect it. A foolish placard was stuck about the streets, professing to come from a knot of "friends of humanity," and calling on the fathers of families, &c. to set their faces against the piece. If this bill was seriously intended,—it was ludicrous enough. The answer on the part of the theatre was managerial and absolute;—and *Presumption* fills the theatre still with grumbling and money.

The acting in the two leading characters was perhaps the best ever seen in Melodrame; and, indeed, if it had been feeble, or outrageous, or, anything but what it was,—Frankenstein would soon have got rid of his tall blue Pest, and the long Demon would have perished in his infancy. It required certainly the finest powers of melodramatic acting, to make the extravagance commanding;—and in Mr. T. P. Cooke and Mr. Wallack these powers were, luckily for the author of both Frankenstein and his follower, found. Mr. Wallack was dressed delightfully,—German and scholar-like to the very buckle of his shoe. The fine intelligence of his countenance seemed to warrant the talk about his ardour after knowledge—and the deathy paleness and melancholy thrown into it seemed to speak of the fatality of his pursuits. Mr. P. T. Cooke as (— — — — —) (for he is so described,—and we see no reason for foregoing our own parenthesis because its palings touch those of Mr. Peake's) has proved himself to be the very best pantomime actor on the stage. He never speaks;—but his action and his looks are more than eloquent. The effect of music upon him is affecting and beautiful in the extreme. He looks gigantic—and so contrives his uncouth dress and hair as quite to warrant the belief that he is more than human. While he is on the stage, the audience *dare* not hiss, nay—scarcely breathe—but the moment he is well buried under the avalanche, all the good people in the pit feel for their moralities, and give vent to their disapprobation.

The scenery was old—and the music was taken out of the same *bin*.

Richard H. Horne (1802–1884) was an English poet of sufficient fame that Edgar Allan Poe once sent him a poem hoping for publication in England. Horne undertook *A New Spirit of the Age* (1844) as sequel to William Hazlitt's *The Spirit of the Age* (1825), a book profiling authors; on this he worked with (an uncredited) Elizabeth Barrett (later Browning), who contributed much of the material in it. Horne's book was dismissed by critics as unbalanced in its selections of contemporary authors, but in the following excerpt from his profile of "Mrs. Shelley," Horne makes some interesting observations about the standing of Mary Shelley in the mid-nineteenth century and the rarity of truly good horror, which he called "imaginative romance."

*Excerpt from "Mrs. Shelley"**
R.H. HORNE

"*Out of the depths of Nature—
Substance, shades, or dreams,
Thou shall call up—sift—and take
What seems titling best to make
   A structure, fraught with direful gleams,
   Or one all filled with sunny beams."*

"*Oh you, who sentried stand upon the temple wall;
Holy, and nearer to the glory's golden fall,
Moon-like, possess and shed at large its rays!"*
               CORNELIUS MATHEWS.

"— — — — — — For though
Not to be pierced by the dull eye whose beam
Is spent on outward shapes, there is a way
To make a search into its hidden'st passage."—SHIRLEY.[a]

    The imaginative romance as distinguished from the historical romance, and the actual or social life fiction, is of very rare occurrence in the literature of the present day. Whether the cause lies with the writers or the public, or the character of events and influence now operating on society, certain it is that the imaginative romance is almost extinct among us.

    We had outgrown the curdling horrors and breathless apprehensions of Mrs. Ratcliffe [*sic*], and the roseate pomps of Miss Jane Porter. But why have we no Frankensteins, for that fine work is in advance of the age?

    Perhaps we ought to seek the cause of the scarcity in the difficulty of the production. A mere fruitless, purposeless excitement of the imagination will not do *now*. The imaginative romance is required to be a sort of epic—a power to advance—a something to propel the frame of things. Such is Bulwer's "Zanoni,"[b] a profound and beautiful work of fiction, which has

---

*"Mrs. Shelley," in *A New Spirit of the Age*, ed. R. H. Horne (New York: Harper & Bros., 1844), 317–319, 321.

been reviewed in its place, and in which Godwin's "St. Leon" found a worthy successor. With this single exception, the first place among the romances of our day belongs to the "Frankenstein" of Mrs. Shelley.

The solitary student with whom the longing desire to pry into the secrets of nature ends in the discovery of the vital principle itself, and the means of communicating it, thus describes the consummation of his toils. We quote the passage as illustrative of the genius by which the extravagance of the conception is rendered subservient to artistical effect:—

> "It was on a dreary night of November, that I beheld the accomplishment of my toils. With an anxiety that almost amounted to agony, I collected the instruments of life around me, that I might infuse a spark of being into the lifeless thing that lay at my feet. It was already one in the morning; the rain pattered dismally against the panes, and my candle was nearly burnt out, when, by the glimmer of the half-extinguished light, I saw the dull yellow eye of the creature open; it breathed hard, and a convulsive motion agitated its limbs.
>
> "How can I describe my emotions at this catastrophe, or how delineate the wretch whom with such infinite pains and care I had endeavoured to form! His limbs were in proportion, and I had selected his features as beautiful. Beautiful!—Great God! His yellow skin scarcely covered the work of muscles and arteries beneath; his hair was of a lustrous black, and flowing; his teeth of a pearly whiteness; but these luxuriances only formed a more horrid contrast with his watery eyes, that seemed almost of the same colour as the dun white sockets in which they were set, his shrivelled complexion, and straight black lips."
>
> *Frankenstein*, vol. i., p. 97, 98.

The Monster in "Frankenstein," sublime in his ugliness, his simplicity, his passions, his wrongs and his strength, physical and mental, embodies in the wild narrative more than one distinct and important moral theory or proposition. In himself he is the type of a class deeply and cruelly aggrieved by nature—the Deformed or hideous in figure or countenance, whose sympathies and passions are as strong as their bodily deformity renders them repulsive. An amount of human woe, great beyond reckoning, have such experienced. When the Monster pleads his cause against cruel man, and when he finally disappears on his raft on the icy sea to build his own funeral pile, he pleads the cause of all that class who have so strong a claim on the help and sympathy of the world, yet find little else but disgust, or, at best, neglect.

The Monster created by Frankenstein is also an illustration of the embodied consequences of our actions. As he, when formed and endowed with life, became to his imaginary creator an everlasting ever-present curse, so may one single action, nay a word, or it may be a thought, thrown upon the tide of time become to its originator a curse, never to be recovered, never to be shaken off.

"Frankenstein" suggests yet another analogy. It teaches the tragic results of attainment when an impetuous irresistible passion hurries on the soul to its doom. Such tragic results are the sacrificial fires out of which humanity rises purified. They constitute one form of the great ministry of Pain. The conception of "Frankenstein" is the converse of that of the delightful German fiction of Peter Schlemil,[c] in which the *loss* of his shadow (reputation or honour) leads on the hero through several griefs and troubles to the great simplicity of nature and truth; while in "Frankenstein" the *attainment* of a gigantic reality leads through crime and desolation to the same goal, but it is only reached in the moment of death.

[...]

Mrs. Shelley has published, besides "Frankenstein," a romance entitled "Valperga," which is less known than the former, but is of high merit. She exhibits in her hero, a brave and successful warrior, arriving at the height of his ambition, endowed with uncommon beauty and strength, and with many good qualities, yet causes him to excite emotions of reprobation and pity, because he is cruel and a tyrant, and because in the truth of things he is unhappy. This is doing a good work, taking the false glory from the eyes and showing things as they are. There are two female characters of wonderful power and beauty. The heroine is a lovely and noble creation. The work taken as a whole, if below "Frankenstein" in genius, is yet worthy of its author and of her high rank in the aristocracy of genius, as the daughter of Godwin and Mary Wolstonecraft, and the widow of Shelley.

Notes

a. The anonymous first fragment appears to be by Horne himself, with the latter two being excerpts from "The Preacher" (1843) by Cornelius Mathews and the play *Love Tricks* (1625) by James Shirley.

b. Sir Edward Bulwer-Lytton (1803–1873) was a prolific Victorian writer and poet. He produced sensational novels of mystery and romance, one of which—*Paul Clifford* (1830)—begat the immoral opening, "It was a dark and stormy night," the inspiration for a modern-day bad writing contest. To his credit, he also coined "the pen is mightier than the sword" and "the all mighty dollar." Despite his popularity with the Victorian public, contemporary critics disliked him and his writing, too. (His writing is marked by "the absence of true genius," said *Bentley's Monthly* in 1853. "Sir E. Bulwer Lytton cleaves to the conviction that an after-age will appreciate his genius better than the present," said *The Quarterly Review* in 1865.) *Zanoni* (1842) was an occult mystery centering on the lives of two immortal sorcerers. Among Bulwer's many romances were a few proto-science fiction tales and Gothic fiction.

c. *The Wonderful History of Peter Schlemihl: The Man Who Lost His Shadow* (1814) by the French-German author Adelbert von Chamisso (1731–1838), in which the hero sells his shadow to the devil for a purse that never runs short of gold.

John Polidori's novella *The Vampyre* (sometimes spelled "Vampire") was the prototype for all subsequent vampire fictions and among the first English language vampire stories. Polidori's aristocratic bloodsucker Lord Ruthven was an influence on his more famous cousins, Varney the Vampire and Count Dracula. When first published in the *New Monthly Magazine* in April 1819 without the author's consent, *The Vampyre* was attributed to Polidori's friend, George Gordon Byron (1788–1824), a leading Romantic poet and Polidori's model for Lord Ruthven. Lord Byron, in turn, attempted to clear up the matter but with limited success.

Here from the February 1852 edition of *The Gentleman's Magazine* is an early printing of Byron's protestation, as supplied by "S.E.T." to Sylvanus Urban, the corporate pen name of the magazine's editors. As an interesting side note, when the letter was published in *The Knickerbocker* (1849), *The Gentleman's Magazine* (1852), *The New York Times* (1912), and *The Bookman* (1917) each publication claimed it was a new discovery hitherto unpublished, despite having been in print since at least 1824 and appearing in editions of Byron's letters since at least mid-century.

Letter Denying Authorship of The Vampire*

LORD BYRON

10 Dartmouth St.
Westr. Jan. 17th, 1852

MR. URBAN,—The original of the annexed letter has never been out of the possession of a friend of mine, who received it from a person in the employ of his Lordship's family; and I am not aware that it has ever been published, at least in this country. The Editor of Galignani's Messenger may have inserted it, in the first instance, in his newspaper; but I do not know where in London to find a file of that journal.

"The Vampire" was a composition unblushingly attributed to Lord Byron on its first publication, as appears from the following advertisement, which I copy from the Literary Gazette of the 24th April, 1819:—

Lord Byron.

This Day is published, in 8vo. price 4s. 6d. THE VAMPYRE; a Tale. By the Right Hon. Lord Byron. To which it added, an account of his Lordship's Residence in the Island of Mitylene.

---

*"Letter of Lord Byron Denying the Authorship of *The Vampire*," *The Gentleman's Magazine*, February 1852, 150–151.

Printed, by permission, for Sherwood, Neely, and Jones, Paternoster Row.

The terms of this announcement will render intelligible some of the allusions made by Lord Byron in the letter.   Yours, &c.   S. E. T.

To the Editor of Galignani's Messenger.

Venice, April 27th, 1819.

Sir,—In various numbers of your journal I have seen mentioned a work entitled "The Vampire," with the addition of my name as that of the author. I am not the author, and never heard of the work in question until now. In a more recent paper I perceive a formal annunciation of "The Vampire," with the addition of an account of my "residence in the island of Mitylene," an island which I have occasionally sailed by in the course of travelling some years ago through the Levant, and where I should have no objection to reside—but where I have never yet resided. Neither of these performances are mine; and I presume that it is neither unjust nor ungracious to request that you will favour me by contradicting the advertisement to which I allude. If the book is clever, it would be base to deprive the real writer, whoever he may be, of his honours; and if stupid, I desire the responsibility of nobody's dullness but my own.

You will excuse the trouble I give you; the imputation is of no great importance, and as long as it was confined to surmises and reports I should have received it as I have received many others—in silence; but the formality of a public advertisement of a book I never wrote, and a residence where I never resided, is a little too much, particularly as I have no notion of the contents of the one nor the incidents of the other. I have besides a personal dislike to "Vampires," and the little acquaintance I have with them would by no means induce me to divulge their secrets.

You did me a much less injury by your paragraphs about "my devotion," and "abandonment of society for the sake of religion," which appeared in your Messenger during last Lent—all of which are not founded on fact; but you see I do not contradict them, because they are merely personal, whereas the others in some degree concern the reader.

You will oblige me by complying with my request of contradiction. I assure you that I know nothing of the works in question; and have the honour to be (as the Correspondents to Magazines say) "your constant reader," and

Very obed^t humble serv^t,
BYRON.
A Monsieur, Monsieur Galignani,
18, Rue Vivienne, Paris.

[We add two extracts from Lord Byron's Letters to his publisher Mr. Murray:—

May 15, 1819. "I have got your extract and the Vampire. I need not say it is not mine. There is a rule to go by: you are my publisher (till we quarrel), and what is not published by you is not written by me."—Moore's Letters, &c. of Lord Byron, 1830, 4to. ii. 207.

May 25. "A few days ago I sent you all I knew of Polidori's Vampire. He may do, say, or write what he pleases, but I wish he would not attribute to me his own compositions."—Ibid. p. 211.

In noticing "Ernestus Berchtold; or the Modern Œdipus, a Tale. By J. W. Polidori, M.D." published before the end of the same year, a contemporary critic says, "This is another of the semi-sentimental semi-supernatural productions to which we are now prone—the prose Byroniads which infest the times.... An introduction states Berchtold to be one of the three tales engendered by a travelling junta of our country folks, who agreed to write each a story founded on some superstition. Frankenstein, by Godwin's daughter, Shelley's wife, was the first; the Vampire, of which we have a poor piece at the end of Mazeppa, and a surreptitious whole by Dr. Polidori, instead of its planner Lord Byron, in a separate form, the second; and this novel, the third."—Literary Gazette for 1819, p.546.]

The Scottish journalist Peter Bayne (1830–1896) began writing professionally while still in his twenties, becoming editor-in-chief of Glasgow's *The Commonwealth* newspaper and later the *Edinburgh Witness*, a religious journal. Bayne wrote several volumes of literary essays, collected as *Essays in Biography and Criticism*, beginning in 1857. From the first volume comes "Ellis, Acton, and Currer Bell," a review of the life and works of the Brontë sisters, who wrote under those pen names. Ellis Bell was the pen name of Emily Brontë (1818–1848), the author of *Wuthering Heights* (1847), a late entry in the parade of Gothic novels. In this excerpt, Bayne offers his views on the book and its place in the literature of the macabre.

*Excerpt from "Ellis, Acton, and Currer Bell"**
PETER BAYNE

We make no more than an allusion to Ellis Bell's poetry. It is characterized by strength and freshness, and by that original cadence, that power of melody, which, be it wild, or tender, or even harsh, was never heard before, and comes at first hand from nature, as her sign of the born poet. We have compared the poetry of the three [Brontë] sisters; and in spite of

---

*Peter Bayne, "Ellis, Acton, and Currer Bell," in *Essays in Biography and Criticism* (Boston: Gould and Lincoln, 1860), 404–406.

a prevailing opinion to the contrary, we scruple not to declare, that the clear result of our examination is the conclusion that Ellis Bell's is beyond measure the best.

But, after all, we must pronounce what has been left us by this wonderful woman, unhealthy, immature, and worthy of being avoided. *Wuthering Heights*, we repeat, belongs to the horror school of fiction, and is involved in its unequivocal and unexcepting condemnation. We say not that a mind, inured to the task, cannot, by careful scrutiny and severe discrimination, derive valuable hints and important exercise from such works. You may trace and emulate strength of touch and richness of color, while you detest the subject. You may listen to snatches of woodland music, and thrill to tints of woodland beauty, in the neighborhood of the hyena's den. But we do not for this recall our condemnation. At the foot of the gallows, touches of nature's tenderness may be marked: in the pallid face of the criminal you may note workings of emotion not to be seen elsewhere. Anatomy might be studied, with both novelty and force of instruction, in the quivering of the muscles and wrenching of the forehead of one who lay on the wheel. But it admits not of question, that the general effect of such spectacles is brutalizing, and we would therefore without hesitation terminate their publicity. On exactly the same grounds, would we bid our readers avoid works of distempered excitement. Even when such are of the highest excellence in their class, as those of Ellis Bell and Edgar Poe, we would deliberately sentence them to oblivion. Their general effect is to produce a mental state alien to the calm energy and quiet homely feelings of real life; to make the soul the slave of stimulants, and those of the fiercest kind; and, whatever morbid irritability may for the time be fostered, to shrivel and dry up those sympathies which are the most tender, delicate, and precious. Works like those of Edgar Poe and this *Wuthering Heights* must be plainly declared to blunt, to brutalize, and to enervate the mind. Of the poetry, also, of Ellis Bell, it must be said that it is not healthful. Its beauty is allied to that wild loveliness which may gleam on the hectic cheek, or move while it startles, as we listen to maniac ravings. And wherefore this unchanging wail, whence this perpetual and inexpressible melancholy, in the poems of one so young? What destiny is it with which this young heart so vainly struggles, and by which it is overcome? Is it possible that, under the sunny azure of an English sky, and while the foot is on English moors, so utter a sadness may descend on a girl, whom we expect to find "a metaphor of spring, and mirth, and gladness," the sister of the fawn and the linnet? The spectacle is deeply touching, and, alas! the explanation is at hand; an explanation which, while it leaves untouched the assertion that the beauty of these poems is that of the blighted flower, changes every feeling with which we might momentarily regard their author into pitying sorrow. Her genius was yoked with death. It never freed itself from the dire companionship, never rose into freedom and clearness. As in the old Platonic chariot, her soul, borne by her winged genius, rose strong and daring towards the empyrean; but ere it breathed the pure serene, that black steed, which was also yoked indissolubly to the car, dragged her downwards even to the grave. Her poetry, whatever tones of true and joyful lyric music it may at intervals afford, is, as a whole, but the wild wailing melody to which was fought the battle between genius and death.

3. Poe and His Successors

George Henry Danton (1880–?) was a scholar who wrote about Germany, Romanticism, China, and Confucianism in the first half of the twentieth century. He taught German in China and at several schools in the United States, including Butler College and Union College. In this excerpt from an introduction to "Later German Romanticism" in *The German Classics* (1913), Danton describes relationship between the work of German fantasist Ernst Theodor Wilhelm Hoffmann (1776–1822), who wrote stories of the fantastic, macabre, and outré under the pen name E. T. A. Hoffmann, and the American authors Edgar Allan Poe (1809–1849) and Nathaniel Hawthorne (1804–1864). The extent to which Poe knew of Hoffmann and was influenced by him was actively debated in the late nineteenth and early twentieth centuries.

Excerpt from "Later German Romanticism"*
George H. Danton

E. T. A. Hoffmann (1776–1822) was a thoroughly Romantic person. Like his fellow–Königsberger, Werner, he went through a period of wildest dissipation, and all his life was easily influenced by alcohol. He was a painter, a writer, and a musician. His ability in the pictorial arts was mainly in caricature and his career as a composer is typically Romantic; though he never but once completed a composition that he started, he was thoroughly at home in the theory of the art. Like all Romanticists, Hoffmann was interested in and tried all phases of life and refused to recognize the boundaries between the various parts of existence, between the arts, and between reality and unreality. Hoffmann, with all his North German power of reasoning and his zeal and conscientiousness in public office, was

*George H. Danton, "Later German Romanticism," *The German Classics: Masterpieces of German Literature Translated into English,* vol. V (New York: The German Publication Society, 1913), 159–161.

emphatically *that* Romanticist associated with the night-sides of literature and life. There is something uncanny both in the man and his writings. His power of putting the scene of his most unreal stories in the midst of well-known places, his ability to shift the reader from the real to the unreal and *vice versa*, make some of his stories seem like phantasmagorias.

In all of Hoffmann's stories there is some unpleasant, bizarre character; this is the author's satire on his own strange personality. There is none of Poe's objectivity in Hoffmann, but he uses his subjectivity in a peculiarly Romantic fashion. It is his idea to raise the reader above the everyday point of view, to flee from this to a magic world where the unusual shall take the place of the real and where wonder shall rule. So there are in Hoffmann's stories a series of characters who are really doubles. To the uninitiated they seem every-day creatures; to those who know, they are fairies or beings from the supernatural world. Such characters are found at their best in *The Golden Pot*.

Hoffmann has influenced both French and English literatures more than any other Romantic poet. Hawthorne and Poe read him, and he was felt by the French to be one of the first Germans whom they understood. It was not merely that his clear reason appealed to the French, but that they saw in him one endowed as with a sixth sense. He has a fineness of observation, especially for the ridiculous sides of humanity, together with a tenderness of spirit, that was new in German literature as such men as Sainte-Beuve and Gautier saw it. The soul at war with itself, uncovering its most secret thoughts, the "*malheur d'être poète*," coupled with wit, taste, gaiety, and the comedy spirit all these the French found in Hoffmann as in no other German. Poe was also influenced by Hoffmann, but Poe's whole world is the supernatural, and where Hoffmann slips with fantastic but logical changes from the real to the unreal, Poe's metempsychosis is the real in his world and he has a deeper insight into the world of terror. The difference between Hawthorne and Hoffmann is even more striking, for in the American the supernatural is the embodiment of the Puritan New England conscience. In Hoffmann there is no such elevation of the moral world to the rank of an atmosphere.

In Hoffmann there is no out-of-doors, no lyric love; some of his characters are frankly insane. The musical takes on a supreme significance among the sensations, and music seemed the only art which was able to draw the soul of the man from his earth-bound habitation. Only in music did Hoffmann find the ability to make the Romantic escape from the homelessness of this existence to the all-embracing world of the unreal. But too often in his works does the unreal fail to satisfy the reader. There is an effort felt, an effect sought for, and, while the amalgamation of the two worlds is perfect, the world to which Hoffmann is able to take us proves to be without the cogency which our imaginations expect. Here Hoffmann fails. His world of the imagination cannot always be taken seriously.

The journalist and critic Paul Elmer More (1864–1937) began his career as a professor of classics and Sanskrit at Harvard and Bryn Mawr. He found his calling as editor of *The Independent*, *The New York Evening Post*, and *The Nation*, where he produced erudite literary criticism. He collected his criticism in eleven volumes of *The Shelburne Essays* (1904–1921) and three volumes of *The New Shelburne Essays* (1928–1936), all of which are long out of print. He later wrote works on philosophy and Christian apologies.

The piece under consideration here examines the unique "national consciousness" of early America that gave power and resonance to the works of Nathaniel Hawthorne and Edgar Allan Poe, whom More believed were greater than their British predecessors, whose works he found wanting. "The Origins of Hawthorne and Poe" first appeared in *The Independent* of October 16, 1902 before being collected in the first series of More's *Shelburne Essays* (1904). The "Mr. Lang" mentioned below is Andrew Lang, the critic, anthropologist, and collector of fairy tales and ghost stories. Excerpts of his work appear later in this volume.

The Origins of Hawthorne and Poe[*]
Paul Elmer More

We are credibly told that in years not so very long past young women and even grave men used to read the Gothic tales of Ann Radcliffe with tense brows and trembling lips; and the essays of Carlyle still stand a voluble witness to prove how seriously the grotesque marvels of German romance were once accepted in England. Mrs. Radcliffe is no doubt read occasionally to-day, and the indefatigable Mr. Lang has even attempted to reinstate her in popular favour. But her most generous admirer could hardly aver that she was anything more to him than a curious amusement; the horror of her tales has vanished away like the moonlight she was so

---

[*]Paul Elmer More, "The Origins of Hawthorne and Poe," in *The Shelburne Essays* (1st series) (New York: Knickerbocker Press, 1904), 51–70.

fond of describing. And as for Tieck and Wackenroder and all that dim romantic crew of Teuton *Sturm* and *Drang*—not even an Andrew Lang has arisen for them.

It is a matter for reflection, therefore, that in this country a new life of Hawthorne[1] should be something of a literary event and that there should be a sufficient public to warrant of two new and elaborate editions of Poe[2]; for at first thought it might seem that both Hawthorne and Poe fall in the same class with those forgotten weavers of moonlight and mysticism. What is it, indeed, that gives vitality to their work and separates it from the ephemeral product of English and German Gothicism? More than that: Why is it that the only two writers of America who have won almost universal renown as artists are these romancers, each of whom is, after his own manner, a sovereign in that strange region of emotion which we name the weird? Other work they have done, and done well, but when we call to mind their distinguishing productions we think first of such scenes as *The Fall of the House of Usher*, *The Raven*, and *The Sleeper*, or of such characters as Arthur Dimmesdale with his morbid remorse and unearthly sufferings, the dreamlike existence of Clifford, the hideous unexplained mystery of Miriam's wrong, and the awful search of Ethan Brand—scenes and characters which belong to the real world, for they appeal to a sympathetic cord in our own breasts, but which are yet quite overlaid with some insistent shadow of the fantastic realm of symbolism.

Hawthorne ascribes the superiority of Nature's work over man's to the fact "that the former works from the innermost germ, while the latter works merely superficially," and the same explanation may be given of the genuineness of his own work and Poe's in comparison with the unreality of Mrs. Radcliffe or Tieck; the weird, unearthly substance moulded by their genius is from the innermost core of the national consciousness. Their achievement is not like the Gothic novel introduced into England by Horace Walpole, a mere dilettante; there is in them very little of that recrudescence of mediaeval superstition and gloom which marked the rise of romanticism in Europe, little or nothing of the knights and ladies, turrets and dungeons and all that tawdry paraphernalia, and, fortunately for their reputation, no taint of that peculiar form of sentimentalism which pervades the German *Herzensergiessungen* like the odour of Schiller's

---

1. *Nathaniel Hawthorne*. By George E. Woodberry. [American Men of Letters.] Boston: Houghton, Mifflin & Co.
2. Published respectively by Thomas Y. Crowell & Co. and by G. P. Putnam's Sons.

decaying apples. Their work is the last efflorescence of tradition handed down to them unbroken from the earliest Colonial days, and that tradition was the voice of a stern and indomitable moral character. The unearthly visions of Poe and Hawthorne are in no wise the result of literary whim or of unbridled individualism, but are deep-rooted in American history. Neither Professor Woodberry in his Life of Hawthorne nor Professor Harrison in his Life of Poe has, it seems to me, brought out with due emphasis these spiritual origins of a school of romance which is so unique in its way as to have made for itself a sure place in the literature of the world.

The name of Hawthorne carries us back at once to those grim days of his ancestor in Salem Village when for a season almost the whole community gave itself up to the frenzy of witch hunting. In the earlier days the superstitions of England were concerned chiefly with the fairy folk of hearth and field, a quaint people commonly, and kindly disposed, if mischievous. But with the advent of Puritanism came a change; the fair and frolicsome play of the fancy was discredited and the starved imagination

The Witch. Both Europe and early America experienced witch hunts in which individuals, mostly women, were executed on suspicion of being in league with the devil. As many as one hundred died in seventeenth century New England witch trials, depicted in this 1892 illustration, and up to half a million were executed in Europe's witch hysteria of the fifteenth to seventeenth centuries (Library of Congress, Prints and Photographs Division, LC-DIG-ppmsca-09402).

had its revenge. In place of the elves and goblins of a freer age, instead of "Robin Goodfellow, the spoorn, the man-in-the-oak, the hell wain, the firedrake, the puckle" and all that antic crew, the imagination now evoked the terrific spectre of the Devil and attributed to his personal agency all the mishaps of life. Hence it is that witchcraft became so much more prominent with the Reformation and reached its height where Puritan feelings prevailed. On the one hand it was employed by the Roman Church as an aid in its exterminating fight with the Waldenses and other heretics— the good monks no doubt being easily persuaded, where persuasion was necessary, that the ascetic revolt against the office of the imagination in worship was of diabolic origin—and, on the other hand, the Protestants, and particularly the Puritans with their morbid horror of sin, were quick to accredit to the author of sin every phenomenon they could not understand. Witchcraft, to be sure, is as old as history, and we need go no further abroad than the classic poets for tales of the most abominable night hags. But there is this difference between such monsters as Lucan's Erichtho and the abortions of Christian demonology: Erichtho may haunt the sepulchres and breathe into the cold mouths of the dead the dark secret she would transmit to the Shades, but in the end she is only a product of the imagination brooding on things unclean and hideous; there is in the dread and repugnance she inspires no such added horror as that which the Christian felt at the thought of a soul leagued for infamous ends with the Prince of Hell and doomed as a rebel against God to everlasting tortures.

Considering the history of the Puritan emigrants we shall not be surprised to find these superstitions breaking out with peculiar virulence in the New World. Persecution and insult at home had not tended to soften their temper, nor did flight across a waste of perilous waters to a wilderness where everything was strange and unexplored bring light and cheerfulness to their imagination. In England at least their morbid intensity was to some extent modified by contact with the worldly life about them; in their new home they were completely given up to the working out of their stern purposes. Terrors and difficulties only added fuel to their zeal. "Our faithers were Englishmen which came over this great ocean and were ready to perish in this wilderness," says old Governor Bradford; and "with what difficulties [they] wrastled in going throug these things," we may read in all our school-books. It is easy to see how these hardships and these bitterly-won victories increased the sternness and unyieldingness of the New England Puritans, but perhaps we do not often consider the influence exerted on their imaginations by the wild country and wilder "salvages," as they called the red men, that now engaged their attention. They no longer beheld about them the pleasant vales and green hills of Old England, which the long habitation of man had rendered almost human, but the vast and pathless forests of the wilderness, where nature appeared under a new and forbidding aspect. There is at the best something weird and uncannny about the great woods into whose depths the eye cannot penetrate and from whose interwoven shadows, especially when night has fallen and the ear has grown painfully alert, come forth at intervals sounds that seem to indicate the activity of some nameless secret life within the darkness. What then must have been the feelings of the New England farmer as perchance he made his way homeward at sundown along the border of the gloomy forest. The kindly fancy of his ancestors who peopled the woods with mischievous goblins had yielded to his belief in the extended powers of evil. In these deep shadows he knew not but the very enemy of God might be lurking to lure him to destruction. It was no pleasant *waldeinsamkeit* he felt, such as romantic poets love to indulge, but awe and ghostly terror.

And this feeling was exaggerated by the actual savages who inhabited the woods. The settlers were for the most part thoroughly convinced that these poor, brutal denizens of the wilderness were under the special tutelage of Satan. In times of distress the colonists were ready to charge all their calamities to the machinations of an infernal conspiracy.

> It was afterward by *them* [the Indians] confessed, [says Cotton Mather in his *Magnalia*], that upon the arrival of the *English* in these parts, the *Indians* employed their *sorcerers*, whom they call *powaws*, like *Balaam*, to curse them, and let loose their *demons* upon them, to shipwreck them, to distract them, to poison them, or any way to ruin them. All the noted *powaws* in the country spent three days together in diabolical *conjurations*, to obtain the assistance of the *devils* against the settlement of these our *English*.

It is not strange, therefore, that when the delusion of witchcraft fell upon these people it should have assumed a peculiarly tragic aspect. They were dwelling in the midst of hostile demonic powers, and, feeling themselves attacked, they turned upon the enemy with all the strength and intensity of their souls. And how real and material the phenomena appeared to the bewildered onlookers may be gathered from this sulfurous account written by an eyewitness of the sufferings of one of the victims:

Margaret Rule would sometimes have her jaws forcibly pulled open, whereupon something invisible would be poured down her throat: we all saw her swallow, and yet we saw her try all she could, by spitting, coughing, and shrieking, that she might not swallow; but one time the standers-by plainly saw something of that odd liquor itself on the outside of her neck; she cried out of it, as if scalding brimstone were poured into her, and the whole house would immediately scent so hot of brimstone that we were scarce able to endure it.

Under the stress of this morbid excitement the good people of Salem and the neighbourhood were thrown into a frenzy of fear; crops were abandoned, business stood still, and the only matters considered were the horrible persecutions of Satan in their midst. The general feeling of alarm was aggravated to something like desperation when the Rev. Deodat Lawson in the meeting-house of Salem village preached an inflammatory sermon in which he charged the outburst of the infernal powers directly to the sins of the people.

You are therefore to be deeply humbled, [he said,] and sit in the dust, considering the signal hand of God in singling out this place, this poor village, for the first seat of Satan's tyranny, and to make it (as 't were) the rendezvous of devils, where they muster their infernal forces; appearing to the afflicted as coming armed to carry on their malicious designs against the bodies, and, if God in mercy prevent not, against the souls of many in this place.

No wonder that the people did actually believe "that the devils were walking about our streets with lengthened chains, making a dreadful noise in our ears; and brimstone (even without a metaphor) was making a horrid and a hellish stench in our nostrils."

To stop these terrible inroads of Satan a special court was created, before which those previously examined were tried. Those found guilty were hanged on a conspicuous eminence which thus acquired the ominous title of witch-hill; and how awful was the spectacle there presented to the panic-stricken people may be gathered from the pious ejaculation of the Reverend Mr. Noyes, "What a sad thing it is to see eight firebrands of hell hanging there!" The cruelty engendered by this feeling of insecurity is well indicated by the treatment of Giles Corey, who, refusing to plead either guilty or not guilty, was subjected to the *peine dure et forte*, as the tale is related in Longfellow's *New England Tragedy*; but Longfellow does not relate what we are told in a ballad of the period, that when from the oppression of the stone on his chest Corey's tongue protruded it was rudely thrust back by the staff of a bystander.

In due time this "hellish molestation," as one of the persecuted called it, came to a sudden end; but not before twenty victims had suffered death, many had died in jail, hundreds had endured imprisonment in its worst forms, whole families had been impoverished, and a moral impression had been made upon the community which nothing could efface. The modern historian of the delusion tells us that a sort of curse still rests on the immediate scene of these tragic events and that neglect and desertion still brood on the accursed spot.

Were we to go no further than this episode of Salem history we should find it easy to explain by inheritance that mystic brooding over the dark and intricate effects of sin which the descendant of old John Hathorne has made the substance of his romance, or to account for the realism that underlies the wild fantasies of Poe. And we need only to dip into Cotton Mather's voluminous record of the dealings of Providence in America to see how intensely the mind of the Puritans was occupied with unearthly matters and what a legacy of emotions approaching the weird was left by them to posterity. When the faith of these militant saints was untroubled it often assumed a sweetness and fullness of spiritual content that might even pass into rapturous delight. But always this intoxicating joy bordered on the region of awe—the awe of a soul in the presence of the great and ineffable mysteries of holiness; and the life of Thomas Shepard, which Mather calls *"a trembling walk with God"* may not unfitly be taken to illustrate the peculiar temper of their religion. And if in the wisest and sanest of the Puritan Fathers this trembling solicitude was never far away, there were others in whom the fear of the Lord became a mania of terror. Consider what the impression on the minds of children must have been when in the midst of their innocent sport the awful apparition of the Rev. James Noyes stood before them and rebuked them into silence with these solemn words: "Cousins, I wonder you can be so merry, unless you are sure of your salvation!" Consider the spiritual state of a young man, celebrated for his godliness, who could note down in his diary with curious precision: "I was almost in the suburbs of hell all day."

Literature, in the true sense of the word, could not well flourish among a people who saw in the plastic imagination a mere seduction of the senses, and whose intellectual life was thus absorbed in theological speculation. To be sure, a good deal of verse was written and even printed in early Colonial days; but of all the poets of that age only one attained any real celebrity and has in a way lived on into the present. Michael Wigglesworth, the faithful pastor of Maiden, where in the odour of sanctity he died in 1705, is described as "a little feeble *shadow* of a *man*;" but his diminutive frame harboured a mighty spirit. His poems breathed the very quintessence of Puritan faith, and as such obtained immediate and extraordinary popularity. Professor Tyler calculates that in the first year of publication his *Day of Doom* was purchased by at least one in every thirty-five persons of New England; printed as a common ballad it was hawked everywhere about the country, and its lugubrious stanzas were even taught to children along with the catechism. As late as the year 1828 an essayist declared that many an aged person of his acquaintance could still repeat the poem, though they might not have seen a copy of it since they were in leading strings; and in his own time Cotton Mather had thought it might "perhaps find our children till the day itself arrives"—which God forbid.

The strength of Master Wigglesworth's genius, in this picture of the *Day of Doom*, is, as we should expect, devoted to those who

> void of tears, but fill'd with fears,
>   and dreadful expectation
> Of endless pains and scalding flames,
>   stand waiting for Damnation.

One after another the various kinds of sinners are arraigned at the bar and receive their due reward. Most hideous and most famous of all are the stanzas that describe the pleading and condemnation of unbaptised infants. As an expression of the grotesque in literature they are not without a kind of crude power; as the voice of a real and tremendously earnest faith they elude the grasp of a modern mind, one can only shudder and avert his eyes. We contrast with some curiosity and no little bewilderment the unflinching frankness of this earlier Calvinist with the shifting creed of a recent Calvinistic convention which has attempted to explain away the catechism's abandonment of non-elect infants. Yet Wigglesworth, like the Presbyterians of to-day, had his moment of compunction for the poor souls who

> from the womb unto the tomb
> Were straightway carriëd;—

he at least allowed to them "the easiest room in hell!" Those simple words have of recent years acquired a certain notoriety through literary hand books; indeed, for naked and appalling realism of horror, when all is considered, it would not be easy to find a verse to surpass them.

Wigglesworth's rhymes were, as I said, the intellectual food of the young, and some such strong meat would seem necessary to prepare them for the sermons that nourished their manhood. And at least one of these sermons, Jonathan Edwards's famous Enfield discourse of *Sinners in the Hands of an Angry God*, has gained the unenviable reputation of being perhaps the most tremendous and uncompromising enunciation ever made of the gloomier side of Calvinism. His picture of worldly men hanging over the pit of hell "by a slender thread, with the flames of divine wrath flashing about it, and ready every moment to singe it and burn it asunder," has become classical in its own way.

After the death of Edwards, in 1758, the heart of the country became more and more absorbed in the impending conflict of the Revolution. For a while, at least, religion and the terrors of damnation must give place to the more imminent peril of political subjugation. In New England that other phase of Puritanism, the spirit that had led Cromwell and his Ironsides to victory, and had established the liberties of the English constitution, came to the foreground, and for a time the political pamphlet usurped the place of the sermon. But even then literature did not entirely vanish; and at intervals through the rasping cries of revolution one may catch a note of that pensiveness or gloom, that habitual dwelling on the supernatural significance of life, which had come to be the dominant intellectual tone of the country. Indeed, it was this violent wrenching of the national consciousness into new fields which brought about the change from the old supernaturalism of religion to the shadowy symbolism of literature as exemplified in Hawthorne and Poe. We seem to see the beginning of this new spirit in the haunting pathos that throbs through the anonymous ballad of *Nathan Hale*:

> The breezes went steadily through the tall pines,
>   A saying, "Oh! hu-ush!" a saying, "Oh! hu-ush!"
> As stilly stole by a bold legion of horse,
>   For Hale in the bush, for Hale in the bush.
>
> "Keep still," said the thrush as she nestled her young,
>   In a nest by the road; in a nest by the road;
> "For the tyrants are near and with them appear
>   What bodes us no good; what bodes us no good."

Of all the gentlemen—and women, too—who wrote verse in those stirring times only one can lay claim to any genuine poetic inspiration. Philip Freneau, of New Jersey, has even yet a slight hold on the memory of the reading public, and would be more read and better known were his works subjected to proper selection and editing. Like all the other versifiers of the period Freneau was caught in the wild vortex of political affairs, and, against the protests of his truer nature as he himself avows, gave up the gentler muses for the raucous voice of satire. But here and there through his works we find a suggestion of what he might have accomplished had he fallen on better times. In him we catch perhaps the first note of the weird as it appears in our later literature, of that transition of overwhelming superstition into shadowy haunting symbolism. Not unseldom a stanza, or a single line it may be, wakes an echo in the mind curiously like Poe. Such, for instance, is the spectral beauty of that stanza of *The Indian Burying Ground*, whose last line, as Poe once pointed out, was borrowed intact, and never acknowledged, by Campbell:

> By midnight moons, o'er moistening dews,
>   In vestments for the chase arrayed,
> The hunter still the deer pursues,
>   The hunter and the deer—a shade.

A glance at the titles of Freneau's poems would show how persistently, when relieved from the immediate pressure of politics, his mind reverted to subjects of decay and quiet dissolution. In one of his longer poems, *The House of Death*, he has just failed of achieving a work which might have come from the brain of Poe himself. At the hour of midnight the poet dreams that he wanders over a desolate country:

> Dark was the sky, and not one friendly star
>   Shone from the zenith or horizon, clear,
> Mist sate upon the woods, and darkness rode
>   In her black chariot, with a wild career.
>
> And from the woods the late resounding note
>   Issued of the loquacious whip-poor-will,
> Hoarse, howling dogs, and nightly roving wolves
>   Clamour'd from far off cliffs invisible.

At last he finds himself in the presence of "a noble dome raised fair and high," standing in the midst of "a mournful garden of autumnal hue":

> The poppy there, companion to repose,
>   Displayed her blossoms that began to fall,
> And here the purple amaranthus rose
>   With mint strong scented, for the funeral.

In this strange spot, which has something of the unearthly qualities of Rappaccini's garden or Poe's spectral landscapes, stands the desolate home of a young man whose beloved consort death has recently snatched away, and who now harbours as a guest the grisly person of Death himself. Death, stretched on the couch and surrounded by ghoulish phantoms, lies dying. Over the conversation that ensues and the blasphemies of the ghastly sufferer we may pass without de-laying. At last after Death has composed his own epitaph and described the tomb he is to occupy, in

> A burying-yard of sinners dead, unblest,

the poet flees terror-smitten out of that house into the tempestuous night.

> Nor looked I back, till to a far off wood
>   Trembling with fear, my weary feet had sped—
> Dark was the night, but at the enchanted dome
>   I saw the infernal windows flaming red.

At last the hour of dissolution arrives:

> Dim burnt the lamp, and now the phantom Death
>   Gave his last groans in horror and despair—
> "All hell demands me hence"—he cried, and threw
>   The red lamp hissing through the midnight air.
> Trembling, across the plain my course I held,
>   And found the grave-yard, loitering through the gloom,
> And, in the midst, a hell-red wandering light,
>   Walking in fiery circles round the tomb.

Whereupon with a gruesome picture of Death's interment and a few stanzas of proper exhortation from the author, this remarkable poem comes to an end.

    Between the period of the Revolution and the period that may be called the New England renaissance not much was written which has the distinct mark of the American temperament. Yet it is a significant fact that Charles Brockden Brown's *Wieland*, published in 1798, the first novel of the first American novelist, should be built upon a theme as weird and as steeped in "thrilling melancholy," to use Brown's own words, as anything in the later work of Hawthorne or Poe; and in the proper place it would not be uninteresting to show how far, in his imperfect way, Brown anticipates the very methods and tricks of his greater followers. His immediate inspiration comes no doubt from the mystery-mongering novels then so popular in England, but despite the crudeness of a provincial style there does run through the strange unreality of Brown's pages a note of sincerity, the tongue and accents of a man to whom such themes are a native inheritance, lending to his work a sustained interest which I for my part fail to find in the *Castle of Otranto* or the *Mysteries of Udolpho.* Nor is it without significance that even in New York, where if anywhere this world claims her own, Irving in his genial way could fall so easily into brooding on the dead who sleep in Westminster Abbey or relate with such gusto the wild legends of the Hudson. Bryant, too, has kept his fame chiefly on account of his youthful musings on death and the grandiose pomp of those lines that tell how the rock-ribbed hills, the pensive vales, the venerable rivers, brooks,

> and, poured around them all,
> Old Ocean's grey and melancholy waste,—
> Are but the solemn decorations all
> Of the great tomb of man.

Necessarily this age-long contemplation of things unearthly, this divorcing of the imagination from the fair and blithe harmonies of life to fasten upon the sombre effects of guilt and reprobation, this constant meditation on death and decay—necessarily all these exerted a powerful influence on literature when the renaissance appeared in New England and as a sort of reflection in the rest of the country. So, I think, it happened that out of that famous group of men who really created American literature the only two to attain perfection of form in the higher field of the imagination were writers whose minds were absorbed by the weirder phenomena of life. But it must not be inferred thence that the spirit of Hawthorne and Poe was identical with that of Michael Wigglesworth and Jonathan Edwards. With the passage of time the unquestioning, unflinching faith and vision of those heroic men dissolved away. Already in Freneau, himself born of a Huguenot family, a change is noticeable; that which to the earlier Fathers was a matter of infinite concern, that which to them was more real and urgent than the breath of life, becomes now chiefly an intoxicant of the imagination, and in another generation the transition is complete.

It is this precisely that we understand by the term "weird"—not the veritable vision of unearthly things, but the peculiar half vision inherited by the soul when faith has waned and the imagination prolongs the old sensations in a shadowy involuntary life of its own; and herein too lies the field of true and effective symbolism. If Hawthorne and Poe, as we think, possess an element of force and realism such as Tieck and the German school utterly lack, it is because they write from the depths of this profound moral experience of their people.

Robert Chambers (1802–1871) was a Scottish writer and publisher of reference books, not to be confused with Robert W. Chambers, the later author of the horror cycle *The King in Yellow* (1895). Chambers's last reference work was his *The Book of Days: A Miscellany of Popular Antiquities in Connection with the Calendar, Including Anecdote, Biography & History, Curiosities of Literature and Oddities of Human Life and Character* (1864). This book collected profiles and facts, organized by the day with which they were associated. What follows is part of the entry for October 7, covering the life of Edgar Allan Poe and indicating popular opinion thereof fifteen years after his October 7, 1849, death—namely that authors of morbid works must therefore be insane.

Edgar Allan Poe[*]

Robert Chambers

Edgar Allan Poe, an eccentric American poet, was born at Baltimore, January 1811. It may seem absurd to say that he belonged by birth to the aristocracy, in a country where no aristocracy is recognised. Still, it is a fact that Poe was an aristocrat, and it is also true, that no people are more proud of the advantages of birth and breeding, than citizens of the United States, especially those who belong to the southern division of those states. Poe

Edgar Allan Poe. Nineteenth and early twentieth century critics argued over Edgar Allan Poe's place in the literary canon. Some considered him insane and his works to be unworthy of being called "literature." Others saw genius in Poe and worked to place his writings at the head of the American canon. Only in the twentieth century did the controversy generally resolve in Poe's favor. The dauguerrotype was made in 1848; the photograph of it was taken in 1904 (Library of Congress, Prints and Photographs Division, LC-USZ62-10610).

[*]"Edgar Allan Poe," in *The Book of Days: A Miscellany of Popular Antiquities in Connection with the Calendar, Including Anecdote, Biography & History, Curiosities of Literature and Oddities of Human Life and Character*, ed. R. Chambers (London: W. & R. Chambers, 1882), 421–422.

was a Southerner in manners and feelings, as well as by birth; and there is little doubt, that the greater part of the infamy which was heaped upon him after his death, was owing to the fact that as a man of taste he despised, and as an aristocrat, treated with contempt, a tradesman in literature, who lived by making books of biographies, generally laudatory of living literary persons. This man took his revenge when the opportunity came, as any one may kick a dead lion with impunity. Many have echoed, no doubt honestly, the evil fame which was made for the poor poet by this man, whom he had despised and insulted during his life.

Poe's grandfather was a soldier in the war of the American revolution, and a friend of Lafayette. His father was a student at law. He fell in love with an English actress, named Arnold, and married her. They both died young, and at nearly the same time, leaving three orphan children. Edgar was adopted and educated by John Allan, a wealthy merchant of Virginia. At the early age of five years he was brought to England, and was sent to school near London, till he was ten years old.

Poe's life was a series of eccentric adventures. The reason of this is to be found in his temperament, or physical constitution. He lived, from the cradle to the grave, on the verge of madness, when he was not absolutely mad. A half-glass of wine intoxicated him to insanity. His brain was large, almost to deformity, in the region where phrenologists place the imaginative faculties.[a] Under the influence of slight stimulus, such as would have been inappreciable by a person otherwise constituted, Poe was led on to commit acts, the consequences of which were often distressing, and might at any moment have been fatal, as was finally the case.

At an early age he entered college at Charlottesville, Virginia, but he was expelled for dissipation. He also entered the military school at West Point, New York, but he left in a year. During the excitement in favour of the independence of Greece, he started for that country; but he was next found at St Petersburg, where he fell into distress, as was his fortune almost everywhere, and some friends sent him home.

Soon after his return, he published a volume of poems, entitled *Al Aaraaf, Tamerlane*, and *Minor Poems*. These were written from the age of sixteen to eighteen years.

At one time he enlisted as a soldier, but he soon deserted. He had much partiality for active exercise, and very little for discipline, though he was exceedingly methodical and orderly in all the details of life. He was remarkable for aquatic and gymnastic performances. He was able to leap further than most men, and he once swam seven miles and a half against the tide.

In 1835, Poe was employed to write for the *Southern Literary Messenger*, and about this time he married his cousin, Virginia Clemm, who, at the time of their union, was about fourteen years old. Alter this, we find him engaged on *Benton's Gentleman's Magazine*, at two pounds a week. This engagement was of brief continuance, and he next was connected with *Graham's Magazine*, and wrote *Some Strange Stories*, nearly all of which seem tinged with a sort of semi-insanity. We next find him engaged with Mr Briggs, in establishing the *Broadway Journal*. This was soon discontinued. About 1844, he wrote *The Raven*, which has enjoyed a more extended reputation than any other production of his pen.

After the appearance of the *Raven* in transatlantic periodicals, Elizabeth Barrett Browning wrote to Poe, that '*The Raven* had excited a *fit horror* in England.' He was delighted with the compliment. Indeed this sort of impression appeared to be an object of ambition with him. Poe always seemed to consider *The Raven* as his master-piece, and he was fond of reciting it in company, in a sort of sing-song tone, which was very unpleasant to some.

It would be difficult to calculate the amount of fame that Poe might have earned, if he could have lived, and written one year in undisturbed sanity. After the fame of *The Raven* had brought his name upon every lip, he was invited to lecture before the Boston Atheneum—the highest honour the Athens of America could bestow on the poet. He went before an elegant and most intellectual Boston audience, and instead of giving a lecture, he repeated a juvenile poem that had been published! His friends had no doubt of the cause, or occasion of this strange proceeding, but the audience were indignant. Poe declared that 'it was an intentional insult to the genius of the frog-pond, a small pond on Boston Common'—a further evidence of the madness that he often induced, by taking stimulants, though he knew his fearful liability. After this, his irregularities became so much the rule of his life, that Mrs Clemm, who acted the part of a good genius to the poet and his young wile, her daughter, took a cottage at Fordham, near New York. Here she devoted herself to the care of both with tender and unceasing assiduity. Mrs Poe was dying of consumption. Poe was plunged in a deep melancholy, which did not admit of his writing anything. They were in a state of almost utter destitution, and the malady of the poet was constantly aggravated by witnessing the suffering of his fading lily-like wife, to whom he was tenderly attached. Friends came to their help the moment their condition was known, and it was subsequently brought against Poe, that he took a bribe at this time for a favourable review, which he afterwards wrote of a miserable book of poems. In speaking of this violation of his literary conscience, after he had somewhat recovered the tone of his mind, he said, 'The author gave me a hundred dollars, when my poor Virginia was dying, and we were starving, and required me to write a review of that book. What could I do?'

Let those who have judged him harshly for this, and other sins of his life, place themselves in his condition. When sober and sane, Poe was a gentleman of pure taste and elegant manners, whose conversation was always interesting, and often instructive. He had great personal beauty, and the aristocratic manner and bearing of a southern gentleman, and a descendant of the Cavaliers. In 1848, Poe published *Eureka*, which he first gave as a lecture. It is impossible to give a characteristic description of this and oilier literary performances by Poe. The same sort of extravagance pervades all, and those who knew him most intimately, and were best qualified to judge, believed that he lived and wrote with a shade of madness in all that he did—and yet few men were more methodical and orderly in their habits than Poe. His handwriting was delicately beautiful, and at the same time clear and plain. His study was the perfection of order and neatness. But his fearful proclivities might change all this in a moment. The world cannot believe that half a glass of wine could make a man lose all self-control, and hurry him on to madness, and its fearful consequences. But there is abundant proof that this was true of Poe.

After the death of his wife, Poe gradually recovered from the deep melancholy which had palsied all his mental power during the last portion of her life, and engaged again in literary occupation. Subsequently, he entered into correspondence with a lady of fine genius and high position, with a view to marriage. But here, again, his destiny was against him. The marriage was broken off, and soon after Poe died of delirium tremens, at the age of thirty-eight; that critical period at which it seems natural for an irregular life, combined with excessive brain-work, to bring its victims to an end.

Notes

a. Phrenology was a nineteenth-century pseudoscience that sought to deduce the areas of the brain responsible for cognitive functions and personality traits through the shape of the skull, reading import into the bumps and fissures thereon.

The American poet and satirist James Russell Lowell (1819–1891) was later to become the first editor of the *Atlantic Monthly* and minister to Spain, but in 1845 he was writing anti-slavery pieces for the *Pennsylvania Freeman* and contributing to literary magazines. Edgar Allan Poe and Lowell were friends, and Poe asked Lowell to write about him for *Graham's*, a magazine he once edited and continued to write for. This article, which ran in the edition for February 1845, contained a number of reprinted poems and biographical details here omitted to focus on Lowell's view of Poe as literary genius. After Poe's untimely death, a revision of this article appeared with a new ending: "On the whole, it may be considered certain that Mr. Poe has attained an individual eminence in our literature, which he will keep. He has given proof of power and originality. He has done that which could only be done once with success or safety, and the imitation or repetition of which would produce weariness."

*Excerpt from "Edgar Allan Poe"**
JAMES RUSSELL LOWELL

...Mr. Poe had that indescribable something which men have agreed to call *genius*. No man could ever tell us precisely what it is, and yet there is none who is not inevitably aware of its presence and its power. Let talent writhe and contort itself as it may, it has no such magnetism. Larger of bone and sinew it may be, but the wings are wanting. Talent sticks fast to earth, and its most perfect works have still one foot of clay. Genius claims kindred with the very workings of Nature herself, so that a sunset shall seem like a quotation from Dante or Milton, and if Shakespeare be read in the very presence of the sea itself, his verses shall but seem nobler for the sublime criticism of ocean. Talent may make friends for itself, but only genius can give to its creations the divine power of winning love and veneration. Enthusiasm cannot cling to what itself is unenthusiastic, nor will he ever have disciples who has not himself impulsive zeal enough to be a disciple. Great wits are allied to madness only inasmuch as they are possessed and carried away by their demon, while talent keeps him, as Paracelsus did, securely prisoned in the pommel of his sword. To the eye of genius, the veil of the spiritual world is ever rent asunder, that it may perceive the ministers of good and evil who throng continually around it. No man of mere talent ever flung his inkstand at the devil.

When we say that Mr. Poe had genius, we do not mean to say that he has produced evidence of the highest. But to say that he possesses it at all is to say that he needs only zeal, industry, and a reverence for the trust

*James Russell Lowell, "Edgar Allan Poe," *Graham's Magazine*, February 1845, 51–53.

reposed in him, to achieve the proudest triumphs and the greenest laurels. If we may believe the Longinuses and Aristotles of our newspapers, we have quite too many geniuses of the loftiest order to render a place among them at all desirable, whether for its hardness of attainment or its seclusion. The highest peak of our Parnassus is, according to these gentlemen, by far the most thickly settled portion of the country, a circumstance which must make it an uncomfortable residence for individuals of a poetical temperament, if love of solitude be, as immemorial tradition asserts, a necessary part of their idiosyncrasy.[...]

Mr. Poe has two of the prime qualities of genius, a faculty of vigorous yet minute analysis, and a wonderful fecundity of imagination. The first of these faculties is as needful to the artist in words, as a knowledge of anatomy is to the artist in colors or in stone. This enables him to conceive truly, to maintain a proper relation of parts, and to draw a correct outline, while the second groups, fills up and colors. Both of these Mr. Poe has displayed with singular distinctness in his prose works, the last predominating in his earlier tales, and the first in his later ones.[...]

In his tales, Mr. Poe has chosen to exhibit his power chiefly in that dim region which stretches from the very utmost limits of the probable into the weird confines of superstition and unreality. He combines in a very remarkable manner two faculties which are seldom found united; a power of influencing the mind of the reader by the impalpable shadows of mystery, and a minuteness of detail which does not leave a pin or a button unnoticed. Both are, in truth, the natural results of the predominating quality of his mind, to which we have before alluded, analysis. It is this which distinguishes the artist. His mind at once reaches forward to the effect to be produced. Having resolved to bring about certain emotions in the reader, he makes all subordinate parts tend strictly to the common centre. Even his mystery is mathematical to his own mind. To him x is a known quantity all along. In any picture that he paints he understands the chemical properties of all his colors. However vague some of his figures may seem, however formless the shadows, to him the outline is as clear and distinct as that of a geometrical diagram. For this reason Mr. Poe has no sympathy with *Mysticism*. The Mystic dwells *in* the mystery, is enveloped with it; it colors all his thoughts; it affects his optic nerve especially, and the commonest things get a rainbow edging from it. Mr. Poe, on the other hand, is a spectator *ab extra*. He analyzes, he dissects, he watches

> —————"with an eye serene,
> The very pulse of the machine,"ª

for such it practically is to him, with wheels and cogs and piston-rods, all working to produce a certain end. It is this that makes him so good a critic. Nothing baulks him, or throws him off the scent, *except now and then a prejudice.*

This analyzing tendency of his mind balances the poetical, and by giving him the patience to be minute, enables him to throw a wonderful reality into his most unreal fancies. A monomania he paints with great power. He loves to dissect one of these cancers of the mind, and to trace all the subtle ramifications of its roots. In raising images of horror, also, he has strange success; conveying to us sometimes by a dusky hint some terrible *doubt* which is the secret of all horror. He leaves to imagination the task of finishing the picture, a task to which only she is competent.[...]

His style is highly finished, graceful and truly classical. It would be hard to find a living author who had displayed such varied powers. As an example of his style we would refer to one of his tales, "The House of Usher," in the first volume of his "Tales of the Grotesque and Arabesque." It has a singular charm for us, and we think that no one could read it without being strongly moved by its serene and sombre beauty. Had its author written nothing else, it would alone have been enough to stamp him as a man of genius, and the master of a classic style.[...]

Beside his "Tales of the Grotesque and Arabesque," and some works unacknowledged, Mr. Poe is the author of "Arthur Gordon Pym," a romance, in two volumes, which has run through many editions in London; of a system of Conchology,ᵇ of a digest and translation of Lemmonnier's Natural History, and has contributed to several reviews in France, in England, and in this country. He edited the Southern Literary Messenger during its novitiate, and by his own contributions gained it most of its success and reputation. He was also, for some time, the editor of this magazine, and our readers will bear testimony to his ability in that capacity.

Mr. Poe is still in the prime of life, being about thirty-two years of age, and has probably as yet given but an earnest of his powers. As a critic, he has shown so superior an ability that we cannot but hope that he will collect his essays of this kind and give them a more durable form. They would be a very valuable contribution to our literature, and would fully justify all we have said in his praise. We could refer to [...] his poems [to] prove that he is the possessor of a pure and original vein. His tales and essays have equally shown him a master in prose. It is not for us to assign him his definite rank among cotemporary authors, but we may be allowed to say that we know of *none* who has displayed more varied and striking abilities.

Notes

a. William Wordsworth, "She Was a Phantom of Delight" (1807).
b. The study of mollusks. *The Conchologist's First Book* (1839) bore a preface and introduction by Poe but was otherwise the work of Thomas Wyatt, who paid $50 to have Poe's name attached to a text he produced from an edition of Thomas Brown's *Conchologist's Text Book*. He thought Poe's fame would sell more copies. The result was a century of accusations that Poe had plagiarized the book from Brown.

The following review from *The Knickerbocker* for January 1846 takes Edgar Allan Poe to task for his poetry, which the anonymous critic judges deficient on nearly every level, both qualitatively and quantitatively. His bitterness recalls the old joke about the diner who complained that "the food was awful ... and such small portions!" From the rather lengthy review, I have extracted the specific criticism of Poe's poetry (which he began writing as a boy) and omitted passages dealing with a feud between Poe and the magazine, which he had criticized in an article, but which belongs more properly to a study of Poe rather than horror.

Review of The Raven and Other Poems*
THE KNICKERBOCKER

...According to the biographies of Mr. POE, he must be very near the age at which BYRON died, and beyond that at which all the great poets produced their greatest works; and according to his own story, he began writing poetry at an age much earlier than any poet of whom we know any thing. His whole life has been spent in literary pursuits, and here we have the results of his poetical career.[...] A talent for versification may exist without a genius for poetry; and according to our own estimate of Mr. POE's abilities, his poetical constitution is nothing more than an aptitude for rhythm. We should judge as much, from reading his criticisms of poetry, which seem to have been written after a very thorough cramming of BLAIR's lectures and the essays of Lord KAIMES. In several instances

*Review of *The Raven and Other Poems* by Edgar Allan Poe, in "Literary Notices," *The Knickerbocker*, January 1846, 69–72.

The Raven. Poe explained in "The Philosophy of Composition" (1846) that his poem "The Raven" (1845) was written with careful control and logic and was designed to appeal to both popular and critical tastes. Poe's meter for the poem was partly inspired by Elizabeth Barrett's "Lady Geraldine's Courtship," and he dedicated the volume of poems containing the raven to her. Barrett wrote to Poe that "Your 'Raven' has produced a sensation, a 'fit horror,' here in England." Most contemporary critics found the poem powerful and original. Illustration published 1903 (Library of Congress, Prints and Photographs Division, LC-USZ62-108225).

he has asserted that there cannot be such a thing as a didactic poem. This demolishes at one swoop about nine-tenths of what the world has heretofore considered the highest poetry. If we can glean any distinct meaning from Mr. POE's criticisms and verses, respecting his ideas of what constitutes a poem, it is this: a poem is a metrical composition without ideas.[...] 'The Haunted Palace' and other of his best performances were certainly composed upon such a principle; and the same might be said of many of his prose essays, words being the sole substance in them.[...]

We have no disposition to criticize Mr. POE's poems: such as they are, we give them welcome. His reputation as a poet rests mainly upon 'The Raven,' which, as we have already said, we consider an unique and musical piece of versification, but as a poem it will not bear scrutiny.[...]

We are not much disappointed in the quality of Mr. POE's poems, but the meagreness of his volume as to quantity is really surprising. He is one of the few authors by profession known to American readers; and considering that poetry is 'a passion' with him, and 'not a purpose,' the little of any kind that he has produced is a thing to be wondered at. We do not know what the unhappy circumstances may be which have prevented him from making any 'serious effort' in his favorite pursuit; but his hinderances can hardly be greater than those under which the greater part of that which the world calls poetry has been produced. Has he been blind, like MILTON; has he been mad, like TASSO; been starved, like CHATTERTON; persecuted, like DANTE; exposed, like BYRON; harrassed, like BURNS; depressed, like COWPER? Has he labored like ELLIOT; fought, like KÖRNER; been neglected, like BUTLER; bent, like DRYDEN, or tempted, as many noble poets have been, by luxury and sloth? A real poet will never tell of the hinderances to effort. It is *overcoming* hinderances which gives the surest testimony of ability. Nothing will excuse a poet for non-production but non-ability. Let the author produce his talent and say, ''T is the best I could do'; excuses for not doing better will avail him nothing. Indeed, we are believers in CARLETON's Irish paradox, and think it as applicable to poets, '*who have it in them*,' as to any body else; namely, that 'more men have risen ill tho world from the enmity of their enemies than from tho kindness of their friends.' Poets, like other men, may become 'blue-moulded for want of a *batin*'.' Whatever circumstances the true poet may be placed in, whether worried by affluence or depressed by misery, he will be a poet in spite of them; and his overcoming difficulties will be the best evidence of his 'passion.' Mr. POE's passion for poetry must be a very tender one, or he would not come before, the world at his age with such a volume, and with such an excuse for its meagreness. The history of genius hardly affords an instance of one born upon 'the field of his choice.' Shepherds have become astronomers, shoemakers mathematicians, barbers commanders, physicians architects, ploughmen poets, tailors statesmen, weavers artists. Judging from Mr. POE's memoirs, which must be correct, since he circulates them himself, his opportunities for cultivating his passion have been superior to those enjoyed by any writer of reputation among us. But 'every heart knoweth its own bitterness,' and we doubt not that Mr. POE's complaint is well founded. It is a painful reflection, however, that we have a great poet among us placed in such unhappy circumstances that he cannot develope his genius, nor make a serious effort in that kind of composition for which he has a consciousness of being qualified by nature. The circumstances must indeed be exceedingly unhappy and distressing, which would cause a poet to accept an invitation from a learned society to deliver an original poem at its annual meeting, and after receiving pay therefor, to read a rhapsody composed and published in his tenth year, and afterward bring forward, as a proof of the stupidity of his audience, that they listened to him with civil attention. 'But something too much of this.'

William Crary Brownell (1851–1928) was an American literary critic and an editor at Charles Scribner's Sons, where he edited the works of Edith Wharton. He was influenced by the British critic and poet Matthew Arnold, who held that literature should be a "criticism of life." Brownell sought to raise the standards of American literary criticism accordingly. He thought Poe a genius, but "in the historic rather than the critical estimate," for his influence on literature rather than his production of it. In this excerpt from *American Prose Masters* (1909), Brownell castigates Poe for his "lack of substance" and failure to write "real" literature.

*Poe: Lack of Substance**
W.C. BROWNELL

The truth is it is idle to endeavor to make a great writer of Poe because whatever his merits as a literary artist his writings lack the elements not

*W. C. Brownell, "Poe: Lack of Substance," in *American Prose Masters* (New York: Charles Scribner's Sons, 1909), 231–240.

only of great, but of real, literature. They lack substance. Literature is more than an art. It is art in an extended sense of the term. Since it is the art that deals with life rather than with appearances it is the art *par excellence* that is art plus something else—plus substance. Its interest is immensely narrowed when it can only be considered plastically—narrowed to the point of inanity, of insignificance. Poe was certainly an artist, but the fact that he was exclusively an artist and an artist in an extremely restricted sense, of itself minimizes the literature he produced. Shakespeare, for example, is neither exclusively nor supremely an artist. M. Jules Lemaitre informs us how much better in some respects—in artistic respects—Racine would have written "Hamlet." Every art of course, has its conventions. It rearranges them from time to time, it is subject to the law of evolution, but it depends on them always. And in so far as literature is an art it, too, leans upon them. It has its schools, its phases, its successive points of view, its academic perfections, its solecisms. But the fact that it deals with life itself rather than exclusively with appearances—which may be arranged, organized, systematized, controlled far more easily through their greater preliminary simplification—gives it so much more range, so much greater freedom, such an infinitely greater miscellaneity of material of so much more significance and vitality, that it is comparatively independent of conventions, and finds its supreme justification in giving anyhow, in any way, well or ill one may almost say, the effect of life, the phenomena and significance of life which constitute its substance. Thus it is that in literature substance counts so much more than it counts in any other art, however much any other may also be in its degree "a criticism of life." Mr. Henry James has curiously illustrated the principle in later years. Beginning as pre-eminently or at least conspicuously an artist he has become so overwhelmed by the prodigious wealth and miscellaneity of his material—that is to say, the phases of life which his prodigious penetration has revealed to him—that his art has been submerged by it. The trees have obliterated the forest. All the more important is it, one may argue, to cling to conventions of treatment, that your picture of life may be definite, coherent and effective. Yes, but one of these conventions is a certain correspondence with reality. Life being the subject of literature more fully and directly than it is of any purely plastic art that deals with appearances—which are necessarily more ordered and adaptable and in a sense art themselves, or a stage of it—being indeed the substance as well as the subject of literature, this correspondence with reality is exacted by it of any treatment of it that is, even as art, to have any interest or value. The doctrine of art for art's sake applied to literature is apt to have particularly insipid results.

In short, however extravagant and capricious, any work of art is necessarily subject to its material and the hand of every artist must like the dyer's be subdued to what it works in. But a literary composition, especially, cannot be conceived and executed *in vacuo*. The warp must be "given", however wholly the woof may be invented, or the web will be insubstantial and the pattern incoherent. Poe could transact his imaginings in environments of the purest fancy, in no-man's land, in the country of nowhere, and fill these with "tarns" and morasses and "ragged mountains" and shrieking water-lilies, flood them with ghastly moonlight and aerate them with "rank miasmas." Nevertheless, he could only avoid the flatness of pure phantasmagoria by peopling them with humanity. His landscape might embody extravagance and his atmosphere enshroud caprice, his figures demanded to be made human. The overwhelming interest of fiction is its human interest. Since it is peopled with human figures neglect of its population is a contradiction in terms. Even in the fiction of adventure, in which the personages are minimized and the incidents the main concern, even in fiction in which plot figures as the protagonist of the drama, plot and incident would be sterile but for the characters that figure in them. However subordinate and undifferentiated these may be, they must make some intrinsic appeal, or we should not care what happened to them. The game even as a game is not one that can be played with counters. Yet, that is precisely the way in which Poe played it. And his stories have no human interest because humanity did not in the least interest him. Neither man nor woman delighted him enough to occupy his genius even incidentally. His tales contain, of course, no "character"—that prime essential, and most exacting *raison-d'être* of normal fiction. But what is surprising is the absolute inhumanity of the personages he is compelled to incarnate and the absolutely inhuman way in which he sets them forth. In almost every case of importance, as I have said, the chief personage is the narrator and—perhaps a little from this substantially unvaried practice, though mainly, I think, because of the real resemblance—the narrator suggests Poe himself. Each is very baldly the centre of his universe. The two take pretty much the same view—an astonishingly external one so far as human nature is concerned. The illusion of the story is subserved, but of the story quite apart from the personages. What it gains in illusion, it loses in significance. Indeed, so great is the importance of human character to a story that deals with it at all that I think those of Poe's tales in which the personages are the least shadowy, the least like algebraic symbols, the least characteristic, that is to say, are greatly helped by the fact. The stories in which he figures gain greatly from M. Dupin, who has a pedantic and censorious temperament, though his differentiation is as inferior to that of his successor, M. Lecocq, as the meagre and mathematical medium in which he exists is to the varied and entertaining field of activity, full of character and crowded with incident, that Gaboriau furnished for the latter—without, however, reaching eminence as a "world-author" in the process. "The Fall of the House of Usher" gains greatly from the characters therein, though these are merely sketches for the reader's imagination to fill out. One thinks of

A Martyr of Fanaticism. W. C. Brownell felt that Poe's "The Pit and the Pendulum" (1842) benefitted from its true-life historical setting, which gave its imagined tortures a powerful grounding in reality. The Spanish Inquisition (1478–1834) inflicted innumerable tortures, seen here in a 1901 illustration, upon its victims in order to preserve Catholic orthodoxy. Anywhere from hundreds to thousands died at its hands. When Poe wrote the story, the last vestiges of the Inquisition were only eight years in the past, though the tortures and killings had largely ended by the mid-eighteenth century (Library of Congress, Prints and Photographs Division, LC-USZ62-65697).

"Wuthering Heights" and of the place in literature that would have been assigned to Emily Bronte by Poe admirers, had she had the good fortune to be born an American. "The Pit and The Pendulum," one of the best of the tales, it seems to me, owes much to its exceptional "psychology" as an imaginative study of real torture to which ingenuity gives real point instead of merely displaying itself as ingenuity. It is helped, too, I think, by being localized in real time and space; by the fact that there was such an institution as the Inquisition, a fabric also quite otherwise "thrilling" than any of Poe's imagination, and that the victim's rescuers had an actual and the correct nationality, though I fear these considerations would seem philistine indeed to the true Poe worshipper. Furthermore, "The Murders in the Rue Morgue" forfeits a large part of its interest, the moment it appears that the murderer is an ape and not a human malefactor. *Ce n'est que ça*, one feels like exclaiming—and repeating even when William Wilson's double dissolves into his conscience, though of course allegorically that is the point of the story, as well as being very cleverly, very ingeniously, managed. Finally one of the tales—"The System of Dr. Tarr and Dr. Fether"—has an exceptional interest because it is an intelligent, though it does not pretend to be a profound, study of a phase of mind and character under certain conditions and in a certain environment, executed with a wholly unaccustomed lightness of touch and an aspect of gayety. The scene, however, it will be remembered, is a *maison de santé* and the personages are its inmates. And nothing is more characteristic of Poe's perversity than that his most normal fiction should be the representation of the abnormal. The abnormal was essential to him, and he only varied his practice of achieving it in his treatment by securing it in his material. Taken with the whim of depicting human nature he could at least select its deflected types. Even here, however, his interest is clearly in treating his material in a rather ghastly vein of contrasting and contraindicated *bouffe*. He cares nothing for his "types," and his real success, such as it is, is incidental.

Similarly with his preoccupation with crime—almost an obsession with him. He is never concerned with sin, which is too integrally human an element of life to interest him. Crime on the contrary is in comparison of an artificial nature, and of however frequent still of exceptional occurrence. Undoubtedly it furnishes apposite material to the novelist of character as well as to the portraitist of manners, and is a personal as well as a social factor in human life. But this aspect of it Poe, whose criminals are only criminals, completely ignores. He uses it not naturalistically but conventionally. It is his conventional machinery for his story. Like Mme. Tussaud and Mrs. Jarley he finds in it the readiest instrument of his most cherished effects. And so far as he "psychologizes" it he increases its inherent artificiality by treating it with morbid imaginativeness, endeavoring after his favorite method to give the illusion of reality to its abnormal repellency, and not at all concerned about demonstrating its real character. Here he is measurably successful in such a tale as "The Imp of the Perverse" where he utilizes the well known tendency of the criminal to confess, and totally fails in such absurdity as "The Black Cat," a story that could hardly have "thrilled" Ichabod Crane; but one illustrates his lack of human feeling as well as the other. And of almost all the stories into which the element of humanity enters perforce, it may be said, finally, that the residuum is not so much worth while as to earn neglect of his shortcomings in a respect normally vital to the kind of thing he is doing. In a word the "Poe" in his stories could only be moving and effective, if this element were present also.

For the only thing that can give any significance, any vital interest, any value, in a word, to the weird and the fantastic themselves is to establish them somehow in some human relationship—as Hoffmann does. Otherwise they are simply phenomena that appeal strictly to the nerves. Poe's treatment of them negatives their sole sanction. "He can thrill you as no one else can," says one of his admirers. As to that there are several things to be said. In the first place it depends a good deal on who you are whether you are "thrilled" or not. In the next place how are you "thrilled?" As you are by the knocking at the door in Macbeth, or as you are by a bad dream or a gruesome sight in actual life? Thirdly, are you thus affected because the story *is* thrilling, or because, as I have already noted, your own imagination is set at work as to how you would be affected by experiencing what you are reading of—"The Premature Burial" for example—forgetful of the fact that personal application, than which nothing is more common, notoriously vitiates any objective judgment. Finally of what value after all is "gooseflesh" as a guide to correct estimates in art? Is this hyperæsthetic reaction a trustworthy measure of real æsthetic merit? To ask these questions is of course to answer them. But even accepting this effect on the nerves as evidence of Poe's power, even of his unique power—for I think no other writer ever essayed it so baldly—its essential insignificance must be admitted because it is wholly divorced from any element of interest outside of itself. Instead of itself being an element in a composition, as with Hoffmann, Poe's weirdness is the whole thing. An occasional discord has its uses in a work of harmony, but the scrannel shriek of a locomotive performs no function but that of irritation, though it may "thrill" or even deafen a listener. It is certainly more important to be moved than to be moved pleasantly, but to be moved to no purpose, to be agitated aimlessly in no direction, is an unsatisfactory experience.

It is needless to specify instances among Poe's tales that illustrate this exclusive appeal to the nerves. It would be difficult to find any among those of the weird class that do not. Besides, in them it was his theory, his "scheme," to create this precise effect and no other. The particularly crass one of "Berenice," however, shows his method in particular relief. It is that product of his genius in which a madman recounts his fascination by the beautiful teeth of his mistress and his exhumation of her remains for the purpose of extracting them as a last exercise of his faculties before losing these completely. Poe sometimes went too far and did so in this instance, naively admits one of his earlier editors! As if it mattered where along that line one stopped. The partly ridiculous, partly repulsive, wholly inept quality of the performance is stamped as such at the start. The serious workmanship only emphasizes the fact that the personages are lay figures, the *motif* insane, the story incredible. As a ship-shape and coherent account of incoherent horror it may contain a "thrill" for the predisposed, but it is fully as fitted to wake a smile as a shudder and there is obviously no standard by which to admeasure this sort of thing except that of technical execution. Any reader of "Berenice" not a neurasthenic must inevitably ask, "What of it?" Having no import it has no importance.

An opposing view of Poe comes from Charles Sears Baldwin (1867–1935), a professor of rhetoric at Yale in the first half of the twentieth century. Prof. Baldwin, far from decrying Poe's lack of substance, instead attributes to him the creation of the modern form of the short story, focusing on "Berenice," the bane of W. C. Brownell, as one of the highest examples of horror art. The following piece is excerpted from "Three Studies in the Short Story," which first appeared as "Poe's Invention of the Short Story" in the volume *American Short Stories* (1904). This revised version appeared in Baldwin's *Essays Out of Hours* (1907).

Poe's Fixing of the Short-Story Form*
CHARLES SEARS BALDWIN

For the realization and development of the short-story form lying there *in posse*, the man of the hour was Poe. Poe could write trenchant essays; he turned sometimes to longer fictions; but he is above all, in his prose, a writer of short stories. For this work was he born. His artistic bent unconsciously, his artistic skill consciously, moved in this direction. In theory and in practice he displayed for America and for the world a substantially new literary form. What is there in the form, then, of Poe's tales which, marking them off from the past, marks them as models for the future? Primarily Poe, as a literary artist, was preoccupied with problems of construction. More than any American before him he felt narrative as structure;—not as interpretation of life, for he lived within the walls of his own brain; not as presentation of character or of locality, for there is not in all his tales one man, one woman, and the stage is "out of space, out of time"; but as structure. His chief concern was how to reach an emotional effect by placing and building. When he talked of literary art, he talked habitually in terms of construction. When he worked, at least he planned an ingeniously suspended solution of incidents; for he was always pleased with mere solutions, and he was master of the detective story. At best he planned a series progressively intensifying a single emotion, an edifice of creative, structural imagination.

This habit of mind, this artistic point of view, manifests itself most obviously in harmonization. Every detail of setting and style is selected for its architectural fitness. The Poe scenery is remarkable not more for its original, phantasmal beauty or horror than for the strictness of its keeping. Like the landscape gardening of the Japanese, it is in each case very part of its castle of dreams. Its contrivance to further the mood may be seen in the use of a single physical detail as a recurring dominant,—most crudely in the dreadful teeth of Berenice, more surely in the horse of Metzengerstein and the sound of Morella's name, most subtly in the wondrous eyes of Ligeia. These recurrences in his prose are like the refrain of which he was so fond in his verse. And the scheme of harmonization includes every smallest detail of style. Poe's vocabulary has not the amplitude of Hawthorne's; but in color and in cadence, in suggestion alike of meaning

---

*Charles Sears Baldwin, "Poe's Fixing of the Short-Story Form," in *Essays Out of Hours* (New York: Longmans, Green & Co., 1907), 148–161.

and of sound, its smaller compass is made to yield fuller answer in declaring and sustaining and intensifying the required mood. Even in 1835, the first year of his conscious prose form, the harmonizing of scene and of diction had reached this degree:—

> "But one autumnal evening, when the winds lay still in heaven, Morella called me to her bedside. There was a dim mist over all the earth, and a warm glow upon the waters; and, amid the rich October leaves of the forest, a rainbow from the firmament had surely fallen.
> "'It is a day of days,' she said, as I approached; 'a day of all days either to live or die. It is a fair day for the sons of earth and life—ah, more fair for the daughters of heaven and death!'
> "I kissed her forehead, and she continued:
> "'I am dying; yet shall I live.'
> "'Morella!'
> "'The days have never been when thou couldst love me—but her whom in life thou didst abhor, in death thou shalt adore.'
> "'Morella!'
> "'I repeat that I am dying. But within me is a pledge of that affection—ah, how little!—which thou didst feel for me, Morella. And when my spirit departs shall the child live—thy child and mine, Morella's.'"

If the pattern of the phrase is not yet so masterly as Poe's later habit, it is already almost the last word of adaptation.

Yet in all this Poe simply did better what his predecessors had done already. His harmonizing of scene, of style, was no new thing. The narrative form itself needed more artistic adjustment. To begin with what now seems to us the commonest and most obvious defect, the narrative mood and the narrative progress must not be disturbed by introductory exposition. Not only the ruck of writers for the annuals, but even Irving, but even sometimes Hawthorne, seem unable to begin a story forthwith. They seem fatally constrained to lay down first a bit of essay. Whether it be an adjuration to the patient reader to mind the import, or a morsel of philosophy for a text, or a bridge from the general to the particular, or an historical summary, or a humorous intimation, it is like the juggler's piece of carpet; it must be laid down first. Poe's intolerance of anything extraneous demanded that this be cut off. And though since his time many worthy tales have managed to rise in spite of this inarticulate member, the best art of the short story, thanks to his surgery, has gained greatly in impulse. One can almost see Poe experimenting from tale to tale. In *Berenice* he charged the introduction with mysterious suggestion; that is, he used it like an overture; he made it integral. In *Morella*, the point of departure being similar, the theme is struck more swiftly and surely, and the action begins more promptly. In *King Pest*, working evidently for more rapid movement, he began with lively description. *Metzengerstein* recurs to the method of *Berenice*; but *Ligeia* and *Usher*, the summit of his achievement, have no introduction, nor have more than two or three of the typical tales that follow.

> "True! nervous—very, very dreadfully nervous, I had been and am; but why will you say that I am mad? The disease had sharpened my senses—not destroyed—not dulled them. Above all was the sense of hearing acute. I heard all things in the heaven and in the earth. I heard many things in hell. How, then, am I mad? Hearken! and observe how healthily—how calmly I can tell you the whole story."
> *The Tell-Tale Heart* (1843).

Every one feels the force for this tale of this method of beginning; and to many story-readers of to-day it may seem obvious; but it was Poe, more than any one else, who taught us to begin so.

The idea of this innovation was, negatively, to reject what is from the point of view of narrative form extraneous; positively it was to make the narrative progress more direct. And the evident care to simplify the narrative mechanism for directness of effect is the clue to Poe's advance in form, and his most instructive contribution to technic. This principle explains more fully his method of setting the scene. The harmonization is secured mainly by suppression. The tale is stripped of every least incongruity. In real life emotion is disturbed, confused, perhaps thwarted; in art it cannot be interpreted without arbitrary simplification; in Poe's art the simplification brooks no intrusive fact. We are kept in a dreamland that knows no disturbing sound. The emotion has no more friction to overcome than a body in a vacuum. For Poe's directness is not the directness of spontaneity; it has nothing conversational or "natural"; it is the directness of calculation. So he had little occasion to improve his skill in dialogue. Dialogue is the artistic imitation of real life. He had little use for it. His best tales are typically conducted by monologue in the first person. What he desired, what he achieved, what his example taught, was reduction to a straight, predetermined course. Everything that might hinder this consistency were best away. So, as he reduced his scene to proper symbols, he reduced it also, in his typical tales, to one place. Change of place, lapse of time, are either excluded as by the law of the classical unities, or, if they are admitted, are never evident enough to be remarked. What this meant as a lesson in form can be appreciated only by inspecting the heavy machinery that sank many good tales before him. What it means in ultimate import is the peculiar value and the peculiar limitation of the short story—in a word, its capacity as a literary form. The simplification that he set forth is the way to intensity; but perhaps Hawthorne saw that it might be the way to artificiality.

The history, then, of the short story—the feeling after the form, the final achievement, will yield the definition of the form. The practical process of defining by experiment compiles most surely the theoretical definition. And to complete this definition it is safe to scrutinize the art of Poe in still other aspects. His structure, appearing as harmonization and as simplification, appears also as gradation. That the incidents of a tale should be arranged as progressive to a climax is an elementary narrative principle not so axiomatic in the practice, at least, of Poe's time as to bind without the force of his example. Even his detective stories, in their ingenious suspense and their swift and steady mounting to climax, were a lesson in narrative. But this is the least of his skill. The emotional and spiritual effects that he sought as his artistic birthright could be achieved only by adjustments far more subtle. The progressive heightening of the style corresponds to a nice order of small details more and more significant up to the final intensity of revelation. Little suggestion is laid to suggestion until the great hypnotist has us in the mood to hear and feel what he will. It is a minute process, and it is unhurried; but it is not too slow to be accomplished within what before him would have seemed incredible brevity. The grading of everything to scale and perspective, that the little whole may be as complete, as satisfying, as any larger whole—nay, that any larger treatment may seem, for the time of comparison, too broad and coarse,— this is Poe's finer architecture. But for him we should hardly have guessed what might be done in fifteen pages; but for him we should not know so clearly that the art of fifteen pages is not the art of a hundred and fifty.

Berenice casts a shadow first from the fatal library, chamber of doubtful lore, of death, of birth, of prenatal recollection "like a shadow—vague, variable, indefinite, unsteady; and like a shadow, too, in the impossibility of my getting rid of it while the sunlight of my reason shall exist." The last words deepen the shadow. Then the "boyhood in books" turns vision into reality, reality into vision. Berenice flashes across the darkened stage, and pines, and falls into trances, "disturbing even the identity of her person." While the light from her is thus turning to darkness, the visionary's morbid attentiveness is warped toward a monomania of brooding over trivial single objects. For the sake of the past and visionary Berenice betrothed with horror to the decaying real Berenice, he is riveted in brooding upon her person—her emaciation—her face—her lips—her teeth. The teeth are his final curse. The rest is madness, realized too horribly, but with what final swiftness of force! No catalogue of details can convey the effect of this gradation of eight pages. Yet *Berenice* is Poe's first and crudest elaboration. The same static art in the same year moves *Morella* more swiftly through finer and surer degrees to a perfectly modulated close in five pages. His next study, still of the same year, is in the grotesque. The freer and more active movement of *King Pest* shows his command of the kinetic short story of incident as well as of the static short story of intensifying emotion. By the next year he had contrived to unite in *Metzengerstein* the two processes, culminating intensity of feeling and culminating swiftness of action, for a direct stroke of terror and retribution. By 1836 Poe knew his art; he had only to refine it. Continuing to apply his method of gradation in both modes, he gained his own peculiar triumphs in the static,—in a situation developed by exquisite gradation of such infinitesimal incidents as compose *Berenice* to an intense climax of emotional suggestion, rather than in a situation developed by gradation of events to a climax of action. But in both he disclosed the fine art of the short story in drawing down everything to a point.

For all this was comprehended in Poe's conception of unity. All these points of technical skill are derived from what he showed to be the vital principle of the short story, its defining mark,—unity of impression through strict unity of form. "Totality of interest," an idea caught from Schlegel, he laid down first as the principle of the short poem,[1] and then as the principle of the tale.[2] And what this theory of narrative should imply in

1. In a review of Mrs. Sigourney, *Southern Literary Messenger*, volume ii, page 113 (January, 1836); quoted in Woodberry's *Life of Poe*, page 94.
2. In a review of Hawthorne, *Graham's Magazine*, May, 1842; Stedman and Woodberry's edition of Poe, volume vii, page 30; quoted in the appendix to Brander Matthews's *Philosophy of the Short-Story*. His symbolism is often unified, as it were, by logical summary; for Poe's symbolism summary would be an impertinence. Poe's harmonization, not otherwise, perhaps, superior to Hawthorne's, is more instructive as being more strictly the accord of every word with one constantly dominant impression. His simplification of narrative mechanism went in sheer technical skill beyond the skill of any previous writer in opening a direct course to a single revealing climax. His gradation, too, was a progressive heightening and a nice drawing to scale. All this means that he divined, realized, formulated the short story as a distinct form of art. Before him was the tale, which, though by chance it might attain self-consistency, was usually and typically incomplete, either a part or an outline sketch; from his brain was born the short story as a complete, finished, and self-sufficing whole.

practice is seen best in Poe. For Hawthorne, though he too achieves totality of interest, is not so surely a master of it precisely because he is not so sure of the technic.

Let us stay with Prof. Baldwin for a moment and return to his *American Short Stories* (1904) for a brief assessment of Fitz-James O'Brien (1828–1862), the Irish-American writer whom Baldwin rightly judges as a worthy successor to Poe. We have already met O'Brien in his guise as "Adam Eagle" in the "Fragments from an Unpublished Magazine," but here we consider O'Brien as he is best remembered, as the author of a few startling masterpieces of terror, including "What Was It" (1859), a tale of an invisible monster, to which this piece served as preface.

*Fitz-James O'Brien**
CHARLES SEARS BALDWIN

The facts of O'Brien's life have never been set in order. Even the date of his birth in County Limerick is uncertain. His untimely death was at Cumberland, Virginia, from wounds in the Federal service early in the Civil War. The clearest impression of the man may be had from William Winter's introduction to a collection of his verse and prose, published in Boston, 1881. He seems very like the Thackeray Irishman—generous, impulsive, extravagant with money and words. In the geniality that deserved their warm affection his somewhat Bohemian companions found a touch of genius; but the demands of a spendthrift life hand-to-mouth, and the facility with which these demands could be met, both made against the realisation of this higher promise. That it remained only a promise may be ascribed also to his dying at thirty-four. Youth is evident especially in that his prose is imitative. Poe is suggested almost immediately; and there is often an undertone of Dickens, the Dickens of the Christmas stories. In other aspects, too, O'Brien's writing is the work, not of a craftsman, but of a brilliant amateur. The fancies that he threw upon the periodical press are never quite achieved. Considered as materials, these fancies vary in value all the way from the conceptions of *The Diamond Lens*

---

*Charles Sears Baldwin, "Fitz-James O'Brien," in *American Short Stories*, The Wampum Library of American Literature, ed. Brander Matthews (New York: Longmans, Green, and Company, 1904), 211–212.

and *The Wondersmith*, which are not far from pure imagination, to *Tommatoo* and *My Wife's Tempter*, which are mere melodrama. But whatever their potential value, O'Brien's hand was not steady enough to bring it out. The main scene of *The Diamond Lens*, the microscopic vision, is as delicate as it is original, and as vivid as it is delicate; but the preparation for it is fumbling, and the solution unsatisfying. The tale printed below is exceptionally compact in structure and careful in detail. The obvious general resemblance to Poe's tales of physical horror should not obscure certain original merits. The note of realism, for not merely Poe's verisimilitude: it expresses a differentiation of character more like that of Kipling's similar study, *The End of the Passage*. Prof. Brander Matthews (*Philosophy of the Short-Story*, page 68) points out the similarity in conception of Maupassant's *Le Horla*.

Writing much prose and verse for many magazines now long passed away, and a play or two for Wallack, O'Brien found his steadiest employment with the Harpers between 1853 and 1858, and his most congenial life with the younger journalists and artists of New York.

Henry Seidel Canby (1878–1961) was another professor at Yale, and he was a contemporary of Charles Sears Baldwin. He wrote a number of books of literary criticism, including studies of Thoreau and Whitman. Canby also served as literary editor for the *New York Evening Post* and edited *The Saturday Review of Literature*. In this excerpt from the chapter "The Mid-Century in America" in his *The Short Story in English* (1909), Canby assesses Fitz-James O'Brien and, if anything, praises him more highly than Baldwin did.

*Excerpt from "The Mid-Century in America"**
HENRY SEIDEL CANBY

Fitz-James O'Brien was a brilliant Irishman, who migrated to this country about 1852, at which time he was not more than twenty-five years of age. He became a journalist, a free-lance, whose most regular connection was with *Harper's Magazine* and *Harper's Weekly*, although he contributed to most of the better-known periodicals of the day. Like Poe, he

*Henry Seidel Canby, *The Short Story in English* (New York: Henry Holt and Company, 1909), 282–285.

was poet and critic as well as story-writer. Like Poe, too, his life was Bohemian, nor does the resemblance end here, for O'Brien dealt by preference with the gruesome and *macabre*.

He wrote numerous stories, in this fecundity anticipating the later short-story writers, perhaps because, like them, he was armed with the right technique for the purpose. The memorial volume by William Winter, *The Poems and Stories of Fitz-James O'Brien*, in which alone his work is easily accessible, contains but a selection, but yet enough to form a fair estimate of quality. Some are love stories; others tales of remarkable or horrible incident; but the best and the most characteristic are narratives in which the supernatural is employed in an ingenious fashion to gain the effect desired. *What Was It?* (1859), *The Diamond Lens* (1858), and *The Wondersmith* (1859), are the striking examples of this craft.

Although O'Brien's stories are contemporary with the tales of Mrs. Gaskell, they have a modern ring to them; except for a touch now and then of mid-century sentiment, they are scarcely old-fashioned. If we seek for the reason, we shall find it not so much in any external trait of style as in the skilful adaptiveness of the author. All his stories are somewhat suggestive of earlier masters. There is Dickens clearly in *Milly Dove*; Hawthorne in the same story; Lamb or De Quincey in *The Dragon Fang*; but reminiscences of the new-fashioned Poe lurk in every one. O'Brien was the first author to imitate successfully in English the methods of Poe. Viewed in its external aspects, this memory of his predecessor appears in such idiosyncrasies of tale-telling as the use of an abnormal hero who lives in an abnormal abode and is most irregular in his habits. Both authors, to be sure, were fair models for their own heroes, but Poe, possibly with Byron's aid, began the practice. Far more weighty, however, is another debt owed by O'Brien to the tales of the grotesque, a debt for structure. In spite of wayside palaverings, the best of his stories aim, in every part, straight to the end. The first paragraph implies the last. The mystery ends in a climax as vivid as it is impugnable. *What Was It?* is an account of an invisible man-monster who grapples with an opium-smoker in a New York boarding-house, and is caught. Poe might have been glad to conceive it. *The Diamond Lens*, through which a somewhat diluted Poe hero sees adorable Animula disporting in a drop of water, then loves her, and goes mad when, as the drop evaporates, his beloved dies literally beneath his eye—this story Poe would have approved, would have built up far better, and probably spoiled by an attempt at humor. As it stands, O'Brien is daring and original in the conception; the machinery which makes a story possible is all from Poe. In brief, O'Brien did what no one else in English had done before, really learned the Poe technique. If he was a little too slavish in his use of it, yet his ideas were sufficiently original to strike a balance, and the result is this, that his stories are still readable where less dependent tales have lost their savor.

But we have done scant justice to one of our pioneers in the short story if we leave him here. He died young; his best stories were written before he was much over thirty; their imitativeness might have been a prelude to an achievement like Bret Harte's, the exploitation of such characters as Dickens saw, by the new short-story method. As it is, although so fond of the *macabre*, O'Brien studies life as the novelists of his day were studying it, even when he looks through the glasses of Poe. Consider the pathetic love-affair of the cripple and the gypsy's daughter in *The Wondersmith*, the homely familiarity of the Twenty-sixth Street boarding-house in which the invisible monster is found, the definite New York which is the setting for so many of his stories. This is the manner, not of Poe's fancies, hot from the romantic movement, but of our own imaginings. O'Brien, it is true, succeeded only when he worked up his local color and his contemporary portraits under the stress of a sensationally grim plot, which fused all into one definite impression. But at least, in some measure, he was applying the impressionistic story, hitherto used consciously only in pursuit of the terror of the soul, to reasonably familiar life. Of *The Diamond Lens* and *The Wondersmith*, Mr. Winter says, "They electrified magazine literature, and they set up a model of excellence which, in this department, has made it better than it ever had been, in this country, before those tales were printed."[a] Now Poe's technique had certainly been more original and more perfect, and Hawthorne's stories more fully charged with matter and with meaning. Surely, electrification could only have come from the example of a new story-telling used in tales which, for all their extravagance, had more of the common clay of life than was to be found in earlier examples of the impressionistic short story.

O'Brien's imagination might have carried him far, and did place him unquestionably among the ranks of remarkable narrators. The idea of *The Diamond Lens* is at least unique; the invisible man-monster of *What Was It?* is one of those conceptions which insure a story; but the plot of *The Wondersmith* is still more indicative of power. Mannikin toys are inspired by evil souls and empowered to flesh their tiny swords in the children who loved them. The imagination which conceived and moved this tale without absurdity did much, even in this very unequal narrative. There is nothing else quite like *The Wondersmith* in American literature. Hood might have done it, had he known how to tell a good short story; Hawthorne might have hit upon the fancy, and made the tale far more serious, more gloomy, more sententious, but scarcely so pleasing; neither could have blended so much life, imagination, extravagance in one reasonably coherent whole, and contrived to leave a very definite impression of the heart of the story. O'Brien, with all his journalistic carelessness, accomplished just that because, in his amateur fashion, he really understood Poe's technique for the short story.

Notes

a. William Winter (1836–1917) was an American author and drama critic. The quotation comes from Winter's introduction to *The Poems and Stories of Fitz-James O'Brien* (1881) discussed earlier in Canby's article.

The Rev. Dr. Frederic Rowland Marvin (1847–1918) of Albany, New York, was both poet and clergyman. His famed 1899 sermon "Christ among the Cattle" called for animal rights, and he also wrote books on literary topics. In *Fireside Papers* (1915), he discussed the similarities between Edgar Allan Poe and the French writer Guy de Maupassant (1850–1893), who wrote a small body of weird fiction, including the masterpiece "Le Horla," among his prodigious output of Realist short stories and novels.

*Maupassant and Poe**
Frederic Rowland Marvin

It may be we should never have heard of Guy de Maupassant had there been no Edgar Allan Poe. Both men were masters of the short story; both were gifted with that clear, penetrating intellectual sight which goes at once with unerring certainty to the heart of the thing to be portrayed; both were able to compress a world of meaning into the narrow compass of a few pages; both were cynical and took dark, pessimistic views of life; both passed in youth through the dismal process of endeavoring to adapt

*Frederic Rowland Marvin, "Maupassant and Poe," in *Fireside Papers* (Boston: Sherman, French, and Company, 1915), 67–73.

a highly poetic temperament, fine tastes, and unusual gifts to a commercial pursuit; and both made a failure as dismal as the process itself. But when you come to the substance of their work, the material selected, the situations chosen, and the effect produced, you find in the productions of Maupassant, to remind you of Poe, only here and there a lowering stormcloud that soon dissolves in light and flowers and song. Of Poe's soul of horror, that "mystic obsession" of terror, that weird and desolating beauty that unites in one alluring romance and companionless despair, almost nothing is to be found in the brilliant pages of our French author.

Though both writers were cynical, pessimistic, and at times despondent, Maupassant's view of life had in it some of those brighter and more pleasing features the want of which often renders the work of Poe distressing to the ordinary reader. Maupassant had great delight in nature. He could lie for hours upon the grass or beneath the spreading branches of a leafy tree, perfectly happy in the contemplation of the verdured earth and so much of the blue sky as could disclose itself through interlacing boughs. Flowers gave him exquisite pleasure. The sounds of nature intoxicated him. The moaning of the wind in the tree-tops, the chirp of insects, and the song of birds,—especially that of the nightingale,—filled him with indescribable satisfaction. The roar of the ocean rendered him oblivious of all else. The sights of nature had upon him much the same effect that natural sounds had. Cattle browsing in the fields, the simple life of the peasant, the landscape, and, above all, the joyous existence of children,—of these he could not have too much. His was not the old pagan pleasure; it was rather the artistic delight of the modern mind. His senses were keen and alert. He had what has been called "a joyous animalism," in which the spiritual element was singularly wanting. He reveled in form and color with an artist's joy. His ears were sensitive to every sound. The whisper of love, the cry of passion, the note of terror, and the shout of triumph all seized upon him and held him fast. But the seizure was upon the physical side of his nature.

Of course he reappears in his books. Every man is in a measure the hero of his own story. His life was not pure; why should we expect to find immaculate purity in his work? Where the flame is not without smoke there must be some smudge of soot. His stories are coarse and some of them are, if we mince not our words, libidinous. But they are not all of them evil, and perhaps few that are evil are wholly so. He portrayed vice, but it can hardly be said that he rendered it attractive. There was with it too much of the horror of its fruitage. His descriptive powers were great, but he could describe only that of which he had himself knowledge. Passion he could paint, and as well "the raptures and roses of vice," but of love in its better meaning he knew nothing. Of marriage he had a poor opinion. His soul was incapable of that sacred union. "Boule de Suif," which gave Maupassant his sudden recognition, illustrates what we are saying. The *motif* of the story is certainly not elevating. It presents us with a clear, remorseless, and witty picture of selfishness and insincerity. It brings out the sordid side of human nature. It shows up the meanness and rottenness of those who pretend to a virtue they do not possess. Uncleanness plays a large part, but surely the reader is not made to love evil. The reading brings with it an inward disgust, a loathing, a sense of foulness, but the story is moral in the same way that Daudet's "Sappho" is moral. The latter romance may be played upon the stage in such a way as to make it lascivious to the very last degree,—it was so played. But the tale as we have it from Daudet is good and only good. Any young man reading it may see with fearful distinctness how from first to last a bad woman may ruin a pure life, how under her baneful shadow the most noble and manly virtues may themselves become the servitors of vice.

It is a good thing to know that Maupassant, unlike most young authors, restrained himself from premature publication. For seven long years he toiled at the unattractive duties of a clerk of the navy and education departments. Wearisome work it must have been. The old life in Normandy during all that time haunted his imagination. He dreamed of the dear hills, fields, and brooks of earlier days. He grew homesick and despondent, but still he worked on. Only upon a Sunday could he visit the beautiful environs of Paris. Sometimes a holiday gave him a few hours of canoeing on the Seine—an occasional "holiday and six francs!" During all that time he wrote, but no one knew what he wrote. He entered into no communication with any one, until suddenly the young toiler made his debut, and astonished Paris gave him cordial recognition,—gave him more, for the immediate demand for his work was so great that neither he nor his publishers could meet it. Fortune and fame came with a sudden rush.

The unclean life of the gay French capital was not good for the delicate and sensitive author. Why repeat the sad tale? Suffice it to say that overwork, licentiousness, drugs, alcohol, entire neglect of the ordinary laws of health, were more than his fine temperament could endure. Over the blinded mental vision of our gifted writer the shadows began to fall. Slowly at first, and later with great swiftness, melancholy thoughts pursued him. The mental faculties crumbled, and in a fit of despair he made an assault upon his own life. A watchful friend prevented the suicide, and foreign travel was tried as a remedial agent, but with no marked result. His physician prescribed a period of rest and retirement in a villa at Cannes, but this also failed to benefit him. It was too late. The gifted author,—gifted as few have been, praised and admired by an enthusiastic public,—lingered eighteen months in a strait-jacket, and then died of general paresis.

Poe's life also was one of dissipation. So far as the world knows the author of "Ligeia," "The Fall of the House of Usher," "The Raven," and "Annabel Lee" was pure in all his relations with women. He married the woman he loved, and he faced the great sorrow of her death. Whatever wrongs Maupassant may have committed, he never committed that of wedding a pure and devoted woman. Among the women of Paris who understood him and who chose to live as he lived, he counted, it is said, "his *bonnes fortunes* by the score." Poe's life, as has been said, was pure. If he used narcotics we do not know of it, though true it is the suspicion has been entertained. His one great enemy was alcohol, and of it he died.

Maupassant's sensual enjoyment was restricted by a constant fear of death which, Goncourt thinks, grew out of an intense love of life. Maupassant's theories of both life and death were wholly materialistic. He held that with the last breath one ceased to exist. When a man lost life he lost everything. He found solitude unendurable. Like Aaron Burr, he was unhappy when alone, and preferred almost any company to no company at all. He obtained relief in the presence of other lives, for the presence of such lives seemed to add a measure of stability to his own.

You have the whole of Maupassant's intent and purpose in the story he tells, whatever it may be. The interest centers always in the story, and in the story alone. He introduces no problem and suggests no theories. There are few preachments. He is to be read solely for the story. Since the story is true to life, it conveys its own lesson; but the lesson is always a part of the story, and what may be its contents does not concern the writer.

Here again we come upon a point of resemblance between Poe and Maupassant. Poe makes himself the hero or principal character in many of his tales, and in most of his poems, but you do not feel his personality. So far as the story goes, he is a mere phantom or abstraction masquerading in a personal pronoun. In his tales, as in those of Maupassant, the interest is in the tale itself, and not in any thing it suggests. What moral conclusions may come of the narrative is immaterial to him.

Like Fitz-James O'Brien and Guy de Maupassant, Ambrose Bierce (1842–C. 1914) is often called a successor to Poe. The cynic known as "Bitter" Bierce is justly famous for his careful and precise prose, as well as the wit with which he wrote. Here we see an advertisement for *Tales of Soldiers and Civilians* (1892), later known as *In the Midst of Life*, a book that included some of his best-known horror, including "An Inhabitant of Carcosa," "The Boarded Window," and "An Occurrence at Owl Creek Bridge." This ad from American Publishers originally ran in the back of their publications for 1892.

Advertisement for Tales of Soldiers and Civilians*
AMERICAN PUBLISHERS

Tales of Soldiers and Civilians.
By *AMBROSE BIERCE. 12mo, cloth $1.00; paper 50c.*
American Authors' Series.

A COLLECTION of weird, pathetic, and blood-curdling stories that will be read with avidity not only by the seekers after novelty, but by the more critical readers who appreciate literary merit. Mr. Bierce has no peer in his peculiar vein of satire, and his works will undoubtedly become classic.

Frederic Taber Cooper (1864–1937) was a distinguished editor and writer, as well as a professor of Sanskrit and Latin at New York University. Among his many works were studies of American storytellers and contemporary English novelists. In this excerpt from a lengthy study of Ambrose Bierce as critic, satirist, and storyteller, Cooper presents his case for the greatness of Bierce as a master of the horror story. Later in this volume, we will see Cooper's less flattering opinion of Robert Hichens, a contemporary of Bierce. "Ambrose Bierce: An Appraisal" ran in *The Bookman* for July 1911 and was included in Cooper's *Some American Story-Tellers* that same year.

*Advertisement for *Tales of Soldiers and Civilians* in *In and Out of Three Normandy Inns* by Anna Bowman Dodd (New York: American Publishers Company, 1892), 400.

Excerpt from "Ambrose Bierce: An Appraisal"*
FREDERIC TABER COOPER

In the preface to the fourth volume of his collected works, the volume containing under the title *Shapes of Clay* the major portion of purely personal satiric verse, Mr. Ambrose Bierce emphatically expresses his belief in the right of any author "to have his fugitive work in newspapers and periodicals put into a more permanent form during his lifetime if he can." No one is likely to dispute Mr. Bierce's contention; but it is often a grave question as to what extent it is wise for the individual to exercise his inalienable rights. And in the case of authors the question comes down to this: How far is it to their own best interests to dilute their finer and more enduring work with that which is mediocre and ephemeral? For it is unfortunately true that no author is measured by his high lights alone, but by the resultant impression of blended light and shade; and there is many a writer among the recog-

Ambrose Bierce. The cynical Bierce mastered the short story in all its forms, and was also a brilliant satirist. Echoing Rudolph Ackermann (see p. 67), Bierce joked in his Devil's Dictionary *(1911) that "There is one insuperable obstacle to a belief in ghosts. A ghost never comes naked: he appears either in a winding-sheet or 'in his habit as he lived.' To believe in him, then, is to believe that not only have the dead the power to make themselves visible after there is nothing left of them, but that the same power inheres in textile fabrics." Bierce kept a skull (seen at right in this 1928 photograph of a nineteenth century painting) and a box of ashes on his desk. He told visitors that the skull belonged to a friend and the ashes to a rival critic (Library of Congress, Prints and Photographs Division, LC-USZ62-20182).*

*Frederic Taber Cooper, "Ambrose Bierce: An Appraisal," *The Bookman: A Magazine of Literature and Life*, July 1911, 471, 473–480.

nised classics who to-day would take a higher rank had a kindly and discriminating fate assigned three-quarters of his life work to a merciful oblivion.

To the student of American letters, however, the comprehensive edition of Ambrose Bierce's writings now being issued in ten portly and well-made volumes cannot fail to be welcome. It places at once within convenient reach a great mass of material which, good, bad or indifferent, as the case may be, all helps to throw suggestive side lights upon the author, his methods, and his outlook upon life.[...]

[I]t is as a writer of short stories that Mr. Bierce's future fame rests upon a firm foundation. It is not too much to say that within his own chosen field—the grim, uncompromising horror story, whether actual or supernatural—he stands among American writers second only to Edgar Allan Poe. And this is all the more remarkable when we consider his expressed scorn of new books and modern methods and his implied indifference to the development of modern technique. He does understand and consciously seeks for that unity of effect which is the foundation stone of every good short story; yet in sheer technical skill there is scarcely one among the recognised masters of the short story today, Mr. Kipling, for instance, and the late O. Henry, Jack London and a score of his contemporaries, from whom he might not learn something to his profit. What Mr. Bierce's habits of workmanship may be the writer does not happen to know; it is possible that he has always striven as hard to build an underlying structure, a preliminary scaffolding, for each story as ever Edgar Allan Poe did. But if so he has been singularly successful in practising the art which so artfully all things conceals. He gives the impression of one telling a story with a certain easy spontaneity and attaining his results through sheer instinct. He seldom attempts anything like a unity of time and place; and many of his short tales have the same fault which he criticises in the modern novel, namely, that of having a panoramic quality, of being shown to us in a succession of more or less widely separated scenes and incidents.

Nevertheless, in most cases his stories are their own best justification. We may not agree with the method that he has chosen to use, but we cannot escape from the strange, haunting power of them, the grim, boding sense of their having happened—even the most weird, most supernatural, most grotesquely impossible of them—in precisely the way that he has told them.

The stories, such of them at least as really count and represent Mr. Bierce at his best, divide themselves into two groups: first, the Civil War stories, based upon his own four years' experience as a soldier during the rebellion, and unsurpassed in American fiction for the unsparing clearness of their visualisation of war. And secondly, the frankly supernatural stories contained in the volume entitled *Can Such Things Be?*—stories in which the setting is immaterial because if such things could be they would be independent of time and space. The war stories range through the entire gamut of heroism, suffering and carnage. They are stamped in all their physical details with a pitiless realism unequalled by Stendhal in the famous Waterloo episode in the *Chartreuse de Parme* and at least unsurpassed by Tolstoy or by Zola. Indeed, there is nothing fulsome or extravagant in the statement that has more than once been made that Mr. Bierce is a sort of American Maupassant. And what is most remarkable about these stories is that they never fail of a certain crescendo effect. Keyed as they are to a high pitch of human tragedy, there is always one last turn of the screw, one crowning horror held in reserve until the crucial moment. Take, for example, "A Horseman in the Sky." A sentinel whose duty it is to-watch from a point of vantage overlooking a deep gorge and a vast plain beyond, to see that no scout of the Southern army shall discover a trail down the precipitous sides of the opposite slope, suddenly perceives a solitary horseman making his way along the verge of the precipice within easy range of fire. The sentinel watches and hesitates; takes aim and delays his fire. The scene shifts with the disconcerting suddenness of a modern moving picture and we see the sentinel back in his Southern home at the outbreak of the war; and we overhear the controlled bitterness of his parting with his Southern father after declaring his intention to fight for the Union. A modern story teller would consider this shifting of scene bad art; nevertheless, Mr. Bierce, in theatrical parlance, "gets it over." Back again he shifts us with a rush to the lonely horseman, shows him for a moment motionless upon the brink and the next instant launched into space, a wonderful, miraculous, awe-inspiring figure, proudly erect upon a stricken and dying horse, whose legs spasmodically continue their mad gallop throughout the downward flight to the inevitable annihilation below. This in itself, told with Ambrose Bierce's compelling art, is sufficiently harrowing, but he has something more in reserve. Listen to this:

"Did you fire?" the sergeant whispered.
"Yes."
"At what?"
"A horse. It was standing on yonder rock—pretty far out. You see it is no longer there. It went over the cliff."

The man's face was white, but he showed no other signs of emotion. Having answered, he turned away his eyes and said no more. The sergeant did not understand.

"See here, Druce," he said, after a moment's silence, "it's no use making a mystery. I order you to report. Was there anybody on the horse?"

"Yes."

"Well?"

"My father."

And again, there is that extraordinary *tour de force* entitled "An Occurrence at Owl Creek Bridge." It is the story of a spy caught and about to be hanged by the simple expedient of allowing the board on which he stands to tilt up and drop him between the cross beams of the bridge. The story is of considerable length. It details with singular and compelling vividness what follows from the instant that the spy feels himself dropped, feels the rope tighten around his neck and its fibres strain and snap under his weight. His plunge into the stream below, his dash for life under cover of the water, his flight, torn and bleeding through thorns and brambles, his miraculous dodging of outposts and his passing unscathed through volleys of rapid fire, all read like a hideous nightmare—and so in fact they are, because the entire story of his rush for safety lasting long hours and days in reality is accomplished in a mere fraction of time, the instant of final dissolution—because, as it happened, the rope did not break and at the moment that he thought he had attained safety his body ceased to struggle and dangled limply beneath the Owl Creek Bridge. Variations upon this theme of the rapidity of human thought in the moment of death are numerous. There is, for instance, a memorable story by Morgan Robertson called, if memory is not at fault, "From the Main Top," in which a lifetime is crowded into the fraction of time required for the action of gravity. But no one has ever used it more effectually than Mr. Bierce.

But it is in his supernatural stories that Mr. Bierce shows even more forcefully his wizardry of word and phrase, his almost magnetic power to make the absurd, the grotesque, the impossible, carry an overwhelming conviction. He will tell you, for instance, a story of a man watching at night alone by the dead body of an old woman; a cat makes its way into the room and springs upon the corpse; and to the man's overwrought imagination it seems as though that dead woman seized the cat by the neck and flung it violently from her. "Of course you imagined it," says the friend to whom he afterward tells the tale. "I thought so, too," rejoins the man, "but the next morning her stiffened fingers still held a handful of black fur."

For sheer mad humour there is nothing more original than the tale called "A Jug of Syrup." A certain old and respected village grocer who through a lengthy life has never missed a day at his desk dies and his shop is closed. One night the village banker and leading citizen on his way home drops in from force of habit at the grocery, finding the door wide open and buys a jug of syrup, absent-mindedly forgetting that the grocer who served him has been dead three weeks. The jug is a heavy weight to carry; yet when he reaches home he has nothing in his hand. The tale spreads like wildfire through the village and the next night a vast throng is assembled in front of the brightly lit up grocery, breathlessly watching the shadowy form of the deceased methodically casting up accounts. One by one, they pluck up courage and make their way into the grocery—all but the banker. Riveted to the spot by the grotesque horror of the sight he stands and watches, while pandemonium breaks loose. To him in the road the shop is still brilliantly lighted but to those who have gone within it presents the darkness of eternal night and in their unreasoning fear they kick and scratch and bite and trample upon one another with the primordial savageness of the mob. And all the while the shadowy figure of the dead grocer continues undisturbed to balance his accounts.

It is a temptation to linger beyond all reason over one after another of these extraordinary and haunting imaginings, such for instance, as "Moxon's Master," in which an inventor having made a mechanical chess-player makes the mistake of beating it at the game and is promptly strangled to death by the revengeful being of his own creation. But it is impossible to do justice to all these stories separately and it remains only to single out one typical example in which perhaps he reached the very pinnacle of his strange, fantastic genius, "The Death of Halpin Frayser." The theme of this story is this: it is sufficiently horrible to be confronted with a disembodied spirit, but there is one degree of horror beyond this, namely, to have to face the reanimated body of some one long dead from whom the soul has departed—because, so Mr. Bierce tells us, with the departure of the soul all natural affection, all kindliness has departed also, leaving only the base instincts of brutality and revenge. Now in the case of Halpin Frayser, it happens that the body which he is fated to encounter under these hideously unnatural conditions is that of his own mother; and in a setting as curiously and poetically unreal as any part of "Kubla Kahn" he is forced to realise that this mother whom he had in life worshipped as she worshipped him is now, in spite of her undiminished beauty, a foul and bestial thing intent only upon taking his life. In all imaginative literature it would be difficult to find a parallel for this story in sheer, unadulterated hideousness.

Mr. Ambrose Bierce as a story teller can never achieve a wide popularity, at least among the Anglo-Saxon race. His writings have too much the flavour of the hospital and the morgue. There is a stale odour of mouldy cerements about them. But to the connoisseur of what is rare, unique and very perfect in any branch of fiction he must appeal strongly as one entitled to hearty recognition as an enduring figure in American letters. No matter how strongly he may offend individual convictions and prejudices with the flippant irreverence of his satiric writings it is easy to forgive him all this and much more besides for the sake of any single one of a score or more of his best stories.

The American poet Edwin Markham (1852–1940) wrote nonfiction in between his major bouts of poetry, and thanks to this hobby we have his *California the Wonderful* (1914). In this survey of California history, he includes in the chapter "Intellectual California" an evaluation of Ambrose Bierce, a California native who was even then in the process of disappearing into the Mexican Revolution, never to be seen again. The following is the whole of the section on Bierce excepting a lengthy selection of humorous Bierce quotations appended to the end of the text proper.

*Bierce: Satire, Romance, Philosophy**
EDWIN MARKHAM

Ambrose Bierce looms large in literary California. For years, in the periodicals of the Far West, he reviewed the passing show of humanity, pinking and puncturing in his own fashion whatever offended his principles or his prejudices. There is no doubt he was often too quick on the trigger, too ready to perforate a man or a woman who happened to be "different."

*Edwin Markham, *California the Wonderful* (New York: Hearst's International Library, 1914), 349–353.

The genius of Ambrose Bierce travels in many fields—in romance, satire, poetry, fable, essay, criticism, epigram. We need not look into his books for the learned dullness of the academic Addisons. Wherever we find Bierce we feel the working of a daring intelligence, of an original mind; and we feel this even when we dissent from his striding and crushing opinions.

Bierce stands with the great satirists. Perhaps no one else has ever dealt more lightning strokes at the rats behind the social arras. For quick thrust and parry of wit and sarcasm his rapier hangs beside the unsparing blade of old Dean Swift. Bierce radiates brilliancy; and perhaps no other man of letters ever had a more ready command of condensed expression. For him each word has its unique place in the peerage of words; and he would not use a word out of place any sooner than he would thrust an ape into a captain's saddle. No one has ever surpassed the crystal cleavage and clearness of his sentences. Many of them end like rifle snaps. You don't know that you are struck till you see the blood spurt.

Bierce is also a master of the short story of the supernatural and weird. For his magic of mystery and trembling, he has his seat in the remote and ruby-litten chamber of Hoffmann and Poe. He loves the debatable borderland where dim shapes pass and cryptic voices speak. Yet his realm is not the traveled frontier of the common ghost, but a new, untrodden region of the vast unknown. Moving with invincible logic, he calmly leads us out to an occult realm whose shapes and happenings give us "zero at the bone." If you have nerve for the terrible, if you dare press on, you will find delight in Bierce's rare ingenuity of construction and surprise of climax. More than this, you will feel that you have peered for a breathless moment into the veritable and vast Unseen.

Frequently, Bierce's prose and verse work is only a secretion of pure intellect, and hence it is cold. It comes frosty from the ice-pack of the mind. Cold intellect may create satire, but not the higher literature: great literature can proceed only from *a thinking heart*.

Nevertheless, there are moments in Bierce's work when the fire of emotion throbs through the frost of intellect. This emotion reveals the gentler Bierce who was known to his friends, but who is usually shut out of his books. Hence I once said to him that his chief literary mistake is his habit of merely thinking out the life problems, instead of both thinking and feeling them out. His doctrine of life is too cold, and this gives a hardness to his style: it has brilliancy, but not warmth.

Bierce's philosophy seems at times to be radically wrong, as when he defends the suicide. For a sound philosophy sees that the chief purpose of life is to create character, is to make ready for a higher and nobler existence beyond earth. Life is a school of discipline: it is the testing of man. The beauty of life is in its dangers, its noble hazards, its great adventures. Peril and hardship nobly borne invigorate the virtues. Harken, O soul, to the cry of the bugles! On, on, ever on: let the white plume stream down the wind of the battle!

Moreover, since we go on living after death, it is not possible to end our troubles in the grave. *The suicide does not end troubles: he increases them.* He only makes the life-tangle more complicated, more difficult, more desperate. For there should be a gradual ripening of the spirit of man for the new existence. But in suicide there is a sudden violation of the normal order; so it draws down upon the fleeing spirit *the dread consequences that always follow on violated law.* The suicide forces himself into the Spirit World as an untimely birth, and he cannot escape the consequences of his blind defiance of the fixed order of the universe.

The American man of letters Fred Lewis Pattee (1863–1950) was a literary jack-of-all-trades, producing novels, essays, poems, criticism, and lectures. As a scholar, his preeminent preoccupation was to prove that American literature was a distinct creature, and not a division of British literature. In this excerpt from "The Short Story," a survey written for the *Cambridge History of American Literature* (1918), Pattee makes the case that Bierce was the new Poe, not that he thought that entirely a good thing.

*Excerpt from "The Short Story"**

FRED LEWIS PATTEE,
PROF. OF THE ENGLISH LANGUAGE AND LITERATURE,
PENNSYLVANIA STATE COLLEGE

Another who did much to advance the short story toward the mechanical perfection it had attained to at the close of the century was Henry Cuyler Bunner (1855–96), editor of *Puck* and creator of some of the most exquisite *vers de société* of the period.... In the same group belongs Ambrose

*Fred Lewis Pattee, "The Short Story," in *The Cambridge History of American Literature*, vol. 2, eds. William Peterfield Trent, John Erskine, Stuart P. Sherman, and Carl Van Doren (New York: G. P. Putnam's Sons, 1918), 386–387.

Bierce (1838–1914?), though in mere point of time he is to be counted with the California group of the early *Overland Monthly* days. A soldier of the Civil War, editor of the San Francisco *News Letter* in 1866, associate editor, with the younger Tom Hood, of *London Fun* in 1872, author in London of the brilliant satirical fables *Cobwebs from an Empty Skull* in 1874, then in California again as editor of *The Argonaut* and *The Wasp*, and finally a resident of Washington, D. C., he was one of the most cosmopolitan of American writers. It was not until 1892 that his *Tales of Soldiers and Civilians*, later changed to *In the Midst of Life*, gave him a place with the short story writers, a very prominent place some critics would insist. Power undoubtedly he had, a certain scintillating brilliance, and a technique almost uncanny. His world was the world of Poe, timeless and placeless, ghastly often, chilling always and unnerving. At his best he was Poe returned after a half century equipped with the short story art of the new generation. Few have surpassed him in precision of diction, in reserve, in the use of subtle insinuation and of haunting climax. Some of his tales cling in one's soul like a memory of the morgue. His failure was his artificiality and his lack of sincerity and of truth to the facts of human life. Like Poe, he was a man of the intellect only, a craftsman of exquisite subtlety, an artist merely for the sake of his art.

Irvin S. Cobb (1876–1944) is today best remembered as a humorist, when he is remembered at all, but in his own day he was known for the horror stories he wrote as well as his humor. His best-known story is "Fishhead" (1911), a tale of the murder of the fish-like son of "a negro father and a half-breed Indian mother," which served as a model for H. P. Lovecraft's "The Shadow Over Innsmouth." In this excerpt from an anonymous review in the "Chronicle and Comment" column of *The Bookman* for March 1913, the editors argue that Robert H. Davis, an editor and friend of Cobb, had overestimated the author's talents in a pamphlet praising him.

Excerpt from "Concerning Irvin Cobb"*
THE BOOKMAN

While we are not yet ready to concede to Mr. Irvin S. Cobb the place that has lately been claimed for him by some of his more enthusiastic admir-

---

*"Chronicle and Comment," *The Bookman: A Magazine of Literature and Life*, March 1913, 14–15.

ers, we do not question the fact that he must be regarded rather seriously. He is still a young man, and, in the natural course of events, should have many years' more activity. Therefore, his achievement, which up to the present time has been considerable, is of secondary importance. What counts is what he may eventually accomplish. Then, while regarding his admirers as somewhat extravagant, it is impossible not to be a little impressed by what they profess to think of him. For example, one cannot entirely ignore a little pamphlet entitled *Who's Cobb and Why*, written by Mr. Robert H. Davis. Now Mr. Davis's opinion may have been somewhat influenced by personal friendship, or by his liking for the particular flavour of Mr. Cobb's stories. But we can't forget that during the last ten years Mr. Davis has probably read, or at least accepted and rejected, more fiction than any other editor on earth. To Irvin Cobb he pays the following extraordinary tribute:

> [...] I know of no single instance where one man has shown such fecundity and quality as Irvin Cobb has so far evinced, and it is my opinion that his complete works at fifty will contain more good humour, more good short stories, and at least one bigger novel than the works of any other single contemporaneous figure.

* * *

Now this is lavish praise indeed, so lavish that we are inclined to shy from it. There have been men in the history of the writing of books to merit it. But as yet we hesitate to endorse it in the case of Mr. Irvin Cobb. We have in mind one particular story by Mr. Cobb about which Mr. Davis's opinion is not our opinion. That story is called "Fishhead." "Fishhead," according to Mr. Cobb, is the best horror story he has ever written, and yet it was the one manuscript that he was unable to sell until the *Cavalier* printed it as a so-called "daring experiment" in its issue of January 11th [1913]. With the story appeared the letters of a number of magazine editors to whom it had been sent, who had admired it for its qualities, but had feared to print it, for, as one of them wrote: "I like red blood stories, but our readers are not educated up to raw beef—yet." Mr. Davis's comments leave little room for doubt that he regards "Fishhead" as one of the great short stories of the world, and one of the great horror stories of all time. That is just one of the reasons why we hesitate to accept Mr. Davis's judgment.

* * *

Now "Fishhead" is a good story—there is not any doubt about that. But it is not a great story, and it is not even a big horror story if we gauge such a story by the thrill it inspires. As a matter of fact, on that basis, the world has not produced very many great horror stories. Poe in America, and Guy de Maupassant in France, are regarded as the masters of that type of tale. But how many of Poe's stories inspire in a reader the feeling of actual terror? The mere quality of the story does not count. For example, take Poe's "The Fall of the House of Usher" and Conan Doyle's "The Adventure of the Speckled Band." Poe's tale is literature, and Doyle's is not. Poe's tale is art from the first line to the last, and Doyle's tale is a crude, illogical and slovenly written narrative. Yet the most impressionable reader is not likely to derive from "The Fall of the House of Usher" more than a passing thrill, while the most hardened reader cannot go through "The Adventure of the Speckled Band" for the first time without a positive creeping of the flesh. The reason is that with Poe the high key is struck at the beginning and maintained throughout. The warning of impending horror neutralises the final effect. And Mr. Cobb's "Fishhead" is neither "The House of Usher" in its quality, nor "The Speckled Band" in its thrill.[...]

Irvin S. Cobb. In the horror story "Fishhead," Cobb described his monster fish man as having a face "as near to being the face of a great fish as any face could be and yet retain some trace of human aspect.... His eyes were small and round with shallow, glazed, pale-yellow pupils, and they were set wide apart in his head, and they were unwinking and staring, like a fish's eyes.... His mouth was the worst of all. It was the awful mouth of a catfish, lipless and almost inconceivably wide, stretching from side to side." Twelve magazines rejected the story as too gruesome or sophisticated (!) for their readers. When finally published in 1913 in the Cavalier, *the editor, Bob Davis, included a warning that the story might offend some readers. Photograph ca. 1916 (Library of Congress, Prints and Photographs Division, LC-Digggbain-20856).*

4. Monsters of the Gilded Age

"The London Hermit" was the pen name of Walter Parke, who otherwise wrote humorous poetry. Here, the Hermit's humor is put to a different use, exploring the rise of the "Penny Awful," or "Penny Dreadful," paperbound volumes sold for the title price or less to a mid–Victorian mass audience and featuring a "dreadful" or "awful" story. Descendents of the Gothic chapbooks, these works delivered sensation and horror with ample illustration, though often with a minimum of literary virtue. The most famous was probably *Varney the Vampire; or, the Feast of Blood* (1845–1847). It ran 237 chapters.

An intriguing record of this lost literary genre, "The Physiology of 'Penny Awfuls'" first appeared in *The Dublin University Magazine* for September 1875 and was collected in Walter Parke's *Peeps at Life* (1875). Parke's quotations from the penny awfuls are real and belong to the works cited, though O'Riginal's works are fictitious.

*The Physiology of "Penny Awfuls"**
THE LONDON HERMIT (WALTER PARKE)

> "On horror's head horrors accumulate,
> Do deeds to make heaven weep, all earth amazed!"
> SHAKESPEARE

> "Fond wretch! and what can'st thou relate
> But deeds of sorrow, shame, and sin?
> Thy crime is proved, thou know'st thy fate,
> But come, thy tale begin, begin."
> CRABBE[a]

---

*The London Hermit (Walter Parke), "The Physiology of 'Penny Awfuls,'" *The Dublin University Magazine*, September 1875, 364–376.

What is a "Penny Awful?" The term, like that of "Ethereal Cuss," which I have attempted to expound on a previous occasion, is etymologically devoid of any reason or congruity. The word "awful" used in its legitimate, instead of its prevalent slang sense, is applied generally to things great in magnitude and of a sublime and impressive character, with which the copper coinage of the realm can have no sort of connection. Neither is there any warrant for using "awful" as a noun substantive. The term, therefore, not only defies grammar, but is a violent bringing together of the immense and the minute, the solemn and the trivial, which can only be paralleled by the name of a hostelry, "The Flea and Earthquake," mentioned in one of our comic comtemporaries' [sic] burlesques. Still the phrase is so aptly expressive of the thing signified, that it would be difficult, if not impossible, to improve it by any substitute.

It was through the agency of my friend, Mr. Strayshot, that I became initiated into the meaning and mystery of "Penny Awfuls." As to the still greater mystery of that erratic gentleman's means or mode of subsistence, I am as much in the dark as ever, and his profound knowledge of the ins and outs of London life, and especially of the various aspects and characteristics of Bohemianism in all its branches, continues to awaken my interest and astonishment. A short time ago, I happened to be in one of the many turnings betwixt Chancery Lane and Fleet Street, endeavouring to increase my knowledge of the ways of men by listening to Strayshot's shrewd and pregnant remarks thereon, when, interrupting himself abruptly, and with his hand indicating a not remote object, he exclaimed, "Bless my soul! here's the O'Riginal!" "The what?" I asked. "The O'Riginal—Irishman—good family—clever, but very wild—you ought to know him—quite a character."

And "quite a character" he indeed proved to be. It happens that I have as yet been brought into contact with but few natives of the Sister Isle; but from all I have gathered concerning the national character, I should judge the O'Riginal to be by no means a fair or favourable specimen of the race. Indeed, as I subsequently discovered, he was not purely an Irishman, his mother having been French, while paternally he was descended from a long line of O'Riginals, or O'Reginalds, the descendants of a certain Sir Reginald, a Norman knight who went over with Strongbow.

Outwardly, the O'Riginal was short and dark, with a cast of face far more continental then insular, more Italian than Hibernian. If you can imagine Napoleon the Great at the age of thirty, clad in the garb of the present date; and with a general air of having had a long experience of dissipation and low funds, you will form an idea of the O'Riginal's outward aspect. The smooth face, the square chin, the olive complexion, the aquiline nose, closely-cropped dark hair, and piercing deep-set eyes, all combined to produce this Bonapartean resemblance. He spoke very colloquial English, with the most singular blending of a French and Irish accent, and with occasional inversions of sentences, misplaced emphasis, abundant gesticulation, and wild play of the eyes, which altogether had a most astonishing effect, and one impossible to convey an idea of by written description. "How do?" he said. "Haven't seen you for an age; been very busy—up to the eyes!" and he significantly flourished some printed matter which he carried tightly rolled up in his left hand.

This remarkable being greeted Strayshot with a hearty slap on the shoulder, accompanied by a startling shout of recognition,—

"How is Gallows Jack?" asked Strayshot.

"In splendid condition. Smith is working up his Awfuls now, and no mistake. Did sixty of Jack last week; what do you think of that?"

Strayshot appeared to think it was the fulfilment of a consummation devoutly to be wished, but I found myself utterly unable to judge of the merits of the case. Who was "Gallows Jack?" who also was "Smith?" and what were the "sixty" he had been "doing?" above all, what in the name of goodness was the process of "Working up his Awfuls?" Before these problems could be solved, the O'Riginal, playfully poking Strayshot in the ribs with his roll of papers, exclaimed, "Come up to my crib—it's just round here," and he darted down a narrow court, and through the side entrance of a small baker's shop. Strayshot followed hurriedly, saying to me, "Come along, he won't mind." So I brought up the rear. We had to mount three flights of a dingy staircase, the construction and state of which showed the house to be a very old one, and sadly in want of repair, before the O'Riginal, throwing open a door, exclaimed,—

"Here we are, in the Lion's Den, where I do all my murders; walk in!"

At this tempting invitation we entered the room. It was an attic with a low roof, sloping on one side, and an old-fashioned lattice window, commanding an extensive view of slates and chimneys. A rude bench near the window served as a table, and was covered with writing materials; piles of books, papers, and manuscripts lay about all over the floor, the boards of which were otherwise uncovered, and on the white-washed walls were pasted glaring and repulsive prints, both plain and coloured, and all treating of subjects apparently out of the "Newgate Calendar."

"Yes, this is my slaughterhouse," said the O'Riginal, seating himself upon a pile of books and papers, and motioning Strayshot to take a tall and rather rickety four-legged stool.

"O, I forgot," exclaimed Strayshot, turning to me; "permit me to introduce the London Hermit to the O'Riginal, of Castle Reginald, in the county of Carlow, Ireland, the successful author of 'Gallows Jack; or, the Knight of the Cord,' 'Claude Turpin; or, the Hero Highwayman,' 'Blood and Crime; or, the Hangman's Curse,' and other thrilling periodical romances, too numerous to mention."

The O'Riginal, thus introduced, greeted me with the bow of a prince, and was so polite as to abdicate the pile of books in my favour, seating himself crosswise on an old curiously-carved high-backed chair, which was always consecrated exclusively to his own use. Every minute developed some fresh peculiarity in this remarkable being. He seemed able to talk like an adept upon any subject possible to be conceived or named. He had the volubility of a Cheap Jack, and the vivacity and high spirits of a child; although at times he would lapse into such deep and stony abstraction that there was no rousing him. When he did begin to speak he generally monopolized the conversation, which, however, he made as full of variety as if a dozen had been engaged in it. Flights of imagination, not only poetic, but actually reaching the sublime, were alternated with jests and anecdotes of sparkling humour; sometimes, it must be owned, sounding the depths of grossness and obscenity. Anon, by way, I suppose, of antidote, the O'Riginal, standing upon his one chair, and addressing us over the back, as from an extempore pulpit, preached one of the most touching and beautiful sermons I ever heard.

He was in the constant habit of carrying about and showing to every one a huge roll of paper, containing a full historical and genealogical account of the family of O'Riginals, traced back as far as the illustrious founder, all printed, and illustrated with a view of Castle Reginald, a chart of the estates, and an enumeration of the tenants. Of this interesting document he was very proud, producing it as his credentials where any were supposed to be required, and always adding that he was the sole and rightful heir of the family wealth and honours, of which he would even now be in full enjoyment, but that the potent injustice of law had awarded them to a wealthy usurper, whom he was unable to dispossess. "I am the last of my race," he would then remark, with a mournful pathos in his tone,—

> "But now the old house is no dwelling for me,
> The home of the stranger henceforth it must be,
> And never again shall I rove as a guest.
> In the time-honoured halls that my fathers possess'd."[b]

He omitted to inform me (as Strayshot afterwards did) that for years his own family had disowned him, and that he had played the part of an incorrigible prodigal son, until there was no one left to kill the fatted calf. By more than one indication I discovered that the O'Riginal, of Castle Reginald, was not perfectly sober, and that his eccentric excitation and wildness of manner proceeded in part from artificial causes. This I subsequently learnt was almost his normal condition, for he was one of those persons, alas! too numerous in the lower walks of the intellectual professions, who indulge too freely in material stimulants—inferior De Quinceys, whose "accursed chain" is of alcohol instead of opium.

"Yes, Smith *is* working up his 'Awfuls,'" the O'Riginal repeated, eliding down so as to sit astride on the chair backwards, for he had finished his sermon, and intended to return to mundane things. "It's marvellous how Smith does it," he added, lurching slightly on either side before he could settle himself in his new position, "he has now no less than six 'Awfuls' abreast, all going like wildfire; I'm doing three, Blithers two, and Fennington one."

"Astonishing!" exclaimed Strayshot.

By this time, of course, I had unearthed the mysteries buried beneath all this professional slang. A "Penny Awful" is, it seemed, a sheet of eight or sixteen pages, containing a continuous romance of a highly sensational and adventurous character, garnished with striking and even horrifying illustrations, and retailed for the small sum of one penny per week. The publication is continued as long as a paying circulation can he secured, both by sustaining the interest of the story itself, and by the additional stimulus of gifts in the form of coloured plates or supplements. Some adepts call them "Penny Dreadfuls," but "Awfuls" seems to me by far the more expressive term, and this was what the O'Riginal invariably used. "Gallows Jack" was his latest and most successful performance. Smith was the publisher of that and sundry other "Awfuls;" "working them up" meant energetically pushing the sale, and "doing sixty" was an elliptic mode of signifying that the circulation had reached 60,000 weekly.

Strayshot now privately intimated to me his intention of "drawing out" the O'Riginal for my especial behoof; so he presently turned to that erratic gentleman, and remarked, "It's always astonishing to me however you can manage to keep on filling penny numbers with suitable matter week after week."

"Easy enough, dear boy, easy enough; look at the vast amount of material there is. I work up anything I can get hold of, new or old, true or false, high or low; I've all the volumes of the Newgate Calendar; I watch the current police cases; I have a guinea ticket for Mudie's; I dip into old plays, and forgotten novels and travels; ransack Scott, Bulwer, Braddon, Wilkie Collins, Ainsworth, especially Dumas, and Eugene Sue. Then look at the vast fund there is in untranslated French literature! Difficult to find stuff to fill 'Awfuls!' Why, there is a teeming mine, an *El Dorado*, a perennial fountain—an embar-*rass*-ment of riches!"

"But don't you get fogged, and mix up the incidents and events together, or lose the identity of your characters?" asked Strayshot.

"Not a bit, my dear fellow—practice, you know, practice. My memory is ex-*cel*-lent, but to keep sure, I put all names down, and file my back numbers. Pile on your incident, vary it in each number, and pay attention to your *con*-nection, that's the whole secret."

"What do you mean by your *con*-nection?" asked Strayshot, accenting the word after his friend's manner."

Bottom of last page of number, where story breaks off," the O'Riginal replied; "it *must* be something startling, so as to lead them on to take next number, even if you have to cut a chapter out of the middle to make it fit in. It never matters what plot you take, or whether you have any at all, so long as the incidents are sensational, and an air of mystery thrown in here and there. I always make up my plots as I go along. Plagiarism counts for nothing. I once, when pressed for time, copied a story out of a current high-class magazine, changing only the names, and worked it bodily into—let me see, it was the 'Hangman's Curse'—it filled a number and a half, nobody discovered the trick, and it went beautifully."

I was turning over the leaves of some of these ingenious compositions, and actually beginning to be absorbed in a "striking" incident, obviously leading to murder, when the O'Riginal asked suddenly, close to my ear, and in a deep and solemn voice,—

"Do you know Varney the Vampire?"

170   4. Monsters of the Gilded Age

I was for the moment startled and appalled at this strange and terrible query, but answered that I had not the pleasure of Varney's acquaintance.

"Oh, he's a beauty!" enthusiastically exclaimed the O'Riginal; "one of the earliest 'Awfuls,' and the best of his kind. Look at the title, 'Varney the Vampire; or, the Feast of Blood.' Isn't that magnificent? That alone ought to be the making of it. I am sorry I have no number here to show you. Do you know 'Villeroy'?"ᶜ

"Yes!" I exclaimed, feeling a sudden and intense interest, "I *do* know 'Villeroy.'"

The O'Riginal had, unwittingly, touched a tender chord. He had made my thoughts fly back years and years to the happy days of childhood, ere

Vileroy; or, the Horrors of Zindorf Castle. The motif of snakes emerging from a skeleton's eye sockets recurs in several illustrations used in Vileroy. *The "Penny Awful" trade was well known for its sensational illustrations (like this one, ca. 1842–1850), which appealed especially to young readers. Critics worried that the stories were "awakening nervous or superstitious feelings" (in Parke's words) in young readers and contributing to a decline in literacy, a critique later repeated against pulp magazines, comic books, television, and video games—all, like the Penny Awful, popular culture media reliant on visual imagery for their appeal (courtesy Justin Gilroy).*

I had mastered the dubiously-advantageous art of extracting meaning from alphabetic characters. I remembered that there used to be lying about in the kitchen at home an old dogs-eared romance, bearing the appalling title of "Villeroy; or, the Horrors of Zindorf Castle!" For me this terrific tale had a fearful fascination. The portions read to me by Mary Jane (the owner or borrower of the book) were quite sufficient to "freeze my young blood," make my hair "stand on end," and cause me to lie awake at night, a prey to ghostly terrors, and, I have no doubt, did much to produce that tendency to nervousness from which I have never since wholly recovered. But it was the pictures that most contributed to this result. These I could read for myself. I was continually becoming absorbed in their ghastly details. They were full of murderers, skeletons, ghosts, and doomed victims chained in horrible subterraneous vaults, in company with mouldering bones, toads, snakes, and water-rats. I remember in particular one picture of a skeleton with snakes crawling out of its eyeless sockets, the thoughts of which has many a time and oft caused me in early life to hide my throbbing breast and chattering teeth under the bedclothes.

All this made me receive "Villeroy" as an old friend, or rather, perhaps, enemy, but at least as something fraught with considerable personal interest, when the O'Riginal handed me a complete volume of that work in company with several other "Penny Awfuls." All the old impressions were for the moment revived as I turned over its pages, and asked the O'Riginal whether he knew anything of the author.

"Of course I did—old Billy Pottinger—a most successful man with 'Penny Awfuls' in their early days. At one time he was writing eight a week, and making heaps of money. But Billy was one of those who never could keep it, and in his latter days he had run out both of coin and ideas. He lived then in a garret up a court (this place is a palace to it), and it was as much as he could do to get through one 'Awful' a week, and even *that* proved a decided 'frost.' I used to help him at his work. Sometimes he would dictate to me, and sometimes sit up in bed and write himself, using an old tea-tray as a desk, for want of a better. In fact, poor old Billy, the kindest but most improvident man I ever knew, was 'played out.' This couldn't last. He died, and was buried by the parish."

"A sad story," I commented, half to myself. "So this, then, was the author of the terrific 'Villeroy'?"

"It was very different with Spalding, and the way he worked up *his* 'Awfuls'!" proceeded the O'Riginal; "Spalding was one of the best hands in the whole business, and worked for Smith ever so many years. Spalding knew how to stick to money when he'd got it. His celebrated romance of 'Edgeworth Bess; or, the Night-Riders of Hounslow Heath,' was the beet and most successful highwayman story ever written. It had such an enormous run that it kept on for five years. The publisher made his fortune over it, and the author retired on £20,000."

"Is it possible?" I exclaimed. "Why, Milton did not get much more than £20 for the immortal 'Paradise Lost.'"

"My dear sir, Milton couldn't write 'Penny Awfuls,' nor did he live in an age when literature was a branch of commerce," returned the O'Riginal. "There is a knack in 'Awful' writing as in everything else. It requires special capacities to do it with success. The faculty of skilful construction is essential; but original genius is rather in the way than otherwise."

At the conclusion of our visit, the O'Riginal, finding me interested in the subject, insisted upon my borrowing a pile of 'Awfuls,' taking them home to read, and giving him afterwards my opinion thereon. When Strayshot and I left him, our Anglo-Franco–Hibernian entertainer had begun "pegging away" (as he expressed it) at "Gallows Jack," whom he had the task of rescuing, for about the dozenth time, from the hands of the hangman.

The calm and careful perusal of the various specimens of the "Penny Awful" genus I found to be an occupation not without interest or instruction, as it opened to my view a field of literature much patronized by large masses of the community, but seldom subjected to the examination of the critical.

Of course I gave my first attention to the long-remembered "Horrors of Zindorf Castle." Yes, there were the old, old mysteries and horrors, once so powerfully impressive to my youthful mind. How well I remembered the double frontispiece—two pictures facing each other. In one, the wicked Baron of Zindorf is furiously knocking an imaginary enemy down what appears to be a stage trap-door, thereby much disconcerting a living black skeleton, surrounded by white smoke, who seems to object to such violence, while a lady is turning away and weeping—as well she may—at such a startling condition of affairs.

"No, Claudio," exclaims the wicked baron, "hadst thou a thousand lives, I would sacrifice them all. This stroke precipitates thee to the lowest hell!"

In the other picture there is a conference between a venerable man and a young lady in a deep dungeon, with all the cheerful accompaniments of skulls, rusty chains, and mouldering bones, and a *tableau* is formed by the usurping tyrant rushing in, armed and furious, just as the aged prisoner is disclosing himself as the real baron, who has for years been, "by his villany, confined within this living tomb." After which opening the reader will not be surprised to find, further on, that the heroine is disturbed by a mysterious portrait on the wall, which turns out to mask the entrance to a secret passage, leading to a gloomy bedchamber, where a skull adorns the dressing-table; that another skull is used as a drinking-cup by the bad baron, who forces her to drink out of it; and that another of these sad relics of mortality is discovered on the shelf of a long disused closet, together with a parchment which throws some light on the fate of the skull's original owner. From these specimens, and a glance through the text, it is obvious that the Romance of "Villeroy" (or "*Vile*roy," as I find it is spelt) is a close imitation of the "Mysteries of Udolpho," with a certain admixture of the "Castle of Otranto." A small edition of "Udolpho" was familiar to my childhood, but though one plate represented the heroine discovering "a corpse, stretched on a kind of low couch," the frightening power of the work utterly paled before the accumulated horrors of "Villeroy." At what period of history the events in "Zindorf Castle" are supposed to have occurred, is a point left delightfully vague. Travelling carriages and coffee-houses are spoken of, and the heroine reads Corneille's tragedies, which would make us assign the story to a comparatively modern era.

We are, therefore, rather puzzled further on to meet with a condition of things only applicable to the middle ages. The author seems to have heedlessly or wilfully neglected chronological as well as all other probabilities. The male costumes in general resemble those of the days of Charles II., but sometimes approach nearer to the Henry VIII. era; and anon recede as far back as the times of the Crusaders. At all times, they partake strongly of that highly adorned, conventional, and theatrical character suggestive of old east-end melodramas. The ladies' dress, still more inaccurately, approximates to the date when the book itself was produced—during the early days of Queen Victoria. But all these inconsistencies are fully in accordance with the perplexing mysteries of Zindorf Castle. It must have been a charming place to reside in. In addition to the skeletons, ghosts, &c., the inmates were liable at any time to come upon a stranger in a dark cloak, with slouched hat and black mask, whose demeanour was at least calculated to alarm a timid person, even if he did not whip out a dagger and plunge it into somebody's heart previous to disappearing mysteriously through a spring-door. Just such a personage in one picture is pointing (the characters in "Zindorf" are always pointing) down a subterranean passage, through which a lady in white very properly refuses to accompany him. Of course numerous "hardened ruffians" are in the pay of the iniquitous baron. One is murdering an unfortunate man in a forest so dark that the blood, dripping from his dagger, comes out *white* in comparison. Another cuts the throat of a lady in a gondola; and throughout the book headless bodies lying in pools of blood are extremely common.

Several numbers are taken up by the adventures of Claudio and Maurice, two friends who pass an indefinite period wandering about the vaults, dungeons, and subterranean passages of the terrible castle, which, by all accounts, must have been equal in extent to the catacombs of Egypt. Horrors of all kinds await the explorers at every turn. They come to one particularly damp vault, the flooring of which is covered by a stagnant pool, and they are instantly surrounded by a perfect aquarium of strange and loathsome creatures; groans and stifled shrieks as of tortured victims fall upon their ears, and the mouldering walls give forth the exhalations of the grave. But a few extracts from this portion of the book will best convey an idea of its intense "horrors."

> "I feel sick at heart in this place," said Maurice.
> "Let us leave it then," replied Claudio; "we cannot pursue inquiry further in this direction; we may find some other opening from the first passage."
> "Beware!" said a hollow voice, which sounded from behind them. Claudio started, and turned instantly round. He tried to pierce the obscurity of the passage, and his heart beat with excitement,
> ..."This is as awful," said Maurice, "as it is inexplicable."
> A dead silence now ensued, and neither Claudio nor Maurice moved a limb, but waited in wrapt expectation of again hearing some sound which should influence their movements; but, no! all was still save the monotonous pattering of the water, as it dropped from the roof, with a sullen sound, into the pool below.
> Claudio drew a long breath as he said, "There are, indeed, horrors and mysteries connected with the castle of Zindorf, which can by Heaven alone be unravelled."
> Presently their souls were again harrowed.
> "Hark!" cried Maurice, "Good heavens! what sound was that?" A sound reached Claudio's ears, like the low growling of some wild beast, and *before he could bestow a thought upon its particular character*, it was succeeded by a yell so loud and terrific, that it would seem to have proceeded at once *from the mouths of millions of demons!*"

This naturally frightens Maurice, so that he drops the lamp, and darkness odds to the horrors of the scene; fortunately Claudio is provided with a tinder-box, and by the *blue gloom* of the match ("blue gloom" is a fine phrase, full of ghastly and sulphurous suggestions) lie is able to find the lantern and rekindle it. The scene already alluded to, in which they discover the remains of one of the baron's victims, is ghastly and repulsive enough to please even the author of "L'homme qui rit."

> "The flesh had rotted from the bones, which were of a dull yellow colour, and covered with an unwholesome dampness. The skeleton still hung to the pillar, suspended round the waist by an iron hoop, and the long bony fingers were twined round an iron chain, which was twisted us many times round the fleshless bones. As Claudio and Maurice continued to gaze on the sad remains, a long, slimy, shining reptile, of a kind they had never before seen, crept from one of the sockets of the eyes, and dropped among the bones beneath."

Over this "mouldering form" Claudio proceeds to soliloquize, *à la* Hamlet.

> "Sad emblem of mortality!" he cried, ... "what schemes may not have been devised within the hollow chamber of thy now fleshless skull ? The smile of beauty may have brought sunshine to thine heart, which has resolved itself into its elements, and now forms but a portion of the noxious air of a dungeon. Alas! those eyes, which now shine no more, may they not have at one time flashed with celestial fire?" &c., &c.

I cannot stay to quote half the unique gems of expression which are scattered through the 400 pages of "Villeroy." One of the characters has "an *universal* shudder pass over his frame;" an old recluse is addressed as "respectable sire;" a villain "seethes his soul in crime;" the "bad baron" is perpetually either "turning pale with guilty terror," or "hissing furiously through his clenched teeth," or "shrieking is his excess of auger;" anon he puts on "a sneer which makes him look like a scowling demon;" and when by chance he node himself looking at all amiable, he "pauses a moment *to restore the habitual sternness of his demeanour*;" but his companion in guilt even outdoes all this on one occasion, by assuming "an expression of ferocity *which the archenemy of mankind might have envied!*"

"Villeroy," as I discovered, belongs to an old-fashioned order of "Penny Awfuls," which reflected the Gothic style in vogue in the days of Radcliffe, Maturin, and Monk Lewis. This class of narrative is now less prevalent, although the same horrors, mixed with more modern elements, are still retained. Another, of the same date, is a close imitation of Scott's "Ivanhoe," of which, indeed, most of the events, scenes, and characters, judiciously mixed with those of the "Talisman," are taken almost bodily. The adventures of Robin Hood seem also a favourite subject with those who patronize these cheap serial fictions.

But, above all, highwaymen stories—those illegitimate descendants of the poems and romances in which Byron, Bulwer, and Ainsworth have given immortality to sublimated outlaws and ideal felons—are the most popular.

The real and apocryphal deeds of the chevaliers of industry who formerly infested the king's highway never seem to pall upon "Penny Awful" readers. Amongst the specimens submitted to me by the O'Riginal was a portion of the famous "Edgeworth Bess; or, the Night-Riders of Hounslow Heath," that successful romance which had made the fortunes of its producers, and become a standard work. In the number I read the narrative had reached the seventeen hundred and twentieth page, and the thousand and second chapter, and was still in the high tide of its adventurous career—a fact alone speaking eloquently of its favourable reception. It is a peculiarity of these fictions that they bring all the most notorious leaders of felonry upon the field at once; and we find Jack Sheppard, Dick Turpin, Claude Duval, Jack Kann, Tom King, Sixteen-string Jack, and even the fabulous Captain Macheath and Paul Clifford, seeking adventures in concert, in defiance not only of chronological possibility, but of the unlikelihood that these stars of the murky firmament of crime would consent to shine so amicably together. In the course of the adventures, intrigues, and hairbreadth 'scapes that follow each other in rapid and endless succession, these worthies are brought in contact with all classes and conditions of men, from "King George upon his throne," to the vilest outcast in Newgate. There can be little doubt that this department of "gutter literature," as it has been aptly termed, is more harmful than, any other, since it paints in glowing hues, and holds up to admiration, the achievements of those who were, in sober reality, mere vulgar ruffians. The authors seem fully aware that they are open to this charge, as the following noteworthy argument in the "Night-Riders," will show:—

> "We wish, if possible, to combat in a few lines the objections which have been raised to making a highwayman the hero of romance. It has been urged, *and with some apparent reason*, that the narration of such romantic incidents as pertain to highwaymen's career would tend to make the thoughtless endeavour to imitate them. But it should be borne in mind

that much of the interest of such tales is due to the fact that the highwayman is essentially a thing of the past, and that time has softened and thrown a gloss over his exploits. Surely it is impossible that any one could be ridiculous enough, in these days, to attempt to imitate their deeds. In fact, the bold highwayman has got to be considered as a species of knight-errant, whose chief business *was to redress such social wrongs* as he encountered during his adventures(?).... It is not his obnoxiousness to the laws of the land, nor the crimes of which he may have been guilty, that rivets the reader's attention, hut his *courage, address, single-mindedness, and opposition to all sorts of oppression....* Besides, the person who was weak-minded enough to think he could achieve the feats ascribed to heroes such us ours would be just as likely, after reading some romance of chivalry, to don a suit of armour and set out in quest of adventures, like Don Quixote. No one thinks of stigmatizing as improper the romances in which mailed warriors and crusaders take a part, and yet it appears to us that the objection raised applies to them with equal force."

This is specious reasoning, and not readily refuted, until we remember that the point of the argument lies in the question, "to what kind of readers do such romances appeal?" The writers surely cannot hope to blind themselves or others to this fact. Here is another remarkable sentence, from a "Penny Awful" which, not being a highwayman story, but a species of popular calendar of current crimes, does not mind apparently siding against its rivals:—

"The following account of a burglary and brutal murder, which took place during the same year as the above, will give a yet clearer idea of the utter villany and dastardly cowardice of your 'gallant cracksman.' How would the gold lace and cocked hat excuse such villany as this? And those dashing heroes, *whose false adventures fill so many books*, are men of the same stump as these wretches who perpetrated the fearful crime detailed in the following report."

But what can such paragraphic apologies or disclaimers avail against the thousands of pages of mischievous matter which environ them? How can they weaken the force of each pictures as the subjoined enticing description of a "famous highwayman"?—

"Macheath was a gentleman by taste, habit, and instinct. His refinement was inherent. He did nothing coarsely or offensively—nothing in any way calculated to shock or convey a disagreeable impression. His smile was always winning, his manner incomparably graceful. The scabbard of his sword was jewelled, so was the hilt of the weapon itself. The long polished barrels of his pistols were richly chased, the stocks beautifully set and graved.

"His dress was very captivating. The most exquisite lace fell softly over his wrists, and the wrists themselves were white and round to feminine perfection. Then, on the fourth finger of the slim, snowy hand, which he was wont to extend for the reception of such gifts as travellers chose to present, there flashed one magnificent gem—a red stone of limpid light. Altogether, he was the beau ideal of a wayside cavalier, just the gentleman to stop and plunder a king with princely grace."

The natural effect of such writing upon the class of readers appealed to by "Penny Awfuls" would be a deep admiration, if not a desire to emulate these brilliant and dashing heroes, and an impression that such a gorgeous and dazzling exterior must in itself be almost sufficient to atone for a career of deadly crimes. Far less demoralizing, but equally misleading to the mind, are such stories as the O'Riginal's serial of "Young King Crusoe; or, the Boy Rover of the Pacific." The charms of "a life on the ocean wave," under adventurous circumstances, are seldom lost upon boys, especially English boys, and "Robinson Crusoe," an early friend of us all, is not only himself immortal, but lives in a constantly increasing number of imitators. Defoe's great romance owed its charm to a close following of nature, if not of actual facts, but its cheap prototypes are altogether wild and outrageous, representing things as they are not, and never could be.

"Young King Crusoe" commences with a wreck, whereby the hero is cast ashore—of course, alone, as all but heroes inevitably perish on these occasions—upon one of the "ten thousand islands of the Indian Archipelago," where he shifts for himself after the fashion of his immortal predecessor. The island, which is only a few miles in circumference, proves to be "one in ten thousand," in a double sense; for besides being of most extraordinary beauty and fertility, it teems with animal life to an extent surpassing anything on record. Not only do monkeys, snakes, parrots, "and such small deer," abound, but crocodiles, gorillas, lions, tigers, peccaries, zebras, tapirs, and bears of enormous size, while the coasts are infested with sharks and other creatures very like whales—which, indeed, prove to be such. How all these creatures came to be in a small and remote island in the South Pacific it is difficult to conceive, unless it be presumed that some enterprising but mistaken person had at some time or other imported a menagerie there. This is the more probable as the animals seem to have been collected from different quarters of the globe. But the question how they had contrived to find subsistence in such close quarters without the weaker races at least being exterminated by the stronger, or killed by starvation, is utterly incomprehensible. At all events, being there, they were likely to interfere a great deal with the comfort of any merely human emigrant; and so, indeed, they did in the present case, for scarcely a day passes without our gallant Crusoe (who appears to be about fourteen years of age) coming into violent contact with some of them.

But he never gets killed, and very rarely wounded. A single blow from his cutlass is always sufficient to dispose of a lion or a gorilla—or, for the matter of that, I suppose, a whale or an elephant. At one time he was "ALONE IN THE WILD BEASTS' LAIR" (this is printed in capitals), where, "gathered around the cave, were the fierce denizens of the adjacent forest—the terrible-looking puma, the sleek but deadly jaguar, were there in every size and age," all of which attack the young adventurer, who, however, manages to get off with his life. The constant recurrence of these surprisingly narrow escapes let me into one important secret in the construction of "Penny Awfuls." Your hero must bear a charmed life. Ever on the brink of destruction, he never oversteps it, and rescue arrives at the nick of time with mathematical certainty. In like manner, the hero's friends and sweethearts are rescued by him or by each other. In short, all foes and obstacles, however formidable they may appear at the time, are to the favoured youth like so many ninepins which are set up for the sole object of being knocked down again. The O'Riginal told me that he once, by mistake, killed a favourite hero, causing a "row" with the publishers and many angry remonstrances on the part of "millions of readers," and was obliged to resuscitate him in the next number, after he had had his skull cleft in two with a tomahawk, and been thrown down a precipice thirty feet high. This mischance, which would have been irremediable in a narrative of more sober cast, was easily got over in the "Penny Awful," where it became only one in a thousand improbabilities, just a little more improbable than the rest. The veracious chronicler had only to write:—

> "He sank to rise no more!—*so, at least, it seemed* to his relentless foes; but was every spark of life really extinct in that gallant breast? No, thank heaven! When drawn from the dark waters of the lake, he was exhausted, senseless, and bleeding, *but his hour was not yet come!*"

The "Boy Rover"'s after existence on the wonderful island is diversified by the advent of cannibals, and of an old sailor who becomes his companion. This conventional character has, of course, an aptitude for "spinning yarns," and for ingeniously improving the comforts of Crusoe-life. He has also a deep practical knowledge of the animal and vegetable kingdoms, and the characteristics of different countries, for there is always a vast amount of natural (?) history and geography in these adventurous stories, which would be instructive if it were in any instance correct. Our juvenile hero manages, single-handed, to rescue a certain beautiful savage from the claws first of a couple of lions, and next from a whole tribe of cannibals. This leads to the introduction of another conventional character indispensable in stories of this kind—the "Indian Maiden"—so called, to whichever of the dark races she may belong. She is a creature at once savage and refined, whose manners and appearance are those of an English lady masquerading as Pocahontas. It is a remarkable fact that the savages in these wild romances, in whatever part of the world the scene is laid, invariably talk after the fashion of Fenimore Cooper's North American Indians. Communication between them and the white adventurers is established with surprising quickness. We are told that "the old sailor, *to be ready for any emergency*, began to teach our hero the Indian language, such as is spoken by the various tribes of North, South, and Central America," conveying the idea that *one* language not only serves for all that extensive region, but is also understood in the "ten thousand islands of the South Pacific."

Afterwards the "young King Crusoe" extends his travels throughout all latitudes and longitudes—even as far as the North Pole, meeting with pirates, slavers, wrecks, waterspouts, and ships on fire; in short, encountering adventures without end, and, ere he is yet a man, going through more perils and excitements than a veteran of eighty.

Amid all the amusement that may be caused by applying a critical test to these preposterous fabrications, we should never forget the serious objections there are against their moral tendency. Simply absurd and puerile to adult readers of ordinary intelligence, they may be powerful for harm in the hands of the uninstructed juvenility for whom they are mostly written. From immorality—in the restricted sense of that term, as commonly used—the "Penny Awful" is generally free, although licentious scenes, incidents, and suggestions are sometimes to be found. But, in other respects, and mainly by instilling in the youthful mind an antagonism to law and order, and the duties of everyday life; by exciting vain expectations, and false notions of life, and giving highly-coloured pictures with neither the value of truth nor the refining power of poetic romance, their effect cannot but be baneful. Whether the "Penny Awful" be a highwayman story, likely to lead a boy to turn amateur robber, or a Crusoe story, calculated to make him run away to sea in the hope of encountering pirates and savages, or a ghost and murder story, awakening nervous or superstitious feelings, it is, to say the least, far from wholesome reading. All the qualities which romance should hold up to the emulation of youth, steadfastness, courage, generosity, presence of mind in danger, and an adventurous spirit in a right cause, can be powerfully exemplified without making the hero either a felon or a companion of felons; and the wonders of nature are sufficient in themselves without distorting geography and zoology into nonsense.

The vast amount of such deleterious fiction produced of late years, and the fact that, by the very manner of its publication, its circulation must be extensive, and its effects powerful and immediate, makes this subject one of serious importance. We cannot doubt that we have here an evil of considerable magnitude, for which a remedy is urgently needed. The law has evidently no power to stop it, or to decide precisely how far it is calculated to deprave the minds of readers. It is useless to cast the entire blame upon such persons as the O'Riginal, who write only to live, whose sole care is to suit their market, whether the moral results be good or bad, and who are equally ready to write sermons if that would serve their turn better. Nor can we even throw the entire onus upon the publishers or projectors of such trashy compositions, for, in an age when literature is dealt with so completely in a commercial spirit, when even religious publications are not above making friends with the "Mammon of unrighteousness," it would be unreasonable to expect the lower classes of literary traders to be overscrupulous. As long as a large and paying public can be obtained for them, "Penny Awfuls" will be produced. Nor should we censure the readers for their depraved taste, for which, indeed, considering that in most cases no other has ever been fostered in them, they rather deserve pity. The only effectual remedy lies in the spread of education, not only in its useful and intellectual, but in its purely imaginative branches. It would, indeed, be a national benefit if there were to arise some original genius, with a power of writing for the masses in such a manner as to sweep away the whole catalogue of horrors, crimes, and unwholesome excitements in which they at present delight, and substitute something which should combine the fascinations of the "Penny Awful" with adherence to truth and nature, and evince both a healthy imagination and a sound moral purpose.

Notes

a. The first epigraph comes from *Othello* (Act III, scene iii), and the second from George Crabbe's (1754–1832) "The Hall of Justice" (1807).
b. From Thomas Haynes Bayly's (1797–1839) popular ballad "The Old House at Home."
c. *Varney* is variously attributed to John Malcolm Rhymer or Thomas Preskett (or Peckett) Prest. Recent evidence favors Rhymer, though at 247 chapters, the work was likely the result of many hands. *Vileroy; or, the Horrors of Zindorf Castle* (1842) shares the same set of suspected authors and Elizabeth Caroline Grey, with Rhymer most likely. Parke attributes *Vileroy* to a Billy Pottinger, possibly a mocking reference to Sir William Pottinger, who wrote about juvenile delinquency in the 1850s.

The British-Irish writer J. Sheridan Le Fanu (1814–1873) composed a number of famous horror stories, including the one described here, the vampire novella *Carmilla* (1872), often thought of as a "lesbian" tale because both vampire and victim are female. The reviewer for the *Saturday Review*, looking back on Le Fanu in 1881, considered this a masterpiece though made no mention of the homoerotic aspects of the tale. This review first ran in the *Saturday Review* for June 19, 1881, and was reprinted in *Additions to the Library*, a publication of the Boston Athenæum, on November 16, 1881.

Review of The Purcell Papers *by J. Sheridan Le Fanu*[*]

THE SATURDAY REVIEW

The genius of the late Mr. Sheridan Le Fanu was of a chill and curdling nature. No author more frequently caused a reader to look over his shoulder in the dead hour of night. None made a nervous visitor feel more uncomfortable in the big, bleak bedrooms of old Highland houses. Mr. Le Fanu did not deal much in actual ghosts. His apparitions were much more fearful. Carmilla is a tale that every parent should make haste not to place in the hands of the young. Neither Poe nor Richepin[a] ever invented anything more horrible than the dusky, undulating, nocturnal shape of her who was a fair woman by daylight and an insatiate fiend at night. Mr. Le Fanu's skill in the weaving of plots was greater, we think, than that of Mr. Wilkie Collins,[b] as his humor was more spontaneous and less mechanical. "Wylder's hand" is a very well managed story.

[*]Review of *The Purcell Papers* by J. Sheridan Le Fanu, *Boston Athenæum Additions to the Library*, 1877–1886 (Boston, 1887), 307.

Notes

a. Jean Richepin (1849–1926) was a French novelist, poet, and playwright who wrote mostly about the lives of the poor. He was jailed for producing offensive poems and was criticized for "crude and revolting realism" in his stories of debauchery and misery, in the words of his contemporary, the Columbia professor Mathurin M. Dondo.

b. Wilkie Collins (1824–1889) was a writer of dozens of sensational novels, including mystery, suspense, and detection, as well as dozens more short stories. His most famous works are *The Woman in White* (1859) and *The Moonstone* (1868).

Continuing in the vein of Le Fanu, we come to this odd little passage from an otherwise unremarkable article about tea, the British national beverage. Here, E. V. Lucas (1868–1938), the prolific English writer and the biographer of Charles Lamb, refers in his discussion of the beverage to the plot of Le Fanu's horrific tale "The Green Tea" (1872), in which the beverage makes the supernatural antics of a demon monkey visible to a harried priest. At the time, green tea was sometimes thought to be poisonous. This excerpt comes from "Concerning Tea," which first ran in *Cornhill Magazine* and was reprinted in the *Eclectic Magazine* for February 1897.

*Excerpt from "Concerning Tea"**

E. V. LUCAS

For the full appreciation of afternoon tea there is no preparation to compare with a picture gallery. Certain social critics profess to have discovered that many art galleries exist solely in the interests of neighboring tea resorts, and the memory of pictures sometimes found on their walls almost inclines one to accept the theory as a fact. It is a compliment to this divine fluid when the drinker is a little fatigued. But perhaps a cup of tea "the first thing in the morning" is best of all. Then, pre-eminently, as Browning says, is it the time and the place and the loved one altogether. Tea in one's bedroom is a luxury which brings the humble person into line with the monarch and millionaire. It is akin to the luxury of staying away from church.

The happiest tea drinkers are they who have generous friends in China. No tea is like theirs. That inscrutable humorist, Li Hung Chang, left presents of priceless tea in his wake as he passed smiling through the West— tea of integrity hitherto unsuspected by the few persons whose glory it was to taste it. Among these was Mr. Gladstone, who is great among tea

*E. V. Lucas, "Concerning Tea," *Eclectic Magazine of Foreign Literature, Science, and Art*, February 1897, 267.

drinkers, and whose pleasant humor it is to speak of a cup as a dish. Dean Stanley was among the tea giants, and Dr. Johnson's prowess is a by-word. Hartley Coleridge was another colossus of the caddy. One who knew him tells that asking him on a certain occasion how many cups he was in the habit of drinking, the poet replied with scorn, "Cups! I don't count by cups. I count by pots." Once a man looks upon tea when it is green, his fate is sealed. Hyson and "Gunpowder" between them have shattered many a nerve. Green tea numbers among its opponents Miss Matty. It will be remembered that when she set up her tea shop in Cranford, the whole countryside seemed to be out of tea at the same moment. "The only alteration," says the chronicler, "I could have desired in Miss Matty's way of doing business was that she should not have so plaintively entreated some of her customers not to buy green tea—running it down as a slow poison, sure to destroy the nerves, and produce all manner of evil." According to a story by Sheridan Le Fanu, one of the effects of green tea is to be visited o' nights by an impalpable monkey with red eyes. "Punch,"[a] with that happy, witty way it has, calls this state "delirium tea-mens."

Telling Fortunes by Tea Leaves. Tea has long been associated with supernatural properties, associations J. Sheridan Le Fanu drew on when creating his story "The Green Tea," in which the beverage drives a man to madness. Since the seventeenth century, the reading of tea leaves was used to divine the future, as seen in this 1897 photograph of a tea reading party. Green tea, though, was considered dangerous. The Edinburgh Medical Journal *reported in 1818 that green tea had "injurious effects in some." An 1866 household guide warned that green tea could be used to make toxins that "killed a dog almost instantly" and a poison good for "killing flies." In 1883,* The Book of Health *warned that green tea causes "such a disturbance of the nervous system that the patient suffers from hallucinations of vision and trembling of the muscles," just like the character in Le Fanu's story (Library of Congress, Prints and Photographs Division, LC-USZ62-121562).*

Notes

a. *Punch* was a long-running (1841–1992) British satirical magazine.

The Rev. J. Charles Cox (1843–1919) wrote most frequently on matters religious, but he also contributed critical reviews to contemporary periodicals. In this excerpt from "The New Gallery" report in a column called "The Antiquary among the Pictures," Cox reviews the installation of Philip Burne-Jones's (1861–1926) painting *The Vampire* (1897) in London's New Gallery. The painting inspired Rudyard Kipling's poem of the same name. This review first ran in *The Antiquary* for June 1897. The numbers in the text refer to the numbers assigned to the works in the 1897 exhibit.

Excerpt from "The New Gallery"*
J. CHARLES COX

The exigencies of space compel the curtailment of our notes on this exhibition. It contains nothing so startling or contentious as on some occasions, and is assuredly above the average. In proportion to its far smaller numbers, the New Gallery of 1897 has more distinguished pictures than its elder sister at Burlington House.

The West Room is dominated by Sir Edward Burne-Jones's great picture of "The Pilgrim of Love" (134). It is a masterpiece of his allegorical style, but scarcely needs any description, as it is but another phase of that which he has several times produced. The South Room, in its turn, is also pervaded by a single picture; but whilst the imaginative recollection of Sir Edward's painting must be, on the whole, of a helpful nature, and yielding much artistic enjoyment, the impressions raised by the big picture of Mr. Philip Burne-Jones, "The Vampire" (15), cannot fail to be unwholesome, or, at the best, uselessly morbid. The man or woman who would like to have such a thing hung in a gallery should be shunned. It is not, probably, nearly so creepy or ghastly as its designer and executor expected, but the sickly livid green light over all the details is a most befitting colour. In all true senses of the word, this laboriously achieved picture is distinctly low art. Rudyard Kipling, a relative of the artist, has written a "poem" of three stanzas expressly for the picture, which is printed in the catalogue. The poem in no ways

*J. Charles Cox, "The Antiquary among the Pictures," *The Antiquary*, June 1897, 173.

The Vampire by Robert Burne-Jones. The painting (1897) inverts the traditional image of the male vampire preying on a female victim, and this depiction of a predatory female disturbed contemporary critics, who found the painting distasteful, morbid, and unwholesome. The painting inspired Kipling to write a short poem, also called "The Vampire." This in turn inspired the 1915 film A Fool There Was, which gave rise to so-called "vamps" in theater and film, powerful, non-supernatural women who drained the life out of the men they encountered.

detracts from the nasty morbidness of the apparent ideas of the artist, or succeeds in making them intelligible. The rhymes accompanying the picture can only be described as Swinburne and dirty water.

The British clergyman William James Dawson (1854–1928) was a prolific writer and compiled several books on subjects ranging from religion to literature, both fiction and nonfiction, prose and poetry. Here the Rev. Dawson surveys the work of Robert Louis Stevenson (1850–1894), with special emphasis on *The Strange Case of Dr. Jekyll and Mr. Hyde* (1886), to look for underlying morality and religiosity. Rev. Dawson believed Stevenson was a classic, and in this he was proved right. "The Religion of Robert Louis Stevenson" appeared in *The Bookman* for September 1896 and was reprinted in 1910.

*The Religion of Robert Louis Stevenson**
W. J. DAWSON

It was the fortune of Robert Louis Stevenson, dying untimely as he did, to be treated as a classic before his death, and there is something in the circumstance singular and extraordinary. It is a fate which has happened to few, to scarcely any one indeed whose period of earthly toil has been so brief. It is quite possible that more distant generations may not endorse our spirit of laudation, and may accuse us of lack of perspective and hastiness of judgment. But I am not one of those who entertain such forebodings. Stevenson is for me the most vivid, brilliant, and suggestive figure in our later literature, and his writings possess an element of charm which I find in no others. Preeminently he is a great master of style. It would he hard indeed if he were not, considering the immense pains which he took to write perfectly. He is entirely frank in confessing that he does not wield an easy pen. He never thinks of the immense fecundity and power of Walter Scott without despair. He says frankly, "I cannot compete with that." In a darker mood he cries, "What makes me sick is to think of Scott turning out *Guy Mannering* in three weeks! What a pull of work! heavens, what thews and sinews! And here am I, my head spinning from having only rewritten seven not very difficult pages—and not very good when done." But he has certainly written as Scott never did, with a

*W. J. Dawson, "The Religion of Robert Louis Stevenson," Reprint, *The Bookman: A Magazine of Literature and Life*, September 1910, 89–93.

precision and subtlety of style which at its best is nearly inimitable. The swing and case of Scott he has not; but he has contrived so to interpret himself in all his work that there is scarcely a page which does not throw over us the spell of something intimate and spiritual—a nameless aroma of genius which all sympathetic to him must feel, though few can describe.

Perhaps it is because this curious essence of personality which pervades his work is so elusive that few critics have discovered the right word to say of it, and have found it easier to fall back upon a general analysis of Stevenson's qualities as story-writer. That these qualities are of supreme excellence no one will deny. He himself justly felt that his power as a novelist lay in the direction of the grim and terrible. Give him a scene of savage passion and bloodshed, and no one can handle it so convincingly. Invalid as he was all his life, no man had more of the spirit of the adventurer. His was the spirit which loved adventure for its own sake. In one of his last letters to Mr. Colvin he rejoices that there is no more Land of Counterpane for him, and suggests what a find ending it would be if, after all, he could contrive for

Robert Louis Stevenson. Stevenson's reputation has waxed and waned over the past century. In his time, he was both a popular writer and critically acclaimed. Though Stevenson never lost his popular appeal, modernist authors like Virginia Woolf disapproved of Stevenson's neo-romantic writings, and for much of the twentieth century scholars excluded him from the accepted canon of major authors. Only recently have scholars reevaluated Stevenson and seen in him a peer of Joseph Conrad, Henry James, or Thomas Hardy. 1916 (Library of Congress, Prints and Photographs Division, LC-USZ62-96126).

himself a violent death. It was probably by a sort of reaction from the actual conditions of his life that he became a writer of adventure stories. He wrote them superbly. Some of his scenes, some of his phrases even, live enduringly in the memory. Almost all the scenes in *Treasure Island*; the fight upon the deck in *The Wrecker*; the dreadful picture of the abominable Huish in *The Ebb-Tide* going to his doom, with the packet of dynamite concealed in his simious hand; the murder of Case in *The Beach of Falesá*, the body of the man giving "like a spring-sofa" under the knees of his assailant; the immortal duel of the two brothers on the snowy lawn, the candles burning clear beside them in the windless air, in *The Master of Ballantrae*—these and many more scenes might be quoted as examples of Stevenson's extraordinary power in dealing with the grim and terrible. In the Celtic imagination the weird is always a potent force, and Stevenson was pure Celt. But he who does not see much more than this in Stevenson sees little. Any good writer could describe a duel or a murder with some degree of power and accuracy; but there are few writers who can make us feel that Death and Eternity surround the scene. Stevenson does this. He has a powerful and persistent sense of the spiritual forces which move behind the painted shows of life. He writes not only as a realist, but as a prophet. His meanest stage is set with Eternity as a background. Take, for example, the astonishing subtlety and truth of the scene in which he pictures Herrick as attempting suicide by drowning, in *The Ebb-Tide*. The moment the wretched man takes the water, he begins to swim by a sort of instinct. He is about to "lie down with all races and generations of men in the house of sleep;" there will be plenty of time to stop swimming presently. But could he stop swimming? He knew at once that he could not.

> He was aware instantly of an opposition in his members, unanimous and invincible, clinging to life with a single and fixed resolve, finger by finger, sinew by sinew; something that was at once he and not he—at once within and without him; the shutting of some miniature valve within his brain, which a single manly thought should suffice to open—and the grasp of an external fate ineluctable as gravity.... There were men who could commit suicide; there were men who could not: and he was one who could not.

There is not a hint here of the sort of imagination which a commonplace novelist would indulge in—the marching before the mind of the drowning man of his past life, and so forth; but there is something infinitely more terrible. Stevenson admits us into the very soul of the miserable man. He makes us partners in his extreme self-contempt, the utter self-loathing which makes him feel "he could have spat upon himself." He gives us a momentary glimpse of far-off powers that watch the spectacle: a city "along whose distant terraces there walked men and women of awful and benignant features, who viewed him with distant commiseration." This is one of the greatest pieces of imaginative writing in our literature, but it is much more than this. It is the work of a man profoundly impressed by spiritual realities, and only such a man could have produced it.

It would be easy to arrange in opposing categories the novelists who have a religious sense and those who are destitute of it. The first usually spoil their art by making it the abject vehicle of something that they want to teach: the second usually fail of the most difficult success, because when they come to the greatest episodes of life they lack the spirituality which can alone interpret them aright. Stevenson belongs to neither of these classes. He does not profess that he has anything to teach, and has no temptation to the didactic. He aims at one thing only, to tell his story in what seems to him the completest and most perfect manner. His ethical views are to be found in his essays, and of these we are not speaking now. But nevertheless Stevenson is a moralist or nothing. The Scot can rarely escape the pressure of those profound and serious thoughts which constitute religion; and Stevenson carried religion in his very bones and marrow. That which gives his great scenes their most impressive element is not merely their force of imagination or of truth; it is this subtle element of religion which colours them. The awful, the distant, the eternal, mix themselves in all his thoughts. The difference between a great scene of Scott and a great scene of Stevenson is that the first impresses us, but the second awes us. Words, phrases, sudden flashes of insight, linger in the mind and solemnise it. We feel that there is something we have not quite fathomed in the passage, and we return to it again to find it still unfathomable. Light of heart and brilliant as he can be, yet not Carlyle himself moved more indubitably in the presence of the immensities and eternities. Wonder and astonishment sit throned among his thoughts, the wonder of the awestruck child at divine mysteries, the enduring astonishment of the man who moves about in worlds not recognised. It is this intense religious sense of Stevenson which sets him in a place apart among his contemporaries; it is, to use his own phrase, a force that grasps him "ineluctable as gravity."

Sometimes, though but rarely, he permits himself a wider latitude. Thus he puts into the lips of Attwater thoughts which no doubt had moved his own heart deeply. Attwater is very far from being a perfectly conceived or rendered character; indeed, he must stand among Stevenson's failures. But he is useful in showing us the mysticism of his creator's mind. He is a man who walks awestruck through the labyrinth of life. He hears across the desolate lagoon eternity ringing like a bell. He ponders life and death with insistence, with passion and absorption. He preaches to the wretched fugitives who are his guests; he uses the very words which might express Stevenson's own sense of the unseen—"We sit on this verandah on a lighted stage with all heaven for spectators. And you call that solitude." To Herrick, who has implied his total disbelief in God, he replies that it is by the grace of God we live at all:

> The grace of your Maker and Redeemer, He who died for you, He who upholds you, He whom you daily crucify afresh.... Nothing but God's Grace! We walk upon it; we breathe it; we live and die by it; it makes the nails and axles of the universe; and a puppy in pyjamas prefers self-conceit!

A trifle grandiloquent, perhaps; but then Attwater is meant to be a grandiloquent personage, a half-barbarous and half-evangelical South Sea Hercules. Yet surely these words of his are a deep cry out of Stevenson's own heart. A man whose daily breath was a sort of miracle, and who felt that every hour he lived he was cheating the grave of its proper prey, might well feel that he lived literally by the grace of God.

Nowhere does the spiritual genius of Stevenson express itself with such force and fulness as in his *Strange Case of Dr. Jekyll and Mr. Hyde*. And incidentally it may be remarked that nothing which he has written has laid hold so strongly on the public mind. When one comes to think of it, there are very few, even of the greatest writers, who have created figures so vital and so real that they have become familiar and alive to the great world of readers. Dickens has done it: hardly any one else of our time. There is certainly no firm in England so well known as Spenlow & Jorkins, and no public personage half so familiar to us as Micawber, perpetually waiting for something to turn up. The politician or the speaker has but to use these names, and instantly his parable is perceived: on the mimic stage of memory and imagination there struts forth a figure, better known to us than the clerk in our office, or the friend who talks with us at dinner. And thus to seize upon certain living traits of character and certain catchwords of speech, and so mould the whole that the result is a personage so thoroughly alive and so delightfully human that we can sum up whole stages of observation and experience by the mention of his imaginary name, is the crowning skill of great creative art. No novelist can expect a higher triumph than this; but this triumph has certainly been Stevenson's. "Dr. Jekyll and Mr. Hyde" has already become a password: men utter the phrase and declare a parable. It has become, in fact, a synonym for the dual nature of man, and the deadly war of opposites which is always going on in human character. But there is this difference—and it is a typical one—between the creatures of Dickens's stage and those of Stevenson's: Micawber and his fellows spring out of humorous fancy, Hyde and Jekyll from the womb of a sombre and terrible imagination. Here, again, we come upon that profound seriousness of soul that underlies all Stevenson's best work; the questioning and philosophic mind groping at the intricate coil of things; the intense imagination of the Celt, fascinated by the grim and subtle mysteries of human nature. The seed-thought of this appalling fable of *Dr. Jekyll and Mr. Hyde* is familiar enough: it is the ancient Pauline description of a war in our members, so that the thing we would, that we do not; and the thing we would not that we do. The summary of the whole—it might well form the inscription for the title-page—is that great cry wrung out of the very agonised heart of this internecine conflict, "O wretched man that I am! who shall deliver me from the body of this death ?" We have heard the words many times on the lips of preachers and theologians, but one would certainly have doubted if they were capable of being vitalised by the art of the novelist. But in the mind of Stevenson there existed just that combination of faculties to which they most powerfully appealed. He has told us that the fable was a form of literary art which always fascinated him, and in the truest sense *Dr. Jekyll and Mr. Hyde* is a fable. But what a fable! There is the weirdness of Poe, his eloquence too, and his power of piling up detail, but a power of analyses and a psychologic subtlety which he never reached. It may be doubted if any novelist has ever cut so deep into morbid psychology as Stevenson in this short story of one hundred and fifty pages. What an awful picture is this of a man torn between his good and evil natures; in his right mind given to religions and serious thoughts, in the guise of Mr. Hyde greedy of abominable vices; repenting and sinning in turn; conscious all the time that the ape-like thing within him grows stronger for each fresh indulgence and liberation, and yet incapable of restraining him; to the last desirous of good, but impotent of achieving it. Fantastic, all but grotesque as the story is, yet it has all the firm outline of reality. Reading it, we readily permit ourselves to be convinced that such a thing could be. The horror grows with every stage: it becomes palpable, tremendous. The ape-like thing called Hyde, the incarnated evil of the soul of Jekyll, pursues our very dreams. And with what solemn and lamenting eloquence does the allegory close:

This was the shocking thing; that the slime of the pit seemed to
utter cries and voices; that the amorphous dust gesticulated and sinned;
that what was dead, and had no shape, should usurp the offices of life.
And this again: that that insurgent horror was knit to him closer than
a wife, closer than an eye; lay caged in his flesh, where he heard it
mutter, and felt it struggle to be born; and at every hour of weakness,
and in the confidence of slumber, prevailed against him, and deposed
him out of life.

A piece of writing like this is a unique achievement in the art of letters. It is really comparable with nothing else; it stands alone. And it is conclusive evidence of that subtlety and force of spiritual genius which gives Stevenson a place apart, and high above all contemporaries, as an interpreter of the deepest things of the human soul.

A sort of foreshadowing of *Dr. Jekyll and Mr. Hyde* may be found in another and earlier story, of Stevenson's, called *Markheim*. As a story this is briefer and less elaborated, but it is scarcely less powerful and tragic. In this instance it is the soul of a man who appears to him immediately after he has done a cruel murder, and calmly analyses all the slow moral disintegration which has led up to this crowning infamy, and finally extorts from the man a confession of the truth of the analysis.

"You have grown in many things more lax," says the accusing spirit: "possibly you do right to be so; and at any account it is the same with all men. But granting that, are you in any one particular, however trifling, more difficult to please with your own conduct, or do you go in all things with a looser rein?"
"In any one?" repealed Markheim, with an anguish of consideration.
"No," he added with despair, "in none! I have gone down in all!"

But here again, powerful as the story is, and told with an incomparable realism and suggestiveness, it is not the story which holds us spellbound so much as the moral drama which it displays. It probes deep into the intricacies of human motive, and the mystery of human sin. No one who has read pages such as these in Stevenson with the least degree of right appreciation can ever mistake him for the idle story-teller of an idle hour. Most readers will be far more inclined to say that nowhere in our literature is there to be found a writer who displays such mastery over the secrets of the soul, or speaks with a voice more undoubtedly prophetic.

It is an astonishing thing that a writer who has deliberately set himself to write pure adventure stories should possess such a gift of spiritual subtlety, and it begets in us a doubt whether, after all, Stevenson was rightly aware of the nature of his own genius. But this at least must be admitted, that he has contrived to lift the adventure story to a quite new elevation by the powers which he has brought to bear upon it. That which gives his books their enduring hold upon the mind is precisely this spiritual subtlety which informs them. We read them once, we read them twice; we read them again after the lapse of years during which many things have happened in the development of our own minds, and we still find them fascinating. Nor is it altogether the clearness and beauty of the style that compels attention: still less is it the narrative. It is rather a compulsion which arises from the spirit of the man; something in the turning of a phrase, in the felicity of an epithet, in the imaginative force of a sentence that has the effect of being flashed upon the brain, which opens up profound depths of thought, and calls the mind to solemn speculations. Stevenson was too modest a man to pose as a thinker; yet a thinker he was, and of great originality and insight. And in the truest sense of the word he was an entirely pious man. He knew what it meant, as he has put it, to go up "the great bare staircase of his duty, uncheered and undepressed." In the trials of a life unusually difficult, and pierced by the spear's points of the sharpest limitations, he preserved a splendid and unbroken fortitude. No man ever met life with a higher courage; it is safe to say that a man less courageous would not have lived nearly so long. There are few things more wonderful and admirable than the persistence of his energy; ill and compelled to silence, he still dictates his story in the dumb alphabet, and at his lowest ebb of health makes no complaint. And through all there runs a piety as invincible as his fortitude; a certain gaiety of soul that never deserts him; a faith in the ultimate rightness of destiny which holds him serene amid a sea of troubles. Neither his work nor his life have yet been justly apprehended, nor has the time yet come when a thoroughly accurate and balanced judgment is possible. But it will be a painful surprise to me if coming generations do not recognise his work as one of the chief treasures of our literature, and the man himself as one of the most original, rare, and entirely lovable men of genius of this or of any time.

An anonymous review of *Dr. Jekyll and Mr. Hyde* from the *Dublin Review* of April 1886 offers a glimpse of the critical reception of Stevenson's novel.

Review of The Strange Case of Dr. Jekyll and Mr. Hyde*

THE DUBLIN REVIEW

Mr. Stevenson's vivid realism of style enables him to frame a fascinating tale on a basis of fable as weirdly extravagant as a nightmare. A man, originally driven to lead a life of dissimulation by the desire to combine external decorum with secret self-indulgence, attains at length to the concoction of a philtre by which he can dissever the two opposite strands of his existence; and the respectable and benevolent Dr. Jekyll thus transmutes himself at will into the monster of wickedness, Edward Hyde, in whom till the evil of his nature is incarnated. As a complete bodily transformation accompanies his change of identity, the vices and crimes of the latter can never be brought home to the man in his original character, and he thus acquires complete irresponsibility for his actions. The subtle process by which the lower nature, thus fostered, gradually dominates and crushes the higher, refusing to be bound by the laws that had given it a separate existence, effects a tremendous retribution, as the man becomes, in the end, liable to transformation at any time, without the act of will signified by drinking the philtre, into his worse and outlawed self. We may thus, if we so choose, regard the extravaganza as a profound allegory, personifying the good and evil tendencies of every individual, and the moral transformation deliberately invoked by the surrender of the faculties to the demon of excess. The gradual deterioration of the better nature, through toleration of the misdeeds of its evil shadow, is finely marked, and the hero's eventual helplessness to recover his original shape accents the meaning of the parable, as the enslavement of will by passion.

British barrister Alfred Bailey was the author of *The Succession to the English Crown: A Historical Sketch* (1879), but in a piece entitled "Novelists' Law," he sought to judge "the goodness or badness of the law which ... novelists have introduced in their works" as well as to answer outstanding legal questions raised by the plots of contemporary novels. In this excerpt Bailey surveys some vexing legal issues raised by *Jekyll and Hyde*.

*Review of *Strange Case of Dr. Jekyll and Mr. Hyde* by Robert Louis Stevenson, *The Dublin Review*, April 1886, 422–423.

"Novelists' Law" first appeared in *The Gentleman's Magazine* for July 1886, not long after *Jekyll and Hyde* saw publication.

Excerpt from "Novelists' Law"*
ALFRED BAILEY

Many of my readers will have recently read with much interest the weird story of the "Strange Case of Dr. Jekyll and Mr. Hyde," "where more is meant than meets the ear." Early in the tale we find Mr. Utterson, Dr. Jekyll's friend and lawyer, pondering over the singular document which the doctor has committed to the lawyer's keeping.

"The will was holograph, for Mr. Utterson, though he took charge of it now that it was made, had refused to lend the least assistance in the making of it. It provided not only that in case of the decease of Henry Jekyll, M.D., D.C.L., LL.D., F.R.S., &c., all his possessions were to pass into the hands of his 'friend and benefactor Edward Hyde'; but that in case of Dr. Jekyll's disappearance or unexplained absence for any period exceeding three calendar months the said Edward Hyde should step in the said Henry Jekyll's shoes without further delay and free from any burthen or obligation, beyond the payment of a few small sums to the members of the doctor's household." The author seems to have had some misgiving as to the character of this instrument, for later on we read: "On the desk among the neat array of papers a large envelope was uppermost, and bore in the doctor's hand the name of Mr. Utterson. The lawyer unsealed it, and several enclosures fell to the floor. The first was a will, drawn in the same eccentric terms as the one which he had returned six months before, to serve as a testament in case of death, and as a deed of gift in case of disappearance."

I must own that I should feel considerable difficulty in framing an instrument which should operate at once as a will, and as a deed of gift in case of the testator's disappearance.

Proof of Dr. Jekyll's death would, I think, have been necessary before the instrument could have been acted on.

If a similar case of a person being able to change himself into two shapes should arise, I would venture to advise such a bi-formal individual to dispose of his property by two separate instruments, one a will and the other a deed of gift.

---

*Alfred Bailey, "Novelists' Law," *The Gentleman's Magazine*, July 1886, 27.

Jekyll and Hyde was easily the most popular and resonant of nineteenth century horrors, spreading across the Atlantic and pervading popular culture. During the bitter campaign for the American presidency in 1888, in which Benjamin Harrison defeated the sitting president Grover Cleveland (who in turn defeated Harrison four years later), the *New York Herald Tribune* published the following editorial. In it, the paper describes Cleveland as a Jekyll-and-Hyde, publicly torn over whether to accept his party's nomination to run for a second term (acceptance came long after nomination in those days) while privately contributing $10,000 to further his campaign. The editorial ran September 4, 1888.

*The Secret Out**

THE NEW YORK HERALD TRIBUNE

The explanation of the extraordinary delay in Mr. Cleveland's letter of acceptance is easy. Like the rest of mankind, the President is afflicted as we long ago made known, with a dual personality; but in his case the ordinary conditions are reversed. The Jekyll, who favors reform and is animated by patriotic and statesmanlike purposes is feeble and small of build. The Hyde is large and powerful and fat. When Mr. Cleveland was first nominated he was touched by this mark of confidence on the part of his fellow-man. Jekyll came uppermost. He saw, knowing as he did the irrepressible wickedness of Hyde, that unless he were checked at the outset he would use every cunning and wicked device to bring about his re-election. So Jekyll wrote the passage in the letter of acceptance which served notice on Hyde that he must not dare to think of a second term. But the ink was hardly dry before that wily and unscrupulous character began his evil machinations, and Hyde, being by far the stronger personality of the two, invariably gains the victory in the end. The sending of that ten thousand-dollar check to the Democratic National Committee was a critical point in this tremendous struggle, of which no hint so far has escaped to the outside public. Jekyll knows that he cannot consistently or with any propriety accept the nomination, and is making a brave fight for a clean record. But what are consistency and propriety to Hyde? When, therefore, he succeeded in sending the ten-thousand-dollar check, it was with a chuckle of ghoulish glee, for he knew then that he had committed Jekyll, and while the final acceptance might be long delayed, it must come sooner

*"The Secret Out," in *The Republican Campaign Text-Book for 1888*, George Francis Dawson (New York: Brentano's, 1888), 247.

or later. It is even said that the check was signed by Edward Hyde, and not by Dr. Jekyll at all. But the national committee accepted it without question, because they know that Mr. Cleveland has bank accounts in both names, and draws on Hyde's much more frequently than on Jekyll's.

This disclosure must arouse a great popular sympathy with Mr. Cleveland. We can easily imagine now what fearful struggles have been going on in the White House, at the dead of night, when Jekyll was straining every nerve to conquer his familiar demon, If Jekyll could have had his way we might have had a model administration, within its intellectual limitations, but Hyde's unconquerable depravity has kept his wretched victim continually in hot water. It was Jekyll who promised to be a civil-service reformer, but Hyde made the appointments, and so it was that about two hundred persons directly connected with the criminal classes got into Federal office in three years. It was Jekyll who wrote such beautiful letters to George William Curtis, but to what end? Hyde had no sooner been inaugurated than he struck up a violent friendship with Gorman, and sat up late nights with him planning political rascality. It is Hyde who writes all the pension vetoes, and sneers at the soldiers and their widows. It was Hyde who wanted to return the rebel flags, but the outcry frightened even him. It was Hyde who, after a long and frightful combat, succeeded in getting possession of the President's pen last December and wrote the free-trade message, because it is the one craving of his nature to smash things. It was Hyde who determined that there must be a bid made for the Irish vote, and so wrote the retaliation message in spite of Jekyll's wailing remonstrances that his entire policy on this question was being revised and made ridiculous. It was Hyde, too, who dictated the new anti–Chinese bill.

For ninety-one long days now this contest has lasted, and it cannot continue much longer. The sending of the ten-thousand-dollar check was a sign that Jekyll is fast losing his strength and must soon succumb. It will not be many days now before we shall have a letter in which nothing will be said concerning "the allurements of power" and "the temptation to retain public place once gained," but in which the nomination for a second term will be eagerly, even greedily, accepted. The letter will be signed by Jekyll, but we shall all recognize between the lines the cunning and unscrupulous hand of Edward Hyde.

The abnormal ferocity of Stevenson's Mr. Hyde seemed all the more plausible in light of the Jack the Ripper killings two years after the novella's publication. At the time, the American actor Richard Mansfield (1857–1907) was performing the title role in a stage production of *Jekyll and Hyde*. As the next two excerpts show, the similarities between stage and real life did not go unnoticed in Victorian London. This excerpt comes from a profile of Mansfield in *Famous American Actors of To-day* (1896) by William Henry Frost (1863–1902), a reporter and drama critic for the *New York Tribune*.

*Excerpt from "Richard Mansfield"**
WILLIAM HENRY FROST

An invitation from Henry Irving to Mr. Mansfield to occupy his theatre in London for some months prevented a summer engagement in New York in 1888. He began his season at the Lyceum Theatre, late in the

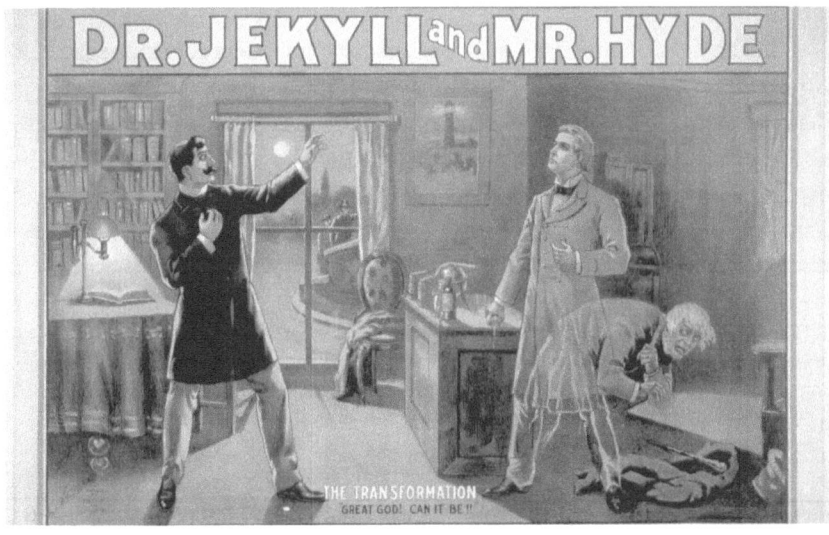

Dr. Jekyll and Mr. Hyde. *Theatrical adaptations of* Jekyll and Hyde *began not long after the book's 1886 publication, as seen in this poster for an American production likely from 1888 or 1889. The play was on offer in London at the time of the Jack the Ripper murders, and critics quickly grasped the similarities between the story of a man who looses his inner monster and the savagery of the serial killer (Library of Congress, Prints and Photographs Division, LC-USZC4-8267).*

*William Henry Frost, "Richard Mansfield," in *Famous American Actors of To-Day*, eds. Frederic Edward McCay and Charles E. L. Wingate (New York: Thomas Y. Crowell and Company, 1896), 141.

summer, with "Dr. Jekyll and Mr. Hyde." Later he gave "A Parisian Romance" and "Prince Karl." All of these created no small comment; and the ferocious wickedness of Mr. Hyde gained more attention than would perhaps have been the natural share, from the fact that two or three of the Whitechapel murders were committed in Mr. Mansfield's early days at the Lyceum.

Our second view on the Jekyll-Ripper connection is the work of Richard Le Gallienne (1866–1947), a writer and poet associated with the Decadent publication *The Yellow Book* and active from the 1890s through the 1920s. It comes from a discussion of Robert Louis Stevenson in *Retrospective Reviews* (1896), a book collecting his literary journalism. The profile was first published in May 1892.

*Excerpt from "R.L. Stevenson"**
RICHARD LE GALLIENNE

In the light of later days, such readers have doubtless come to regard *The Strange Case of Dr. Jekyll and Mr. Hyde* as a prophecy of the Whitechapel murders. In fact, I know that for certain members of Mr. Mansfield's audience, at one of his representations of Hyde, 'Jack the Ripper' was the one possible explanation—in spite of some most painstaking psychology on the play-bill.

Though Bram Stoker (1847–1912) is best known as the author of *Dracula*, his first novel was *The Snake's Pass* (1890), a Gothic-style romance filled with menace, dread, and terror. Here we observe the recommendation the short-lived *Murray's Magazine* (1887–1891) gave Stoker seven years before *Dracula*. The review ran in the January 1891 issue.

Excerpt from "Our Library List"†
MURRAY'S MAGAZINE

THE SNAKE'S PASS. By BRAM STOKER (*Sampson Low & Co.*) Mr. Bram Stoker's name is by no means unknown in literature. A few years ago he published a little volume entitled 'Under the Sunset,'

---

*Richard Le Gallienne, "R. L. Stevenson," in *Retrospective Reviews: A Literary Log by Richard Le Gallienne, vol. I, 1891–1893* (London: John Lane, 1896), 113.
†"Our Library List," *Murray's Magazine*, January 1891, 142.

containing some clever and interesting stories for children, which showed him possessed of a graceful and versatile fancy. 'The Snake's Pass' is a melodramatic tale of Ireland, the title referring to a cleft in the rocks of the coast connected with the old banishment by St. Patrick of the snakes from the Emerald Isle. The story is very skilfully narrated, and the author's knowledge of Irish manners and modes of life has enabled him to produce a vivid, and indeed, brilliant romance which will carry the reader's interest without pause from the first page to the last. Mr. Stoker's powers of description are shown in his remarkable account of the central catastrophe in the book, the details of which we will, however, leave to be discovered by readers themselves.

When Bram Stoker published *Dracula* in 1897, the British press gave it mixed reviews. This one by the pseudonymous "Baron de Book-Worms" in the June 26, 1897, edition of the satirical magazine *Punch* shows the ambiguous feelings the novel generated. Here, the reviewer clearly enjoyed reading the book, though he finds fault with its narrative structure and feels discomfort with the book's employment of religious symbolism in dispatching the vampire menace. The final six words of the review became a tag-line used in most subsequent advertisements of *Dracula* during its initial run.

Review of Dracula*
The Baron de Book-Worms

"I wants to make your flesh creep," might Mr. Bram Stoker well say as a preface to his latest book, named *Dracula*, which he has given in charge to Constables (& Co.) to publish. The story is told in diaries and journals, a rather tantalising and somewhat wearisome form of narration, whereof Wilkie Collins was a past-master. In almost all ghostly, as in most detective stories, one character must never be absent from the *dramatis personæ*, and that is the Inquiring, Sceptical, Incredulous Noodle. The Inquiring Noodle of Fiction must be what in comedy "Charles, his friend" is to the principal comedian, "only more so," as representing the devoted, admiring slave of the philosophic astute hero, ever ready to question, ever ready to dispute, ever ready to make a mistake at the critical moment, or to go to sleep just when success depends on his remaining awake. "Friend John"[a] is Mr.

*Baron de Book-Worms, "Our Booking-Office," *Punch*, June 26, 1897, 327.

202   4. Monsters of the Gilded Age

BRAM STOKER's Noodle-in-Chief. There are also some secondary Noodles; Noodles of no importance. This weird tale is about Vampires, not a single, quiet, creeping Vampire, but a whole brood of them, governed by a Vampire Monarch, who is apparently a sort of first cousin to *Mephistopheles*. Rats, bats, wolves and vermin obey him, but his power, like that of a certain well-advertised soap, "which will *not* wash clothes,"[b] has its limits; and so at last he is trapped, and this particular brood of vampires is destroyed as utterly as would be a hornets' nest when aroused with hot pitch. It is a pity that Mr. BRAM STOKER was not content to employ such supernatural anti-vampire receipts as his wildest imagination might have invented without rashly venturing on a domain where angels fear to tread. But for this, the Baron could have unreservedly recommended so ingenious a romance to all who enjoy the very weirdest of weird tales.

Notes

a. The character of Dr. John Seward, who in the novel disbelieves in vampires until his mentor, Prof. Abraham Van Helsing, provides overwhelming evidence of their reality.

b. "Monkey Soap—It Won't Wash Clothes!" The soap, meant for cleaning pots, pans, and glass, was advertised in the 1880s and 1890s with pictures of a monkey holding a frying pan.

While the early British reviews of *Dracula* are frequently included in critical editions of Stoker's novel, the book's American reception is less widely remembered. When the book was published in the United States in 1899, it received rather good press under the publisher's tag-line, "A thrilling book for the jaded reader." Our next two pieces are reviews from this side of the Atlantic. The first comes from Charles F. Lummis (1859–1928), a journalist, adventurer, and passionate defender of Native American rights. It first ran the magazine he edited, *The Land of Sunshine: The Magazine of California and the West,* in December 1899.

Supped Full with Horrors[*]
CHARLES F. LUMMIS

It is economically certain that Mr. Bram Stoker is a sober man. Drunkenness would have no charms, nor delirium any news, for a person of his imagination. His novel, *Dracula*, is a most surprising affair—and not its

[*]Charles F. Lummis, "That Which Is Written," *The Land of Sunshine: The Magazine of California and the West,* December 1899, 261.

Dey Flewed an' Dey Flewed. Dracula was neither the first nor the last of the vampires and devils in Victorian literature. Drawing inspiration from Polidori's Lord Ruthven and Rhymer's Varney, Dracula became the epitome of the demonic being. The bat-creature illustrated here comes from Virginia Frazer Boyle's African American–themed "Dark er de Moon" (1899), one of many tales of demons, devils, vampires, voodoo, and the occult published in the years following Dracula *(Library of Congress, Prints and Photographs Division).*

least surprise is that of finding yourself clutched and dragged along by so grisly an impossibility. Mr. Stoker has a steady and rather adroit hand to steer and display the paces of his hasheesh fancy; and though the story never convinces, it never loosens its peculiar grip on the reader. "Dracula" is a human vampire—literal vampire of the folkmyths—and with this repellant *motif,* the author has spun a web of horrors I do not remember the mate to. Perforce, all turns out well in the end; else one would have every right to resent so persistent racking of whatever nerves one may have. Doubleday & McClure Co., New York. C. C. Parker, Los Angeles. $1.50.

Our second American review of *Dracula* is an unsigned piece from the "Current" fiction column of *The Literary World,* a Boston literary review, for January 20, 1900.

Review of Dracula*

THE LITERARY WORLD

Bram Stoker's *Dracula* is the most exciting old-fashioned story of horrors we have read in a long time. Vampires in modern London, as well as in Transylvania, are prolific of delightful thrills to the sensation lover, and we confess that our favorite among these vampires is the worldly one who resided in Piccadilly and had a card-case; our most vivid imagination had never associated card-cases and vampires, but the two make a weird and attractive combination. The interest of the story is kept up from the first page to the last, and although we should hesitate to recommend Mr. Bram Stoker as a steady literary diet, one feast from him is a relief from the "tendency" and "temperamental" fiction of our day and generation. [Doubleday & McClure Co. $1.50.]

In an era before computers made retrieving information easy, publications used to make a virtue of answering their readers' questions. In the March 1903 edition of *Current Literature,* the editors gave a rather unsatisfactory answer to the 943rd query they had addressed, a charmingly misspelled question about Bram Stoker's *Dracula.*

*Review of *Dracula, The Literary World,* January 20, 1900, 26.

Excerpt from "Open Questions: Talks with Correspondents"*

CURRENT LITERATURE

943 (1) Is there any allegorical signification in Straker's [sic] story, Dracula? Is there any hidden meaning in the book?

(2) Who are Thomas Hardy's publishers in America—L. F. Valentine, Clay Center. Kan.

[(1) Never having read the work, we do not know whether it has any hidden meaning or not. We are curious, and shall try to read it. (2) Harper & Brothers, New York.]

J. Richardson Parke, S.B., Ph.G., M.D., suffered the indignity of arrest for sending his *Human Sexuality: A Medico–Literary Treatise on the Laws, Anomalies, and Relations of Sex with Especial Reference to Contrary Sexual Desire* (1906) through the mail, on the grounds that said book was obscene. (A grand jury refused to indict.) While the majority of the text is medical in nature, a footnote on page 333 is of special interest, though of a very strange sort. The two texts besides *Dracula* mentioned are credulous eighteenth century reports about real-life vampires and their nocturnal activities.

Excerpt from Human Sexuality[†]

J. RICHARDSON PARKE

...[T]here is little doubt, in my mind at least, that the origin of such *outre* fictional characters as Bram Stoker's Dracula, and the Slavonic and Albanian beliefs so gravely set forth in Ranft's "De Masticatione Mortuorum in Tumulis," and Calmet's "Dissertation on the Vampires of Hungary,"

---

*"Open Questions: Talks with Correspondents," *Current Literature: A Magazine of Contemporary Record*, March 1903, p. 383.

[†]J. Richardson Parke, *Human Sexuality: A Medico–Literary Treatise on the Laws, Anomalies, and Relations of Sex with Especial Reference to Contrary Sexual Desire* (Philadelphia: Professional Publishing Co., 1906), 333.

is to be found in the nocturnal depredations of *sexual sadists*, whose abnormality escaped detection through the fact that it was not then recognized or known.

Edmund Clarence Stedman (1833–1908) worked in newspapers early in life and became a noted poet, essayist, and critic. He later became an editor of the standard edition of Poe's work. Here, in a private letter, he reveals some of his feelings on *Dracula* to Julian Hawthorne (1846–1934), the son of Nathaniel Hawthorne and an author in his own right. "The Were-Wolf" discussed here is one of Julian's poems, a chilling portrait of the title creature (first published in *Chap-Book* for May 1, 1895), which Stedman later included in *An American Anthology* (1900).

Letter to Julian Hawthorne[*]
EDMUND CLARENCE STEDMAN

August 5, 1899.

Not so d—d hospitable I wish you to understand. Please rub off that stigma from that mental image of me, evolved by your own inner consciousness years ago. Nor does hospitality have to be "boundless" to ask *you*[1] over the door-sill along with your "Were-Wolf." Not that I know you to set up as a poet, although I have long suspected that the poet in you, more or less hampered the novelist, but I happened on that "Were-Wolf" in the *Chap-Book* some years ago, and overcame my indolence sufficiently to store it up against a day of need. I am anything but hospitable as a critic or an editor with the platitudes of the big figure–heads in poetry, but I often find some one poem written by a man of brains, who doesn't belong to the perfesh, that comes up in our rule of admission to an Anthology because it can't be left out. By the way, that is the Golden Rule for a "Golden Treasury," which my Anthology is not going to be, although I may make up a "Golden Treasury" from it on some leisure evening.

The "Were-Wolf" has an apt, irregular and seemingly inevitable power that makes it necessary to my collection. Instead of being the occasional poem of a prose-writer, I would think it the successful effort of a life-long

---

[*]Edmund Clarence Stedman, *Life and Letters of Edmund Clarence Stedman*, vol. 2, eds. Laura Stedman and George M. Gould (New York: Moffat, Yard and Company, 1910), 264–265.

1. Vampires, so Bram Stoker tells me in that Masterpiece of Terror, "Dracula," can't cross one's threshold unless they are (invited). [E. C. S.]

verse-writer, who in the matter of art had learned to unlearn. I suppose it is not a translation or paraphrase, and wonder what put it into your head. You really ought to have written "Dracula" years ago, and not have let Stoker get ahead of you. The infernal book haunted me nights during the early stages of my illness.

Please write me at once that I can use the "Were-Wolf," and remember that the novelist who is by blood and choice a romancer is a confessed poet.

Mignon, my granddaughter, and right hand man, says that you needn't think that I am well because I am swearing, for I have been a splendid swearer straight through; but we both acknowledge that the fact that I am dictating my own letters, etc., to a staff of three secretaries and editors, is a still better symptom, though the doctor keeps me flat on my back....

This strange little paragraph sits in a 1904 book by the occultist and simplified spelling advocate A. Osborne Eaves otherwise devoted to exposing the dangers of "modern vampirism" in the nineteenth century world.

Excerpt from Modern Vampirism[*]
A. OSBORNE EAVES

Perhaps the most sensational fiction with regard to the Vampire after Sheridan le Fanu's "Carmilla" is to be found in "Dracula," but it is very morbid reading. Evidently the author has been working the subject up, judging from the story, and by means of a vivid imagination an exciting narrative has been produced. The book is quoted here because so much information in reference to the Vampire is given which want of space forbids enlarging upon here. Robert Louis Stephenson's [sic] romance of the *Strange Case of Dr. Jekyll and Mr. Hyde* illustrates other phases and may interest the reader.[...] The dangers arising from the class of entity we have been considering are naturally limited, but there are other dangers to which a very large number of people are exposed. Truth, as is generally the case, supplies us with example which fiction cannot easily equal, but is not always easily accessible; whereas fiction is, and often, unwittingly, it may be, places the less-known facts of life in a clearer light.

---

[*]A. Osborne Eaves, *Modern Vampirism: Its Dangers and How to Avoid Them* (Harrogate: Talisman Publishing Company, 1904), 31.

A small notice in *The Bookman* for June 1912 shows us the period when *Dracula* began to become a classic, but the magazine's comments on *Frankenstein* indicate that horror was losing its literary respectability in the last years before the Great War. This early pairing of two horror classics that would soon become inseparable thanks to iconic movie versions leaves neither novel sounding like a must-read.

Frankenstein*

THE BOOKMAN

Since the death of Bram Stoker several writers in the weekly and daily journals have thought to bestow high praise upon his *Dracula* by saying that it will eventually take its place with Mrs. Shelley's *Frankenstein*. We wonder how many of these writers have read *Frankenstein*, which, despite the fact that it is remembered after one hundred years, is one of the most badly constructed and written of stories. When the voice of pessimism over the degenerate library conditions of our time is particularly loud we can console ourselves with the thought that *Frankenstein*, in the form in which it was written, could not be published to-day. There is probably hardly a "publicity" man in any of our leading American publishing houses who could not be trusted to edit and "touch it up" to good effect. At any rate there could be very little harm done by revision.

Dracula, by the way, had some curious vicissitudes in the United States. At first no American publisher would take it and Bram Stoker himself went to considerable expense in copyrighting it in this country. Time went on, and it looked as if this money—hard-earned, as was all Stoker's money—would be utterly wasted. Then suddenly a publisher took the book, and from the very first its sales were enormous, not only in the States, but in Canada also.

---

*"Chronicle and Comment," *The Bookman: A Magazine of Literature and Life*, June 1912, 347–348.

5. Fin de Siècle Science, Detection, and Terror

By mid-century, critics had begun to tire of Gothic horrors, then entering their second century of literary life. The following is an excerpt from an unsigned article from *The Dublin Review* for January 1872. The majority of "Fictions of the Future" explores the emergence of science fiction as a genre of literature, but in this excerpt from the beginning of the article, the unnamed author explains how the future became an exciting terra incognita for writers and readers tired of Gothicism's backward gaze.

*Excerpt from "Fictions of the Future"**
THE DUBLIN REVIEW

Sensational fiction has taken various forms within this century. Bulwer,[a] who happily half belongs to ancient literature, led the way by introducing us to aristocratic and intellectual criminals. Ainsworth, and now Miss Braddon,[b] have followed suit with their criminals, less intellectual and less aristocratic, if we may say so with Lady Audley's leave. Dickens gives us a murder or a violent death with the circumstantial details of a coroner's inquest. Through all these productions, to name no others, runs the vein of horror which constitutes the sensation. It is a horror interwoven with various other matters, grave and gay; but we know it is coming, and look out for it. It flavours the preceding passages, to readers who delight in such mental experiences. So, in lionizing the ruinous and haunted mansion, visitors are restless until they have reached *the* one thrilling room, with the ineffaceable stain upon its floor.

*"Fictions of the Future," *The Dublin Review*, January 1872, 76–78.

But the sated Roman emperor announced a prize to him who should invent some new pleasure. And so, in the literary epicurism of readers who have supped full of horrors, and who have come to yawn even in face of the grinning death's-head at their banquet, a something was needed to spur the jaded appetite into a fresh sensation. Into what region, then, shall the caterer travel for "pastures new"? Whence shall he procure for his imperial patron, the many-headed public, a pabulum, a dainty, yet unknown? To an ordinary imagination, the prospect might seem discouraging. Every crime in the Newgate Calendar has been already presented to the young ladies and gentlemen of England for their affectionate admiration and hearty acceptance. Every production of an unfettered Parisian fancy has found an English translator or plagiarist on the spot. The characters in our fictions have been flung into wells, hurled from steeples, cut into pieces on railways, roasted alive; which catastrophes they have abundantly deserved, inasmuch as they have fired houses, forged wills, starved widows and orphans, put their nearest relatives out of the way, and shown vivacity of spirit and muscular Christianity by playful peccadilloes of a like trifling nature, till we weary of the monstrous that has even become a monotony. *Ohe, jam satis*, we exclaim, with a yawn. Violence, according to the sensational writer, is the normal condition of human life. But even violence can weary, as the howling tempest can lull.

Only, before we throw aside our shilling volume, let us glance beyond it at the results. Schiller's "Robbers"[c] was the sensational novel of the day; and behold, the youth of Germany turns out, hault sentiment on its lips, and pistol in hand, to enact the hero on the highway. Turpin[d] rides to York on his famous black mare; and young brains have reeled with excitement to follow his adventures. Jack Sheppard,[e] the delight and glory of youthful aspirant cracksmen, has reappeared in the conviction of 'prentice burglars, long since inappreciative justice cut short his brilliant career. And the Bulwer and Braddon sensations may have borne fruit, partially unknown to us hitherto. Truth may yet in actual life be displaced from its well by the body of some victim of a lady murderess, hurled in thither by the force of powerful fiction. The field of sensational literature being thus already occupied by industrious tillers, and even exhausted by their succession of crops, it has become necessary to escape beyond it, through some gap in the hedge, if writers are to glean a harvest. And lo! a bright thought flashes, all but simultaneously, on several minds. *Eureka*! the Future! A sensation of what may possibly come; or what, though impossible, may be represented under certain extravagant conditions as coming.

Le Sortie de l'opéra en l'an 2000 (Leaving the Opera in the Year 2000). As Gothic horror flooded the market and grew clichéd, a new type of fiction seized the public and critical imagination, science fiction. While the Gothic looked back to a medieval past of horror, science fiction looked forward to a future of wonder, like this fanciful ca. 1882 Belle Époque scene of flying cars taking patrons from the opera. However, in time science fiction would take on darker hues and impinge on the territory of the Gothic, giving new life to the horror genre (Library of Congress, Prints and Photographs Division, LC-DIG-ppmsca-13553).

Notes

a. Sir Edward Bulwer-Lytton (see note, page 102, n.2).
b. Mary Elizabeth Braddon (1835–1915), author of *Lady Aubrey's Secret* (1862), a novel about a bigamist murderess.
c. Friedrich Schiller (1759–1805), Weimar author, philosopher, and historian. His play (not novel) *The Robbers* (1781) has been called the first melodrama, focusing on the conflict between two brothers.
d. Dick Turpin (1705–1739), famed highwayman and subject of popular ballads and plays. Legend has it that he rode his mare, Black Bess, from London to York so fast he outpaced news of his crimes.
e. Jack Sheppard (1702–1724), famed robber. He and Dick Turpin both gained renewed notoriety when William Harrison Ainsworth (1805–1882) wrote about them in the novels *Jack Sheppard* (1839) and *Rockwood* (1834), respectively.

Herbert George Wells (1866–1946) is primarily remembered as a founder of the science fiction genre, a title he shares with Jules Verne. While Verne's scientific romances were filled with wonder and awe, Wells's stories were frequently darker, occupying the territory where science fiction and horror overlap. This is best illustrated in *The Island of Dr. Moreau* (1896), a *Frankenstein*-like tale of a mad scientist who creates monsters in his own image through the vivisection of animals. Here, *Punch*'s "Baron" book reviewer renders his verdict on the book that Wells called his best in an 1897 interview and "not good" in 1901. The review first ran in *Punch*'s "Our Booking-Office" on April 18, 1896.

Review of The Island of Dr. Moreau[*]
THE BARON DE BOOK-WORMS

If H. G. WELLS, whilst writing *The Island of Dr. Moreau*, had only preserved the courage of his original idea, he might have produced a romance out–Haggarding HAGGARD,[a] and relegating *Zanoni* and the "Vril" people[b] to keep company with *Lemuel Gulliver, Ferdinand Count Fathom*, and Co.,[c] in the shades of the Almost Forgotten Ones. But after going through two-thirds of his uncanny tale, the author, apparently satisfied so far with his undoubted success in producing such grotesque and fantastic effects as could be only attributed to a training course of heavy suppers and a superficial study of anatomical subjects, resulting in dream-fits of violent indigestion, became frightened by his own monsters, and thought his best course would be to announce to his readers that he had "only been purtendin' all along," and that these awful creatures of his imagination were in reality only intended to represent the stupidity, selfishness, sensuality, and all the lower qualities of animal man; and that, in fact, the whole story, from beginning to end, was a parable, and not the true record supposed to have been made by the uncle of *Charles Edward Prendrick*, and subsequently published, for the benefit of society and science, by his enterprising nephew. When the author himself shows you how it's done, there is an end of the mystery, the interest in the tale is dead, and the author in giving himself away causes the reader to regret ever having taken him at his own valuation.

Notes

a. H. Rider Haggard (1856–1925), author of such adventures as *King Solomon's Mines* (1885).
b. *Zanoni* (1842) was by Edward Bulwer-Lytton (see p. 102, n.2), as was *The Coming Race* (1870), a science fiction novel featuring the subterranean Vril people.
c. Gulliver from Swift's *Gulliver's Travels* (1726/1735); *The Adventures of Ferdinand Count Fathom* (1748) was Tobias Smollet's (1721–1771) third novel, about an immoral adventurer.

---

[*]The Baron de Book-Worms, "Our Booking-Office," *Punch*, April 18, 1896, 185.

Review of The Island of Dr. Moreau (The Baron de Book-Worms) 213

Merchant's Gargling Oil for Man and Beast. In the years before Wells wrote The Island of Dr. Moreau, *a story about a scientist's attempts to surgically remake animals into humans, controversy about Charles Darwin's theory of evolution raged. Popular culture responded with a wave of images and writings that explored the implications of the blurring line between man and beast, something* Moreau *shares with this 1873 ad for gargling oil (Library of Congress, Prints and Photographs Division, LC-USZ62-48534).*

William Morton Payne (1859–1919) taught high school in Chicago and college in three states, was a literary critic, and was an editor for *The Dial*. In this excerpt from the "Recent Fiction" column of the December 16, 1897, edition of *The Dial*, Payne gives his opinion of the prolific author H. G. Wells's hybrid science fiction and horror novel, *The Invisible Man* (1897), which he published after his success with *The Time Machine* (1895) and *The Island of Dr. Moreau* (1896).

Review of The Invisible Man[*]

WILLIAM MORTON PAYNE

The peculiar vain of fantastic romance based upon scientific conceptions, which has been cultivated of late so successfully by Mr. H. G. Wells, reaches what is perhaps a climax of daring in his story of "The Invisible Man." The idea of the story is by no means new, but the treatment is distinctly novel, for Mr. Wells's hero is no magician with the gift of fernseed,[a] but a practical student of physics and physiology, who has hit upon a course of treatment whereby the refractive index of the human tissues may be equalized with that of the atmosphere, thus making the body invisible, just as certain jelly-fishes are practically invisible in the medium which they inhabit. Mr. Wells has not hesitated to think out his problem, and to face squarely all the minor details incident to this fantastic conception, which makes his treatment totally different from the hazy method of his predecessors who have attempted the same subject. For example, his invisible man must eat, and the food remains grotesquely visible until it is assimilated, thus necessitating his retirement from the neighborhood of men for some hours after a meal. Again, his blood, although invisible when in vital circulation, turns red when it is spilt and allowed to coagulate, as his entire body becomes visible at the end after he has been hunted down and killed. For the hero of this story is a monster as devoid of moral sentiment as the one created by Frankenstein, and he robs and slays without compunction until his career is rudely brought to an end. The whole thing is extremely well managed, and all the probability possible is given to a situation which is inherently impossible.

Notes

a. Fernseeds, the spores of ferns, were once thought to grant their bearer invisibility.

---

*William Morton Payne, "Recent Fiction," *The Dial: A Semi-Monthly Journal of Literary Criticism, Discussion, and Information*, December 16, 1897, 890.

The American scholar and critic William Lyon Phelps (1865–1943) taught at Yale for more than forty years, producing a number of works of literary criticism. In this excerpt from "Love, War, and Pseudo-science" in *The Book Buyer*'s February 1898 number, he savages Wells's *Invisible Man* (1897).

Excerpt from "Love, War, and Pseudo-science"*
WILLIAM LYON PHELPS

The "grotesque romance" by Mr. Wells is a combination of Jules Verne and Dickens, and is very far from being successful. There can be no doubt that Mr. Wells is writing too much. Since the publication of his delightful skit, "The Wheels of Chance," he has produced a new book every few weeks. Like many other prominent authors of the present day, he is apparently willing to sacrifice real repute and solid merit for immediate cash sales. *The Invisible Man* is a mere thing of the moment, an amusing trifle that is scarcely worth reading. It is, furthermore, embellished with horrid details that seem wholly out of place in a book that is meant and should be taken only as a jest. The pseudo-chemistry and the parade of scientific terminology remind one of Jules Verne, but are not so well managed; and the artistic unity of the little book is destroyed by the unconscionable length of the invisible man's autobiography, which begins right in the middle of the story. Some of the characters and conversation pleasantly remind one of Dickens, as the dialogue between Mr. Marvel and the mariner, and all the early scenes at the inn. On page 128 Mr. Wells remarks, "A black-bearded, man in grey ... conversed in American with a policeman off duty," but a study of his conversation fails to reveal anything strikingly "American" except the use of the word "guess," which was good enough English for Wordsworth. *The Invisible Man* is too manifestly a forced attempt at originality to be a genuinely attractive book. And on every page it bears the marks of haste.

Clement Shorter (1857–1926) is best remembered for his works on the life and times of the Brontë sisters, but he was also a journalist and editor. In this review for *The*

*William Lyon Phelps, "Love, War, and Pseudo-science," *The Book Buyer: A Review and Record of Current Literature*, February 1898, 69–70.

Bookman of May 1898, Shorter praises H. G. Wells's extraterrestrial invasion novel, *The War of the Worlds* (1898).

Mr. Wells's War of the Worlds*
Clement Shorter

"A gun which shoots electricity is the latest invention of an enterprising American, and Mr. John Hartman, the inventor of the automatic carbine socket, which has been used in the United States Army for sixteen years, and who himself served in the Civil War, is the inventor of this new device. It is said that he has discovered conditions by which the rays of a search-light can be charged with electricity, the beam of light thus taking the place of an ordinary wire. The individual coming within the light rays completes the circuit and falls dead. Experiments have been tried on rabbits, and with a current from a lamp of only fifty voltage he succeeded in killing a rabbit at fifty feet. We shall certainly await the details of this remarkable invention with curiosity."

I cut the above from a copy of the *Westminster Gazette* the other day, when engaged in reading Mr. Wells's new story. It set me thinking that if the Martians did not war on the world some human enemy armed with those heat-rays might, and instead of killing rabbits might kill men, until London became the silent, empty city that Mr. Wells's imagination has pictured with so much force.

That is one of the most striking points about Mr. Wells's work, that he always kindles the imagination. The thief who behind every hedge sees a constable is in a better plight than the average reader of *The War of the Worlds*, who, in every thunderstorm or convulsion of nature, will, for long years to come, think of those grim and impressive creatures from another world. There is an enormous gulf between Mr. Wells's wild imaginings and the imaginings of the men who are by some described roughly as his predecessors. The travels of Baron Munchausen and the adventures which we owe to Jules Verne are on an entirely separate plane. With these writers we are simply in fairyland; it is no disparagement that our delight in their adventure stories does not in the least disturb our sense of the fitness of

---

*Clement Shorter, "Mr. Wells's 'War of the Worlds,'" *The Bookman: A Literary Journal*, May 1898, 246–247.
The War of the Worlds. By H. G. Wells. New York: Harper & Brothers. $1.50.

things in our daily humdrum life. But Mr. Wells has set our minds agog; I do not say he has done it with that perfection of sanity which so great a subject might have called forth. A war of the worlds, if it really came, would bring us face to face with noble aspects of heroism, with infinite depths of terror, with a mingling of exquisite pathos, and—in spite of the horrors afforded—of grim humour, of a kind which do not come into the ken of Mr. Wells. I do not even deny that in *The War of the Worlds* there are certain small numbers of pages over which many readers may be excused for yawning, whereas to thoroughly convince us of so dire a catastrophe of nature as is here presented an inferior writer, equipped with some of Mr. Wells's material, would have prevented our interest from waning for a moment.

H. G. Wells. Both H. G. Wells and Jules Verne are honored as the "fathers of science fiction," but Wells's stories of monsters, aliens, and the unchecked consequences of technology were frequently much darker than Verne's fantasies. As a result, Wells's more terrifying stories form a bridge between science fiction, fantasy, and horror, a territory shared by later writers like H. P. Lovecraft. Photograph undated (Library of Congress, Prints and Photographs Division, LC-DIG-ggbain-21320).

Personally, I confess to being frankly sorry that here, as in other of Mr. Wells's books, he is so little of an optimist. It has been a dream of good men for countless ages that swords shall be beaten into ploughshares and spears into pruning-hooks, and although Tennyson in our own day has talked of "the canker of peace," and told us roundly that the wars of armies are not more deadly than the wars of capitalists, he also has filled two or three generations with an aspiration for the time "when the war-drum throbs no longer." And yet Mr. Wells, the first novelist to turn to account for purposes of fiction the great revival of science—the New Learning—which we owe to Darwin and Lyell, to Huxley and Tyndall, unlike his masters, who were all optimists, has painted, and continues to paint, developments where life is more full of pitfalls than in our own time, and where great convulsions of nature find us morally not one whit better prepared than the eruption of Vesuvius found the people of Pompeii nearly two thousand years ago. None the less do I count the work of Mr. Wells as one of the most distinctly individual achievements of our time, on a lower literary plane, it may be, but as distinctly an individual achievement as the work of Swift in the eighteenth century, with which it has much in common.

I note in passing as an interesting fact, that Mr. Wells, among the many interpolations that he has made since his book appeared in the pages of a popular magazine, has expressed his distaste for the impossible illustrations with which the magazine serial was adorned. "I recall particularly," he says, "the illustration of one of the first pamphlets to give a consecutive account of the war. The artist had evidently made a hasty study of one of the fighting machines, and there his knowledge ended. He presented them as tilted, stiff tripods, without either flexibility or subtlety, and with an altogether misleading monotony of effect. The pamphlet containing these renderings had a considerable vogue, and I mention them here simply to warn the reader against the impression they may have created. They were no more like the machines I saw in action than a Dutch doll is like a human being. To my mind, the pamphlet would have been much better without them." In wishing for the absence of the illustrations, Mr. Wells only expresses the feeling of most readers concerning the illustrations to stories by their favourite authors. Who is there, since Fred Barnard illustrated Dickens's novels, and Mr. Tenniel *Alice in Wonderland*, that has entirely satisfied us in the illustration of our most approved authors? But all this is to digress from my main point, which is to reiterate the conviction that among the younger writers of the day Mr. Wells is the most distinctly original, and the least indebted to predecessors. *The War of the Worlds* is a very strong and a very powerful book.

William Morton Payne enjoyed *The Invisible Man*. However, he was less enthusiastic about *The War of the Worlds*. This review ran as part of a longer overview of the month's new fiction in the June 1, 1898, edition of *The Dial*.

Review of The War of the Worlds*
WILLIAM MORTON PAYNE

The story of "The War of the Worlds" is contrived with an ingenuity of invention that outdoes M. Jules Verne, yet it remains almost as unconvincing as the pseudo-scientific imaginings of that entertaining Frenchman. It is difficult to take seriously these Martians who look like leather polyps, who go stalking about England in spheroidal long-legged metallic engines, and who deal death and destruction by means of heat-rays and poisonous suffocating vapors. The best parts of the story are those that describe the advent of the Martians in cylinders shot from our neighbor planet, and those others that make the terrible visitors succumb to the ravages of the terrestrial microbe. In this book, as in such others as "The Time Machine" and "The Invisible Man," Mr. Wells accepts to the full the logical implications of his primary postulate, and works in a good deal of effective realism in the detailed description of occurrences. The imagination displayed is somewhat unusual in intensity, although of a cheap sort, and if his account of "The War of the Worlds" does not actually thrill, it may at least be admitted to entertain.

Along with science fiction, the mystery genre relates closely to horror. Author of more than one hundred and seventy works, the prolific Carolyn Wells (1862–1942) is best known as a poet and mystery novelist. In 1913, she prepared a book for the Home Correspondence School Writer's Library instructing would-be mystery writers in that literary art. She does not distinguish between the ghost story and the detective tale, though, calling both mysteries, and as such discusses the relationship between the genres in the "Detective Stories" chapter of *The Technique of the Mystery Story*.

Excerpt from The Technique of the Mystery Story[†]
CAROLYN WELLS

[W]e must agree that for devotees the Detective Story sets a stirring mental exercise, with just enough of the complex background of life to

---

*William Morton Payne, "Recent Fiction," *The Dial: A Semi-Monthly Journal of Literary Criticism, Discussion, and Information*, June 1, 1898, 356.
†Carolyn Wells, *The Technique of the Mystery Story*, The Writer's Library, Springfield, Mass.: The Home Correspondence School, 1913, 63–64.

distinguish it from a problem in mathematics. Whatever thrills of horror are excited come by way of the intellect, never starting directly in the emotions. The reader divests himself of sympathy, and applies to every situation the dry light of reason. It is only when one's reason is baffled, leaving the murder unexplained or the ghost at large, that one feels privileged to shudder. And such a shudder is remarkably different from a start that is unthinking. The Detective Story applies reason to some of the big half-mysteries of human conduct; and the result for the ordinary reader is not dissimilar to that felt by the philosopher when trying to square with his poor apparatus the secrets of Nature and Providence.

Sir Arthur Conan Doyle (1859–1930) is best known as the author of the Sherlock Holmes detective stories, but Doyle, himself a Spiritualist, was also a devotee of horror, producing a number of macabre stories of the supernatural in counterpoint to his rationalist detective. Here *The Literary World* reviews *My Friend the Murderer* (1893), a collection of horror tales. The review ran on November 18, 1893.

Review of My Friend the Murderer*
THE LITERARY WORLD

A volume containing a dozen short stories by A. Conan Doyle is certain to furnish abundant excitement, but no other tale in the group proves to be quite so grewsome as that which gives the title. Unrelieved horror is not satisfactory material for fiction, and least of all is it desirable as an opening chapter. Even if this be a true narrative, as possibly it may be, like the one succeeding it and somewhat related to it, there was no necessity that the first place in the collection should be given to a study in moral pathology. Several of the stories deal with wild pioneer days in Australasia, when life was held cheap and miners took law into their own hands. Sometimes, as in the history of "Bones, the April Fool of Harvey's Sluice," the elements of lawlessness and cruelty have friendship and loyal love as their foil, but this is not the case with "The Parson of Jackman's Gulch." "Myster-

*Review of *My Friend the Murderer* by Arthur Conan Doyle, in "Fiction," *The Literary World*, November 18, 1893, 386.

Sir Arthur Conan Doyle. Like Wilkie Collins and Edgar Allan Poe, Doyle wrote in both the mystery and horror genres and often crossed between them. He created Sherlock Holmes, the greatest rationalist and skeptic of fiction, but Doyle was himself an adamant believer in Spiritualism, a movement that preached the reality of the supernatural. Doyle would champion such Spiritualist causes as the reality of fairies and later attempted to prove that his friend, the illusionist (and skeptic of Spiritualism) Harry Houdini, had real magical powers. Photograph undated (Library of Congress, Prints and Photographs Division, LC-DIG-ggbain-34027).

ies" or "adventures" are all the themes, whatever the key to which they are pitched. The few that are not darkened by violence are still stimulating to curiosity up to the moment of denouement, and one of them is permitted to end in pure comedy. Dr. Doyle's hand is a strong one and individual in its grasp even when he reminds us of Edgar Allan Poe and Bret Harte.—Lovell, Coryell & Co.

Arthur Bartlett Maurice (1873–1946) was the editor of *The Bookman* from 1899 to 1909, and friend to Frederic Taber Cooper, who appears elsewhere in this volume. In this review of Arthur Conan Doyle's Sherlock Holmes novel *The Hound of the Baskervilles* (serialized 1901–1902), Maurice regrets that Doyle had sidetracked reason in favor of horror. I have omitted a rather lengthy plot summary and some arcane speculation on rumored co-authors of the book to present the heart of the review, which contrasts unfavorably the "new" Holmes of the novel with the old of the nineteenth-century short stories. The author quotes a lengthy passage in which Holmes notices that the pasted-on words of a warning letter are cut from the same article in the previous day's newspaper. We then pick up the review from the May 1902 edition of *The Bookman*.

Excerpt from "Conan Doyle's The Hound of the Baskervilles"*

ARTHUR BARTLETT MAURICE

Here we have a touch of the old Sherlock Holmes of his best days. Ability to distinguish the type of one great newspaper from that of another would undoubtedly be one of Holmes's professional qualifications. It is all very striking and very plausible. At other times, however, the Holmes of this story is not nearly so happy.

In fact, throughout the greater part of the tale, Holmes is but a comparatively small factor. He is baulked in London by the cunning of the black-bearded man in the hansom cab, who recognises him and sends back a derisive message. Not one of his schemes results in any practical success. The narrative shifts from London to North Devon. Watson goes to Baskerville Hall with Sir Henry as a sort of personal guard, and also to describe what is going in weekly letters to Holmes, who remains in London. Mystery is piled on to mystery. False clues are introduced at every turn. A most dangerous convict escaped, and, hiding on the moor, heightens the horror of the situation. When one read this story in its serial form there was something picturesque and thrilling in the very absence and silence of Holmes. To the reader, as to Watson, everything is vague, dark, inexplicable; we feel that it is Holmes in London who is picking up thread after thread, searching among musty archives for certain odds and ends of social history that shall elucidate it all, and rivet the incongruous links into a complete chain. This impression was admirably maintained throughout the greater part of the tale; but when Holmes actually does appear, our belief in his infallibility and in his resemblance to the Holmes of Dr. Doyle's earlier stories is severely shaken. He has done practically nothing, and whatever acumen has been shown has been on the part of phlegmatic, stolid Watson. Even at the end of the narrative itself, at the supreme moment for which all had been waiting, we find that he has only partially guessed; and in that last chapter in which he endeavours to trace for Watson the chain of reasoning by which he reached the heart of the mystery, his explanations are woefully unsatisfactory and insufficient. As a story of mystery and horror, *The Hound of the Baskervilles* is a success; for Sherlock

---

*Arthur Bartlett Maurice, "Conan Doyle's 'The Hound of the Baskervilles,'" in "Seven Novels of Some Importance," *The Bookman: A Magazine of Literature and Life,* May 1902, 255.

Holmes, the Master of the Science of Deduction, whose creator has proclaimed him the peer of Dupin and of Lecoq, it is a *débâcle*.

Arthur Bingham Walkley (1855–1926) was a British drama critic well known in his day for his insightful look at English theatre. George Bernard Shaw dedicated *Man and Superman* to him for being the inspiration for his play. This review of André de Lorde's (1871–C. 1933) and Charles Foley's *Heard at the Telephone* (1902) expresses the critic's disdain for plays whose sole object is horror. Lorde produced more than one hundred plays of terror and horror for the Grand-Guignol, the French theater of horrors, earning him the title "Prince of Terror." *Heard at the Telephone* was an English translation of one of his plays. "Curiosity and Horror in the Theatre" first ran in the *Times* of London in March 1902 before being collected in the author's *Drama and Life* (1908).

Curiosity and Horror in the Theatre*
ARTHUR BINGHAM WALKLEY

Two questions of more than ephemeral interest are suggested by the present playbill of Wyndham's Theatre (March 1902). The main interest of *Cæsar's Wife* is an interest of curiosity; the sole interest of *Heard at the Telephone* is an interest of horror. What are we to think of these two theatrical interests? To crowds of playgoers they are both very real interests. One must take leave, however, to advance the opinion that the interest of curiosity has a very humble place in the region of art, while the interest of horror has no place in that region at all.

And, first, as to curiosity. That is the distinguishing mark of the child in civilised, and of the adult in savage, communities. The state of mind which is always wondering what is going to happen next, rather than forming judgments upon what has happened, is a naïve state. In primitive periods it accounts for the importance of oracles, prophets, and soothsayers. It still makes kitchen-maids the ready victims of "fortune-tellers" and the eager readers of *Zadkiel's Almanac*. In a higher stratum of intelligence it means the popularity of the "detective novel"; curiosity here becoming a mere amusement, a form of dilettantism, so that men of really gigantic intellect, but of a intel-

*A. B. Walkley, "Curiosity and Horror in the Theatre," in *Drama and Life* (New York: Brentano's, 1908), 115–119.

lect which is dormant on the artistic side—Darwin and Bismarck are illustrations of the type—are accustomed to take delight in the stories of Gaboriau, du Boisgobey,[a] and Conan Doyle. To the average mind a "mystery" is always more fascinating than the co-ordination and analysis of ascertained facts. That is why someone or other will always be discovering Bacon "ciphers"; such things appeal to the average man more intimately than the pleasure of reading either Bacon's or Shakespeare's works for what they are. The same feeling, the preference of the mysterious, the unaccountable, to the rational, scientifically explicable, moved the numerous supporters of the Tichborne[b] claimant. So, the interest still taken in the authorship of Junius's letters is an interest wholly unconcerned with the literary or political importance of their contents. The clever "boom" of *An Englishwoman's Love Letters* is another case in point. To return to drama, the aim of the great artist is not to surprise the spectator with an unforeseen, but to gratify him with an "inevitable," action. It is not to provoke his curiosity about what is going to happen so much as to excite in him a keen desire that a certain thing shall happen, and then to satisfy that desire to the full. To the Greek dramatists the interest of curiosity was virtually unknown; or, if they knew it, they despised the use of it. *Œdipus Tyrannus* is perhaps an exception, though even in that play the spectator's feeling is not so much curiosity about what is going to happen as sympathetic anguish for the victim of a fate which the spectator knows, but the victim does not know, to be impending. The state of feeling is very like that excited by Maeterlinck's[c] poignant little play of *Intérieur* wherein the spectator sees a drowned body being brought home. The shadows of the as yet happy family are seen on the window-blind, and the interest is not in what will happen behind that blind when the body is brought in—we all know the commotion, the horror, the grief that will ensue—but in the contrast between the present happiness of the household and the thought of the sudden end to that happiness which is impending. So indifferent were the Greek dramatists to the interest of curiosity that they did not scruple to announce their plot in advance. Euripides used prologues for this very purpose. Lessing, commenting on the practice in his *Hamburg Dramaturgy*, maintains that "the dramatic interest is all the stronger and keener the longer and the more certainly we have been allowed to foresee everything," and he adds, "so far am I from holding that the end ought to be hidden from the spectator that I don't think the enterprise would be a task beyond my strength were I to undertake a play of which the end should be announced in advance, from the very first scene." Lessing was something of a fanatic where the Greeks were concerned, but he had the root of the matter in him. And the fact remains, that the question put in *Cæsar's Wife*—which of two possible women is guilty of an adulterous intrigue?—is a trivial question compared with the questions which the playwright treats as of minor importance—why the guilty woman came to be guilty, and what will be the consequences of her guilt?

As to the theatrical use of sheer horror, there is always a tendency to it. In the first place, the spectacle of helpless physical suffering has a secret attraction for the primeval brute—the *gorille féroce* as Taine calls it—which slumbers in all of us. A poor dog run over in a London street will attract a fascinated crowd, gathered not to assist but to gloat. Burke said that a theatre where a tragedy was a-playing would at once be deserted by an

Hello Central, Give Me Heaven. The telephone was dismissed as a scientific curiosity upon its invention, but by the turn of the century it was a commonplace instrument in many homes, as seen in this staged 1901 photograph. In its first decades, observers marveled at the machine's ability to transmit sound as if by magic. "The effect is weird and almost supernatural," said The New York Herald. *The Providence Press wondered whether "the powers of darkness are somehow in league with it." By the time the telephone made its appearance in* Heard at the Telephone *(1902), it offered a different kind of horror—that of receiving knowledge without the ability to act on it (Library of Congress, Prints and Photographs Division, LC-USZ62-63984).*

audience who learnt that a real execution was going on outside. But in default of the real bloodshed, the audience will content itself with the sham. Dandin, the judge in Racine's comedy of *Les Plaideurs*, offers to amuse Isabelle by the spectacle of a little torturing. "Eh! Monsieur," exclaims Isabelle—"Eh! Monsieur, peut-on voir souffrir des malheureux?" and Dandin, in his reply, speaks for a large proportion of the human race: "Bon! cela fait toujours passer une heure ou deux."[d]

Hence the popularity of the torture scene in *La Tosca*. Besides, there is a law in aesthetics, which corresponds to the physiological law that a steady level of sensation can only be maintained by increasing doses of stimulant. Tastes jaded by the merely terrible crave for the horrible. And so we have such exhibitions as that of *Heard at the Telephone*, wherein a man, conversing with his wife at a great distance by this instrument, is driven raving mad by hearing thieves breaking into the house and murdering her. He can do nothing; it is as though the murder were being committed in his presence, while he is gagged and bound. Now such incidents do not belong to dramatic art, because that art deals with the collision of human wills, whereas in this incident we have merely the spectacle of human powerlessness. They humiliate our common human dignity. A man overwhelmed by an avalanche is no more than a fly or a gnat. Conceive some man revered among men, a Socrates or a John Wesley or a George Washington, fallen among cannibals, tortured before our eyes, then cooked and eaten—You turn with a faugh! even from the mental picture. So there are things in the massacre of Cawnpur[e] which no one to this day dares to think of. There are some calamities so dreadful, so irreconcilable a rational universe, that we can only writhe over the thought of them with an agonised cry of Why? Why? Why? The dramatist who uses such themes as these (and the telephone story is one of them) is travelling outside the region of art. They belong to the region of what Aristotle called ἀτύχημα, sheer accident, misadventure, the irrational element of life. The sensation excited by the picture of them is too violent to be an aesthetic sensation, we are oppressed and shocked by it, whereas the aim of all art, even of tragic art, is to exhilarate and relieve. For the same reason no skill is demanded for such exhibitions. There is skill in the first scene of *Heard at the Telephone*, wherein we see the family of women left unprotected the lonely house, and fear gradually mastering them a sense grows upon them of something uncanny, some hidden presence in the place. It is the same effect which has been attained, on a higher plane of workmanship, in Maeterlinck's *L'Intruse*. But in the actual telephone scene there is no skill.

The idea suffices of itself. The pit receives the scene with "thunders of applause"? Yes, and the fact suggests a train of by no means agreeable reflections. Evidently the primeval man lurking within us is more potent than some of us had thought; evidently the lust for strong emotion is a far more considerable force than respect for art; evidently we still have our Dandins, with their "Bon! cela fait toujours passer une heure ou deux." Once more the commonplace is brought home to us, that our civilisation is only skin-deep.

Notes

a. Émile Gaboriau (1832–1873), French author of detective stories; and Fortune du Boisgobey (1821–1891), French author of police procedurals.
b. Famed British legal case in which Arthur Orton claimed to be the missing Sir Richard Tichborne and was accepted as such despite significant differences, including an inability to speak French, the real Richard's first language. Orton was convicted of perjury for the hoax in 1874 and sentenced to fourteen years in prison. He served ten and died penniless and obscure in 1898.
c. Belgian Nobel laureate Maurice Maeterlinck (1862–1949), author of the play *L'Oiseau Bleu* (The Blue Bird) (1908).
d. *Isabelle*: "O! Sir, how can one see the unfortunate suffer?" *Dandin*: "Indeed, it is always a pastime for an hour or two" (anonymous 1862 translation).
e. The Seige of Cawnpur (also spelled Cawnpore and, today, Kanpur), during the Sepoy Rebellion of 1857, during which Indians killed a large number of British who surrendered to them after a lengthy siege.

The Welsh author Arthur Machen (1863–1947) is well known for such masterpieces of horror as "The Great God Pan" (1894), *The Three Imposters* (1895), and "The White People" (1904), works of horror and fantasy that drew inspiration from aspects of both scientific romance and tales of mystery and detection. Here follows a review of *The Three Imposters*, a loose novel composed of several short stories, including "The Novel of the Black Seal," from the February 1896 edition of *The Bookman*.

Review of The Three Imposters[*]
THE BOOKMAN

THE THREE IMPOSTORS. By Arthur Machen. Keynotes Series. Boston: Roberts Bros. $1.00.

The horrible is sweet to the taste of Mr. Machen. He plays with it a little frivolously at times, but now and then it does seriously take hold of him, and on some of these occasions it impresses us. A curious medley is

[*]"Novel Notes," *The Bookman: A Literary Journal*, February 1896, 533.

this book of the sensational, the trivial, and the occult. Written on an old plan, some idea of its design and tone may be gathered from thinking of Stevenson's *Dynamiters*, with the sprightliness and fun, but not the frivolity, left out, and with dark occult sin substituted for the grotesque. Every now and again we are struck with admiration of the picturesque and suggestive writing, and sometimes we think the same overweights what had been a better story if more plainly and briskly told. We thought for a time that Mr. Machen was fooling us with his horrible hints (we had forgotten the contents of the prologue). The hunt of the gold Tiberius, the ingenious imaginations of the three impostors, we had thought might end farcically. Perhaps his learning in the black arts would so have been wasted, but we wish he had some restraining qualities that would keep him from writing such horrors as those in his last chapter.

Here follows a review of *The Great God Pan and the Inmost Light* (1894), Arthur Machen's slim volume collecting both title stories, by Richard Henry Stoddard (1825–1903), a poet and the literary editor for the New York *Mail and Express*. This review first ran in the *Mail and Express* before being reprinted unsigned in *The Literary News* for February 1895.

Review of The Great God Pan*
RICHARD HENRY STODDARD

Messrs. Roberts Brothers have lately published here, in conjunction with Mr. John Lane, London, "The Great God Pan," and "The Inmost Light," two comparatively short tales by Mr. Arthur Machen, whose name is new to us, though he figures on his title page as the author of "The Chronicle of Clemendy," and the translator of "The Heptameron" and "Le Mozen de Parvenir." It is not easy to say what these tales are, for though they deal, or profess to deal, with men and women of our own day, and with events of real life, it is in such a fantastic way, and with such extraordinary results, that the impression they leave on the mind is rather that of troubled dreams than of actual or possible occurrences in any country, or condition of society, of which we have knowledge. The scenes of both are apparently laid

*Review of *The Great God Pan*, *The Literary News*, February 1895, 44.

The Great God Pan. At the time Arthur Machen wrote "The Great God Pan," George Barnard sculpted the Greek god in bronze (1894–1899), and presented the sculpture to Columbia University in 1907. The goat-man Pan symbolized the natural world and mankind's animal nature, themes Machen drew upon in developing his much more cosmic and horrific take on the deity, which he identified with the Celtic god Nodens (Library of Congress, Prints and Photographs Division, LC-DIG-ggbain-01493).

in London, but they are really laid in a populous *terra incognita* to that which Poe imagined as the home of his Waldemars and Lenores, and the haunt of his Conqueror Worms. The intellectual quality which the production of such things demands is imagination, the activity of which should not be regulated, but encouraged, without regard to consequences, and their most potent motive should be the elucidation of some scientific or psychological problem, no matter what one, provided it be sufficiently profound and recondite. The transference of the soul of one person to the body of another by hypnotism is not a bad subject, when properly and plausibly handled; and the creation of a new soul from the ashes of an old body affords a large scope for the ingenuities of pseudo chemistry and mysticism. His heroine is a beautiful woman, who ruins the souls and bodies of those over whom she casts her spells, being as good as a Suicide Club, if we may say so, to those who love her; and to whom she is Death. Something like this is, we take it, the interpretation of Mr. Machen's uncanny parable, which is too morbid to be the production of a healthy mind. (Roberts. $1.)—*Mail and Express*.

The Victorian art critic and journalist Harry Quilter (1851–1907) was never one to shy away from expressing his opinions. In 1880, Quilter complained about the Pre-Raphaelite art movement, blasting its expressive art in "The New Renaissance—The Gospel of Intensity." Fifteen years later, Quilter expanded his thesis to include literature. In Quilter's mind, literary realism, horror, and sexuality were linked together, part of a constellation of "intense" traits dominating the contemporary arts scene, and derived from the news media, whose pursuit of sensation had driven all art to celebrate "the beast within" at the expense of the higher virtues of humanity's souls and wholesome and demur literature aspiring to art.

"The Gospel of Intensity" first appeared in the *Contemporary Review* of June 1895. To our purpose, the piece singles out Arthur Machen's recent release of *The Great God Pan* as a particularly loathsome specimen, though it is the interplay he sees between horror, sex, and realism that makes this lengthy critical gem worth reading in full.

The Gospel of Intensity[*]
Harry Quilter

There is one misconstruction against which in writing the following article I am desirous of guarding myself. I do not seek nor wish to put the clock back-

[*]Harry Quilter, "The Gospel of Intensity," *Contemporary Review*, June 1895, 761–782.

ward; I have no desire to limit the provinces of art or literature, or to question the right of either to deal with life as a whole in its every manifestation. On the other hand, I do maintain that life can be dealt with fully and honestly only when it is considered from a healthy and manly (or womanly) point of view. I deny that the morbid extravagances of hysterically neurotic and erotic imagination are to be accepted as a sound basis or a proper sphere of analysis for either art or literature; I am assured that there are some subjects in themselves so repellent, so enervating, and so unprofitable, that they should be practically excluded from the domain of literary discussion or artistic representation. And I consider that it is the absolute duty of every public writer who is engaged in the department of criticism to discourage and condemn work of such character, and even work which leads more or less directly towards it.

I have no right, perhaps, to judge men of whose motives and whose necessities I am practically ignorant; but, as a critic of twenty years' standing, I have not only the right but the obligation to judge their work when I believe that work to be vitally affecting the public welfare. It is my sincere conviction that during the past ten years most of the new departures which have been made in the arts, have been mistaken from the æsthetic point of view, and have been injurious from the moral. I know that if our literature and art are to flourish in the future, they must be in accordance with the great work of the past, with the idiosyncrasies of our national character, and with those decencies and restrictions of thought and emotion which have become a part, and the best part, of ourselves. In that assurance, I have written the words which follow, and I have not endeavoured to tone down too cautiously the expression of my feeling. It is my sincere conviction not only that what I have said is true, but that at the present moment it requires to be spoken in the plainest words. Such words, I hope, will be found herein. That in speaking of them I shall give offence to many I am well aware; but in this matter I recognise no obligation so far as public literary or artistic production is concerned—and with that only have I dealt in this paper.

A curious set-back has taken place during the past few weeks in the currents of journalistic criticism. After three years of indiscriminating, vehement, and unmeasured laudation, the various ladies and gentlemen who are kind enough to instruct us, in the columns of the daily Press, what we should eat, drink, and avoid, have, in æsthetic concerns, wheeled about in an irresolute manner, and are now upbraiding their new divinities. For a moment, the cult of the courtesan and costermonger is out of fashion, and the newest developments of blasphemy, indecency, and disease receive only a half-hearted and timid approval. Nay, there are even to be heard here and there tentative murmurs of distaste, and a half-expressed readiness to return—on due encouragement being given—to the ancient ways. A doubt whether the pace has not been made "too hot" for the public, and consequently for profit, is showing itself in Janus-faced articles; and a general "Please, sir, it wasn't me, sir," resounds from the Press and the critics.

Especially with regard to fiction is this apparent, and certain books, as for instance George Egerton's "Discords," have been cast *ad canes*, as loves to the pursuing wolves of Philistia. Mr. Mudie, in one of those periodical spasms of virtue which we all admire, has withdrawn from circulation "The Strange Adventure of Earl Lavender," that most suggestive, though not perhaps most objectionable, of Mr. John Davidson's works; the evening journals are, for the moment, on their best behaviour; theatres and music-halls, too, are in accord with this momentary depression, and a hardy writer in the *Times* has even dared to suggest (clergymen much protesting) that the Phryne of commerce should be whitewashed, not before, but "behind the curtain." Two or three of the least savoury of the illustrated papers have ceased to exist; another, much loved by our gilded youth, has suffered a prosecution for suggestive pictures; and a shadow of reticence, if not of respectability, has darkened the decidedly go-as-you-please sketches of our younger black and white artists.

Posters, it is true, have not improved, and, in the present writer's opinion, the naked, realistically coloured woman, who leers at the by-standers from the portals of Daly's Theatre, is the most unpleasant street advertisement ever placarded in England; but even here there is a comparative arrest of progress—a fear of the County Council and a certain Act of Parliament.

Lastly, rippling backwards over the retreating wave of feeling, the fall of the great high-priest of æstheticism has struck the public imagination—if not aroused its conscience. For this man,[a] connected by his abilities and his tastes almost equally with the arts of fiction, drama, poetry, and painting, was one whose personality and influence have played a great part in recent art criticism and production*—he was the living embodiment of the theory of *l'art pour l'art*. It is not my business to cast a stone at him, nor have I any wish or intention to dwell upon a subject so unpleasant, but it is necessary to remember that his intimate association with certain phases

---

*It is, I think, not generally known that he was also intimately connected with journalism; for obvious reasons I do not mention the periodical or periodicals in which his lucubrations appeared.

of English art and fiction, in speaking of the public estimation of them at the present time.

In truth, the moment is the psychological one for considering the downward tendency of modern art and criticism; the arrest of the movement is apparent rather than real, but it affords an opportunity to gain a hearing for a few plain words. These words I have, perhaps, as good a right to say as any writer in England, for it is about sixteen years since I pointed out, not once or twice, but in many articles in the *Spectator* and various magazines the evil results likely to follow this "Gospel of Intensity,"* though I little thought at the time that those results would affect literature, drama, and social life to the extent which has actually taken place.

Though I saw that the idea at the root of the æsthetic craze was morbid, uncleanly, and unnatural, and had nothing in common with the loveliness and healthiness of fine art, I was far from anticipating that it would so soon spread from painting and art criticism, to poetry, fiction, and drama, and in effect, in all these, a vital and maleficent change. Still less did I anticipate that, in such a change, the foremost actor—the protagonist of the tragedy, would be—the Press. I did not see in the general upsettal of tradition and decay of faith which were taking place, how likely it was that the old criteria of art and literature, resting as they did in no slight measure on authority and faith, should be abandoned or destroyed, and in their stead substituted the new canons of liberty, glorified in proportion to its licence; of beauty, considered as the supreme good; of emotion as the sole and sufficient guide to, and judge of, conduct. That in such a movement the Press should use and adopt the "art for art's sake" theory, and grow daily less tolerant of the old sanctions, was yet natural enough; as natural as that living, as it must do, on and in the sensations of the minute, it should desire to extend their range, analyse their complexity, and dilate upon their virtues. Here was a new ready-made guide to life which had the double merit of being easy to practise, and amusing to describe; which opened up another field for "copy," even wider and more exciting than that of personal journalism, of which, indeed, it was a natural an inevitable development.

Let me dare to speak plainly: I do so with a full sense of responsibility.

---

*Some of these papers were in the *Spectator*: "The Palace of Art," Spots on the Sunflower," "The Higher Criticism," "The *Cornhill* on Coalscuttles," &c.; in the *Art Journal*: "The Nemesis of Art"; and in *Macmillan's Magazine*: "The Gospel of Intensity," from which I have borrowed the title for the present paper.

The genesis of the books which are being criticised with apparent severity just now, is to be found in the standards of literature lately set up by the Press critics, in the praise which those critics have been bestowing day by day, week by week, and year by year upon similar, though less offensive, works. The very periodicals which blame the books, have, in the truest sense of the word, produced them; they are a logical result from journalistic causes. Both by precept and example have the papers fostered this species of literature; they have even, in many cases, trained the men who produce it, and given birth to their earliest efforts.

Nor is it only in positive encouragement the effect has been produced, for the negative position of the critical Press towards the work of alien quality has been at least equally responsible. If there is no immorality, no indecency, no morbidness in fiction and poetry, which has not received a full meed of praise and analysis, so there has been for the old-fashioned storytellers, no sneer too bitter, no misrepresentation too unjust, no neglect too cruel. I am an old journalist, and have never been accused (amongst my many sins) of wishing to restrict the powers of criticism, or of desiring to render it mealy-mouthed, or unduly reticent; but I confess that of late years I have often felt my blood boil with indignation at the unbearable and concentrated impertinence and injustice with which good work, both in painting and literature, is treated by the reviewers of the new school. To say that such writing is criticism, is absurd, for frequently it has not even the decency to disguise its partisanship, and, in fairness, it is analogous to those unscrupulous club-gentlemen who blackball every candidate but the one whom they have themselves proposed.

That the great daily papers are generally free from this last disgrace, I gladly and thankfully admit, but that it is so prevalent, broadly speaking, as to hopelessly invalidate the opinions expressed, is absolutely certain; indeed, it has been proved to demonstration a hundred times of late. So, too, has the converse been proved, and every one knows what the praise is worth which one author-critic showers upon another of the same school.

Every one behind the scenes knows it; but then, and this is "where the laugh (a bitter one) comes in"; so few people *are* "behind the scenes," and of those few, the majority are dumb. Good-fellowship, self-interest, or fear, shuts the mouth, and the conspiracy of silence is practically complete. Louder, shriller, and more audacious blow, day by day, the trumpets of mutual advertisement; dictionaries are ransacked for the laudatory comminatory adjective; the puff preparatory appears for weeks and months beforehand; the detected and exposed lie forms the text of a hundred articles. No flattery is too fulsome, no exaggeration too absurd to describe the merits of A; no insult too coarse or cruel to characterise B's performances.

The worst offenders have been the evening papers and illustrated journals. These have done even more to degrade art, and excite the animal appetites during the last few years, than erotic fiction or suggestive drama. For novel and play have, after all, to be sought out and highly paid for—no one is forced to read or see such art, willy-nilly. This is not so with the periodicals. At clubs, restaurants, hotels, railway-stations, they force themselves upon our attention; their least desirable pictures ornament the bookstalls, and shop-windows. Moreover, the suggestiveness, the immorality of their work is, in view of police prosecutions and commercial prudence, still slightly veiled—occasionally dubious. The women depicted may have every physical and moral characteristic of the courtesan, but they are rarely labelled as such; nor are the absolute indecencies of gesture and expression common in Parisian journals of the same type permitted. It was, indeed, quite a surprise to the public, a short time since, when one of the "illustrateds" laid itself open to police prosecution, and had to burn a too suggestive issue.

There is, however, a wide margin between pictures which are legally guilty of criminal indecency, and those which are desirable and wholesome, and in this borderland disport themselves many, indeed most, of the new "up-to-date" periodicals. Into that wide-meshed net they have, most unfortunately, succeeded in drawing several of the cleverest of our young artists; and it is nothing less than pitiable to these talented young fellows, with all the fair world of art before them, producing, week after week, pictures of drunkards, costermongers, and *cocottes*, vying with one another in the debasement of their best ideals. The artists are not to blame, save so far as any man is to blame who sells his convictions and his beliefs for a means of livelihood; but I cannot acquit the critics who urge them on, the editors who demand such work, and the public who purchase it. For each of these three classes has a distinct duty, which is thereby neglected. The editor of a periodical is no more entitled to make money by debauching public taste, than a publican by selling unsound wine or spirits; a critic's first most imperative duty is to differentiate between pure and impure, ennobling or degrading art; and having differentiated, to hold up the one and discourage the other; and lastly, it is most certain of all that the public owes a duty to itself and those who minister to its pleasure in this connections, and has no more right to employ artists in depicting what is coarse and degrading, than it would have to pay men to commit acts of a like character.

A short time ago a magazine which had been from its commencement in the hands of one of our prominent publishers, and had obtained a high reputation for the character of its contents, was sold by him, and passed, after a short interval, into the hands of a well-known editor of the new type, who was dissatisfied with its circulation. "Do you know what I am going to do with it?" he said to me. "I'm going to *vulgarise* it!" I explained that he would probably succeed—and he did! I may add that this was not said to me in confidence, but as the definite announcement of the policy he considered absolutely necessary to success.

There is the whole matter in a nut-shell. It is vulgarity which is the *raison d'être* of our new illustrated papers, and they are daily vulgarising England; for though London requires and produces these things, they are diffused throughout the country; and their effect is to be seen in the provincial Press, in advertisements, and theatrical entertainments; and though this species of illustration is of such recent growth, I find a difficulty in accounting satisfactorily for its origin, and for the toleration with which it has been hitherto received. So far as I am aware, no voice of preacher or moralist has, as yet, been raised against it; not artist, either from inside or outside the Academy, has pointed out its offensiveness, and it conflict with all the best traditions of our art history; no critic or journalist has uttered even a passing protest. Nor do the public apparently mind one whit. You shall find such papers lying about casually, not only in "smart" houses, but in decent and otherwise well-regulated households; they are noticed with frequent praise and admiration in the daily Press; Mr. Smith, secure of public approval, exhibits their most engaging plates above his respectable bookstalls. Still more wonderful is it to find interspersed in their pages, between, say, one of Mr. Phil May's costers and Mr. Dudley Hardy's trollops, a portrait of this or that young lady who has written a new book, or made a fashionable marriage, or even done nothing in particular except to be the daughter of her mother.

Is it, I wonder, hopelessly, irredeemably old-fashioned, prudish to feel that there is much that is incongruous, and something that is even repulsive in such conjunction? Ten years ago, we all know the way in which the question would have been answered. Why should there be a doubt to-day? Virtue and vice have not changed from what they were in our youth. Do we really wish to break down all barriers between them? Men and women sin, have always sinned, and will always sin; but shall we put their sins and the fruit of them side by side with the innocence that knows no evil, and the purity that knows no spot? If we owe a debt to the Magdalen, and I for one believe that men do owe pity, help, and comfort, do we owe none also to our *un*fallen sister, and is not at least a portion of that debt respect and reverence? If so, let us say boldly that there is neither—no, nor even any decency or good taste in putting the portraits of pure girls side by side with caricatures of drunken men and shameless females; there is only in such juxtaposition insult and injury. If our women would but pause to think what such collocation means (if they would realise its effect upon men's minds and upon their respect for purity), they would sacrifice what can but be the gratification of a momentary vanity, for the sake of preserving for themselves that delicate reverence, that intense whole-souled admiration, which all men worthy of the name not only give but rejoice in giving to modest womanhood. In such an old-fashioned essay, an old quotation may perhaps be pardoned—the special pleading from the Puritan point of view will, at least, have nowadays the merit of novelty:

> "Was there no poetry in his heart at that thought? Did not the glowing sunset, and the reed-beds which it transfigured before him into sheets of golden flame, seem tokens that the glory of God was going before him in his path? Did not the sweet clamour of the wild-fowl, gathering for one rich pæan ere they sank into rest, seem to him as God's bells chiming him home in triumph, with peels sweeter and bolder than those of Lincoln or Peterborough steeple-house? Did not the very lapwing, as she tumbled, softly wailing, before him, as she did years ago, seem to welcome the wanderer home in the name of heaven?
>
> "Fair Patience, too, though she was a Puritan; yet did not her cheek flush, her eye grow dim, like any other girl's, as she saw far off the red coat, like a sliding spark of fire, coming slowly along the strait fen-bank, and fled upstairs into her chamber to pray, half that it might be, half that it might not be? Was there no happy storm of human tears and human laughter when he entered the courtyard gate? Did not the old dog lick his Puritan hand as lovingly as if it had been a Cavalier's? Did not lads and lasses run out shouting? Did not the old yeoman father hug him, weep over him, hold him at arm's length, and hug him again, as heartily as any other John Bull, even though the next moment he called all to kneel down and thank Him who had sent his boy home again, after bestowing on him the grace to bind kings in chains and nobles with links of iron, and contend to death for the faith delivered to the saints? And did not Zeal-for-Truth look about as wistfully for Patience as any other man would have done, longing to see her, yet not daring even to ask for her? And when

she came down at last, was she the less lovely in his eyes because she came, not flaunting with bare bosom, in tawdry finery and paint, but shrouded close in coif and pinner, hiding from all the world beauty which was there still, but was meant for one alone, and that only if God willed, in God's good time?"[b]

It is not with such work, however, that I am concerned in the present paper; and my next point is to show, by description and example, what the actual character of the writings, paintings, &c., which receive the highest praise in the Press, and to give instances of the actual critical opinions which are quoted by the publisher as inducements to the public to buy the books and art in question. Such examination will reveal the fact that reviewers of many first-rate papers are to-day frequently indifferent to the lubricity, brutality, and morbidity of the works submitted to them for criticism, and so a long first step will have been taken toward establishing their partial responsibility for the spread of such work. I shall further prove, by quotation, that these productions, if described in plain terms, cannot fairly be excused, or even tolerated from the point of view of morality or decency, and that even from the æsthetic standpoint we must revolutionise all the established canons of criticism before we can consider them *tolerable*.

My first instance is a book by Mr. Arthur Morrison entitled "Tales of Mean Streets," and this is peculiarly strong evidence for not only was it received by the Press with practically unanimous laudation, but the stories which form the book had previously appeared in the *National Observer*, *Macmillan's Magazine*, and the *Pall Mall Budget*. We may say, therefore, that they had previously received editorial sanction, and such reception from the public as to render it probable that their issue in permanent form would be desirable. It may be noted in passing that during the editorship of Mr. Henley the *National Observer* was peculiarly noted for this species of story, and I believe there is no doubt but that it was the first weekly newspaper in England to insert such tales as, for instance, "Lizerunt" (Elizabeth Hunt) and "That Brute Simmons."

There is not much story in "Lizerunt," which is the first of Mr. Morrison's "Tales," but that little is full of flavour. The heroine is employed in a pickle factory, and is courted by two lads, her successful suitor apparently recommending himself to her by the gentle acts of twisting her arm, bumping her against the wall, and, in a final paroxysm of affection, landing her one under the ear; further endearing himself to her by hiring six or eight other boys to beat and kick his rival almost to death. Billy Chope (such is the euphonious name of this modern Lancelot) marries "Lizerunt"; the happy couple and the bridegroom's mother get comfortably drunk together, and so the pleasant family life is started. A couple more pages, and we arrive at the main incident of the story—one which I prefer to describe in the author's words:—

> "At last Lizer ceased from going to the pickle factory, and could not even help Billy's mother at the mangle for long. This lasted for near a week, when Billy, rising at ten with a bad mouth, resolved to stand no nonsense, and demanded two shillings. 'Two bob! Wot for?' Lizer asked. 'Cos I want it. None o' yer lip!' 'Ain't got it,' said Lizer, sulkily. 'That's a bleedin' lie!' 'Lie yerself!' 'I'll break y'in 'arves, ye blasted 'eifer!' He ran at her throat and forced her back over a chair. 'I'll pull yer face auf! If y' don't give me the money, gawblimy, I'll do for ye!' Lizer strained and squalled. 'Le' go! You'll kill me an' the kid too!' she grunted, hoarsely. Billy's mother ran in and threw her arms about him, dragging him away. 'Don't Billy!' she said, in terror. 'Don't Billy—not now! You'll get in trouble. Come away! She might go auf, an' you'd get in trouble!' Billy Chope flung his wife over and turned to his mother. 'Take yer 'ands auf me,' he said; 'go on, or I'll gie ye somethin' for yerself!' And he punched her in the breast by way of illustration."

The next episode in this cheering tale is the moment of the husband's assault upon his wife, on the day of her confinement; its interruption by the dispenser, who kicks him out-of-doors; and of Lizer's gratitude for this rescue, which again deserves quotation in the original:—

> "When he returned to the room, Lizer, sitting up and holding on by the bed-frame, gasped hysterically: 'Ye bleedin' makeshift, I'd 'ave yer liver out if I could reach ye! You touch my 'usband, ye long pisenin' 'ound you!' Ow! And, infirm of aim, she flung a cracked teacup at his head. Billy's mother said, 'Y'ought to be ashamed of yourself, you low blaggard. If 'is father was alive 'e'd knock yer 'ead auf. Call yourself a doctor—a parcel o' boys—! Git out! Go out o' my 'ouse, or I'll give y'in charge!' ... 'But—why, hang it, he'd have killed her.' Then to Lizer. 'Lie down.' ... 'Sha'n't lie down. Keep auf; if you come near me I'll corpse ye. You go while ye're safe!'
>
> "And he went: leaving the coast clear for Billy Chope to return and avenge his kicking."

The last horrible scene of all which ends this "strange eventful history," is the husband driving forth his wife into the streets, to seek there, in a manner which is not left doubtful, the means of supplying him with drink and tobacco.

Such is "Lizerunt," and such the "Tales of Mean Streets," which the

Athenæum describes as being ["]told with consummate art and extraordinary detail," and of which "the very truth makes for beauty"; and the *World* cries rapturously that it is "a great book," the work of "a master hand"—of "appalling and irresistible genius," and so on, and so on, while even the *Spectator* describes Mr. Morrison's art as "convincing and excellent," and devotes two columns to a mild protest against life in the East End being uniformly as he depicts it.

Are such criticisms and eulogisms in any sense true or just? Leaving out of all account for the moment the effect upon manners and morals of such writing, can it be properly called either Literature or Art?

Well, the first quality of art is to give pleasure—to be delightful. Whatever else may be lacking, that is is a primal necessity. Apply the test here. Can any sane human being take pleasure in, or gain delight from, this squalid story of drunkenness and brutality? But perhaps it may be urged there are elements of excitement and interest in the scenes here depicted which redeem its repulsive aspects, or the construction of the story may be so skilful and elaborate as to give enjoyment; to which it is a sufficient answer to say, that in the relation of these incidents there is, strictly speaking, no attempt at construction whatever, no end achieved or sought for, no working out of character no connection of events. There is not even that sense of the inevitable, that causal relation of personage and circumstances which is of the very essence of a good story, whether it be brought about by the action of character upon events, or traces the effect of events upon character. So, too, is there lacking the element of contrast; there is no shadow in the picture, although the author has used the blackest tints of his palette, because there is no light. All the actors in whom we are asked to take an interest are equally ignoble, and, the author is at some pains to assure us, equally base—the drama has no protagonist, no beginning, no end. Nor, lastly, has it any characters. For character is not realised by giving police-court descriptions of such and such a series of incidents, and it may be confidently asserted that no single reader of this episode would recognise, on meeting, a single individual therein—nor carries away with him the most transient belief in the personal identity of Billy Chope or Lizer Hunt, or any one else. As a city is not a city without inhabitants, so is a story not a story if there are not real people therein, no matter how dull or uninteresting. Indeed, if the people are real, their doings cannot be quite uninteresting, as it would be easy to show by a hundred famous examples.

There remains, perhaps, the contention that though we cannot consider "Lizerunt" a story, it may deserve the name of a work of art; the truth to reality, the very unselectedness, the repulsiveness, even, may demand our admiration from the point of view of realism. The contention is hardly one which any artist would make or uphold, and is also entirely untenable. For no scene can be true imaginatively, in which we lack the elements of belief, and belief in conduct is, in fiction as in drama, an outgrowth from knowledge and personality. The addition of details to a shadow will not make it live; the accuracy with which the coarse language of the streets is reproduced will not show us Billy Chope or Lizer Hunt in *propriâ personâ*, will not differentiate them from the thousands of equally degraded or suffering Billies or Lizers. We have only to make a mental comparison of Mr. Morrison's work with fiction which deals with similar subjects in a truly artistic manner* to perceive the total lack of construction and informing motive, the absence of all epic quality, the powerlessness of the author to arouse in us any emotion of pity for, or sympathy with, his puppets. They dance, it is true, obediently and vigorously enough to his piping, showing, indeed, much superfluity of idiom and gesture; but they fail to move us, and we know them no more that we care for and indentify the figures in one of those strange battle-scenes by Gustave Doré, where heads and limbs chopped off and mangled lie about in every direction.

To further discuss the reason why such stories as these cannot be considered literature is, I think, superfluous; we might as well go through the evidence for a photograph not being a work of art. And in many respects such merits as Mr. Morrison's work possesses are photographic, not literary. The language employed is the lowest slang of the streets. Are we to call that literature because it is printed in a book? "Not along of you, cheeky; you go 'long o' Beller Dawson, like wot you did Easter"; this is the language of literature? But of this and such-like language are the stories mainly composed. The word literature is ridiculous in such a connection; the tales in question are neither more nor less than dramatic journalism of a particularly depressing sort. They are full of acute observation, but observation of the reporting kind; they shed no light upon the East End, awake no sympathies for its sorrows, no understandings of its joys. They might indeed be not untruly said to shed darkness, to widen the breach between those who read them and those whose lives they depict;

*Cf. "The Record of Badalia Herodsfoot," by Mr. Rudyard Kipling.

and this is the root-reason why they are bad art and bad morality. One *may* touch dirt without being defiled, but it must be for a noble and sufficient purpose, not for curiosity, not with indifference; and this holds equally good of readers and writers.

I must leave this analysis incomplete; it has already occupied a proportion of the brief space at my disposal which is only justified because the considerations advanced therein are, in a great measure, applicable to all books of this class, and to much of the illustrated journalism of to-day.

Leaving now Mr. Morrison, who is at least a man, and one whose work is in touch with real life, let us consider the writers who are responsible for a still more unpleasant class of fiction, which has, until the past few weeks, received great and uniform encouragement from the Press. The word sexual has been lately used to describe this work, but not, as I think,

The Battle of Ascalon. Gustave Doré illustrated editions of Dante's Inferno, *Milton's* Paradise Lost, *and Poe's* "The Raven." *In his best work, his style combined highly detailed and realistic techniques with fantastic and horrific subject matter to produce uncanny works of art. Speaking of the uncanny effects of Doré and the Romantic painter Henry Fuseli (who painted the well-known* Nightmare *[1781]) in the story "Pickman's Model" (1926), H. P. Lovecraft wrote, "I don't have to tell you why a Fuseli really brings a shiver while a cheap ghost-story frontispiece merely makes us laugh. There's something those fellows catch—beyond life—that they're able to make us catch for a second. Doré had it." Doré's (1881) depiction of the Battle of Ascalon is shown here to illustrate Harry Quitter's allusion to the horrific imagery of Doré's war art (Library of Congress, Prints and Photographs Division, LC-USZ62-99457).*

with any accuracy or propriety. The books are not sexual, but neurotic, and though, after the fashion of the day, there is a preponderance in them of sensual subject, their essence, their differentia is hysteria—induced by morbid conditions of the brain and heart. Nor is it the sexual instinct which gives to these books their power for evil; it is the disguise, the transformation of this instinct; the alliance of it with art, with religion, with a species of bastard socialism, and the abandonment, under the pretence of introducing a higher morality, of all restriction upon emotional feeling. The worst of these books rely for their attractiveness and subject matter upon those morbidities of desire which are as repugnant to healthy men as they are to pure-minded women; they are, so to speak, from first to last, quivering with nervousness, for ever seeking the purpler blood of pain which throbs through the heart of pleasure*—seeking it, yes, and lingering over it, making it the cadence of the song, striving to persuade the reader that this, and this alone, is life and beauty. In this attempt, the younger school of critics and journalists have aided and inspired the writers; indeed, the writers themselves have, in many instances, turned critics for the occasion, and praise one another with a splendour of laudation which almost defeats its object.

Let us take, as instance, the *Keynotes* series, so named after the first volume by George Egerton. I have read all the most important of these, and it is not an exaggeration to say that there is not one, which is not morbid, painful, and depressing. Leaving altogether out of the question the morality or good taste of the sketches of prostitution, imaginaries devilries, or loathsome eccentricity which form the subject matter of such books as "Discords," by George Egerton, "The Parasite," by Conan Doyle, "The Great God Pan," by Arthur Machen, and "The Woman who Did," by Grant Allen,† and, even assuming for the moment that subjects of this kind are not in themselves totally unfit for treatment in story-form, what can we think of the critical faculty and veracity which describe such stories in the highest terms of praise; which claim for them a place beside the masterpieces of our literature; and, for each author known or unknown, the position of high genius and supreme literary excellence? Yet those publishers who bring out these books, and many others of similar quality, have not difficulty in filling their circulars with such verdicts, and that not from

---

*Pace Swinburne.
†A dozen others equally objectionable might easily be cited, including the various volumes of the *Yellow Book*.

obscure provincial journals, but from the most important daily and weekly papers. For instance, "The Great God Pan" is, I have no hesitation in saying, a perfectly abominable story, in which the author has spared no endeavour to suggest loathsomeness and horror which he describes as beyond the reach of words. Here are two specimens, that readers may judge for themselves:

> "Though horror and revolting nausea rose up within me, and an odour of corruption choked my breath, I remained firm. I was then privileged or accursed, I dare not say which, to see that which was on the bed, lying there black like ink, transformed before my eyes. The skin, and the flesh, and the muscles, and the bones, and the firm structure of the human body that I had thought to be unchangeable, and permanent as adamant, began to melt and dissolve.
> "I knew that the body may be separated into its elements by external agencies, but I should have refused to believe what I saw. For here there was some internal force, of which I knew nothing, that caused dissolution and change.
> "Here too was all the work by which man had been made repeated before my eyes. I saw the form waver from sex to sex, dividing itself from itself, and then again reunited. Then I saw the body descend to the beasts whence it ascended, and that which was on the heights go down to the depths, even to the abyss of all being. The principle of life, which makes organism, always remained, while the outward form changed.

* * * * * *

> "I watched, and at last I saw nothing but a substance as jelly. Then the ladder was ascended again ... for one instant I saw a form, shaped in dimness before me, which I will not further describe. But the symbol of this form may be seen in ancient sculptures, and in paintings which survived beneath the lava, too foul to be spoken of ... as a horrible and unspeakable shape, neither man nor beast, was changed into human form; there came, finally, death."

Surely it is strange that a book not only contains these things, but which contains nothing else save the preparation for their elucidation, should be praised and recommended for its very vices, for its horror and bestiality, by respectable newspapers. Yet here they are, all apparently delighted with what the *Telegraph* calls these "blood-chilling masterpieces." Who can blame the poor chap whose imagination has here run riot, if he considers himself, and is considered by his friends for the future, as a very clever fellow, the pioneer of a new class of literature? Who can blame young writers if, seeing such things win praise and success, they follow in his footsteps, and endeavour to surpass him in his own strain? Who can

Frontispiece to The Great God Pan. *Aubrey Beardsley's Art Nouveau style and erotic subject matter scandalized conservative social critics at the end of the nineteenth century, but today his works often appear tamer and more tasteful than the Victorians would have viewed them. This illustration (1895) from the title page of Arthur Machen's* The Great God Pan *depicts an androgynous Pan with his mythological accoutrements, goat horns and the Pan pipes.*

wonder even at the nasty little naked figure of dubious sex and humanity with which Mr. Aubrey Beardsley[c] has prefaced the story—in all truth a most fitting introduction.

There is but one point of view from which such writing can be tolerated, and that is the point of view of those who deny that there is any obligation, any responsibility laid upon a writer not to produce unwholesome work. If this be so, it seems to me absolutely necessary that all restrictions whatsoever as to decency and propriety must also be removed. Why should we tolerate in our fiction that which we could not tolerate in our conversation or our life? Why should we allow a novelist to describe abortions, moral and physical, which in reality would fill us with horror and disgust? What conceivable right have two men, author and publisher, to collaborate together for the purpose of writing, printing, and distributing stories which can conceivably do no good, and which, in all human probability, will do a great deal of harm? Here in this book, "The Great God Pan," there are two tales in which there is no attempt to do anything but suggest a nameless horror—a horror which the author foams himself into a frenzy in the attempt to describe. Why should he be allowed, for the sake of a few miserable pounds, to cast into our midst these monstrous creations of his diseased brain?* A very grave responsibility rests with the publishers of such work, and still more with the public critics. There is no doubt whatever but that the appetite for such productions increases in proportion to the supply; there is no doubt also that the Press could practically stamp out such fiction in a few months if so disposed. And that disposition *must be acquired, must even be enforced;* the school of criticism which, for the last few years, has been fostering such fiction and art must be detected, exposed, and destroyed; and the interested verdicts, chiefly of personal friends, which have succeeded in causing such work to be momentarily accepted, must no longer find a place in respectable journals.

It is ridiculous to talk about the power of the Press, and its claims upon our admiration and gratitude, if that power is not to be exerted beneficially in matters which are distinctly of public importance. And I fear there can be no doubt that much of the writing and art which is today receiving its first blast of unfavorable criticism, has had its origin in the sensational journalism, which may be said to have started with the first publication of the *World* newspaper in 1874, and which has from that to this increased in volume and extravagance—has become almost daily more unscrupulous and more irresponsible. It is not only that newspapers of this kind have multiplied in number and deteriorated in quality, but it is demonstrably the fact that there is scarcely one of the older newspapers which has not been injuriously affected by the new journalism. Readers accustomed to sensational writing and sensational art are scarcely able to tolerate the old-fashioned style of news, in which the events are simply and soberly told, and the comments upon them are made with moderation and some degree of impartiality. Exaggeration is the very essence of the modern journalistic article, the very use of the headline† almost enforces it. Is it not, therefore, most natural that the writers of fiction and poetry should follow in their accounts of imaginary life the system which their journalistic comrades daily prove to them to be the most popular? Does it not stand to reason that if we cannot tolerate the plain account of a fact, we can still less tolerate the plain account of a fiction; that if we force ourselves to use habitually the most vehement, the most coloured

---

*The second story is called the "Inmost Light," and is, if anything, more detestable than the first.
†From America.

words in our vocabulary in reporting the simplest occurrences, we shall also use a similar intensity of phrase in describing our imaginary concepts? And from using these phrases the step is very short to a similar exaggeration of incident—a similar indifference to ordinary reticence and selection.

Let us take a single instance of the manner in which this affects poetry; and to make this the more fairly illustrative, I will select, not the work of any of the less able and less meritorious of our minor poets, but the verse of one who has distinct traces of genius, who has undoubtedly a fine ear for melody, and who has also that eminent poetic gift of selecting the impressive, and, if I may use the phrase, the inevitable word. With all these merits, with a strong, almost dominant personality, with plenty of ideas, and apparently great facility in expressing them, with an utter absence of platitude, and few traces of imitative quality, this author has yet nevertheless, within the last few months, produced some work which appears to me to be frankly blasphemous, and unprovokedly immoral. He has done this in poetry, and in prose he has written a book which positively beggars description, but of which the character may be guessed from the frontispiece by Mr. Aubrey Beardsley, which represents a half-naked woman with pendulous breasts, flogging the back of a man who kneels before her. The name of this work, which the *Times* mildly mentions as being descriptive of a new order of Flagellants, is "The Strange Adventure of Earl Lavender," and the name of the poet-author is Mr. John Davidson. I do not propose to say any more of this story than that I am pleased to see Mr. Mudie has at length removed it from his lists. But that it should have been written by a man of Mr. Davidson's literary pretentions, and published by a respectable firm, appears to me most wonderful. Turning to Mr. Davidson's poetry, here is the story, in plain English, of the Ballad which has received most praise in the daily and weekly Press, and to the analysis of which even the once cautious editors of the *Spectator* devote more than a column of laudatory notice. A young nun grows discontented with the convent life as animal passion increases within her. She leaves the convent by night in carnival time, and running half-naked to the town, offers her virginity (in so many words*) to the first man who takes her fancy. Her fall accomplished, she continue her amatory pilgrimage throughout the other towns of the province, till she has worn out her desire. Then she

---

*"'Your love, your love, sweet lord,' she said;
'I bring you my virginity.'"

returns to the convent, also by night, the door is opened to her by a portress, identical in appearance with herself before the days of her fall, but who speedily discovers herself to be the Virgin Mary, who has come down from heaven for the express purpose of preventing the discovery of the nun's absence. The Virgin explains to the nun that she is now sister to God, as well as sister to the mountains, and the day and night, whatever that relationship may mean, and so disappears.

Perhaps there may be something hopelessly puritanic and narrow-minded in my view of this poem, but I do think that the idea is one of the most thoroughly nasty ones which I have ever seen put into verse or prose. If taken as an allegory, the obvious lesson taught is that the more utterly we give way to the beast with us, the more surely we receive the grace of the divinity above. And if this be not a most objectionable and misleading doctrine, I should like to know what can be called so. To my mind the sensuality of the poem, though it is intense, and thrust upon the reader in every verse, is made infinitely more intolerable by the introduction of the religious element, and the connection of spiritual emotion with what is, in plain words, nothing but the gratification of lust.

In saying these words I am not unaware that one of our purest singers anticipated in "The Legend of Provence" the subject of Mr. Davidson's ballad. There is, however, between Miss Proctor's[d] treatment of the theme, and that of our modern author, an essential difference; not only is the motive of the nun's fall removed from the desire to gratify a purely sensual impulse, but the whole working out of the succeeding disenchantment, repentance, and final return is reticent, dignified, and absolutely free from offensiveness. Moreover, the point of the whole poem in Miss Proctor's version is that on the nun's return the figure which greets her (also the embodiment of the Blessed Virgin) is not herself as she was when she left the convent, but as he *might have been* had she stayed:—

> "She saw—she seemed to know
> A face that came from long long years ago;
> Herself; yet not as when she fled away,
> The young and blooming novice, fair and gay,
> But a grave woman, gentle and serene,
> The outcast knew it,—what she might have been."

And lest her meaning should even then be missed, the authoress points out in her own person (as was the fashion then) the inner meaning of her legend, the eternal possibility of repentance:

"But still our place is kept, and it will wait
Ready for us to fill it, soon or late;
No star is ever lost we once have seen,
We always may be what we might have been."

Some readers of this paper will possibly be aware of the opinions which the present writer has not infrequently expressed concerning the latest developments of English painting, such as are seen, to take a typical instance, at the so-called New English Art Club. And as these developments are intimately connected with the character of modern illustrated journalism, it is necessary to briefly consider their origin and meaning. This is the more desirable, as one species of art, which promises to be greatly extended in the immediate future—that is, the art of pictorial advertisement, has, chiefly owing to the recommendation of the Press, fallen almost entirely into the hands of artists of this new Anglo-Gallic school. Indeed, several of the New English Art Club men are prominent designers of street posters, play-bills, and other advertisement placards. They are also rapidly coming to the front as book illustrators; and journals like the *Sketch, Pick-Me-Up, To-day, In Town, St. Paul's, et id genus omne,* rely almost exclusively upon the services of eight or ten draughtsmen, all of whom are of this school, though the majority do not actually belong to the club in question. The most prominent of these are, Mr. Phil May, Mr. Dudley Hardy, Mr. Rothenstein, Mr. Maurice Greiffenhagen, Mr. Raven-Hill, Mr. Townsend, Mr. Lewis Baumer, Mr. Birkenreuth, and "Mars."

It may be as well to mention here that some of the signatures to these picture are wholly fanciful ones, and occasionally in the same paper there may be two drawings, of which one signed by the artist's real name, and the other by some *nom de plume* assumed for that occasion only. I think that this is a most objectionable practice, and one which editors should strongly discourage. Mr. Aubrey Beardsley confessed in a recent interview that he had similarly deceived the public in one issue of the *Yellow Book.* I did not see the drawings in question myself.

But it would be most unfair, whatever may be the faults of the ordinary black and white illustrator, to class him with one artist whose work has received of late the highest praise, especially from the art critics. This is Mr. Aubrey Beardsley—a prominent member of the New English Art Club, who first became known to the public by his illustrations to a book entitled, "Bells and Pomegranates," written by Mr. Oscar Wilde, and who subsequently illustrated an edition of the "Morte d'Arthur," and has since been employed to design frontispieces and other illustrations to many works of the erotic and decadent schools. Mr. Beardsley is a young man of decided and original ability, but I do not think there can be any two opinions as to the use he has made of his genius. There is, to the present writer, something absolutely repulsive in this artist's renderings of humanity, and in the general savour of his compositions. By the side of them, the most up-to-datedly improper of Dudley Hardy's young ladies, the most vehemently vulgar of Phil May's 'Arriets are wholesome and cleanly. Much of the form of the drawing has been borrowed from Burne-Jones, and, as I believe Mr. Beardsley himself admits, from Puvis de Chavannes, but the spirit belongs entirely to the artist himself, and I dare express it no more definitely, than by saying that however unnatural, extravagant, and morbid are the stories and poems of the modern decadence, which I shall have occasion to mention in this paper, there is not one of them which is more perverted in what it says and suggests than these grotesques, in which the types of manhood and womanhood are, as it were, mingled together, and result in a monstrous sexless amalgam, miserable, morbid, dreary, and unnatural. Mr. Beardsley says, in defence of his sensual conceptions, that most human faces are sensual, and that he goes for his types to a certain *café*, It is a pity, methinks, that the address of that *café* should not be made public, for very certainly if the men and women in these drawings, with these expressions, are its habitual frequenters, a whiff of grape-shot would do the whole establishment good, and clear the moral atmosphere into the bargain. I am not going to dwell upon this subject, but I beg all readers who may think that my words are upon these points exaggerated, to examine these drawings for themselves and form their own conclusion. And I remind all critics who have tolerated, and even praised, Mr. Beardsley's work for its ingenious eccentricities, that the first duty of a writer upon art is remember that the worst offenders against the cause of fine and healthy art, are those who seek to exalt debased types of humanity, and to delineate unnatural and unwholesome emotions. Think, for one moment, only of what art has been in the past, of the intense elevating pleasure if has given to millions, and shall yet give in the days to come; and then say whether it is tolerable that we should permit and favour a species of design which is corrupt to the last degree, enfeebling and enervating. Just fancy a nation of Beardsleys! Conceive politics, commerce, law, and religion approached from this standpoint, applied in this manner. And yet, why not? Art is, we are told with sickening reiteration, but a reflection of life; why should we not have a Beardsley bishop addressing a Beardsley congregation, or, say, Mr. Gully, *à la* Beardsley, reproving an emasculated House of Commons? It is easy to see the ridiculous side of this work; easy and, of course, pleasant to disregard it altogether; but the neglect does harm, and the ridicule passes lightly over those who are likely to enjoy such conceptions. And since it is beyond doubt that this art has been made the handmaid of a very morbid species of literature, and has in that service achieved great success and emolument, it is essential that all those who attempt to point out the demoralising effect of the fiction and poetry in question, should point out also this artistic connection.

In comparison with such work one is almost tempted to praise the spirit which distinguishes the drawings of Mr. Phil May and Mr. Hardy, and their numerous imitators, especially since the fine technical quality of these artists do so much to disguise the coarseness of the scenes and the vulgarity of the people with which they present us. But though I do not for a moment class their work from the emotional and moral point of view with that of the above-mentioned artist, it must, nevertheless be acknowledged that it is of distinctly deteriorating character. The spirit of it is the Parisian Boulevard spirit, and is in no sense either national, refined, or desirable. I should like, had not the word been so discredited of later, to say that it is not even respectable. Indeed, Mr. May may be said to absolutely revel in a sort of comic disreputability, which, I am sorry to say, his genius frequently renders most amusing.

I have no desire to speak harshly of the work of any genuine artist, and I confess to an almost admiring wonder at the extraordinary brilliance and cleverness of Mr. Hardy's advertisement cartoons, and at the intensely vivid and artistic realisations of character and humour of Mr. Phil May.

But when all this is said, the effect upon the public mind of the subjects habitually chosen, and the method in which they are treated, is undoubtedly depraving; for either the pictures deal with, and extract their humour from, coarse and vulgar subjects, or they appeal frankly to the sensual emotions. I say frankly, but the appeal is very frequently neither frank nor direct; the suggestion of the *cocotte* is made. She is not labelled; very often she is disguised as a lady.

But no one who remembers the illustrated papers before the new movement set in, will deny that their general aspect has been entirely changed, and is to-day French, where, ten years ago, it was distinctly and exclusively English. This change necessarily familiarises the readers in general, and young people in particular, with vices and vulgarities which should have no place in their lives at all, and which, if they must be made acquainted with, should not be used as the vehicle of casual amusement.

The deteriorating effects of such drawings, however, does not cease with the drawings themselves, and the actual harm which each or all of them produce; for the constant looking at designs executed in this spirit, creates the appetite which is depicted or suggested, and debauches the taste for work which is less animal and less exciting. In this it is exactly analogous to sensational journalism, and does, as a matter of fact, go hand in hand therewith. Just think in this connection the history of *Punch* for the last fifty years. Not a faultless paper in many respects, but at least there has been this conspicuous merit, that up to the last two or three years there has not been a single picture therein in which vulgarity was predominant. Not a single picture, and as I may say, to the best of my belief, not a single joke. Yet I think no one can well maintain that the new journals mentioned above are more amusing, more manly, or more national.

What is to be the end of this? For as yet we are but at the beginning. Can we contemplate with patience the probability that in another ten years we shall have a "La Vie de Londres," equivalent in intention and grossness to "La Vie Parisienne," and a little laughter journal, which shall do for Phryne of London what its prototype has done for Phryne of Paris. For this must come unless we abandon our present course. I have left out one chief influence which makes such abandonment extremely difficult, and which has been responsible for much of the change above described, and that is the influence of the actor and actress, and of those who regard their profession as alone worthy of serious attention. Here, too, journalists and editors have been much to blame. The dramatic wave which has overspread London, and partially inundated the provinces, has had its volume and its currents increased and multiplied by the press, which has given an amount of attention and glorification to everything connected with the stage which is totally unparalleled in the past, or even at the present time, in any other country than ours.

And this influence has been uniformly bad in its effect upon art, as upon morality. Cheap advertisement is of its essence, and in this game of brag the opportunities afforded by the illustrated interview and the reduplication of actors' and actresses' portraits are of the utmost importance. Some papers may be almost said to exist for the sole purpose of reproducing innumerable likenesses of any dramatic or music-hall artist who may happen to be popular. In many numbers it will certainly not be an exaggeration to say that such interviews, and the illustrations accompanying them, fill half the journal; and, as the pictures are made as flattering as possible, and the interviewer simply reproduces any statements which are made to him by the lady or gentleman in question, the total result is a continual glorification of the stage and its personages, which represents everything in a light as false as it is attractive. And on this subject every mortal being who writes or speaks seems afraid to open his mouth. Editors implore you, almost with tears in their eyes, not to say anything which can possibly reflect upon this immaculate race. "For Heaven's sake, my dear fellow," said one to me but a fortnight since, "don't bring that hornets' nest about my ears!" And he, too, was a bold man, comparatively young in the editorial chair, and with but a slight experience of the thorns in its cushion. So long, however, as this awe and this delirious and almost driveling adulation of the player continues, we must, I suppose, expect that editors, who, after all, are men of business, will swim with the stream, especially when the stream rings them for nothing pictures and copy. *The public have the matter in their own hands.* If they cannot see that they have of their own folly exalted those who were their humble servants into the position of their tyrannical masters; if they continue to accept the manners and morals of the actor and actress as worthy of their deepest admiration and most loving study; if they really think that the most desirable fate for nice English girls is to be flung into that hotbed of egotism, vice, and vanity—then it were folly to expect that those who are interested in the continuance of the present boom, should puncture the bladder.

This paper began with a confession; it shall end with a prophesy; I believe that the day will come, and that very shortly, when the present revolt against belief and modesty will cease to be a distinguishing mark of our art, our literature, and our journalism. I believe that we shall cease to imitate the worst vices of our French neighbours, and to glory in the imitation. I believe that music-hall comiques will cease to receive the wages of Prime Ministers. I believe that actors and actresses will return to their proper place—the place, that is, of paid servants of the public, who are esteemed, not only for excellence in the profession to which they belong, but only in so far as their lives are decent and their abilities genuine. I believe that sensational journalism has had its day, and that the level of the servants' hall is that to which it is doomed quickly to descend. I believe that novelists will soon not dare to publish, what they certainly would not dare to speak. I believe that critics will be afraid to praise such production. I believe that editors will be ashamed to employ the critics who do. I believe that poets will recur to the old beauties of the world, which are *not* identified with what we used to call vice and blasphemy. I believe that painters will find better subjects than are now furnished them in East-End public-houses, and West-End music-halls. And I believe that, partly in consequence of these changes, we shall laugh more and sneer less; that our girls will no longer imitate our manners and our costume, but be content with their own, which are, after all, infinitely better; and that our men will no longer struggle after a pretence of effeminacy which sits upon them extremely ill. And lastly, I believe, that somehow, after some strange, unexpected fashion, there will come back into the world some substitute for the old faith in God, and reverence for those things which are fair, lovely, and of good report. And even if this latter change includes, as well may be, no return of the old hope that once simplified life and sweetened death, I believe that there will remain to us the enjoyment of the simple, natural emotions, and such sense of duty to ourselves and others as may suffice for patience and consolation. In the words of my old master,[e] who taught me most of the things worth knowing which I have ever learnt: "Free-heartedness, and graciousness, and undisturbed trust, and requited love, and the sight of the peace of others, and the ministry to their pain; these, and the blue sky above you, and the sweet waters and flowers of the earth beneath; and mysteries and presences innumerable of living things may yet be here your riches; untormenting and divine, serviceable for the life that now is; nor, it may be, without promise of that which is to come."

Notes

a. Quilter is speaking of Oscar Wilde here; Wilde went on trial for sodomy a few weeks before this article appeared.

b. Quoted from Charles Kingsley's "Plays and Puritans" (1873).

c. Aubrey Beardsley (1872–1898) was an English illustrator best known for his erotic drawings. He illustrated an edition of Wilde's *Salomé* and edited the Decadent publication *The Yellow Book*, which was referenced in Wilde's *Dorian Gray* as an agent of corruption. Quilter discusses Beardsley in greater depth later in the article.

d. Adelaide Anne Procter (1825–1864) was a Roman Catholic convert who crafted poetry celebrating faith and other topics; her poems went through many editions and were praised by Charles Dickens, a family friend.

e. The art and social critic John Ruskin (1819–1900), tireless promoter of neo–Gothic architecture. The following quotation is from *The Crown of Wild Olive* (1866).

The author and book lover A. Edward Newton's (1863–1940) *Amenities of Book Collecting and Kindred Affections* (1918) was a best seller geared to "the tired business man" "who flatters himself that he is fond of reading," moving 25,000 copies in its initial run. In this passage from the chapter on "Oscar Wilde," Newton considers Wilde's (1854–1900) one and only novel, the horror classic *The Picture of Dorian Gray* (1890).

*Excerpt from "Oscar Wilde"**

A. EDWARD NEWTON

[...] "Dorian Gray," Wilde's one novel, appeared in the summer of 1890. It is exceedingly difficult to place: his claim that it was the work of a few days, written to demonstrate to some friends his ability to write a

Oscar Wilde. "No artist is ever morbid," Oscar Wilde wrote in his preface to The Picture of Dorian Gray. *"The artist can express everything."* Critics disagreed, however, and saw Wilde's novel as dangerous, wicked, and an affront to morals, in part due to its homoerotic or *"effeminate"* undertones. Wilde himself received similar treatment when he was tried and convicted of sodomy in 1895. His two years in prison broke his health, and he died three years after his release. Image dated 1882 (Library of Congress, Prints and Photographs Division, LC-DIG-ppmsca-07756).

*A. Edward Newton, *The Amenities of Book Collecting and Kindred Affections* (Boston: The Atlantic Monthly Press, 1918), 329–331.

novel, may be dismissed as untrue—there is internal evidence to the contrary. It was probably written slowly, as most of his work was. In its first form it appeared in "Lippincott's Magazine" for July, 1890; but it was subjected to careful revision for publication in book form. Wilde always claimed that he had no desire to be a popular novelist—"It is far too easy," he said.

"Dorian Gray" is an interesting and powerful, but artificial, production, leaving a bitter taste, as of aloes in the mouth: one feels as if one had been handling a poison. The law compels certain care in the use of explosives, and poisons, it is agreed, are best kept in packages of definite shape and color, that they may by their external appearance challenge the attention of the thoughtless. Only Roosevelt can tell without looking what book should and what should not bear the governmental stamp, "Guaranteed to be pure and wholesome under the food and drugs act."[a] Few, I think, would put this label on "Dorian Gray." Wilde's own criticism was that the book was inartistic because it has a moral. It has, but it is likely to be overlooked in its general nastiness. In "Dorian Gray" he betrays for the first and perhaps the only time the decadence which was subsequently to be the cause of his undoing.

I have great admiration for what is called, and frequently ridiculed as, the artistic temperament, but I am a believer also in the sanity of true genius, especially when it is united, as it was in the case of Charles Lamb, with a fine, manly, honest bearing toward the world and the things in it; but alone it may lead us to yearn with Wilde

> To drift with every passion till my soul
> Is a stringed lute on which all winds can play.[b]

It has been suggested on good authority that it is very unpleasant to wear one's heart upon one's sleeve. To expose one's soul to the elements, however interesting in theory, must be very painful in practice: Wilde was destined to find it so. Why the story escaped success at the hands of the adapter for the stage, I never could understand. The clever talk of the characters in the novel should be much more acceptable in the quick give-and-take of a society play than it is in a narrative of several hundred pages; moreover, it abounds in situations which are intensely dramatic, leading up to an overwhelming climax; probably it was badly done.

It is with a feeling of relief that one turns from "Dorian Gray"—which, let us agree, is a book which a young girl would hesitate to put in the hands of her mother—to Wilde's other prose work, so different in character. Of his shorter stories, his fairy tales and the rest, it would be a delight to speak: many of them are exquisite, and all as pure and delicate as a flower, with as sweet a perfume. They do not know Oscar Wilde who have not read "The Young King and the Star Child," and the "Happy Prince." That they are the work of the same brain that produced "Dorian Gray" is almost beyond belief.

Notes

a. Referring to Theodore Roosevelt, under whose administration the Pure Food and Drug Act (1906) was enacted to regulate the quality of medicines and food.
b. Quoted from Wilde's poem "Hélas" (1881).

A member of the Spanish Generación del 1898, Ramiro de Maeztu (1874–1936) wrote mostly in Spanish but from 1905 lived in England, where he served as a foreign correspondent, until his return to Spain in 1919. During the First World War, he produced *Authority, Liberty, and Function in the Light of the War* (1916) in English, later translated into Spanish as *La crisis del humanismo*, a collection of articles originally written for *The New Age*. In "Art and Luxury," the author writes about Wilde's *Dorian Gray* and concludes that such works no longer satisfy—or horrify—in light of the war. A version of the article first ran in *The New Age* for April 15, 1914—before the war—and was revised for the book in light of it.

*Art and Luxury**
RAMIRO DE MAEZTU

Many artists feel anxious when they think of the possible reaction the war may have on the life of the arts and on culture in general. As war implies destruction of wealth in large proportions, these people have the impression that for many years to come men will devote their activities exclusively to re-making their lost fortunes in an existence of poverty and toil in which there will be neither time for leisure nor money for luxuries. Believing that the function of art is sumptuary or decorative, they conclude that if, in the next few years, there will be no money for luxuries,

---

*Ramiro de Maeztu, *Authority, Liberty, and Function in the Light of the War: A Critique of Authority and Liberty as the Foundations of the Modern State and an Attempt to Base Societies on the Principle of Function* (London: George Allen and Unwin, 1916), 159–168.

there will be none for the arts either; and they fear that, in the absence of Mæcenases, the rose-bush of the arts will wither throughout the lands of Europe, as the flora and fauna of the high steppes of Asia died out when Divine Providence removed to other regions of the globe the clouds that fertilized them with their rain.

This belief that art is one of the articles of luxury is so widespread, not merely among the Philistines but among artists themselves, that if you ask a painter what is the object of a picture you will be told in most cases that "the object of a picture is to adorn a wall." The answer is commendable in its humility. By it the painter is placed in the category of artisans—carpet-weavers, furniture-makers, or paper-hangers; and even when placed in this category the painter is not the first among the artisans, but the last. For, in truth, the most decorative picture ever painted will always be less decorative than a mirror, a panoply of arms, a velvet curtain, or a chandelier, since the material a painter makes use of, his poor colours, will always be less luxurious and less rich than marble and metal and light and velvet.

The curious thing is that this absurd idea that art is an article of luxury has been spread by the same men who gave up their lives to waving the banner of art for art's sake. I say it is a curious thing because the decorative conception of art is expressed by the formula of art for luxury's sake, and this formula is obviously incompatible with that of art for art's sake, unless we are prepared to agree to the proposition that art and luxury are one and the same thing. Shall we agree to this, just for the moment? Anatole France prophesied ironically in one of his books that there would come a day when the famous actresses of Paris, instead of declaiming and singing on the stage, would present themselves at the footlights, completely naked, and each of them carrying a bar of gold; and the public would applaud with the maximum of enthusiasm the naked woman who exhibited the biggest bar of gold. I do not suppose any other arguments are needed to show that luxury is not art. But the fact that the standard-bearers of art for art's sake—Théophile Gautier[a] in France and Oscar Wilde in England—were also the propagandists of art for luxury's sake makes it clear that there was a fundamental error in their attitude, an error that, rendered it unstable; and if we can root out this error we shall have killed two birds with one stone: art for art's sake and art for luxury's sake.

What is most surprising in the formula of art for art's sake is that it refers to a novelty which contradicts the artistic traditions of a thousand years. Beethoven did not write the Heroic Symphony solely for the joy of making music, but he wrote it in the service of the French Revolution and in honour of its hero, General Bonaparte. Milton did not write "Paradise Lost" with the sole aim of bequeathing a poem to us, but in order that—

> I may assert eternal Providence,
> And justify the ways of God to men.

And Michelangelo did not paint the Sistine Chapel only for the purpose of decorating a wall, but to depict before our eyes the omnipotent will of Jehovah. You may tell me that I have chosen examples of our own Christian art. But the Greeks, the most artistic people that ever lived.... "The Greeks had no art-critics," wrote Wilde in his "Intentions." But the truth about Greek art is much deeper than that. The truth is that the Greeks never spoke of beauty as something distinct from knowledge or morality, religion or life. The word "beautiful" was never used by them to designate an autonomous cultural value. The ideal of every good Hellene was to be a perfect gentleman, and a gentleman could not achieve perfection if he did not die a noble death. Both of the perfect gentleman and of a noble death the Greeks said they were beautiful. And the most artistic people the world has known never used the word "beautiful" without giving to it the moral signification of perfection.

The Greeks had no art-critics because they had no æsthetics; but æsthetics is philosophy and not art. The depuration of the conception of beauty, the distinction between the form and matter of the work of art, is necessary for the philosopher, and perhaps also for the art-critic. But for the artist it is unnecessary. Not only unnecessary: it is impossible to achieve. In the heat of artistic creation the form is not and cannot be more than love for the matter of the work. No artist has ever conceived a work from pure love of art, but from love of a given subject. Art is love, and love does not love itself. Not even Gautier and Wilde could practise the doctrine of art for art's sake. Their formula can be accepted only as a battle-cry guiding art towards its emancipation from the tyranny of didactics. It was a device of some value against the people who sought to turn art into a weapon of pedestrian puritanism. But when Gautier and Wilde tried to separate art from morality and knowledge they found that art for art's sake was a wheel of wind wheeling the wind; and to find sustenance for it they had to harness it to the service of luxury, vice, and decoration.

Far from being a pure artist, Gautier was the apostle of a moral idea.

A contemporary of the Sardanapalian pictures of Delacroix, of the "Orientales" of Victor Hugo, of the Orientalist ethics of the Saint-Simonists, and of the first French expedition to Northern Africa, Théophile Gautier preaches the redemption of the world by means of a universal animalism. People are now in the habit of regarding his novels, "Fortunio" and "Mademoiselle de Maupin," as pornographic books; but they are more than that. They are exhortations to pornography. Comte Georges, in "Fortunio," has a politico-social idea, the idea that the State should compel beautiful women to exhibit themselves naked from time to time so that taxpayers should not lose the sense of colour and form. For Gautier, of course, love and lust are the same thing: "No woman resists so obstinately as virtue with ill-shaped knees"; "One woman is as good as another, if she is as pretty"; "Among beautiful and strong natures love is gratitude for satisfaction."

But this animalism of Gautier's is in a way a derivation. Gautier was primarily a reader of the works of other writers. He read with so much impressionability that at the end of a single perusal he was able to repeat by heart 185 lines of Victor Hugo's verses. For his friends he was a kind of dictionary. He hated the reality of his age because "in this civilization, which cares only about raising soap and candle makers on pedestals, one loses the sensation of the beautiful." Thus the formula of art for art's sake had for Gautier no other meaning than that of a mediatization of reality, an escape from it. He could not look at a woman or a landscape without asking himself, "Who would have painted that?" He would call a garden "a Watteau park." He remarked of his Fortunio and his Musidora: "It was a Giorgione beside a Lawrence." Only when he realized that a man could not go on evoking works of art all his life did he get beyond the formula of art for art's sake and annex it to the service of life. But Gautier's idea of life, based, as he based it, on the negation of morality and knowledge, was that of an animalism scarcely disguised under the veil of luxury.

The case of Oscar Wilde is almost identical with that of Théophile Gautier, whom he often quotes in his writings. "The Picture of Dorian Gray" was not written merely for art's sake. Wilde tells us that he wished to express by Dorian Gray "the true realization of a type of mind which they have often dreamed in Eton or Oxford days, a type that was to combine something of the real culture of the scholar with all the grace and distinction and perfect manner of a citizen of the world." Dorian Gray is not merely a character in a novel, but the incarnation of "a new Hedonism that was to recreate life and to save it from that harsh, uncomely puritanism that is having, in our own day, its curious revival." The fact that Dorian Gray comes to an unfortunate end in the novel—and in the life of Oscar Wilde—does not mean that the author repudiates his motto, "to cure the soul by means of the senses, and the senses by means of the soul," formulated again in the phrase, "culture and corruption." Dorian Gray dies as the heroes of tragic dramas and of novels of the first order had to die—"Don Quixote," "Madame Bovary," "Wuthering Heights," or "Anna Karenina." Such heroes die because one of the categories of art is the religious; and the religious category is essentially Death and Resurrection. But Dorian Gray is not killed by Wilde out of punishment, but out of love, because he is a hero; and Wilde expects to see Hedonism arising from his grave, as Christianity arose from the Cross. And there are still people who see in Oscar Wilde the precursor and martyr of the new Hedonism: "culture and corruption."

But that is not to preach art for art's sake, but art for luxury's sake, for pleasure's sake, art for the sake of "refinement" or decoration. And not art alone, but life itself—life as understood by the "smart set." The main chapter of "Dorian Gray" is certainly not more than an idealization of the "smart set." "Like Gautier," writes Wilde, "Dorian Gray was one for whom 'the visible world existed'"; "And, certainly, to him life itself was the first, the greatest, of the arts"; "His modes of dressing had their marked influence on the young exquisites of the Mayfair balls and Pall Mall windows"; "The Roman ritual had always a great attraction for him"; "And for a season he inclined to the materialistic doctrines of the '*Darwinismus*' movement in Germany"; "Yet no theory of life seemed to him to be of any importance compared with life itself"; "And so he would now study perfumes, and the secrets of their manufacture, distilling heavily scented oils, and burning odorous gums from the East"; "At another time he devoted himself entirely to music, and in a long latticed room, with a vermilion-and-gold ceiling and walls of olive-green lacquer, he used to give curious concerts"; "On one occasion he took up the study of jewels"; "Then he turned his attention to embroideries." Here you have the complete circle: dandyism, religion, "*Darwinismus*," perfumes, embroideries, jewels, and music "in a long latticed room."

This description of Dorian Gray, of course, is nothing more than an idealized paraphrase of Théophile Gautier's "Notice" of Charles Baudelaire, prefixed to the definitive edition of "Les Fleurs du Mal," the book that Oscar Wilde's hero possessed, "bound in some Nile-green skin that has been powdered with gilded nenuphars and smoothed with hard ivory." As Baudelaire had really lived, Gautier could not tell us that he went to balls covered with

560 pearls, like Dorian Gray; but he does tell us, giving all the details, that Baudelaire enjoyed symphonies and perfumes, insolent-looking coiffures, "in which something of the actress and the courtesan was mingled," cats which were attracted by essences, "cats that the smell of valerian threw into a kind of ecstatic epilepsy," cold, cunning, and perverse women, " who carry into the soul the vice of the body," and the Black Venus of Madagascar. The coincidence between Gautier and Wilde is due to the fact that there was common to them a strange belief that both Nature and the human mind had exhausted their creative capacities. Life had already engendered its riches: it only remained to enjoy them. Art had already produced its wonders: they had only to be recorded. From this vision of Nature as something finished is born the animalism of Gautier, and from his conception of art comes his technique, which consists in reproducing the image that another artist had wrested from reality. In the case of Oscar Wilde, too, his parasitic Hedonism springs from his retrospective philosophy of life; and from his retrospective æsthetic comes his conception of modern art as a mere evocation of ancient art. In his essay, "The Critic as Artist," he goes the length of declaring resolutely that "as civilization progresses and we become more highly organized, the elect spirit of each age, the critical and cultured spirits, will grow less and less interested in actual life, and *will seek to gain their impressions almost entirely from what art has touched.*" Both in life and in art his ideal was marginal—luxury.

In this cult there was the mistaken but saving conviction that an article of luxury must be carefully elaborated by a skilful artificer. I say "saving" because it led Gautier and Wilde to perfect their manner of using the material they worked with—words—and to give to other artists the sound advice not to be satisfied, when executing a work of art, with their good moral intentions. But I say "mistaken" because in the article of luxury the essential thing is not the form but the rarity of the material—gold, skin, or diamonds—or the quantity of labour displayed at our command. The object of luxury resembles the object of art in that both are expressions of power; but, while the object of luxury is only, the expression of property or monopoly, the work of art tells us, through the power of the means of expression, that man is the master of Nature. Craftsmanship means power. In the object of luxury the thing to be shown is the power of the proprietor. In the work of art the essential thing is the power of the artist.

The world of Gautier and Wilde is dead. The coming generations, whether they like it or not, must be the children of this war that found

The Breath of the Hun. Though the death toll and brutality of the First World War were more horrific than the literary horrors of Victorian fiction, governments and media used the language of literary horror to describe the struggle against the enemy. In The Bookman *in 1917, Florence Finch Kelly described Germany as "the Frankenstein of the twentieth century." On March 28, 1918, as seen here, the* New York Herald *depicted a Germanic figure as a ghostly, monstrous "enemy alien menace" threatening the streets of New York (Library of Congress, Prints and Photographs Division, LC-DIG-ppmsca-07747).*

Europe dancing the Argentine tango and will leave it dancing to the tune of St. Vitus. The horrors and the bloodshed show us that either Nature or the human mind has at any rate lost its powers of destruction. But even now, in the middle of night, one may perceive new streaks of hope and of creation. The very need of knowing the causes and conditions of this catastrophe must bring us nearer the elements of human nature, and hence into the possibilities of a better life. This may involve a whole renovation of politics, ethics, economics, and of all the humanities. We have to think in the next few years for the half-century during which we ceased to think. And with the new ideals will come the desire to realize them immediately.

In this desire immediately to realize ideals we must see one of the categories of artistic creation as distinct from mere evocation. The secret of art will not be unravelled until we have a philosophy capable of constructing a satisfactory aesthetic. All the aesthetics conceived hitherto have told the truth; not one of them saw more than partial aspects of the beautiful. The beautiful is more than a synthesis between what is and what ought to be (Kant), more than the perceptible apparition of the idea (Hegel), more than pure feeling (Cohen), more than the intuition of the individual (Croce), and much, much more than an article of luxury. Humboldt said that a work of art placed human nature "at a point whence rays surged out in all directions into the infinite." It is a union of reality and ideal, of present and eternity, of soul and body, of the empiric and the necessary; a present realization of religious hopes; a reconciliation of man with all the spiritual and material elements, external and internal, past and future, of his life; because it is a sign—but only a sign, not a proof: not even a sincere promise—that this world has a meaning.

That is why art will not cease because Europe may become poorer. The poorer we are the more we shall need it, for it will not be possible for us to lull our souls with the narcotic of luxury. Lyric poetry was never paid for in England, except in the case of Lord Tennyson. No other Mæcenases have fed it but the tears of the poets. And lyrics are one of the things that make of England one of the faces of God upon the earth.

Notes

a. Théophile Gautier (1811–1872) was a poet, playwright, novelist, and critic whose diverse works included historical novels and poetry about death. Gautier followed the philosophy of "l'art pour l'art," art whose sole purpose was to be artistic.

6. Ghosts and Kindred Horrors

Caroline Miles (1866–1951), later Caroline Miles Hill, earned one of the University of Michigan's first doctorates in 1892 and was active in psychology, social work, and literary efforts. The following question was one of fifteen Miles asked of one hundred women, including 71 students and 29 faculty members, at Wellesley College "during the winter of 1893–94." They were then questioned a second time, with 97 responding. The questions covered a broad range of topics intended to provide a psychological profile of the individuals responding. Question F came from the section on "Emotions and Preferences" and deals specifically with horror. Question E had asked respondents to discuss their childhood fears, of which most had feared (in descending order) darkness, animals (dogs and cows), repulsive creatures (like snakes), human beings (including drunks and "rude boys"), the supernatural, thunderstorms, and "everything." The study first ran in the *American Journal of Psychology* in 1893.

Excerpt from "A Study of Individual Psychology"*

CAROLINE MILES

F. Question: Mention a good ghost story, *i.e.*, something that gives you the creepy feeling supposed to characterize ghost stories.

Replies on second questioning (97 cases): Eighty (80) told stories which they thought creepy. Twelve (12) could tell none, were not sufficiently impressed to remember them. Five (5) told stories with a humorous turn at the end, which seemed to be the thing for which they were remembered,

*Caroline Miles, "A Study of Individual Psychology," *American Journal of Psychology*, vol. 6 (1893): pp. 547–548.

not for the mysterious part. The stories mentioned were all read to find the element which gives the creepy feeling. Many, of course, involve several elements of the fearful, but such a classification of elements as can be made gives the following table:

> Of 80 stories which were thought creepy:
> 32 involved something unexplained, *i.e.*, one-third of all the replies were real ghost stories.
> 22 were stories of insanity.
> 16 were stories involving moral horror, as well as other sorts of fear, *e.g.*, Dr. Jekyll and Mr. Hyde.
> 10 were stories of murder, torture, snake stories, or stories about finding a corpse unexpectedly.

While none of the categories under *F* exactly match those of *E* and while *F* asked for stories of one kind of fear only, some general points of resemblance are interesting. The stories of murder, torture, snakes, and the like in *F*, are analogous to the sense fears in *E* and perhaps depend more immediately on sense imagery for their effect than the others. Stories of insanity and the fear of the insane are of common origin. The real ghost stories involve darkness and its fears together with those of the unknown and of mysterious power. An entirely new kind of fear appears in the moral horror group, a mark perhaps of the adult audience for which such stories are written. The feeling inspired by "Dr. Jekyll and Mr. Hyde," or by Mrs. Shelley's "Frankenstein," swallows up the mere physical sensations and makes them instruments of a moral repulsion. Hyde's external appearance and his crimes are repulsive to contemplate, but the story means little to him who sees only the bare incredible facts. Ibsen's "Ghosts" is repulsive as any idiocy is repulsive, but there is more than mere idiocy, there is awe before the forces of nature which make sin its own punishment. This is like the fear of darkness in that it is individual helplessness, but it is much more complex. It includes many kinds of sense-fears plus associations with moral ideals that do not exist for the young child. The ghost stories that affect one most are those in which there is a skillful accumulation and interweaving of all sense-fears. Among these ghost stories Poe's tales, Lytton's "The House and the Brain,"[a] and a story, originally from the German, called "The Gold Arm,"[b] were mentioned equally often. Stories of being watched by a pair of eyes peeping through a rent in a curtain or a crack in the floor received the next highest number of votes, and after them a story in *Harper's Magazine* for 1859, called "What was It?"[c] An examination of the plots of these stories shows most interestingly how the artificial fear is worked up; fears of the sense types are common but generally subordinate, the fears of others are described and excite our own by sympathy or imitation, the whole scene of the story is gradually shifted from the ordinary world of daylight and known forces to a world in which man is the sport of mysterious and unknown powers. The appeal to the senses is never to all at once; a presence can sometimes be felt but not seen, sometimes seen or heard bat not touched; sometimes it is only the effects of its acts which appear. The actual shudder of fear is generally the result of a special sensory appeal.

Notes

a. "The Haunted and the Haunters; or, The House and the Brain" (1859), by Sir Edward Bulwer-Lytton.
b. Most likely a reference to "The Golden Arm," an English fairy tale best known from the works of Joseph Jacobs and Mark Twain about a man haunted by the ghost of his wife, who comes to reclaim the golden arm he stole from her grave. A similar story, "The Golden Leg," comes from Germany and was in circulation in the nineteenth century. In it, a gravedigger steals a dead child's golden artificial leg, and the child's ghost comes to reclaim it.
c. By Fitz-James O'Brien. See page 65 and page 144.

When Lafcadio Hearn, whom we met earlier discussing "Gothic Horror," taught English literature at the University of Tokyo between 1896 and 1903, he spoke slowly so his Japanese students, who were listening to a foreign tongue, could take careful notes for later study. His students' verbatim transcripts allowed Prof. John Erskine to reconstruct his impromptu lectures, which he published in several volumes after Hearn's death. "The Value of the Supernatural in Fiction" explains Hearn's theory that "ghostly" literature is a result of dreams and nightmares, the real origins of supernatural beliefs. It was delivered at the University of Tokyo in 1898 and published in *Interpretations of Literature* in 1915.

*The Value of the Supernatural in Fiction**
LAFCADIO HEARN

The subject of this lecture is much more serious than may appear to you from this title. Young men of your age are not likely to believe in ghosts, nor inclined to consider the subject as worthy of attention. The

*Lafcadio Hearn, "The Value of the Supernatural in Fiction," in *Interpretations of Literature, vol. II*, ed. John Erskine (New York: Dodd, Mead and Company, 1915), 90–103.

first things necessary to understand are the philosophical and literary relations of the topic. Let me tell you that it would be a mistake to suppose that the stories of the supernatural have had their day in fine literature. On the contrary, wherever fine literature is being produced, either in poetry or in prose, you will find the supernatural element very much alive. Scientific knowledge has not at all diminished the pleasure of mankind in this field of imagination, though it may have considerably changed the methods of treatment. The success of writers of to-day like Maeterlinck[a] is chiefly explained by their skill in the treatment of the ghostly, and of subjects related to supernatural fear. But without citing other living writers, let me observe that there is scarcely any really great author in European literature, old or new, who has not distinguished himself in the treatment of the supernatural. In English literature, I believe there is no exception—even from the time of the Anglo-Saxon poets to Shakespeare, and from Shakespeare to our own day. And this introduces us to the consideration of a general and remarkable fact, a fact that I do not remember to have seen in any books, but which is of very great philosophical importance; there is something ghostly in all great art, whether of literature, music, sculpture, or architecture.

But now let me speak to you about this word "ghostly"; it is a much bigger word, perhaps, than some of you imagine. The old English had no other word for "spiritual" or "supernatural"—which two terms you know, are not English but Latin. Everything that religion to-day calls divine, holy, miraculous, was sufficiently explained for the old Anglo-Saxons by the term ghostly. They spoke of a man's ghost, instead of speaking of his spirit or soul; and everything relating to religious knowledge they called ghostly. In the modern formula of the Catholic confession, which has remained almost unchanged for nearly two thousand years, you will find that the priest is always called a "ghostly" father—which means that his business is to take care of the ghosts or souls of men as a father does. In addressing the priest, the penitent really calls him "Father of my ghost." You will see, therefore, that a very large meaning really attaches to the adjective. It means everything relating to the supernatural. It means to the Christian even God himself, for the Giver of Life is always called in English the Holy Ghost.

Accepting the evolutional philosophy which teaches that the modern idea of God as held by western nations is really but a development from the primitive belief in a shadow-soul, the term ghost in its reference to the supreme being certainly could not be found fault with. On the contrary, there is a weirdness about this use of the word which adds greatly to its solemnity. But whatever belief we have, or have not, as regards religious creeds, one thing that modern science has done for us, is to prove beyond all question that everything which we used to consider material and solid is essentially ghostly, as is any ghost. If we do not believe in old-fashioned stories and theories about ghosts, we are nevertheless obliged to recognise to-day that we are ghosts of ourselves—and utterly incomprehensible. The mystery of the universe is now weighing upon us, becoming heavier and heavier, more and more awful, as our knowledge expands, and it is especially a ghostly mystery. All great art reminds us in some way of this universal riddle; that is why I say that all great art has something ghostly in it. It touches something within us which relates to infinity. When you read a very great thought, when you see a wonderful picture or statue or building, and when you hear certain kinds of music, you feel a thrill in the heart and mind much like the thrill which in all times men felt when they thought they saw a ghost or a god. Only the modern thrill is incomparably larger and longer and deeper. And this is why, in spite of all knowledge, the world still finds pleasure in the literature of the supernatural, and will continue to find pleasure in it for hundreds of years to come. The ghostly represents always some shadow of truth, and no amount of disbelief in what used to be called ghosts can ever diminish human interest in what relates to that truth.

So you will see that the subject is not altogether trifling. Certainly it is of very great moment in relation to great literature. The poet or the story-teller who can not give the reader a little ghostly pleasure at times never can be either a really great writer or a great thinker. I have already said that I know of no exception to this rule in the whole of English literature. Take, for instance, Macaulay,[b] the most practical, hard-headed, logical writer of the century, the last man in whom you would expect to find the least trace of superstition. Had you read only certain of his essays, you would scarcely think him capable of touching the chords of the supernatural. But he has done this in a masterly way in several of the "Lays of Ancient Rome"—for example, in speaking of the apparition of the Twin Brethren at the battle of Lake Regillus, and of Tarquin haunted by the phantom of his victim Lucretia. Both of these passages give the ghostly thrill in a strong way; and there is a fainter thrill of the same sort to be experienced from the reading of parts of the "Prophecy of Capys." It is because Macaulay had this power, though using it sparingly, that his work is so great. If he had not been able to write these lines of poetry which I referred to, he could not even have made his history of England the living history that it is. A man who has no ghostly feeling can not make anything alive, not even a page of history or a page of oratory. To touch men's souls, you must know all that those souls can be made to feel by words; and to know that, you must yourself have a "ghost" in you that can be touched in the same way.

Now leaving the theoretical for the practical part of the theme, let us turn to the subject of the relation between ghosts and dreams.

No good writer—no great writer—ever makes a study of the supernatural according to anything which has been done before by other writers. This is one of those subjects upon which you can not get real help from books. It is not from books, nor from traditions, nor from legends, nor from anything of that kind that you can learn how to give your reader a ghostly thrill. I do not mean that it is of no use for you to read what has been written upon the subject, so far as mere methods of expression, mere effects of literary workmanship, are concerned. On the contrary, it is very important that you should read all you can of what is good in literature upon these subjects; you will learn from them a great deal about curious values of words, about compactness and power of sentences, about peculiarities of beliefs and of terrors relating to those beliefs. But you must never try to use another man's ideas or feelings, taken from a book, in order to make a supernatural effect. If you do, the work will never be sincere, and will never make a thrill. You must use your own ideas and feelings only, under all possible circumstances. And where are you to get these ideas and feelings from, if you do not believe in ghosts? From your dreams. Whether you believe in ghosts or not, all the artistic elements of ghostly literature exist in your dreams, and form a veritable treasury of literary material for the man that knows how to use them.

All the great effects obtained by poets and story writers, and even by religious teachers, in the treatment of super-natural fear or mystery, have been obtained, directly or indirectly, through dreams. Study any great ghost story in any literature, and you will find that no matter how surprising or unfamiliar the incidents seem, a little patient examination will prove to you that every one of them has occurred, at different times, in different combinations, in dreams of your own. They give you a thrill. But why? Because they remind you of experiences, imaginative or emotional, which

El sueño de la razon produce monstruos (The Sleep of Reason Produces Monsters). Goya's "The Sleep of Reason" (1799) depicts the artist asleep while dangerous, demonic animals approach. Horror writers like Mary Shelley and H. P. Lovecraft found inspiration in their dreams, where the irrational is given free rein and the cold light of reason yields to wilder impulses. Lafcadio Hearn found in dreams the source of all supernatural tales. This is an 1868 print of a 1799 Goya work (Library of Congress, Prints and Photographs Division, LC-USZC4-13029).

you had forgotten. There can be no exception to this rule—absolutely none. I was speaking to you the other day about a short story by Bulwer Lytton, as being the best ghost story in the English language. The reason why it is the best story of this kind is simply because it represents with astonishing faithfulness the experiences of nightmare. The terror of all great stories of the supernatural is really the terror of nightmare, projected into waking consciousness. And the beauty or tenderness of other ghost stories or fairy-stories, or even of certain famous and delightful religious legends, is the tenderness and beauty of dreams of a happier kind, dreams inspired by love or hope or regret. But in all cases where the supernatural is well treated in literature, dream experience is the source of the treatment. I know that I am now speaking to an audience acquainted with literature of which I know practically nothing. But I believe that there can be no exception to these rules even in the literature of the Far East. I do not mean to say that there may not be in Chinese and in Japanese literature many ghost stories which are not derived from dream-experience. But I will say that if there are any of this kind, they are not worth reading, and can not belong to any good class of literature. I have read translations of a number of Chinese ghost stories in French, also a wonderful English translation of ghostly Chinese stories in two volumes, entitled "Strange Stories from a Chinese Studio," by Herbert Giles. These stories, translated by a great scholar, are very wonderful; but I noticed that in every successful treatment of a supernatural subject, the incidents of the story invariably correspond with the phenomena of dreams. Therefore I think that I can not be mistaken in my judgment of the matter. Such Japanese stories as I could get translations of, obeyed the same rule. The other day, in a story which I read for the first time, I was very much interested to find an exact parallel between the treatment of a supernatural idea by the Japanese author, and by the best English author of dream studies. The story was about a picture, painted upon a screen, representing a river and a landscape. In the Japanese story (perhaps it has a Chinese origin) the painter makes a sign to the screen; and a little boat begins to sail down the river, and sails out of the picture into the room, and the room becomes full of water, and the painter, or magician, or whoever he is, gets into the boat and sails away into the picture again, and disappears forever. This is exactly, in every detail, a dream story, and the excellence of it is in its truth to dream experience. The same phenomena you will find, under another form, in "Alice in Wonderland," and "Through the Looking Glass."

But to return to the point where we left off. I was saying that all successful treatment of the ghostly or the impossible must be made to correspond as much as possible with the truth of dream experience, and that Bulwer Lytton's story of the haunted house^c illustrates the rule. Let us now consider especially the literary value of nightmare. Nightmare, the most awful form of dream, is also one of the most peculiar. It has probably furnished all the important elements of religious and supernatural terror which are to be found in really great literature. It is a mysterious thing in itself; and scientific psychology has not yet been able to explain many facts in regard to it. We can take the phenomena of nightmare separately, one by one, and show their curious relation to various kinds of superstitious fear and supernatural belief.

The first remarkable fact in nightmare is the beginning of it. It begins with a kind of suspicion, usually. You feel afraid without knowing why. Then you have the impression that something is acting upon you from a distance—something like fascination, yet not exactly fascination, for there may be no visible fascinator. But feeling uneasy, you wish to escape, to get away from the influence that is making you afraid. Then you find it is not easy to escape. You move with great difficulty. Presently the difficulty increases—you can not move at all. You want to cry out, and you can not; you have lost your voice. You are actually in a state of trance—seeing, hearing, feeling, but unable to move or speak. This is the beginning. It forms one of the most terrible emotions from which a man can suffer. If it continued more than a certain length of time, the mere fear might kill. Nightmare does sometimes kill, in cases where the health has been very much affected by other causes.

Of course we have nothing in ordinary waking life of such experience—the feeling of being deprived of will and held fast from a great distance by some viewless power. This is the real experience of magnetism, mesmerism; and it is the origin of certain horrible beliefs of the Middle Ages in regard to magical power. Suppose we call it supernatural mesmerism, for want of a better word. It is not true mesmerism, because in real hypnotic conditions, the patient does not feel or think or act mentally according to his own personality; he acts by the will of another. In nightmare the will is only suspended, and the personal consciousness remains; this is what makes the horror of it. So we shall call the first stage supernatural mesmerism, only with the above qualification. Now let us see how Bulwer Lytton uses this experience in his story.

A man is sitting in a chair, with a lamp on the table beside him, and is reading Macaulay's essays, when he suddenly becomes uneasy. A shadow falls upon the page. He rises, and tries to call; but he can not raise his voice above a whisper. He tries to move; and he can not stir hand or foot. The spell is already upon him. This is the first part of nightmare.

The second stage of the phenomenon, which sometimes mingles with the first stage, is the experience of terrible and unnatural appearances. There is always a darkening of the visible, sometimes a disappearance or dimming of the light. In Bulwer Lytton's story there is a fire burning in the room, and a very bright lamp. Gradually both lamp and fire become dimmer and dimmer; at last all light completely vanishes, and the room becomes absolutely dark, except for spectral and unnatural luminosities that begin to make their appearance. This also is a very good study of dream experience. The third stage of nightmare, the final struggle, is chiefly characterised by impossible occurrences, which bring to the dreamer the extreme form of horror, while convincing him of his own impotence. For example, you try to fire a pistol or to use a steel weapon. If a pistol, the bullet will not project itself more than a few inches from the muzzle; then it drops down limply, and there is no report. If a sword or dagger, the blade becomes soft, like cotton or paper. Terrible appearances, monstrous or unnatural figures, reach out hands to touch; if human figures, they will grow to the ceiling, and bend themselves fantastically as they approach. There is one more stage, which is not often reached—the climax of the horror. That is when you are caught or touched. The touch in nightmare is a very peculiar sensation, almost like an electric shock, but unnaturally prolonged. It is not pain, but something worse than pain, an experience never felt in waking hours.

The third and fourth stages have been artistically mixed together by Bulwer Lytton. The phantom towers from floor to ceiling, vague and threatening; the man attempts to use a weapon, and at the same time receives a touch or shock that renders him absolutely powerless. He describes the feeling as resembling the sensation of some ghostly electricity. The study is exactly true to dream-experience. I need not here mention this story further, since from this point a great many other elements enter into it which, though not altogether foreign to our subject, do not illustrate that subject so well as some of the stories of Poe. Poe has given us other peculiar details of nightmare-experience, such as horrible sounds. Often we hear in such dreams terrible muffled noises, as of steps coming. This you will find very well studied in the story called "The Fall of the House of Usher." Again in these dreams inanimate objects either become alive, or suggest to us, by their motion, the hiding of some horrible life behind them—curtains, for example, doors left half open, alcoves imperfectly closed. Poe has studied these in "Eleonora" and in some other sketches.

Dreams of the terrible have beyond question had a good deal to do with the inspiration both of religious and of superstitious literature. The returning of the dead, visions of heavenly or infernal beings,—these, when well described, are almost always exact reproductions of dream-experience. But occasionally we find an element of waking fear mixed with them—for example, in one of the oldest ghost stories of the world, the story in "The Book of Job." The poet speaks of feeling intense cold, and feeling the hairs of his head stand up with fear. These experiences are absolutely true, and they belong to waking life. The sensation of cold and the sensation of horror are not sensations of dreams. They come from extraordinary terror felt in active existence, while we are awake. You will observe the very same signs of fear in a horse, a dog, or a cat—and there is reason to suppose that in these animal cases, also, supernatural fear is sometimes a cause. I have seen a dog—a brave dog, too—terribly frightened by seeing a mass of paper moved by a slight current of air. This slight wind did not reach the place where the dog was lying; he could not therefore associate the motion of the paper with a motion of the wind; he did not understand what was moving the paper; the mystery alarmed him, and the hair on his back stood up with fear. But the mingling of such sensations of waking fear with dream sensations of fear, in a story or poem, may be very effectually managed, so as to give to the story an air of reality, of actuality, which could not be obtained in any other way. A great many of our old fairy ballads and goblin stories mixed the two experiences together with the most excellent results. I should say that the fine German story of "Undine" is a good example of this kind. The sight of the faces in the water of the river, the changing of waterfalls and cataracts into ghostly people, the rising from the closed well of the form of Undine herself, the rising of the flood behind her, and the way in which she "weeps her lover to death"—all this is pure dream; and it seems real because most of us have had some such experiences of fancy in our own dreams. But the other part of the story, dealing with human emotions, fears, passions—these are of waking life, and the mixture is accomplished in a most artistic way. Speaking of Undine obliges me also to speak of Undine's predecessors in medieval literature—the medieval spirits, the *succubæ* and *incubi*, the sylphs and salamanders or salamandrines, the whole wonderful goblin population of water, air, forest, and fire. All the good stories about them are really dream studies. And coming down to the most romantic literature of our own day, the same thing must be said of those strange and delightful stories by Gautier, "La Morte Amoureuse," "Arria Marcella," "Le Pied de Momie." The most remarkable is perhaps "La Morte Amoureuse"; but there is in this a study of double personality, which complicates it too much for purposes of present illustration. I shall therefore speak of "Arria Marcella" instead. Some young students visit the city of Pompeii, to study the ruins and the curiosities preserved in the museum of Naples, nearby. All of them are familiar with classic literature and classic history; moreover, they are artists, able to appreciate the beauty of what they see. At the time of the eruption, which occurred nearly two thousand years ago, many people perished by being smothered under the rain of ashes; but their bodies were encased in the deposit so that the form was perfectly preserved as in a mould. Some of these moulds are to be seen in the museum mentioned; and one is the mould of the body of a beautiful young woman. The younger of the three students sees this mould, and romantically wishes that he could see and love the real person, so many centuries dead. That night, while his companions are asleep, he leaves his room and wanders into the ruined city, for the pleasure of thinking all by himself. But presently, as he turns the corner of a street, he finds that the city looks quite different from what it had appeared by day; the houses seem to have grown taller; they look new, bright, clean. While he is thus wandering, suddenly the sun rises, and the streets fill with people—not the people of to-day, but the people of two thousand years ago, all dressed in the old Greek and Roman costumes. After a time a young Greek comes up to the student and speaks to him in Latin. He has learned enough Latin at the university to be able to answer, and a conversation begins, of which the result is that he is invited to the theatre of Pompeii to see the gladiators and other amusements of the time. While in this theatre, he suddenly sees the woman that he wanted to see, the woman whose figure was preserved in the Naples museum. After the theatre, he is invited to her house; and everything is very delightful until suddenly the girl's father appears on the scene. The old man is a Christian, and he is very angry that the ghost of his daughter should deceive a young man in this manner. He makes a sign of the cross, and immediately poor Arria crumbles into dust, and the young man finds himself alone in the ruins of Pompeii. Very beautiful this story is; but every detail in it is dream study. I have given so much mention to it only because it seems to me the very finest French example of this artistic use of dream experience. But how many other romances belong to the same category? I need only mention among others Irving's "The Adalantado of the Seven Cities," which is pure dream, so realistically told that it gives the reader the sensation of being asleep. Although such romances as "The Seven Sleepers," "Rip Van Winkle," and "Urashima," are not, on the other hand, pure dreams, yet the charm of them is just in that part where dream experience is used. The true romance in all is in the old man's dream of being young, and waking up to cold and grave realities. By the way, in the old French lays of Marie de France, there is an almost precisely similar story to the Japanese one—similar, at least, at all points except the story of the tortoise. It is utterly impossible that the oriental and the occidental storytellers could have, either of them, borrowed from the other; more probably each story is a spontaneous growth. But it is curious to find the legend substantially the same in other literatures—Indian and Arabian and Javanese. In all of the versions the one romantic truth is ever the same—a dream truth.

Now besides the artistic elements of terror and of romance, dreams certainly furnish us with the most penetrating and beautiful qualities of ghostly tenderness that literature contains. For the dead people that we loved all come back to us occasionally in dreams, and look and talk as if they were actually alive, and become to us everything that we could have wished them to be. In a dream-meeting with the dead, you must have observed how everything is gentle and beautiful, and yet how real, how true it seems. From the most ancient times such visions of the dead have furnished literature with the most touching and the most exquisite passages of unselfish affection. We find this experience in nearly all the ancient ballad-literature of Europe; we find it in all the world's epics; we find it in every kind of superior poetry; and modern literature draws from it more and more as the years go by. Even in such strange compositions as the "Kalevala" of the Finns, an epic totally unlike any other written in this world, the one really beautiful passage in an emotional sense is the coming back of the dead mother to comfort the wicked son, which is a dream study, though not so represented in the poem.

Yet one thing more. Our dreams of heaven, what are they in literature but reflections in us of the more beautiful class of dreams? In the world of sleep all the dead people we loved meet us again; the father recovers his long-buried child, the husband his lost wife, separated lovers find the union that was impossible in this world, those whom we lost sight of in early years—dead sisters, brothers, friends—all come back to us just as they were then, just as loving, and as young, and perhaps even more beautiful than they could really have been. In the world of sleep there is no growing old; there is immortality, there is everlasting youth. And again how soft, how happy everything is; even the persons unkind to us in waking life become affectionate to us in dreams. Well, what is heaven but this? Religion in painting perfect happiness for the good, only describes the best of our dream life, which is also the best of our waking life; and I think you will find that the closer religion has kept to dream experience in these descriptions, the happier has been the result. Perhaps you will say that I have forgotten how religion teaches the apparition of supernatural powers of a very peculiar kind. But I think that you will find the suggestion for these powers also in dream life. Do we not pass through the air in dreams, pass through solid substances, perform all kinds of miracles, achieve all sorts of impossible things? I think we do. At all events, I am certain that when, as men-of-letters, you have to deal with any form of supernatural subject—whether terrible, or tender, or pathetic, or splendid—you will do well, if you have a good imagination, not to trust to books for your inspiration. Trust to your own dream-life; study it carefully, and draw your inspiration from that. For dreams are the primary source of almost everything that is beautiful in the literature which treats of what lies beyond mere daily experience.

Notes

a. See note p. 227, n.3. In an article on true-life ghosts for *Harper's*, Maeterlinck noted that ghost stories in fiction differ from "real" ghost encounters: "It is worthy of remark, in the first place, that these authentic narratives bear no relation whatever to the legendary and sensational ghost-stories that still linger in many English and American magazines, especially in the Christmas numbers. They mention no winding-sheets, coffins, skeletons, graveyards, no sulphurous flames, curses, blood-curdling groans, no clanking chains, nor any of the time-honoured trappings that characterize this rather feeble literature of the supernatural. On the contrary, the scenes enacted in houses that appear to be really haunted are generally very simple and insignificant, not to say dull and commonplace" (Maurice Maeterlinck, *The Unknown Guest*, translated by Alexander Teixeira de Mattos [New York: Dodd, Mead and Company, 1914], 29–30).

b. Thomas Babbington Macaulay (1800–1859), British poet, historian, and parliamentarian.

c. "The Haunted and the Haunters; or, The House and the Brain" (1859), by Edward Bulwer-Lytton.

In this essay Andrew Lang (1844–1912) looks at the Chinese and Japanese literary and artistic treatment of ghosts and other things that go bump in the night and their relationship to their European literary counterparts. The Scotsman Lang was a critic, poet, anthropologist, and novelist with a deep interest in folklore and mythology, as well as "psychical research," the quest to prove the existence of ghosts and the supernatural, which he advocated as president of the Society for Psychical Research in 1911. "Some Japanese Bogie-Books" originally ran in *The Magazine of Art* before being reprinted in his collection of literary essays, *Books and Bookmen* (1886). The illustrations and captions accompanying this article are original to it.

*Some Japanese Bogie-Books**
ANDREW LANG

There is or used to be a poem for infant minds of a rather Pharisaical character, which was popular in the nursery when I was a youngster. It ran something like this:—

> I thank my stars that I was born
> A little British child.

Perhaps these were not the very words, but that was decidedly the sentiment. Look at the Japanese infants, from the pencil of the famous Hokusai. Though they are not British, were there ever two jollier, happier small creatures? Did Leech, or Mr. Du Maurier, or Andrea della Robbia ever present a more delightful view of innocent, well-pleased childhood? Well, these Japanese children, if they are in the least inclined to be timid or nervous, must have an awful time of it at night in the dark, and when they make that eerie "northwest passage" bedwards through the darkling house of which Mr. Stevenson sings the perils and the emotions. All of us who did not suffer under parents brought up on the views of Mr. Herbert Spencer have endured, in childhood, a good deal from ghosts. But it is nothing to what Japanese children bear, for our ghosts are to the spectres of Japan as moonlight is to sunlight, or as water unto whisky. Personally I may say that few people have been plagued by the terror that walketh in darkness more than myself. At the early age of ten I had the tales of the ingenious Mr. Edgar Poe and of Charlotte Brontë "put into my hands" by a cousin who had served as a Bashi Bazouk, and knew not the meaning of fear. But I *did*, and perhaps even Nelson would have found out "what fear

*Andrew Lang, "Some Japanese Bogie-Books," in *Books and Bookmen, A New Edition* (London: Longmans, Green, & Co., 1892), 46–68.

280   6. Ghosts and Kindred Horrors

was," or the boy in the Norse tale would have "learned to shiver," if he had been left alone to peruse "Jane Eyre," and the "Black Cat," and the "Fall of the House of Usher," as I was. Every night I expected to wake up in my coffin, having been prematurely buried; or to hear sighs in the area, followed by light, unsteady footsteps on the stairs, and then to see a lady all in a white shroud stained with blood and clay stagger into my room, the victim of too rapid interment. As to the notion that my respected kinsman had a mad wife concealed on the premises, and that a lunatic aunt, black in the face with suppressed mania, would burst into my chamber, it was comparatively a harmless fancy, and not particularly disturbing. Between these and the "Yellow Dwarf," who (though only the invention of the Countess D'Aulnoy) might frighten a nervous infant into hysterics, I personally had as bad a time of it in the night watches as any happy British child has survived. But our ogres are nothing to the bogies which make not only night but day terrible to the studious infants of Japan and China.

Chinese ghosts are probably much the same as Japanese ghosts. The Japanese have borrowed most things, including apparitions and awesome sprites and grisly fiends, from the Chinese, and then have improved on the original model. Now we have a very full, complete, and horror-striking

Japanese Children. Drawn by Hokusai.

account of Chinese *harnts* (as the country people in Tennessee call them) from Mr. Herbert Giles, who has translated scores of Chinese ghost stories in his "Strange Tales from a Chinese Studio" (De la Rue, 1880). Mr. Giles's volumes prove that China is the place for Messrs. Gurney and Myers, the secretaries of the Psychical Society.

Ghosts do not live a hole-and-corner life in China, but boldly come out and take their part in the pleasures and business of life. It has always been a question with me whether ghosts, in a haunted house, appear when there is no audience. What does the spectre in the tapestried chamber do when the house is *not* full, and no guest is put in the room to bury strangers in, the haunted room? Does the ghost sulk and complain that there is "no house," and refuse to rehearse his little performance, in a conscientious and disinterestedly artistic spirit, when deprived of the artist's true pleasure, the awakening of sympathetic emotion in the mind of the spectator? We give too little thought and sympathy to ghosts, who in our old castles and country houses often find no one to appear to from year's end to year's-end. Only now and then is a guest placed in the "haunted room." Then I like to fancy the glee of the lady in green or the radiant boy, or the headless man, or the old gentleman in snuff-coloured clothes, as he, or she, recognises the presence of a spectator, and prepares to give his or her best effects in the familiar style.

Now in China and Japan certainly a ghost does not wait till people enter the haunted room: a ghost, like a person of fashion, "goes everywhere." Moreover, he has this artistic excellence, that very often you don't know him from an embodied person. He counterfeits mortality so cleverly that he (the ghost) has been known to personate a candidate for honours, and pass an examination for him. A pleasing example of this kind, illustrating the limitations of ghosts, is told in Mr. Giles's book. A gentleman of Huai Shang named Chou-t'ien-i had arrived at the age of fifty, but his family consisted of but one son, a fine boy, "strangely averse from study," as if there were anything strange in *that*. One day the son disappeared mysteriously, as people do from West Ham. In a year he came back, said he had been detained in a Taoist monastery, and, to all men's amazement, took to his books. Next year he obtained is B.A. degree, a First Class. All the neighbourhood was overjoyed, for Huai Shang was like Pembroke College (Oxford), where, according to the poet, "First Class Men are few and far between." It was who should have the honour of giving his daughter as bride to this intellectual marvel. A very nice girl was selected,

282 6. Ghosts and Kindred Horrors

but most unexpectedly the B.A. would not marry. This nearly broke his father's heart. The old gentleman knew, according to Chinese belief, that if he had no grandchild there would be no one in the next generation to feed his own ghost and pay it all the little needful attentions. "Picture then the father naming and insisting on the day;" till Kʻo-chʻang, B.A., got up and ran away. His mother tried to detain him, when his clothes "came off in her hand," and the bachelor vanished! Next day appeared the real flesh and blood son, who had been kidnapped and enslaved. The genuine Kʻo-chʻang was overjoyed to hear of his approaching nuptials. The rites were duly celebrated, and in less than a year the old gentleman welcomed his much-longed-for grandchild. But, oddly enough, Kʻo-chʻang, though very jolly and universally beloved, was as stupid as ever, and read nothing but the sporting intelligence in the newspapers. It was now universally admitted that the learned Kʻo-chʻang had been an impostor, a clever ghost. It follows that ghosts can take a very good degree; but ladies need not be afraid of marrying ghosts, owing to the inveterate shyness of these learned spectres.

The Chinese ghost is by no means always a malevolent person, as, indeed, has already been made clear from the affecting narrative of the ghost who passed an examination. Even the spectre which answers in China to the statue in "Don Juan," the statue which accepts invitations to dinner, is anything but

A Storm Fiend.

a malevolent guest. So much may be gathered from the story of Chu and Lu. Chu was an undergraduate of great courage and bodily vigour, but dull of wit. He was a married man, and his children (as in the old Oxford legend) often rushed into their mother's presence, shouting, "Mamma! mamma! papa's been plucked again!" Once it chanced that Chu was at a wine party, and the negus (a favourite beverage of the Celestials) had done its work. His young friends betted Chu a bird's-nest dinner that he would not go to the nearest temple, enter the room devoted to coloured sculptures representing the torments of Purgatory, and carry off the image of the Chinese judge of the dead, their Osiris or Rhadamanthus. Off went old Chu, and soon returned with the august effigy (which wore "a green face, a red beard, and a hideous expression") in his arms. The other men were frightened, and begged Chu to restore his worship to his place on the infernal bench. Before carrying back the worthy magistrate, Chu poured a libation on the ground and said, "Whenever your excellency feels so disposed, I shall be glad to take a cup of wine with you in a friendly way." That very night, as Chu was taking a stirrup cup before going to bed, the ghost of the awful judge came to the door and entered. Chu promptly put the kettle on, mixed the negus, and made a night of it with the festive fiend. Their friendship was never interrupted from that moment. The judge even gave Chu a new heart (literally) whereby he was enabled to pass examinations; for the heart, in China, is the seat of all the intellectual faculties. For Mrs. Chu, a plain woman with a fine figure, the ghost provided a new head, of a handsome girl recently slain by a robber. Even after Chu's death the genial spectre did not neglect him, but obtained for him an appointment as registrar in the next world, with a certain rank attached.

The next world, among the Chinese, seems to be a paradise of bureaucracy, patent places, jobs, mandarins' buttons and tails, and, in short, the heaven of officialism. All civilised readers are acquainted with Mr. Stockton's humorous story of "The Transferred Ghost." In Mr. Stockton's view a man does not always get his own ghostship; there is a vigorous competition among spirits for good ghostships, and a great deal of intrigue and party feeling. It may be long before a disembodied spectre gets any ghostship at all, and then, if he has little influence, he may be glad to take a chance of haunting the Board of Trade, or the Post Office, instead of "walking" in the Foreign Office. One spirit may win a post as White Lady in the imperial palace, while another is put off with a position in an old college library, or perhaps has to follow the fortunes of some seedy "medium"

284   6. Ghosts and Kindred Horrors

through boarding-houses and third-rate hotels. Now this is precisely the Chinese view of the fates and fortunes of ghosts. *Quisque suos patimur manes.*[a]

In China, to be brief, and to quote a ghost (who ought to know what he was speaking about), "supernaturals are to be found everywhere." This

A Snow Bogie.

is the fact that makes life so puzzling and terrible to a child of a believing and trustful character. These Oriental bogies do not appear in the dark alone, or only in haunted houses, or at cross-roads, or in gloomy woods. They are everywhere: every man has his own ghost, every place has its peculiar haunting fiend, every natural phenomenon has its informing spirit; every quality, as hunger, greed, envy, malice, has an embodied visible shape prowling about seeking what it may devour. Where our science, for example, sees (or rather smells) sewer gas, the Japanese behold a slimy, meagre, insatiate wrath, crawling to devour the lives of men. Where we see a storm of snow, their livelier fancy beholds a comic snow-ghost, a queer, grinning old man under a vast umbrella.

The illustrations in this paper are only a few specimens chosen out of many volumes of Japanese bogies. We have not ventured to copy the very most awful spectres, nor dared to be as horrid as we can. These native drawings, too, are generally coloured regardless of expense, and the colouring is often horribly lurid and satisfactory. This embellishment, fortunately perhaps, we cannot reproduce. Meanwhile, if any child looks into this essay, let him (or her) not be alarmed by the pictures he beholds. Japanese ghosts do not live in this country; there are none of them even at the Japanese Legation. Just as bears, lions, and rattlesnakes are not to be seriously dreaded in our woods and commons, so the Japanese ghost cannot breathe (any more than a slave can) in the air of England or America. We do not yet even keep any ghostly zoological garden in which the bogies of Japanese, Australians, Red Indians, and other distant peoples may be accommodated. Such an establishment is perhaps to be desired in the interests of psychical research, but that form of research has not yet been endowed by a cultivated and progressive government.

The first to attract our attention represents, as I understand, the common ghost, or *simulacrum vulgare* of psychical science. To this complexion must we all come, according to the best Japanese opinion. Each of us contains within him "somewhat of a shadowy being," like the spectre described by Dr. Johnson: something like the Egyptian "Ka," for which the curious may consult the works of Miss Amelia B. Edwards and other learned Orientalists. The most recent French student of these matters, the author of "L'Homme Posthume," is of opinion that we do not all possess this double, with its power of surviving our bodily death. He thinks, too, that our ghost, when it does survive, has but rarely the energy and enterprise to make itself visible to or audible by "shadow-casting men." In some extreme cases the ghost (according to our French authority, that of a disciple of M. Comte) feeds fearsomely on the bodies of the living. In no event does he believe that a ghost lasts much longer than a hundred years. After that it mizzles into spectre, and is resolved into its elements, whatever they may be.

A somewhat similar and (to my own mind) probably sound theory of ghosts prevails among savage tribes, and among such peoples as the ancient Greeks, the modern Hindoos, and other ancestor worshippers. When feeding, as they all do, or used to do, the ghosts of the ancestral dead, they gave special attention to the claims of the dead of the last three generations, leaving ghosts older than the century to look after their own supplies of meat and drink. The negligence testifies to a notion that very old ghosts are of little account, for good or evil. On the other hand, as regards the longevity of spectres, we must not shut our eyes to the example of the bogie in ancient armour which appears in Glamis Castle, or to the Jesuit of Queen Elizabeth's date that haunts the library (and a very nice place to haunt: I ask no better, as a ghost in the Pavilion at Lord's might cause a scandal) of an English nobleman. With these *instantiæ contradictoriæ*, as Bacon calls them, present to our minds, we must not (in the present condition of psychical research) dogmatise too hastily about the span of life allotted to the *simulacrum vulgare*. Very probably his chances of a prolonged existence are in inverse ratio to the square of the distance of time which severs him from our modern days. No one has ever even pretended to see the ghost of an ancient Roman buried in these islands, still less of a Pict or Scot, or a Palaeolithic man, welcome as such an apparition would be to many of us. Thus the evidence does certainly look as if there were a kind of statute of limitations among ghosts, which, from many points of view, is not an arrangement at which we should repine.

The Japanese artist expresses his own sense of the casual and fluctuating nature of ghosts by drawing his spectre in shaky lines, as if the model had given the artist the horrors. This *simulacrum* rises out of the earth like an exhalation, and groups itself into shape above the spade with which all that is corporeal of its late owner has been interred. Please remark the uncomforted and dismal expression of the *simulacrum*. We must remember that the ghost or "Ka" is not the "soul," which has other destinies in the future world, good or evil, but is only a shadowy resemblance, condemned, as in the Egyptian creed, to dwell in the tomb and hover near it. The Chinese and Japanese have their own definite theory of the next world,

Some Japanese Bogie-Books (Lang) 287

The Simulacrum Vulgare.

and we must by no means confuse the eternal fortunes of the permanent, conscious, and responsible self, already inhabiting other worlds than ours, with the eccentric vagaries of the semi-material tomb-haunting larva, which so often develops a noisy and bear-fighting disposition quite unlike the character of its proprietor in life.

A Well and Water Bogie.

The next bogie, so limp and washed-out as he seems, with his white, drooping, dripping arms and hands, reminds us of that horrid French species of apparition, "la lavandière de la nuit," who washes dead men's linen in the moonlit pools and rivers. Whether this *simulacrum* be meant for the spirit of the well (for everything has its spirit in Japan), or whether it be the ghost of some mortal drowned in the well, I cannot say with absolute certainty;

Raising the Wind.

6. Ghosts and Kindred Horrors

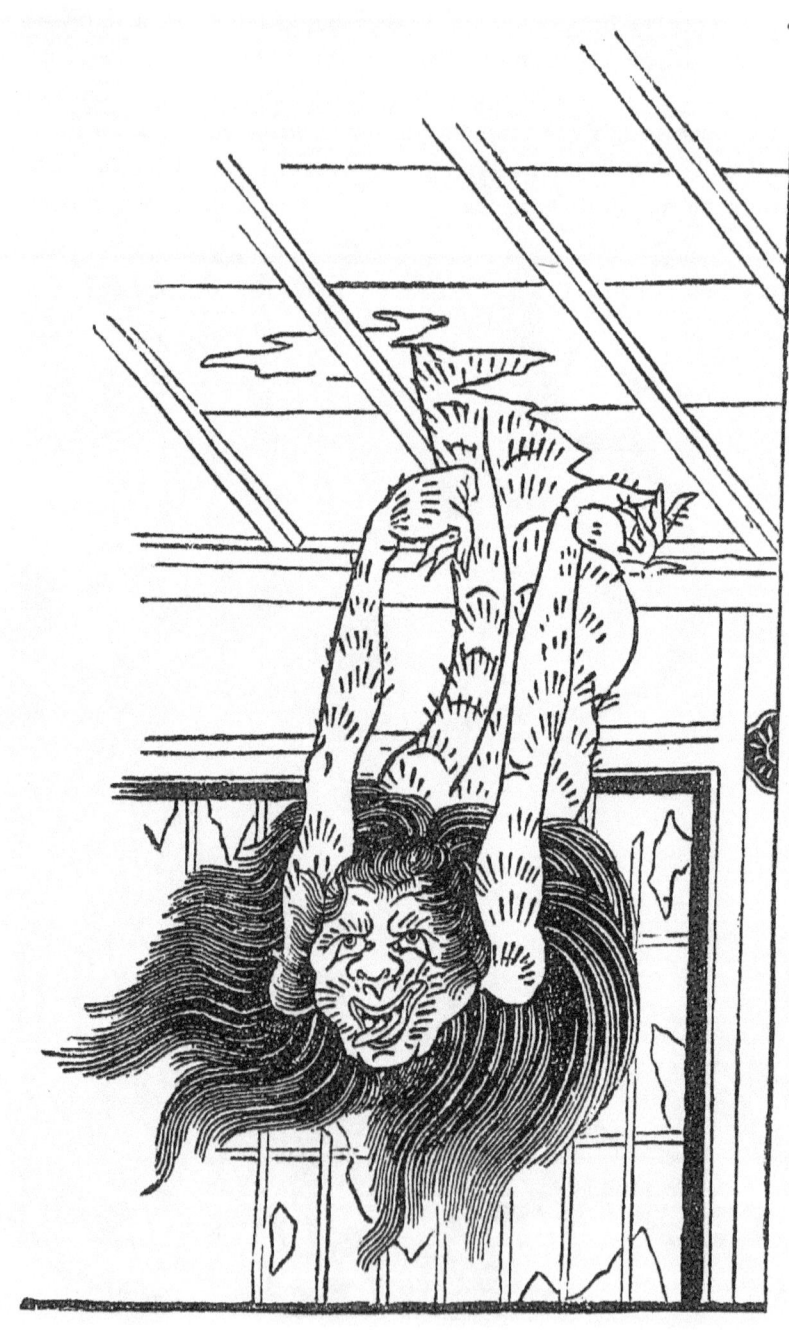

A Chink and Crevice Bogie.

but the opinion of the learned tends to the former conclusion. Naturally a Japanese child, when sent in the dusk to draw water, will do so with fear and trembling, for this limp, floppy apparition might scare the boldest. Another bogie, a terrible creation of fancy, I take to be a vampire, about which the curious can read in Dom Calmet, who will tell them how whole villages in Hungary have been depopulated by vampires; or he may study in Fauriel's "Chansons de la Grèce Moderne" the vampires of modern Hellas.

Another plan, and perhaps even more satisfactory to a timid or superstitious mind, is to read in a lonely house at midnight a story named "Carmilla," printed in Mr. Sheridan Le Fanu's "In a Glass Darkly." That work will give you the peculiar sentiment of vampirism, will produce a gelid perspiration, and reduce the patient to a condition in which he will be afraid to look round the room. If, while in this mood, some one tells him Mr. Augustus Hare's story of Crooglin Grange, his education in the practice and theory of vampires will be complete, and he will be a very proper and well-qualified inmate of Earlswood Asylum. The most awful Japanese vampire, caught red-handed in the act, a hideous, bestial incarnation of ghoulishness, we have carefully refrained from reproducing.

Scarcely more agreeable is the bogie, or witch, blowing from her mouth a malevolent exhalation, an embodiment of malignant and maleficent sorcery. The vapour which flies and curls from the mouth constitutes "a sending," in the technical language of Icelandic wizards, and is capable (in Iceland, at all events) of assuming the form of some detestable supernatural animal, to destroy the life of a hated rival. In the case of our last example it is very hard indeed to make head or tail of the spectre represented. Chinks and crannies are his domain; through these he drops upon you. He is a merry but not an attractive or genial ghost. Where there are such "visions about" it may be admitted that children, apt to believe in all such fancies, have a youth of variegated and intense misery, recurring with special vigour at bed-time. But we look again at our first picture, and hope and trust that Japanese boys and girls are as happy as these jolly little creatures appear.

Notes

a. "Each of us bears his own hell" (Vergil, *Aeneid*, Book VI).

6. Ghosts and Kindred Horrors

In 1902 William Francis Dawson published a lengthy treatise on the origins of Christmas celebrations after discovering that there were no such works then extent. As part of *Christmas: Its Origins and Associations*, Dawson dealt with the popular yuletide tradition of telling ghost stories in a chapter on "Modern Christmases at Home." Here he explains the relationship between Christmas and horror, which in the United Kingdom remains to this day, while in the United States Halloween absorbed all of Christmas's creepiness.

Ghost Stories*

W. F. DAWSON

Everybody knows that Christmas is the time for ghost stories, and that Charles Dickens and other writers have supplied us with tales of the true blood-curdling type. Thomas Hood's "Haunted House," S. T. Coleridge's "Ancient Mariner," and some other weird works of poetry have also been found serviceable in producing that strange chill of the blood, that creeping kind of feeling all over you, which is one of the enjoyments of Christmastide. Coleridge (says the late Mr. George Dawson)[1] "holds the first place amongst English poets in this objective teaching of the vague, the mystic, the dreamy, and the imaginative. I defy any man of imagination or sensibility to have 'The Ancient Mariner' read to him, by the flickering firelight on Christmas night, by a master mind possessed by the mystic spirit of the poem, and not find himself taken away from the good regions of 'ability to account for,' and taken into some far-off dreamland, and made even to start at his own footfall, and almost to shudder at his own shadow. You shall sit round the fire at Christmas time, good men and true every one of you; you shall come there armed with your patent philosophy; that creak you have heard, it is only the door—the list is not carefully put round the door, and it is the wintry wind that whistles through the crevices. Ghosts and spectres belong to the olden times; science has waved its wand and laid them all. We have no superstition about us; we walk enlightened nineteenth-century men; it is quite beneath us to be superstitious. By and bye, one begins to tell tales of ghosts and spirits; and another begins, and it goes all round; and there comes over you a curious

*W. F. Dawson, *Christmas: Its Origins and Associations* (London: Elliot Stock, 1902), 274–275.
1. "Biographical Lectures."

feeling—a very unphilosophical feeling, in fact, because the pulsations of air from the tongue of the storyteller ought not to bring over you that peculiar feeling. You have only heard words, tales—confessedly by the storyteller himself only tales, such as may figure in the next monthly magazine for pure entertainment and amusement. But why do you feel so, then? If you say that these things are mere hallucinations, vague air-beating or tale-telling, why, good philosopher, do you feel so curious, so all-overish, as it were? Again, you are a man without the least terror in you, as brave and bold a man as ever stepped: living man cannot frighten you, and verily the dead rise not with you. But you are brought, towards midnight, to the stile over which is gained a view of the village churchyard, where sleep the dead in quietness. Your manhood begins just to ooze away a little; you are caught occasionally whistling to keep your courage up; you do not expect to see a ghost, but you are ready to see one, or to make one." At such a moment, think of the scene depicted by Coleridge:—

A Christmas Frolic. Ghost stories were an integral part of yuletide in Great Britain, as seen in Dickens' A Christmas Carol *and this scene (1814) of a boy using a "ghost" to frighten guests at a Christmas party. In the United States, Halloween gradually subsumed the ghostly aspects of Christmas, while in Britain the tradition of the Christmas ghost continues, though increasingly challenged by Halloween (Library of Congress, Prints and Photographs Division, LC-DIG-ppmsca-07805).*

"'Twas night, calm night, the moon was high:
The dead men stood together.

All stood together on the deck,
    For a charnel-dungeon fitter:
All fixed on me their stony eyes,
    That in the moon did glitter.

The pang, the curse, with which they died,
    Had never passed away:
I could not draw-my eyes from theirs,
    Nor turn them up to pray."

With this weird tale in his mind in the mystic stillness of midnight would an imaginative man be likely to deny the reality of the spirit world? The chances are that he would be spellbound; or, if he had breath enough, would cry out—

"Angels and ministers of grace, defend us!"[a]

Notes

a. *Hamlet*, Act I, scene iv.

Because of the tradition of Christmas ghost stories, the holidays were high time for publishers to release works of horror. Noah Brooks (1830–1903) was a lifelong journalist and longtime friend of Abraham Lincoln. In this review for *The Book Buyer*, Brooks discusses *Modern Ghosts* (1890), a collection of European ghost stories, including Maupassant's "The Horla," and a separate volume by the macabre fantasist E. T. A. Hoffmann, *Weird Tales*, reissued in translation from the German. This review is part of "Books of the Christmas Season," which ran in *The Book Buyer* for December 1890.

*Excerpt from "Books of the Christmas Season"**
NOAH BROOKS

The latest addition to Harper's Odd Number series of stories is a volume of short tales by various hands, entitled "Modern Ghosts." These clever stories are really ghostly, and not very modern in their realism. Their

*Noah Brooks, "Books of the Christmas Season," *The Book Buyer: A Summary of American and Foreign Literature*, December 1890, 531.

modernity lies rather in their being of "contemporaneous human interest" than in their conforming to the latest fashion in ghosts. Were they less romantic than they are, they would remind one more of Robert Dale Owen[a] and less of Monk Lewis and the author of that hair-lifting tale, "The Three Spaniards."[b] But these are all fascinating to the lover of the weird and the mysterious, and they may be used to send a circle of terrified auditors to bed shivering as the wind roars down the chimney or shrieks and sobs around the gables of a country house at night. Two of these seven stories are from the French, two from the Spanish, one from the German, one from the Swedish, and one from the Italian. The two from the French are written by Guy de Maupassant, and have all of his deftness of touch; his "On the River" being the better of the two. Mr. George W. Curtis writes a pleasant introduction, but it is hardly fair to credit Robert Dale Owen, as he does, with inventing the phrase, "the night side of nature." Mrs. Crowe[c] borrowed that from the German, more than fifty years ago. To be read with these modern ghost stories while one is in the humor, is Hoffmann's "Weird Tales," a new edition of which has just been issued by Charles Scribner's Sons. These tales, after all, are classics in their peculiar field, and nothing that Poe or other fantastic dreamers have ever written in this vein will take their place in the affections of the world of ghostseers and readers of strange tales. This edition is enriched with a fine portrait and biography of Hoffmann and eleven etchings by Lalauze.

Notes

a. Robert Dale Owen (1801–1877), Scottish expatriate and American socialist who helped found the New Harmony Utopian community with his father, Robert Owen, proposed ending slavery to Lincoln, and helped draft the Fourteenth Amendment. Here Brooks is referring to Owen's well-known works on Spiritualism, *Footfalls on the Boundary of Another World* (1859) and *The Debatable Land Between this World and the Next* (1872).

b. Gothic novelist George Walker (1772–1847), whose *The Three Spaniards* was published in 1800.

c. Catherine Crowe (1807–1876), author of *The Night-Side of Nature* (1848), a book of supposedly true ghost stories that helped launch the mid–Victorian Spiritualist craze.

Henry Wysham Lanier (1873–1958) was the son of the poet Sydney Lanier and a writer in his own right. As an editor he founded *Golden Book Magazine*. Here he reviews the novelist Henry James's (1843–1916) *The Turn of the Screw* (1898), the famed psychological ghost story. The review first ran as part of "Fiction, Poetry, and the Lighter Note in the Season's Books" in *The American Monthly Review of Reviews* for December 1898.

Two Volumes from Henry James*
HENRY WYSHAM LANIER

Mr. Henry James is represented this year by two volumes, exhibiting the extremes of his art. *In the Cage* (Stone), if any name less well known appeared on the title-page, might be pronounced stupid, strained, and overdrawn without much compunction. In the light of Mr. James' former work one can recognize some of its subtlety, some of its laboriously intricate analysis and complex psychology.

What a relief is it to turn from this dreary monotone to *The Two Magics!* This astonishing book contains two stories, "The Turn of the Screw" and "Covering End," and the present reviewer must confess to no little racking of brains in the search for the author's meaning in classing them together. Apparently the first shows the mysterious legacy of evil that may continue in force after death: the second that peculiar, manifold, and irresistible influence which breathes from a dwelling for many generations the habitation of a line of sturdy ancestors—or is it the "magic" of a charming woman's personality? Although, if either happen to be the right guess, the general title is not at all felicitous, and the two tales might far better go merely as a couple of stories; although the introduction to "The Turn of the Screw" seems a needlessly awkward method of starting the story. In spite of any criticisms that may be made, it is impossible to read this horribly absorbing narrative without recognizing that it is a notable achievement. It is in an entirely new vein for Mr. James and one in which his delicate, subtle psychology shows to best advantage, for the foul breath of the bottomless pit itself, which strikes the reader full in the face as he follows the plot, puts to shame by its penetrating force and quiet ghastliness the commonplace, unreal "horrors" of the ordinary ghost-story; it does indeed give an extra "turn of the screw" beyond anything of the sort that fiction has yet provided. There is something peculiarly against nature, something indescribably hellish in the thought of the beautiful little children holding unholy communion with the wraiths of two vile servants who had, when alive, corrupted them; and it would be difficult to find anything so unpretentious capable of producing such a living, vivid, indelible impression upon the mind. Let us hope that Mr. James will

*Henry Wysham Lanier, "Fiction, Poetry, and the Lighter Note in the Season's Books," *The American Monthly Review of Reviews*, December 1898, 732–733.

soon again give his unique gifts another chance in a field so congenial. To my mind it is the finest work he has ever done: there is a completeness, a finish, a sense of easy mastery and boundless reserve force about this story which are entirely fascinating. Looking back upon the tale when one has finished it, one instinctively compares it to a beautiful pearl: something perfect, rounded, calm, unforgettable. It would not require a rash prophet to predict that *The Two Magics* (Macmillan) will outweigh a score of such books as *In the Cage* in the future estimate of later nineteenth-century literature.

Amy Leslie (1855–1939) sang soprano to some renown before becoming a drama critic for the *Chicago Daily News*. She was one of Stephen Crane's lovers, and some say she bore him a child. She collected her *Daily News* profiles of famous actors in a volume called *Some Players: Personal Sketches* (1899), from which comes this excerpt from the profile of the actor William Gillette (1853–1937) on his desire for a great horror play. Gillette, an longtime stage Sherlock Holmes, invented the phrase "elementary, my dear fellow," later amended on film to "elementary, my dear Watson."

Excerpt from "Gillette"*

AMY LESLIE

Something of the soothing completeness which lies upon a still and twilight sea invigorates the personality of William Gillette and socially gives him a rare, gracious, and potential attractiveness of a sort not quite possessed by any American actor of the hour.

There is a restless fire in his eyes and a note of vigilance touching his forehead and mouth, the note David and Abel de Pujol give to their soldiers and martyrs; but the smile in Gillette's eyes quiets the impatient smolder and softens the lines until his fine, sympathetic face is a pleasant study as he talks. He never says any more than does commonplace things, though he accomplishes this special magic without a trace of eccentricity or ever seeming to be either unusual or exceptional. It is only in the calm pleasure of the impression that Mr. Gillette leaves among the favored few

---

*Amy Leslie, *Some Players: Personal Sketches* (Chicago: Herbert S. Stone & Company, 1900), 301, 313.

298   6. Ghosts and Kindred Horrors

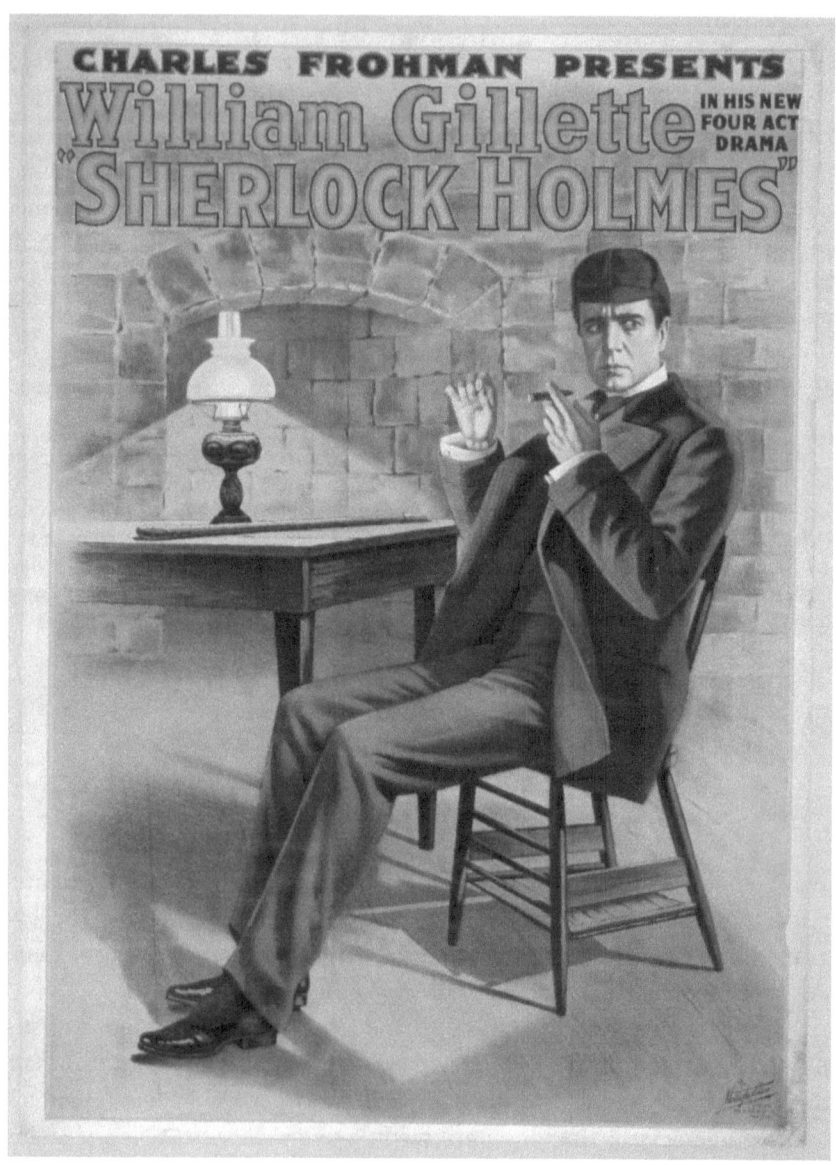

Charles Frohman Presents William Gillette in His New Four Act Drama, "Sherlock Holmes." William Gillette is best remembered for his portrayal of Sherlock Holmes, whose deerstalker cap and pipe he helped make synonymous with the character. Gillette played the character on stage around 1,300 times in Europe and the United States, and later in silent films and on the radio. He told Amy Leslie that he had hoped to create the world's most convincing theatrical ghost, but feared it could not be done. This advertisement is from 1900 (Library of Congress, Prints and Photographs Division, LC-USZC2-1459).

upon whom he bestows his companionship that the real charm of his own self is revealed.

He is diffident, and in panic takes flight at the shadow of adulation, but to-day perhaps there is no other man of Gillette's eminence as an actor who is so universally beloved.[...]

One of the plays Gillette thinks about is an apparition drama.

"You know," said Gillette, telling of his fancy, "it has been my ambition for years to invent a means of putting a scary ghost story before an audience so that people would turn white and shriek with fright; but, really, it cannot be done—even children know the devices and usually laugh. It is because of the people themselves out there; perhaps if the spiritistic seance arrangement of dark room and joined hands could be introduced with the audience my ghost play would do; but I don't see my way to a finish grewsome as the subject demands, do you?"

The idea of Mr. Gillette brooding over such a sanguinary and tortureful mission in the drama is amusing, for a gentler, finer, more sympathetic soul does not exist; but he might start a holding-hands-coupon distribution. A whole lot of ingenuous creatures would hold hands in the dark for the sake of Professor Gillette and his spooks.

Our next two pieces are short notices reporting the republication of Robert W. Chambers's (1865–1933) horror classic *The King in Yellow* (1895), the loosely linked collection of tales focusing on a mysterious play that brings its readers terror and death. A prolific author of historical romance, Chambers's few weird stories are often considered his best work. The first notice is from the "Chronicle and Comment" column of *The Bookman* for July 1902.

Excerpt from "Chronicle and Comment"*
THE BOOKMAN

We are very glad to hear that a new edition of Mr. Robert W. Chambers's *The King in Yellow* is to appear. Mr. Chambers has written a great many books. Some of them we have liked. Some we have not liked at all.

*"Chronicle and Comment," *The Bookman: A Magazine of Literature and Life*, July 1902, 411.

6. Ghosts and Kindred Horrors

Easily at the head of the first class is *The King in Yellow*. For sheer horror and weirdness some of the stories of this book have seldom been surpassed.

Our second take on *The King in Yellow* is from the "Fiction" column of *The Literary World* for August 1, 1902.

Review of The King in Yellow*
THE LITERARY WORLD

THE KING IN YELLOW. By Robert W. Chambers. Illustrated. Medium. Pp. 373. Harper & Brothers. $1.50.

It is difficult to imagine who the readers may be whose "thousands of unsolicited requests" have impelled Mr. Robert Chambers to issue a fresh edition of *The King in Yellow*. A more unsavory and deleterious book, as it appears to dispassionate criticism, it would be hard to find, and its most suitable fate would seem to be permission to sink out of recollection. No marked ability or originality distinguish it; it is simply erotic, ghastly, sensational.

Mary E. Wilkins (1852–1930; after 1902, Mary E. Wilkins Freeman) was an author of short stories and novels, many dealing with the conflicted inner lives of New England women, for which she remains somewhat well known. This review of her ghost story collection, *The Wind in the Rose Bush* (1902), ran in the May 1903 edition of *The Literary News* after first being published in the *Brooklyn Times*.

Review of The Wind in the Rose Bush†
THE LITERARY WORLD

Downright creepy, genuine old-fashioned ghost stories are these half dozen stories, which reveal Miss Wilkins in an entirely new field. They

---

*"Fiction," *The Literary World*, August 1, 1902, 126–127.
†Review of *The Wind in the Rose Bush* by Mary E. Wilkins, *The Literary News*, May 1903, 142.

are well told; although lacking in subtlety and gruesomeness, they have the fascination of the uncanny. The majority of the spirits seem to revisit the scenes of their earthly dwelling places out of a kind of perversity. The stories introduce many quaint characters, drawn with the author's customary skill. "Luella Miller" is the strongest story of the collection.

Mr. Newell's[a] illustrations are especially ugly, and utterly fail to convey even the faintest idea of the supernatural. His peculiar gifts lend themselves very kindly to caricature or the purely fantastic. The choice of illustrator for this particular volume could hardly hart been more unfortunate.

The cover design is entirely in keeping with the spirit of the story, which gives the title to the book. (Doubleday, Page & Co. $1.50)—*Brooklyn Times.*

Notes

a. Peter Newell (1862–1924), best known for his illustrations of children's books like *Topsys and Turvys* (1893), which featured reversible pictures.

Gouverneur Morris (1876–1953) shared the name of his great-grandfather, the early American statesman, but was otherwise a novelist in his own right, of sufficient fame that *Time* magazine reported his becoming a bank president in California. His writing, though, is largely forgotten today. Ward Clark, reviewing Morris's short story collection *The Footprint* (1908) in *The Bookman* echoed Harry Quilter in declaring that horror has "no rightful place" among wholesome, mainstream English letters. This review ran as the seventh of "Nine Books of the Month" in May 1908.

Mr. Morris's "The Footprint"*
WARD CLARK

Mr. Morris's book of short stories is one that tempts the reviewer to the giving of good advice. It is known that he is young; it is in evidence that he is prodigiously clever; it is indisputable that he has chosen in these tales to exercise his talent on subjects that will not endear him to the rab-

*Ward Clark, "Mr. Morris's 'The Footprint,'" *The Bookman: A Magazine of Literature and Life*, May 1908, 283–284.
The Footprint. By Gouverneur Morris. New York: Charles Scribner's Sons.

ble. A number of these stories are frankly studies in the horrible or the terrible or the fantastic. It is on the whole a grewsome, *macabre* collection. Such morbid efforts have no rightful place in our healthy Anglo-Saxon literature. No English author has ever achieved a real success who dealt with such matters—at least, none but Shakespeare and Marlowe, and Dickens and Hardy, and Poe and Hawthorne, and a few others of their ilk. It is plain that Mr. Morris ought to change his course, and turn his undoubted talents to the writing of stories more like those that the great American public is used to reading.

Nevertheless, I am glad that before mending his ways he has given us this volume. If these stories are not great, they are at least different, and their rather highly spiced originality is welcome to a jaded appetite. Nearly every one is a *tour de force*—a "trick" story, so to speak, in which some phase of a highly developed technic is displayed almost for its own sake. "The Footprint" is a sombre drama in which the setting of the desert is admirably realised; but the sharpness of the interest it evokes is due to the skill with which a supernatural element is suggested but never quite confirmed. "Paradise Ranch" is a virtuoso study in madness. "The Execution" is a curious refinement of horror; both this story and "The Explorers" are sketches in the ironic mood. In "Simon l'Ouvrier" Mr. Morris allows a fantastic idea to run its own course to an extreme that suggests fascinating possibilities. In all these stories the setting, the manner, the outer envelope, remain wholly realistic. "The Little Heiress" is a delightful fantasy—not a story, but an extended paradox. Its whimsical tenderness supplies the needed relief in an otherwise rather strenuous volume.

In candour it must be admitted that Mr. Morris is far from being typically American or English in his work. His models are plainly French, and there are discernible traces in more than one story of the French spirit. He is conspicuously witty, and his touch has at times a Gallic lightness. Every story is striking in idea, nearly every one is refined in workmanship. Not always is there solid substance behind them. One may read the volume through with a great deal of pleasure, and yet not wish the author to continue too long in precisely the same path. With three or four volumes to his credit, Mr. Morris has emerged from the ranks of beginners; but he has by no means done the work yet that his abilities warrant us in expecting. Beyond the present pleasure to be had from *The Footprint*, it is welcome as showing its author on the road to better things.

Remembered after her death as a translator and editor, Grace Isabel Colbron (1869–1943) was also a journalist, playwright, and novelist. In this piece she published in *The Bookman* for February 1915, she profiles Algernon Blackwood (1869–1951), whom she rightly recognizes as a major author of the weird, and even more rightly describes as more popular with readers than with critics. Blackwood's stories, such as "The Willows" (1907) and "The Wendigo" (1910), are now considered high points in the art of horror.

*Algernon Blackwood—An Appreciation**
GRACE ISABEL COLBRON

In these days when popularity, for an author, means that his books are read some, but are talked about a great deal more, and that he himself is talked about more than his books, it comes with a shock of pleasing surprise to discover a writer who is read more than he is discussed. This has been Algernon Blackwood's fate thus far. The majority of his books have gone into several editions in England and in this country, and yet they are little talked about and the man himself even less. He has escaped requests for his opinion on all the multifarious subjects, from Esoteric Buddhism to the width of women's skirts, which our popular authors are expected to elucidate in the daily and weekly journals, a deadly result of wide advertising. Algernon Blackwood has been little advertised, except by readers who have come under the spell of his unique literary personality.

It is scarcely ten years since the first book over the name of Algernon Blackwood appeared in England, and already there are twelve volumes of remarkable stories bearing his name, stories that haunt one after reading, tales that are heady as new wine. His imagination and insight are as rare as his choice of subjects is unusual. But there is no pose about this choice, we feel the man could not express himself in any other way. His rather unique life experience, if one may judge from the few biographical facts he is willing to give, has kept him singularly free from the trammels of the Obvious. From a childhood and youth spent in a Moravian school in the Black Forest, he went to the Canadian wilds and to the life of the man who has only his own exertions upon which to depend. This in spite of titled ancestry which would seem to chain him to conventional habits. Every sort of work came his way, even newspaper work in New York, until

*Grace Isabel Colbron, "Algernon Blackwood—An Appreciation," *The Bookman: A Magazine of Literature and Life*, February 1915, 618–621.

he returned to Europe and began to express in literary form some of the rich experiences that had piled in upon a brain of rare sensitiveness. Having apparently entirely escaped the usual sort of life that should have fallen to his lot, there was little to interpose between the eyes of his mind and the Core of Things. The physical eye became the immediate receiver of impressions that registered themselves on a brain which did not have to forget prejudices and the superimposed opinions of others. The result is one of the most remarkable literary personalities of the present day, a personality too powerful to be imbibed in large doses even by the most hardened reader. To criticise this personality calmly, by the canons of accredited literary criticism, is a task that taxes self-control. One's pen limps lamely after his ten-league strides and in a moment of exhaustion one acknowledges that to do Algernon Blackwood justice one should be—Algernon Blackwood himself.

At first it seems that it is the subject which enthralls, then comes appreciation of rare insight and finally a realisation of remarkable stylistic power, rich and exuberant, a rush of words like a mountain torrent, suiting sound to sense poignantly, hypnotising like some Eastern drug. The reader's progress to understanding follows the writer's progress of achievement. In his earlier books the subject sometimes taxes his power of expression. But with growing practice the gift of interpretation in words grows and grows—until his tendency to linger over the soul conflict and hurry with a sentence past actual happenings is handled with such mastery that it gives the chosen theme its greatest charm. There are few others who dare to do this. No one else comes to mind just now who ventures it in such degree unless it be that wonderful Danish prose stylist J. P. Jacobsen, who dislikes actualities and lingers lovingly over realities as Blackwood does.

Algernon Blackwood's chosen theme is the Unknown, the great realm that lies beyond the world of the Known and the Obvious. He finds it in many places, in the forest depths of pathless Canadian wilds, in Egyptian desert sands, in smiling mountain valleys, and even in London streets and offices. It comes to the adult with a tinge of horror, because the adult dislikes and fears all that will not fall in line with his notions of what the world should be like. It comes to the child as something exquisitely sweet, in dreams of Star Dust Caverns, of beautiful beneficent Beings that understand one's play. And it comes to the cat—but then, the cat is half in that world always and often has to come back from it when we would call her attention to our humble human selves! For Algernon Blackwood is one of those rare adults who can so sink his own consciousness of self that he can find his way into the psychology of the little child and the cat. They have taken him into the secret garden where they really live and he has interpreted it for us in tales of poignant sweetness. The child and the cat are the supreme non-conformists of a world which spends its energies trying to conform to some set pattern changing with the decades. They simply *don't* try, that's why so few adults understand them. In *A Prisoner in Fairyland*; *Jimbo*; some of the stories in *Pan's Garden* (New York: The Macmillan Company), and *The Education of Uncle Paul* (New York: Henry Holt and Company), Blackwood has given us lyrics of childhood that will last. Children themselves may not understand them until they grow up, and then only if they are the sort of children that never grow up. But the adult who Knows will find great store of riches, and the lover of cats will find much delight, in these books.

Oregon National Forest. Algernon Blackwood's distinctive fiction draws on the awe-inspiring power of the unknown which lies just beyond our ken. Unlike Gothic writers, Blackwood located his most successful fiction in the wilderness, the desert, or the forest, "a spot held by the dwellers in some outer space, a sort of peep-hole whence they could spy upon the earth, themselves unseen, a point where the veil between had worn a little thin," as he wrote in "The Willows." Blackwood drew upon his belief in Theosophy and Spiritualism, and his membership in the Golden Dawn (a secret society), which were enjoying a fashionable acceptance around the turn of the twentieth century. Photograph undated (Library of Congress, Prints and Photographs Division, LC-USZ62-100994).

But when the adult mind finds itself approaching or crossing the borderland that parts the Known from the Unknown, sorrow or horror even take the place of joy. And in the expression of this creeping horror that chills the heart when the human comes face to face with what is not human, Algernon Blackwood excels. It is not done sensationally, it seems to come from the man's inmost heart, as an expression of personal beliefs and experiences, and his stories have little dealing with organised or accredited spiritualism. He has only scorn for such futile mental debauches, he has no interest in ghosts that are ticketed and classified, and have even become fashionable. He lays no claim to "scientific research," but he can enthrall the reader until the sweep of unseen or dimly glimpsed Presences crowd thick upon us in the silent room and we long to get back, in sheer shrinking fear, into the "sweet wholesome business of To-day." Every degree of emotion felt by the mind and heart under stress of such experience figures in the many stories that deal with this subject. For sheer naked concentrated horror, unexplained and unexplainable, such tales as "The Wendigo" (*Lost Valley*, New York: Vaughan and Gomme) and "The Willows" (*The Listener*, New York: Vaughan and Gomme) may be said to lead among the stories of the supernatural. But many others are a gorgeous, haunting riot of imagination and creepiness, mingling terror and a sense of splendid free life, Real and Unreal, in bewildering confusion. "The Regeneration of Lord Ernie" and the stupendous "Descent into Egypt" in the book *Incredible Adventures* (New York: The Macmillan Company), "Ancient Sorceries," "Secret Worship," and "The Camp of the Dog" in *John Silence* (New York: Vaughan and Gomme) are some of the most noteworthy among these, although many others have power to hold and thrill unendurably. *The Centaur* (Macmillan Company) has sustained power of imaginative writing equal to the best Blackwood has produced. Arnold Böcklin, the Swiss painter, had such an imagination. And many a sentence in the best of the Blackwood stories takes the form of a Böcklin picture to the inner vision. One wishes Böcklin were still among us to illustrate these conceptions of a kindred spirit that can see the teeming life just beyond the Border of what human vision, hampered by human prejudices, considers fitting limit for the soul's sight.

And yet through all these tales of the power of What Lies Beyond to act upon human lives, there is a note of splendid courage in the appeal to the mind of man to understand that he may control—by controlling himself—all these powers, and take their strength into himself to form it over for Good. It is this note and the sincerity of the style which free the tales entirely from any reproach of desired sensationalism, and which also relieve the strain of horror, that might otherwise prove too strong to be wholesome. Algernon Blackwood stands in a class by himself. What effect it will have on his work if he should ever become popular and Sunday-supplemented, cannot now be foretold. But somehow there is that about his writing which arouses the hope that the good in it may survive even such a fate.

We have already met the editor and critic Frederic Taber Cooper through his assessment of Ambrose Bierce. Here, in a chapter from *Some English Story Tellers: A Book of the Younger Novelists* (1912), Cooper evaluates Robert Smythe Hichens (1882–1940), the English novelist and journalist. Largely forgotten today, Hichens was the author of *The Green Carnation* (1894), a scandalous satire of Oscar Wilde that helped propel Wilde's prosecution for sodomy. Later, Hichens turned his hand to melodrama, mysteries, and the supernatural, producing works like the melodrama *The Garden of Allah* (1904) and the supernatural *The Dweller on the Threshold* (1911). His best-known horror work is "How Love Came to Professor Guildea" (1900), a short story beloved by anthologists, and possibly one of the greatest ghost stories of its age, but which Cooper calls "a hideous bit of morbidity" and the mid-twentieth century critic Edmund Wilson called "trash."

A version of Cooper's "Robert Hichens" ran in *The Bookman* for July 1912 and was collected with a revised ending in *Some English Story Tellers* (1912). Though it is a lengthy piece, the depth of the critical argument marshaled against a man now obscure makes it worth resurrecting in full.

*Robert Hichens**

FREDERIC TABER COOPER

It is almost a score of years since Mr. Robert Hichens first sprang into local notoriety through *The Green Carnation*, which set all London buzzing hotly anent the identity of its bold literary and social lampoons. It was just ten years later that he obtained at last an international recognition, with *The Garden of Allah*, in which for the first time, and perhaps for the last, the inherent bigness of his theme and the titanic majesty of his setting shook him out of his studied pose of aloofness and sardonic cynicism, and

*Frederic Taber Cooper, "Robert Hichens," in *Some English Story Tellers: A Book of the Younger Novelists* (New York: Henry Holt and Company, 1912), 342–375.

raised him to unexpected heights. And almost at the close of a second decade, Mr. Hichens visited America, to find himself, for the passing hour, one of the most widely discussed of modern novelists, with his latest novel giving promise of becoming a "best seller," his earlier triumph, *The Garden of Allah*, demanding a second recognition in dramatic form, and he himself receiving the doubtful tribute of full-page interviews in the Sunday supplements. Accordingly, Mr. Hichens seems to be one of the contemporary British story tellers about whom it is distinctly worth while to ask: How much of this popular acclaim is merited on sound literary grounds, and how much of it is not?

Before attempting to answer specifically this natural and legitimate question, it seems profitable to call attention to the treatment which Mr. Hichens has received at the hands of his critics during the past eighteen years as an illuminating example of the average professional reviewer's shortness of memory and lack of prophetic intuition. A glance over the files of the leading English literary reviews leaves the reader amazed at the suavity with which the critics of Mr. Hichens's more recent popular triumphs ignore the many harsh aspersions they cast upon his earlier volumes, and the completeness with which most of them seem to have forgotten their one-time aversion to certain salient features of his style, his technique and his attitude towards life, all of which are just as marked and most of them just as offensive to-day as in the days when he was trying to startle a sated public into attention, by eccentricities like *Flames*, *The Londoners* and *The Slave*.

For, if we examine Mr. Hichens with dispassionate frankness, refusing to be dazzled by those physical and moral mirages of the desert, of which he possesses the incomparable and magic trick, we must realize that, although he has gained immensely in sheer craftsmanship, and although his instinct for the unerring right word has become surer with practice, his verbal color more brilliantly lavish, his style more fluent and less epigrammatically crystalline, his development has nevertheless been peculiarly homogeneous and consistent. That he has grown, it would be idle to deny; but the growth has been logical, and on certain definite and predestined lines. His gifts, and some of his faults as well, have attained ampler dimensions with the passage of years; but gifts and faults alike, there is scarcely one of them, the seeds of which might not have been found already germinating and taking vigorous root in the now almost forgotten *Green Carnation*. It is worth while, as a bit of pertinent literary history, to call to mind the terms in which Mr. Arthur Waugh first brought this volume to the attention of American readers, in his monthly London letter to the New York *Critic*:

> At last London has a sensation. The quiet of the early autumn is broken by the explosion of a genuine bombshell, and every one is rushing to read *The Green Carnation*.... It is a satire, brilliant and scintillating, upon the literary and social affectations of the hour; and a more daring, impertinent and altogether clever piece of work has not been produced for many years.... The writer remains anonymous and his preference for secrecy is not surprising, for if it is possible for good-humored satire to make enemies, he would scarcely find a friend left. Nobody is spared. Mr. Oscar Wilde is, as the title implies, the principal butt of the brochure, but almost every conspicuous writer and personage is touched to the quick.

From the very nature of its naked and unashamed personalities, this first volume was handled rather gingerly by the reviewers, most of whom were fain to dismiss it, after the euphemistic manner of the *Academy*, as a mere "caricature of an affectation in life and literature, an abnormality, a worship of abstract and scarlet sin, which must by its very nature pass away with the personality that first flaunted it before a wondering, half-attracted, half-revolted world." To-day the unwholesome interest of its theme has passed away like a whiff of foul gas; and in its place remains the interest of the human document, for it shows that the author was even then, just as he is to-day, concerned primarily with the abnormalities of life, seeking by preference the tainted mind, the stunted soul, the pathological body. In spite of a life-long straining after startling effects, Mr. Hichens has no great and original fertility of plot. Many another novelist before him has built stories upon the themes of metempsychosis; of a woman's slavery to the glitter of jewels or to the fool's paradise of opium; of hereditary fires of passion, that betray a bridegroom on his honeymoon into forgetting the marriage service, or a renegade monk into breaking his vows. Mr. Hichens's distinction lies rather in his special gift for taking world-old problems and modernizing them, warming them over to suit a jaded palate, with a dash of the decadent spirit and a garniture of *Fleurs de Mal*. Any one who has read Henry James's *Ambassadors* must remember the sensations of the mild and scholarly Mr. Strethers during his first afternoon in Chad Newsome's Paris apartment, while he listens to the conversation going on blithely and carelessly around him, and wonders helplessly whether all those well-dressed, well-mannered guests really mean all the unspeakable things that they seem to be uttering, or whether his own mind has suddenly become strangely perverted and is playing him tricks. The episode inevitably comes to mind in connection with Mr. Hichens's novels, for it precisely portrays the impression that, with malice aforethought, he contrives to leave upon the mind of his readers. He seems to delight in bringing them to a sudden full stop, with a gasping protest, "Surely, he never could mean that!"—and then, at the turn of the page, leaving them with a bewildered and shamefaced wonderment how they could have entertained, even for a moment, such outrageously indecent thoughts!

That this is no arbitrary and one-sided view of Robert Hichens, any one may readily convince himself by merely taking the trouble to glance over the contemporary reviews of his several books. These reviews, with few exceptions, and quite regardless of their favorable or unfavorable tone, form a rich thesaurus of the various English synonyms, and sometimes the French synonyms as well, when Anglo-Saxon resources run low,—of such words as morbid, neurotic, pathological, decadent, salacious and unclean. It is true that since the appearance of *The Garden of Allah*, less emphasis has been laid upon the unwholesomeness of Mr. Hichens's themes, and more upon the vivid color and scintillating brilliance of his style. It may even be conceded that there is justice in this change, and that, on the whole, his later books are more normal, more human, than his earlier. Nevertheless, the taint persists. There is no escaping the obvious fact that his interest is always in the exceptional, rather than in the average, type. Strange people, bizarre customs, alien skies, men and women vainly struggling against some overmastering obsession, physical disability or mental lesion, a long nightmare procession of the socially and morally unfit,—such, as they mentally file before us, is the impression left by the leading characters of Mr. Hichens's novels.

Now the fault with Mr. Hichens is not too great a frankness about life. It is not that he looks upon the world without illusions, recognizing the plague-spots of human nature and ruthlessly stripping them bare. A bold, uncompromising handling of hypocrisy and avarice, frailty and vice is one of the canons of the realistic creed. There is more disease and degradation in Zola's *Lourdes* than in all the pages ever penned by the author of *The Black Spaniel*. And the reason why *The Black Spaniel* is an unwholesome book, while *Lourdes* is not, is simply this: That when he has occasion to expose the ugliness of life, Mr. Hichens, unlike Zola, either cannot or will not emulate the purely scientific zeal of the surgeon, dissecting away a diseased tissue. Underneath the surface impersonality of the realist, one discerns a spirit of prying and unwholesome curiosity, gloating over the forbidden and the unclean. "When I am what is called wicked, it is my mood to be evil," are the words that Mr. Hichens puts into the mouth of Reggie Hastings, in *The Green Carnation*. "I must drink absinthe, and hang the night hours with scarlet embroideries; I must have music and the sins that march to music." And, if we are content not to stretch the comparison unduly, these phrases are not a bad characterization of the salient qualities of much of Mr. Hichens's fiction. He, too, is fond of hanging the night hours with scarlet embroideries, of showing us sins that keep pace to sensuous rhythms. Like the French artist, Fromentin, one of Mr. Hichens's forerunners in discovering and interpreting Algeria, he has suffered from an innate tendency to see what is picturesque, spectacular, even pretty, rather than what is truly great; and, as with Fromentin, Algeria taught him how to do the bigger thing. It was not until he replaced his "scarlet embroideries" with the vast monochrome of the African sky, the tinkle of drawing-room music with the sublimity of desert silence and solitude, that he attained, for once at least, an epic amplitude of canvas and of theme.

As a bold and effective colorist, Mr. Hichens deserves cordial commendation. His skill in vivid pictorial description is beyond dispute. Whether it be a glimpse of a crowded London street, the turquoise blue of Italian sea and sky, or the burning reach of sun-ravished desert, his printed words seem to open up a vista of light and warmth, a moving picture wrought of dissolving and opalescent hues. His colors lack the riotous romanticism of a Théophile Gautier, the wistful melancholy of a Pierre Loti, the frankly pagan sensuousness of a d'Annunzio,—yet he owes something of its varied richness to each of these. It is obvious that he loves color for its own sake, much as his heroine in *The Slave* loves the gleam of jewels,—and flings it on lavishly, just as he flings on other forms of ornamentation, purely decorative in purpose, with the result that his backgrounds are often crowded with superfluous and confusing detail. This tendency has grown upon him year by year; it is only in his shorter stories that he has learned the value of restraint. *The Garden of Allah*, *Bella Donna*, *The Fruitful Vine*, one and all would have gained much by a well-advised and ruthless pruning.

There is a popular impression that Mr. Hichens is a writer of uncommon versatility; and when we consider that his themes range from the morphine habit to the transmigration of souls, and his stage settings from a London drawing-room to the Sahara desert, and from the Nile to the Italian lakes, this impression seems at least superficially justified. But when we begin carefully to sift them over and mentally slip each plot into its respective pigeon-hole, we find that, underneath all his shifting scenes and varied topics, Mr. Hichens's interest in life narrows down to just one form of obsession, namely, the study of human imperfection, the analysis of those various lesions in body, mind or soul which, like a flaw in the heart of a gem, brand certain men and women as unfit,—at best, to be classed as eccentrics, and at worst as monstrosities. Viewed from this point, his themes fall naturally under three heads: first, his social satires, or studies of the passing fads, foibles, petty vices and hypocrisies on which the world of fashion smiles indulgently; secondly, certain mental delusions, occult phenomena, psychopathic hallucinations, such as form the underlying idea of stories of *The Black Spaniel* type,—in which each reader must decide for himself whether he is reading an allegory, a diagnosis of a curious form of insanity, or a report to the Society for Psychical Research; and, thirdly,— and to this class belong practically all of Mr. Hichens's later serious novels,—studies in moral depravity, chronic and often incurable maladies of the human soul.

Because of this threefold classification of his stories, it is impracticable to survey Mr. Hichens's writings in anything approaching chronological order. His sardonic enjoyment of the social extravagance of the passing hour is more or less apparent in every book that he writes, and lends sharp characterization to many an unforgettable minor character. Yet the only volume since *The Green Carnation* in which it would be fair to say that social satire is, first, last and all the time, the main issue, is *The Londoners*, in which the pretensions of smart society, the pomps and vanities of Mayfair, are, as Mr. Hichens's own sub-title implies, reduced to an absurdity. Of the second class of plots, or those dealing with occultism and pseudo-psychic phenomena of the Jekyll-Hyde order, we have, besides *The Black Spaniel*, a number of weird and fantastic short tales and two novels, *Flames: A London Phantasy*, one of his earliest efforts, and *The Dweller on the Threshold*, which is one of his most recent. This group of stories represent various degrees of cleverness; but they one and all leave the impression that the author has not put the best of himself into them. They simply are the embodiment of certain fantastic ideas which in hours of perversity happened to riot through his brain, and which later he could not bring himself wholly to reject. There is a loathsome and uncanny horror about a theme like that of *The Black Spaniel*, that obviously fastened leech-like upon the abnormal side of Mr. Hichens's nature and refused to let go its hold. Yet, even in this instance, the strongest of all his occult horror tales, the thing is not quite achieved. By over-insistence upon obvious details, by under-estimating the intelligence of his readers and explaining his meaning in words of one syllable, as though to an audience of little children, he defeats his purpose, and destroys the last vestige of plausibility. Mr. Hichens is too much of the earth, earthy; he is far too interested in the frailties and perversions of the flesh, to gain credence when writing of the transmigration of souls or the vagaries of disembodied spirits. Consequently, it is with his third class of stories, serious studies of human delinquency, that we must mainly concern ourselves, in order to take a fair measure of Mr. Hichens, as artist and as student of human nature.

Neither is it worth while to linger over his shorter stories, in any of the three subdivisions. What has so often been said in regard to the collection of Egyptian and Algerian tales that swell the volume containing *The Black Spaniel* to its required three hundred and odd pages, namely, that they were fugitive pages from his note-book for *The Garden of Allah*, applies in the main to most of his shorter efforts. He is essentially a writer of the sustained effort type; and it is consequently only fair to judge him by his full-length volumes. If evidence were needed to support the contention that, other things being equal, he ministers by preference to a mind diseased, then such a collection of tales as *Tongues of Conscience* would furnish fertile illustrations. There is, for instance, the story of the famous painter whose peace of mind is destroyed because he holds himself responsible for having inspired a street urchin with a passion for the sea, and the boy subsequently was drowned; or again, in "The Cry of the Child," we have a young doctor, in whose ears there rings ceaselessly the dying cry of his own child, whom he had cruelly neglected in its last hours; and still again, in "How Love Came to Professor Guildea," we are told how a materialistic man of science becomes subject to the obsession of a degraded spirit,—a hideous bit of morbidity, which might pass for a study in insanity, if the author had not precluded that explanation by showing us the Professor's parrot offering its crest to the caresses of unseen fingers, and mimicking the endearments of the invisible and loathsome visitant.

But, as it happens, the longer stories are even more to our purpose than the short tales. Already in 1895, his second published volume, *An Imaginative Man*, clearly reveals the author's natural bent. Briefly, it is the story of an intellectual and highly cultivated man who is destitute of natural affections:

> He (Denison) had never loved his kind, and never even followed the humane fashion of pretending to love them.... It amused him to observe them under circumstances of excitement, terror or pain, in a climax of passion or despair.... He liked people when they lost their heads, when they became abnormal. Anything bizarre attracted him abnormally.

This curiously unnatural personage marries a charming and devoted wife, because he chooses to suspect something enigmatic about her. Later, when he is forced to recognize that she is normal and simple and truehearted, his interest turns to a dislike akin to hatred. Accordingly, he leaves her, and, after amusing himself for a time in Egypt, watching the impotent rebellion of a boy in the last stages of consumption, he ends his useless career by dashing out his brains against the Sphinx, with which he has perversely become enamored. Among the press-clippings of that period there is one opinion upon which it would be presumptuous to try to improve:

> It is a story to remain a splendid monument to unwholesome fancy, a thesaurus of morbid suggestion, which exalts mere vulgar suicide into an intellectual resource of the weary-minded, and degrades the humanity of virtue into mere animal instinct.

As a companion picture to this unnatural man, Mr. Hichens shortly afterwards gave us an equally unnatural woman, in the person of Lady Caryll Allabruth, the heroine of *The Slave*. Lady Caryll is obsessed by one consuming passion, jewels,—by which, of course, Mr. Hichens wishes to symbolize all the futile luxuries for which women, from time immemorial, have sold themselves. She is fortunate in meeting, while still quite young, an Anglicized Oriental of great wealth, who can lavish upon her diamonds, pearls and rubies, who understands her through and through, without one remnant of flattering illusion, and who actually wins her by the dazzling splendor of one huge and matchless emerald. It is her own husband who, in the course of the story, sums her up as follows:

> "She was born to live in a harem, petted, as an animal is petted, adorned with jewels as a sultan's favorite is adorned. Such a life would have satisfied her nature. Her soul shines like a jewel and is as hard.... A certain class of women has breathed through so long a chain of years a fetid atmosphere, of intellectual selfishness, has sold itself, body, mind and soul, so repeatedly for hard things that glitter, for gold, for diamonds, for the petted slave-girl's joys, that humanity has absolutely dwindled in the

race, just as size might dwindle in a race breeding in and in with dwarfs. In Caryll, that dwindling light of humanity has gone out. My wife is not human."

Now, it is extremely convenient for a woman who happens not to be human to have a husband who, although aware of the fact, does not seem to mind; so it was rather unfortunate for Caryll Allabruth that her husband died, ruined by her monomania for jewels. In her poverty, however, Lady Caryll managed to retain the one matchless emerald with which he had won her. This emerald is subsequently stolen; and, since it is the one thing left in life for which she cares, and all other means of recovering it fail, Lady Caryll consents to become the burglar's bride, in order that the emerald's green fires may once more burn upon her breast. All of which, in spite of its melodramatic extravagance, rests upon a foundation of perverse and sardonic logic that is eminently characteristic.

The next two volumes, in point of time, while unmistakably expressing the same outlook upon life, show a distinct gain in the direction of sobriety and self-restraint. *Felix* and *The Woman with the Fan*, although neither of them a book of real importance in itself, at least revealed Mr. Hichens as a novelist worth watching for better reasons than merely because he could attract attention with a flow of epigram, as insistent as the cracking of a whip. Moreover, although he had not learned to draw sympathetic characters,—and it is seriously to be questioned whether he ever will learn,—he at least began to get rather nearer the average human level of understanding than in the case of Denison or Lady Caryll. The heroine of *Felix* is not naturally inhuman; she is simply a victim of the drug habit, an unfortunately common and pitiable human weakness, although repulsive and rather nauseating when forced in intimate detail upon our notice. If Mr. Hichens's purpose was to do for the opium habit what Zola did for alcohol in *L'Assommoir*, it is a pity that his misunderstanding of the realistic method has resulted in defeating his object. Zola got his effects by tireless and uncompromising accumulation of facts, flung at us almost defiantly, with no attempt to palliate or to obscure. What his characters made of these facts, whether they understood them, believed them, acted upon them or not, was all of secondary importance; facts, as nearly as he could get them, were the be-all and the end-all of his novels, their excuse and apology for existence. Mr. Hichens, on the contrary, cannot be frank, even if he wants to be; he always proceeds by indirection. It is so much easier to suggest than to tell plainly an unsavory fact, and then trust the reader's mind to go to greater lengths than the printed page would dare to go!

In *Felix* we have probably the best and most extreme case of this method to be found in the whole range of its author's writings. Felix himself is in no wise abnormal; on the contrary, he is just the plain, ordinary variety of young fool, the Kipling type of fool, whose rag and bone happens, to his more complete undoing, to be further complicated with a hypodermic needle. Felix pays a brief visit to Paris, where fate wills it that he shall meet a certain little tailor who in youth had the honor to make Balzac a "pair of trousers without feet," and who initiates Felix into the endless delights of the *Comédie Humaine*. This whole episode of the little tailor stands out luminously against a background of human slime. It is the sort of thing that Mr. W. J. Locke can do so supremely well, a page that might have fluttered loose from *The Belovèd Vagabond*. When the final reckoning of Mr. Hichens's achievements is to be cast up, this little masterpiece of Balzac's tailor ought to count heavily on the credit side.

As for the story of Felix as a whole, it is undeniably strong,—as strong as escaping sewer gas. Having read the *Comédie Humaine*, Felix flatters himself that human nature holds no secrets from him; he plunges, hotheaded, into the turbulence of London's fast set, men drugged with ambition, women drugged with vanity, with avarice, with opium. There is an all-pervading sense of something unexplained and inexplicable. Felix's inexperience hangs like a heavy veil before our eyes, and we are forced to grope with him, to piece fragments of evidence together, just as he does, and, like him, often to piece them wrong. Especially, out of the other loathsome and unclean horrors, there looms up, as nauseously offensive as some putrescent fungoid growth, a certain corpulent, bloated, blear-eyed little dog, symbolic of human bestiality. The present writer can recall no episode in modern fiction, not even in the audacities of Catulle Mendès, which, after a lapse of some years, still brings back the same sickening qualm of physical illness.

The Woman with the Fan, although not by any means lacking in audacities, came as a welcome contrast to its predecessor. In addition to its odd title, it had a somewhat startling cover design, the nude figure of a woman apparently going through some sort of a drill with an open fan. This figure, which proves to be a marble statuette known as *Une Danseuse de Tunisie*, plays a rather important part in the development of the story. It is the fan which makes the statuette wicked, one of the characters repeatedly insists; and the thought which is symbolized by the statue is that of the Eternal Feminine degraded by the artificial and the tarnish of mundane life. In applying the symbolism of this statuette to his heroine, Lady Holme, Mr. Hichens seems to have taken a perverse pleasure in confusing right and wrong, idealism and sensuality. Lady Holme's friends constantly identify her with the statuette, and beg her to "throw away her fan," meaning that there is a taint of wickedness about her, and that she is capable of higher things. The facts in the case, however, hardly fit in with this theory. Stripped of its symbolism, the book is a study of the two elements which go to make up human love, the physical attraction and the psychological. Viola Holme is a woman in whom the finer elements of character lie dormant. She is married to a man of the big, athletic, primitive sort, "a slave to every impulse born of passing physical sensations." She knows that of poetry, music, and all the finer things of life he has not, and never will have, the slightest comprehension. She knows, too, that he loves her only for the surface beauty of her hair, her eyes, her symmetry of face and form, and that if she lost that beauty on the morrow, his love would go with it. And yet she loves him, in spite of his crudeness and his many infidelities, because he satisfies the demands of that side of her nature which is the strongest,—the side which "holds the fan." Other men, the men who urge her to "throw the fan away," offer her a different kind of love, because there are times when they see in her eyes and hear in her voice, when she sings morbid little verses from d'Annunzio, the promise of deeper emotions than her husband ever dreamed her capable of. Now, a woman of Viola Holme's temperament would never voluntarily "throw aside her fan," and Mr. Hichens is a sufficiently keen judge of women to be aware of it. Nothing short of an accident in which the statuette is broken will accomplish this miracle. So fate is invoked, in the shape of an overturned automobile, and Lady Holme struggles back to consciousness, to find her famous beauty gone forever. In its place is a mere caricature of a human face, a spectacle so repellent that, of all the men who formerly professed to worship the "inner beauty of her soul," only one has the courage to renew his vows, and he a poor, broken-down inebriate, as sad a wreck as herself. Such, in bare outline, is the story of *The Lady with the Fan*, and each reader may apply the symbolism to suit himself. A hasty, snap-shot interpretation would be that Lady Holme would have become a better woman, mentally and morally, if she had discarded her coarse-minded husband and replaced him with a lover of more artistic temperament. But such an interpretation would do scant justice to Mr. Hichens's subtlety. The physical and spiritual elements of love, he seems to say, are too curiously intermeshed to be readily separated; there is no love so earthly that it does not get a glimmer of higher things, no love so pure and idyllic that it does not crave some slight concession to the flesh. If she would hold love, the modern woman must be content to remain a little lower than the angels, she must hold to her fan.

In spite of the implied confession of weakness in solving a rather big problem with the unsatisfactory makeshift of an accident, *The Woman with a Fan* is obviously, even now as we look at it in the light of his later achievements, so much bigger and stronger and more vital than all that went before it, that *The Garden of Allah*, when it followed shortly afterwards, ought not to have been the surprise that it actually was. Of this book, the one really big and enduring contribution that Mr. Hichens has made to modern fiction, there is really absurdly little to say. It is so simple, so elemental, so inevitable in all its parts. It may be epitomized with more brevity than many a short story. There is a certain Trappist monk, Androvsky, who, after twenty years of silent obedience to his order breaks his vows, escapes from bondage, and, meeting Domini Enfilden, an independent English girl with a lawless strain of gipsy blood in her veins, woes her with a gauche and timid ardor, and carries her off for a mad, fantastic honeymoon into the heart of the African desert. The desert, so says a Moorish proverb, is the Garden of Allah; and here the renegade monk, fleeing from his conscience, with confession ever hovering on his lips, and doubly punished through dread of the anguish awaiting his innocent bride when enlightenment comes to her, finds the solitude too vast, the isolation too terrifying, the imminence of divine wrath too overwhelming to be borne. It drives him back to the haunts of men, even in the face of a premonition that amounts to certainty, that his secret must be laid bare and his short-lived and forbidden joy be ended. Now the theme of a man breaking the holiest vows for the unlawful love of a woman is one of the commonplaces in the history of fiction. It is the majestic simplicity of his materials, the isolation of his man and his woman, the sublimity of his remote, unfathomable background, that combine to raise this exceptional book almost to the epic dignity of the First Fall of Man. As has already been insisted, in connection with each succeeding book, Mr. Hichens does not possess the faculty of frankness. That Boris Androvsky is a sinner, bearing the burden of an unpardonable and nameless misdeed, is a fact that we grasp almost at the outset; but Mr. Hichens would have been false to his own nature, if he had not, before revealing the secret, forced us to suspect his hero of every known crime against man, nature and God. But suddenly his theme seems to have taken possession of him, to have raised him against his will, perhaps without his knowledge, out of the pettiness and subterfuge that have dwarfed so much of his work, into the full light of truth and sympathy and understanding. In a certain sense, the book seems to have written itself; it is a fantastic piece of word-painting, done with a tropical luxuriance of color, a carnival of Algerian pageantry and African sunshine; and everywhere and all the time, is an all-pervading sense of the mystery, the languor, the thousand blending sights and sounds and scents of the Orient. Long after the final page is turned, you cannot shut out from your eyes the memory of the desert, "with its pale sands and desolate cities, its ethereal mysteries of mirage, its tragic splendors of color, of tempest and of heat"; you cannot forget the throbbing pulsations of burning air, the vast endless monochrome of earth and sky, the primeval tragedy of an erring man and woman, helpless motes in the glare of universal sunshine, impotently fleeing from an avenging God. It is this one book which entitles Mr. Hichens to a serious consideration among the novelists of to-day. Without it, he could have safely been passed over in silence.

It follows that, in various degrees, all the books that Mr. Hichens has given us since *The Garden of Allah* are in the nature of an anti-climax; and for that reason they may be somewhat briefly and summarily dismissed. One recalls with a certain amount of cordial appreciation another and briefer story of Algeria called *Barbary Sheep*,—a book that owes its charm chiefly to its delicate and almost flawless artistry, and its lack of any pretension to be more than it actually is. Just a bit of idle playing with fire, a young English couple gaining their first glimpse of African life and African temperament; and while the husband spends his days, and sometimes the nights, tirelessly hunting Barbary Sheep, the young wife, restless, unsatisfied, craving excitement, is drifting rashly into an extremely dangerous intimacy with a cultured and suave young Arab, an officer in one of the native regiments. What might so easily have become a tragedy is brought to a safe and final solution by the removal of the Arab from further participation, through his death at the hands of a fanatical dervish. And to the end we have the delicious irony of the utter unconsciousness of the phlegmatic English husband, so intent on Barbary Sheep that he passes his wife, where she crouches among the rocks, in the desert moonlight, equally unsuspecting, as he passes, the menace of her Arab lover, and the death-blow that an instant later removes that menace.

Then we have the much overpraised Sicilian story, *The Call of the Blood*, and its stronger and more sanely appraised sequel, *A Spirit in Prison*. Aside from an almost pagan frankness in their unashamed, recognition of physical passion, these are conspicuously clean volumes, with little if anything of the author's earlier perversity. The chief weakness in *The Call of the Blood* lies in the unconvincing character of the leading episode, the one upon which the whole structure of the story hinges: namely, the fact that Hermione, the young English wife of Maurice Delarey, feels herself compelled to leave him before their honeymoon in Sicily is half over, in order to hasten to the bedside of Émile Artois, the Frenchman who has long been in love with her, and who is said to be dying. During the brief weeks of her absence, her husband, who has inherited through his grandmother a strain of Sicilian blood, yields to the call of this remote strain and falls under the spell of a young peasant girl's transient beauty, promptly paying the penalty of death at the hands of the peasant girl's kinsmen. Of the true facts of this tragedy Hermione is never told; she knows only that her husband was drowned, and that she lost some precious weeks of happiness by her absence at the bedside of the Frenchman whom she did not love and who has lived, while the Englishman whom she did love has died. So, believing him to be the perfect type of honor and fidelity, she consecrates herself to lifelong widowhood.

It is at this point that *The Call of the Blood* breaks off, with a young and still beautiful woman wasting her best years in mourning for an unworthy man, while the right man, who knows the truth and might easily win her if he chose to speak, feels that his lips are sealed by his unwillingness to destroy her ideal. *A Spirit in Prison* takes up the story some seventeen years later. The scene is no longer Sicily, but a tiny island in the Bay of Naples, to which the widowed bride retired at the time of her bereavement, to await the birth of her child, and in which she and Vere, the daughter, now a girl of sixteen, still have their home. The Sicilian peasant girl, for whom Hermione's husband proved false to her, also had a child, who is now a sturdy young fisher lad, with eyes that are strangely reminiscent of some one whom Hermione has known, some one in the distant past whom she either cannot or will not name even to herself. Her attention is first called to the fisher lad by the interest that he awakens in her daughter, Vere; for the girl, by some curious instinct, has recognized the ties of kinship and has made the boy her protégé and comrade. It takes very little time for Artois, who still loves Hermione with patient hopelessness, and for Gaspare, her faithful old servant, to learn the truth about the boy's parentage; and these two men instinctively conspire to keep Hermione in ignorance. But by doing so they unconsciously prolong her suffering; because her spirit is struggling in the prison of delusion, and can win freedom, and with it love and happiness, only through full knowledge of the truth. Altogether, these two volumes make up a strong, clean, tender human story, admirably handled to bring out all the values that the plot contains. It revealed Mr. Hichens as an interpreter of Italian life somewhere midway between Richard Bagot and Marion Crawford, less pedantic than the former, yet lacking the geniality of the creator of *Saracinesca.*

Mr. Hichens might, had he chosen, have gone on indefinitely from this point, doing the fairly innocuous, fairly entertaining sort of story, and letting us little by little forget the days when a new volume from his pen meant an alternate gasp and shudder at the turn of each page. But it is not in his nature to be content with doing the innocuous thing. He insists upon being conspicuous; and if the only way of being conspicuous is to shock a startled world into attention, he stands ready to do so. Just two more novels demand a passing word: *Bella Donna* and *The Fruitful Vine.* Of these two, the former is of no special importance, either in theme or in detail, although in its heroine he has created one more unwholesome and abnormal type that lingers in the memory. At the opening of the story, Mrs. Chepstow is summed up as "a great beauty in decline":

> Her day of glory had been fairly long, but now it seemed to be over. She was past forty. She said she was thirty-eight, but she was over forty. Goodness, some say, keeps women fresh. Mrs. Chepstow had tried a great many means of keeping fresh, but she had omitted that.

The facts about Mrs. Chepstow, which Mr. Hichens regards as of moment, are that in the zenith of her youth and beauty she was divorced by her husband; that, having made a failure of one life, she resolved that she would make a success of another; that for a long time she kept men at her feet, ministering to her desires,—and then suddenly, as she approached forty, "the roseate hue faded from her life, and a grayness began to fall over it." In other words, to catalogue the book roughly, it is one more of the many studies devoted to *L'Automne d'une Femme*. And so, at the opening of the volume, we meet Mrs. Chepstow, in the consulting-room of a famous specialist, Dr. Meyer Isaacson, confiding to him certain facts about herself, physical, mental and moral facts, which the reader is not allowed to overhear, which the woman herself never alludes to again, but which Mr. Hichens has no intention of allowing the reader to cease for one moment to ponder over, with a more or less prurient curiosity. Incidentally,—and to this extent alone is her confession justified structurally,—it is the memory of what she confided to him that at a crucial hour hurries Dr. Isaacson on a desperate, headlong Odyssey to the Nile, in order to save a friend and keep Mrs. Chepstow from the sin of murder. But all of this is, frankly, rather cheap stuff, and quite unworthy of the author of *The Garden of Allah*. It makes a normal-minded reader somewhat exasperated to see a rather rare talent deliberately misused.

Only one other volume, *The Fruitful Vine*, remains for discussion. The setting is modern Rome, the leading characters two married couple, both English, Sir Theodore Cannynge and his wife, Dolores, Sir Theodore's closest friend, Francis Denzil and his wife Edna—and just one Italian, Cesare Carelli. Cannynge, having lost his first love in a painful tragedy years before, remained unmarried almost until middle age. At the opening of the story Dolores has for ten years been his wife, but no children have come to them. Whatever regrets he may have felt have remained unspoken; until within a year his whole interest seemed to center in his diplomatic career, first in one European capital, then in another. But when the inheritance of an independent fortune came almost simultaneously with the loss of his great ambition, the Austrian Embassy, in a moment of pique he resigned, and from that time on had more time for thought than was good for him. Finally comes the day when, fresh from a visit to Denzil's home, full of the merriment of children's voices, he catches up his wife's Chinese poodle by the throat and, while the miserable little beast writhes and coughs and blinks, tells her violently: "Look at it! This is all we've got, you and I, to make a home—after ten years!" Dolores is not surprised; she has felt instinctively that sooner or later this outbreak was bound to come. None the less it hurts her just as every one of his almost daily visits to Denzil's home, blessed with a fruitful vine in place of a barren one, has hurt her. She is not jealous of Edna, Denzil's wife, although she knows that the idle gossip of Rome has settled their relations for them. The Roman world would be incapable of understanding that the attraction might be the children and not the woman. Dolores's troubles, however, are only just beginning. Francis Denzil, husband of "the happiest woman in Rome," is suddenly stricken down with cancer of the larynx, is operated upon and never rallies. His last request is that Sir Theodore will be a second father to his little son—and Sir Theodore promises. From this time onward, Dolores sees less and less of her husband; a vicarious fatherhood has taken possession of him, absorbed him, made him a new man. When the summer comes, he disappoints her regarding her long-cherished plan to visit London, and insists upon taking a villa at Frascati, so as to be near the Denzil children. Then comes a day when Dolores rebels, packs her belongings and goes by herself to Lake Como, to escape the torture of neglect. Meanwhile Roman gossip has been busy in coupling her name with that of another man, that of Cesare Carelli. Since he was a mere boy, Carelli has been faithful to just one woman, the Mancini. But suddenly and quite recently it has become common knowledge that he has definitely broken with her. Why? asks Rome insistently; Romans do not do such things; a man may be untrue to his wife, but a lover remains faithful. There must be some other woman—and Rome is quick to find her in Dolores. As the Countess Boccara tells Dolores to her face, with a malicious little stress on the pronoun: "The rupture happened in the summer, very soon after you left Rome, *cara*." Now it is while Dolores is in hiding at Como, and just at the crucial moment when the insistent thought has first taken possession of her, "If I could only give Theodore a child!" that Carelli tracks her down—and this is the beginning of the tragedy that the reader at once foresees is inevitable. What actually follows may be put into a dozen words. Dolores does give a child to Sir Theodore—a child of alien parentage—but she never reaps the harvest that she has hoped for, the harvest of reawakened love; because the child costs the mother her life, or rather, not the child, but her own loosened hold upon life itself, due to a loathing of her own deed. As for Carelli, he is truly Italian in his inability to conceive of Dolores's real motive. For love, yes, that he could understand; but for motherhood, never! And when the woman is dead, and the stricken husband is just awakening to his loss, the Italian thinks to square accounts by claiming his child. But his revenge misses fire. His revelation simply results in quickening Sir Theodore's own self-knowledge, and he says at last in all humility: "She was better than I, better than I!"

Such is the story of *The Fruitful Vine*, analyzed as generously and as sympathetically as possible. It is written with extraordinary power, and it is thrown into strong relief against a background of rare richness, the vari-colored background of the Roman world. Of the inherent bigness of his theme, the pathos of barrenness, the tragedy of a woman who sees her husband's love alienated because she fails to give him sons and daughters, there can be no question:—just as there can be no question that Mr. Hichens has, perhaps unwittingly, done his utmost to debase it. He has given his theme certain perverse twists that put it on a level even lower than that of Elinor Glyn's much-discussed *Three Weeks*. It was cheap workmanship, and not an unworthy plot, that made *Three Weeks* the ephemeral, negligible book that it was. But in *The Fruitful Vine* we are asked to believe that a delicately nurtured, refined and cultivated Englishwoman, who worships her husband, is willing to do him the ultimate, crowning wrong that any wife can do, and foist upon him, as his son and heir, an interloper that has not even the redeeming grace of being a child of love, but one more basely begotten, more purely meretricious than half the nameless waifs that crowd the asylums! And in asking this, he simply insults our intelligence. All his finished craftsmanship cannot make the volume otherwise than futile.

To sum him up in a few words, we have in Mr. Hichens a story teller of much brilliance who has deliberately chosen to prostitute his gifts to the gratification of unhealthy tastes. He has preferred the sensational notoriety of the passing hour to the less flamboyant successes of enduring worth. He has given us a few books that are fairly innocuous and just one book that deserves to live. And the danger of according the full measure of praise to *The Garden of Allah* lies in this: that by granting its greatness, we may seem by implication to put the stamp of approval on the author's other works, so many of which, unfortunately, are mentally and morally unclean.

Henry Duff Traill (1842–1900) was a British author and journalist who wrote for a number of prominent newspapers and magazines. He produced a series of volumes of literary criticism among his numerous works, and he coauthored with Robert Hichens a play, *The Medicine Man* (1898). In this excerpt from the "Et Cætera" column in *The English Illustrated Magazine* for July 1889, Traill discusses the dismal state of ghostly literature in the 1880s. The title "The Creeps" is the one given the piece when reprinted in *The Bookmart* for August 1889.

The Creeps*

H. D. TRAILL

"What constitutes the 'creeps'?" to throw a famous poetic question into a slightly different form. What was the secret of the Fat Boy in *Pickwick*, and how may it be acquired by the author of the "dreadful"? For it must be admitted that the secret development of the "creepy-story" business has not been accompanied by a corresponding improvement of methods. It may be that method has not very much to do with it, and that a natural gift for the gruesome bestowed upon few, availeth more than art. Whatever the cause (which also, by the by, may be personal to myself), it is the fact that the professional blood-curdler much more often leaves my blood flowing at its normal rate of speed and fibrinous consistency, than he was wont to do, and that where formerly I crept I now creep not at all. What—if it be not a purely subjective one—is the reason of this? I am not sure that I have had a really good shudder—a single refreshing rill of ice-cold

A Graveyard. By the end of the nineteenth century, horror stories known as "curdlers" were a regular feature in newspapers and magazines. Their popularity at century's end helped firmly establish horror as a literary genre and testified to the pleasures inherent in experiencing "the creeps," which the horror genre had been marketing for more than a century and would continue to market for a century to come. The genre remained conservative, though, employing the same ideas and signifiers again and again so that in 1800, 1900, or 2000 an overgrown graveyard still served as shorthand for the aesthetic of terror Edmund Burke described in 1757.

*H.D. Traill, "Et Cætera," *The English Illustrated Magazine*, July 1889, 760–761.

water down the spinal column since the late lamented M. Lefanu quitted this earthly scene—the only writer of the kind of literature, as it seemed to me (with perhaps the exception of the unknown author of a certain story entitled, I think, "Cousin Anastasius,"[a] in the far back pages of *Household Words*), who had caught anything of the Poesque trick. A recent volume of "curdlers"[b] has been highly commended by certain critics in the press. I have tried with every desire to be appalled by it, but if I were asked whether it gave me tremors, I should honestly have to reply that it has signally failed to do so. There is a story of "spirit possession" which is very well for you if you are an Esoteric Buddhist—only then it wouldn't frighten you—but will never wash, I feel convinced, in the Western world. And there is another entitled "Dog or Demon," which is certainly a dismal treatise enough to cause one's fell of hair to rouse and stir as life were in't. But not *my* fell: It no more roused and stirred than the judge's horse-hair at the touch of the black cap. I didn't believe in that dog a bit. He was not to be mentioned along with—not in the same spectral Zoo so to speak with—that delightful phantom monkey whom the hero of one of M. Lefanu's last stories[c] saw for the first time in a midnight omnibus, his sole travelling companion, squatting in one of the corner seats next the conductor, while he himself was sitting dozing at the further end of the 'bus, and who never quits him until he drives the haunted wretch to suicide. That monkey was a convincing and a creepy monkey—but a dog. In the first place, no true lover of the canine race—and I have no sympathy with any one who is not—would mind being haunted by a dog. He would like it, and would make friends with the animal, and chuckle at having escaped the license duty. In the next place—but it is needless to labour a point, which after all must be impossible to prove—if a spectre fails to appal you he fails, and it is not much good in inquiring whether it is your fault or the spectre's. If you are polite you will take the whole blame of the failure upon your prosaic and unimaginative self; but the spectre if he is a "spook" of good sense and self-respect will lose no time in taking himself off.

In spite however of the demon dog having fallen flat, I am inclined to think that the future is with the lower-animal ghost rather than with the human apparition. Perhaps the Psychical Society have taken the fun out of the ghost story of the old-fashioned kind: but whether or no, it can not be made to go in these days in any but a master's hand. It is in vain that the supposed narrator of the story laboriously endeavours to impress you with such a conception of his own character as may make you feel that anything which convinces him ought to convince you. Sometimes he is a doctor—the very man who is most familiar with the tricks that the senses may play on the imagination, and therefore the least likely to become the victim of mere optical illusions. Or again, he is a hard-headed, cynical lawyer, trained by his long experience of fools and knaves to know how easily man may be deceived, and how ready he is to practise deceit upon his fellows. But whether doctor, lawyer or what not, he is always a sceptic by conviction and habit, and moreover—this is invariable—the ghost-seer who is going to tell you his plain tale disclaims any sort of literary ability whatsoever. It follows partly from this and partly from a certain morbid reserve which afflicts all ghosts seen in ghost stories, that he is most reluctant to tell you the story at all. His reluctance indeed is in some cases almost painful, and the reader feels a positive delicacy about prying into secrets which it apparently costs the narrator so distressing an effort to recall. He is "strongly urged by his friends," he says, "to give to the world"— ghost-seeing apparently produces much the same effect on a man's friends as verse-scribbling—"the history of the painful episode which," &c, and much against his will he has at last consented. But these well-meant attempts to impress the reader impress him no longer. Instead of hanging breathless and awe-stricken on the story which is thus being wrung from these unwilling lips, the reader with difficulty suppresses a smile at the thought of the number of times he has heard the same thing before. "No," he says to himself, "it is too thin. This sceptical lawyer, this doubting doctor, I have met too many times before. So far from being what they represent themselves, I believe them to be men of unbounded credulity. I suspect the doctor of being a spiritualist, and the lawyer of believing in the Tichborne claimant."[d] Their ghost story in consequence gains nothing at all in credit from their personal character, and has to depend solely on its natural verisimilitude for its effect on the reader. And this verisimilitude somehow or other is not great. The modern phantom-maker either overdoes the transcendental side of the matter, or he sticks too closely to the old-fashioned Mrs. Radcliffe business. One does not know which is the worse mistake. Clanking chains and other such spectral properties have of course had their day; ghosts who pit-a-pat with their feet on the terraces of country houses; ghosts who are heard washing their hands, as the poet says, "with invisible soap in imperceptible water"[e] in dressing rooms adjoining haunted chambers; ghosts who blow out candles on the stairs; ghosts who smile and roll their eyes from the canvases of old family

328   6. Ghosts and Kindred Horrors

portraits, behind which of course there turns out to be an unsuspected spiral staircase, "constructed in the thickness of the masonry, and leading to," &c.; ghosts who light up the windows of long-deserted rooms in ancient mansions, to the dismay of the villagers; ghosts (female) clad in white, with a stain of crimson on the breast; ghosts (male) of the Elizabethan or early Jacobean period, middle-aged, with a peaked, slightly grizzled beard, and grave melancholy eyes; ghosts who breathe on the cheeks of sleepers, lightly and yet in a manner quite distinguishable from an ordinary "infernal draught"; ghosts who do nothing particular but make the occupants of haunted rooms undefinably uncomfortable, and cause them to wake suddenly in the night with "the feeling, how produced I cannot explain, but strong, overmastering, irresistible, no more to be doubted or questioned than the consciousness of my own existence, that there was SOME ONE (in capitals) *sitting* (in italics) *by the side of the bed*"—to all these ghosts it may be kindly but firmly notified that they need not apply. But in declining their services and repudiating their ancient and discredited properties, the seeker after the awful need not go to the other extreme, and instead

The Vigil of Arms. Ghost stories and their trappings had become so clichéd that they had long since become objects of humor and ridicule. In this illustration from the satirical Bill Nye's History of England *(1896), a knight is shown encountering all the traditional accoutrements of terror. If* Dracula *had proved the Gothic still held on to its power to frighten, it was equally true that sophisticated readers had grown tired of over-reliance on hackneyed set-pieces and wanted new, more innovative horrors.*

of spectres who palpitate too much with actuality, giving us vague, impersonal, inconceivable phantoms of whom we are not sure whether they are the simulacra of themselves or the actual bodies of somebody else. What we want is the ghost who is neither a piece of mechanism nor a strip of hazy mind-mist. The ghost of what may be called the "middle period" of ghost stories hit this happy mean. He was not, as in the old days, a mere scooped turnip with a lighted candle stuck in its interior, nor was he like the spook of the present era, "defecated to a pure transparency." He lived and mixed among us, and sat, if he did not eat, at our tables. He did not depend upon haunted rooms or historic and unpunished murders like his predecessors; nor did he, like his successors, postulate in those who are to be appalled by him a previous course of Madame Blavatzky [sic] and Mr. Sinnett.[f] He would have turned up his phantasmal nose at Esoteric Buddhism, and "gin he had met an 'astral body'" would have made very short work of him. But this *revenant* has, I fear, departed, never to return.

Notes

a. "M. Anastasius" (1857) by Dinah M. Mulock (1826–1887).
b. *Not for the Night-Time* (1889) by Theo Gift (Dorothy Henrietta Boulger; 1847–1923), from which comes "Dog or Demon?," which Traill discusses next.
c. "The Green Tea."
d. See note page 227, n.2.
e. From Thomas Hood's (1799–1845) poem *Miss Kilmansegg and Her Precious Leg* (1842), in the section "Her Christening."
f. Helena Blavatsky (1831–1891) and Alfred Percy Sinnett (1840–1921), famed Theosophists. Blavatsky founded the Theosophical movement, which mixed Eastern mysticism with Western Spiritualism and influenced many thinkers of the era. Sinnett wrote books about the occult.

The novelist and women's suffrage advocate Olivia Howard Dunbar (1873–1953) wrote a number of feminist-influenced supernatural stories in the early twentieth century, including "The Long Chamber" (1914). Her stories were rich in psychological detail and grew directly out of the following essay, in which she lamented the decline of ghostly fiction and called for a new, reinvigorated literature of horror. Of course, what she meant was that horror had vanished from mainstream, respectable magazines. It was still doing gangbuster trade in the "pulps," the cheap magazines aimed at working class readers, to which twentieth century horror would migrate. "The Decay of the Ghost in Fiction" ran in *The Dial* for June 1, 1905.

The Decay of the Ghost in Fiction*
OLIVIA HOWARD DUNBAR

"For one, I cannot purge my mind of that forlorn faith."—ANDREW LANG.

For approximately a generation, the ghost has been missing from fiction; after a disappearance so sudden and of such far-reaching implications that it is a matter of some amazement that those who profess to concern themselves with the phenomena of imaginative literature should have paid so little attention to it. It is a commonplace that ever since literature began, as well as considerably before that interesting period, what we call 'the supernatural' has been a staple material of the tellers of tales. As there has always been a literature of love, so there has always been a literature of fear; and until the development of the present narrow and timorous popular taste, one had perhaps as strong an appeal as the other. Ghosts in their most literal acceptation—not as the more or less impersonal shades we have sometimes indifferently pictured them—have always been held an essential complement of tangible everyday life, inextricably bound up with religion, with love for the dead, with hunger for the unknown, with many of the most intimate and profound emotions; and their literary use has seemed, to the greater public, not only no less, but even more 'realistic,' than the modern exploitation of the commonplace.

Twenty-five years ago, even, the reader of magazine fiction was still able to shudder to his heart's content. Spectres glided with the precision of long-established custom through the pages of the more conventional compendiums of light literature. The familiar paraphernalia of supernatural incident,—draughty chambers, tempestuous nights, blood-stains, wan-faced women,—were still in constant and elaborate requisition. And while there was a discreet dribbling of phantoms from week to week or from month to month, a magnificent convocation of the spectral tribe occurred annually. That is to say, a curious association of ideas connected the maximum of ghostly prevalence with Christmas, the season of popular rejoicing; and by way of making sure of these dismal but doubtless salutary companions, it was customary, as Mr. Anstey once remarked, 'to commission a band of ingenious littérateurs to turn out batches of ready-made

*Olivia Howard Dunbar, "The Decay of the Ghost in Fiction," *The Dial: A Semimonthly Journal of Literary Criticism, Discussion, and Information,* June 1, 1905, 377–380.

spectres for the Christmas annuals."ᵃ The business of chilling the popular spine was taken with due seriousness and was all the more effectually brought about in that the "magazine ghost" as this source of popular refreshment was termed, was as stereotyped and conventional as the old-fashioned novel-heroine. Its looks, manner, haunts, companions, and alleged errands were those long since laid down by tradition; it evinced no sensational modern unexpectedness.

But suddenly, and it must surely have seemed mysteriously, the magazine ghost vanished; nor were its eerie footprints traced. Whether by a concerted action of magazine editors, or by a swift and complete paralysis of the contributors' imaginations, or by a profound alteration of popular sentiment, or by the operation of a principle presently to be suggested, the literature of the supernatural ceased to be produced. Can this have happened without protest, without comment, even? The subject is rich in its possibilities of speculation. For if the acceptance and enjoyment of ghost-

The Case Against Spiritualism. For much of the nineteenth and early twentieth centuries, ghosts were believed to be as real as electricity, to which they were frequently compared. Mediums, like the one seen in this 1918 charcoal drawing, believed they could contact the dead at darkened séances, and the Society for Psychical Research tried to prove the existence of ghosts and psychic phenomena scientifically. Despite repeated debunking by skeptics like the illusionist Harry Houdini, Spiritualism, as the ghost belief of the age was called, found devoted followers in some of the era's best minds, and the best mediums performed for the crowned heads of Europe (Library of Congress, Prints and Photographs Division).

lore imply a childish quality of mind, as one sometimes hears superior persons assert, then our rejection of them would argue that we are the wisest generation that ever lived. If, again, the reading or writing of such tales demand a freshness of imagination that in our little day has become desiccated, then our plight is pitiable indeed.

There is at hand, of course, an easy but superficial explanation to the effect that a prevalence of ghost-stories must depend upon a stout popular belief in ghosts; and that having lost the one, we must forego the other. The slightest reflection shows that this position is untenable. Not believe in ghosts? We believe in them with all our hearts. Never before, since spectral feet first crossed a man-made threshold, have ghosts been so squarely, openly, and enthusiastically believed in, so assiduously cultivated, as now. We have raised ghost-lore to the dusty dignity of a science. The invocation of the spirits of the dead, far from having its former suggestion of vulgar mystery, is one of the most reputable of practices, which men of learning carry on publicly, with stenographers conveniently at hand. There even flourishes a 'Haunted House Committee' appointed and maintained by the foremost society for the promotion of ghosts, and this for the express purpose of encouraging the presence of the shyer and less aggressive spectres in what seem their appropriate habitations,—of making them, as it were, feel at home. We believe in ghosts as sincerely as we believe in the very poor; and in similar fashion we endeavor to live among them, establish a cordial understanding, and write about them in our notebooks. Nor do we believe in them the less because, when on our learned behavior, we may refer to them as 'phantasmogenetic agencies.' Not believe in ghosts? They are our fetish. Let it never be imagined that ghost-stories have suffered decline because of our indifference to their subject-matter, 'material' though our age is commonly held to be. By our very zest in their pursuit, we have possibly proved the reverse of Scott's mistaken theory that to see ghosts it is only necessary to believe in them,—to wish to see. Much truer is the proposition that the seer of ghosts commonly does not premeditate his vision; that spectres manifest themselves by preference to 'unimaginative people in perfect health.'

No small share of the fascination exerted by the ancient and outgrown ghost of fiction was due to its invariable and satisfactory conformity to type. However frequent its intrusion, or however familiar, it was never suffered to deviate from its character, so deeply rooted in human consciousness, as a source of dread. It was the function of the ghost to be consistently unpleasant, and that function was relentlessly fulfilled. No one personal characteristic of the ghost as we know it in song or story or as we learn from the unimpeachable testimony of our friends' friends, can explain its unequalled power to arouse the emotion of fear. Distasteful as is the ghostly habit of reducing its unfleshly essence to a threadlike, infinitely ductile filament—like a bit of transsubstantial chewing-gum—in order sneakily to penetrate keyholes; disturbing as is its fashion of upsetting our gravely accepted 'laws of nature'; intolerable as is its lack of vocal organs (for phantoms, with few exceptions, cannot or will not speak);—neither one nor all of these undesirable characteristics can completely solve the interesting riddle of its fear-compelling power. And it is undoubtedly almost as remarkable that having for centuries, in and out of fiction, maintained this consistent and extremely prevalent personality, the ghost should have dropped out of literature altogether. Now, how can this have been?

To go as far back as the early English folktales and ballads, when the wherefore of phantoms was even better understood than now, and when fiction more essentially took its origin from life, ghost-tales gained their grim effectiveness from the accuracy with which they reflected popular belief. The audiences of that simple day had not attained a sufficient refinement of imagination to delight in vague, casual, incoherent spectres; every ghost had a name and date. What is more important is that there was no ghost that had not a reason for being. The ingenious notion that the spirits of the dead return from an allegedly peaceful Elysium simply to make themselves disagreeable, by way of easing their minds, had not yet suggested itself. On the contrary, the animistic trend of popular thought, which of course greatly favored the appearance of ghosts in general, assigned them likewise adequate and intelligible motives, among the chief of which were: to reveal treasure, to reunite happy lovers, to avenge a crime, and to serve as 'a primitive telegraphic service for the conveyance of bad news.' Ghosts were therefore not only the recognizable shades of the familiarly known dead; they were sinister symbols of crime, remorse, vengeance. If you shuddered at sight of them, it was for a better reason than weak nerves. Horror was not piled on horror, in early ghost-tales, merely to satisfy the artist's own sense of cumulative effect. Each detail had a powerful conventional significance, and the consequent power to arouse a strong primitive emotion. This system not only lent an artistic strength and symmetry to the early literature; it was intensely satisfactory to the Anglo-Saxon mind.

But inevitably, when the motives and the language of literature became more complex, the *rationale* of ghost-lore became affected. Phantoms began to lose their original force, fell into the habit of haunting from motives relatively unworthy. Evidences multiplied of their degeneration into a morbid and meddlesome tribe, with a sadly diminished sense of the fitting and the picturesque. Their visits were even concerned with the payment of debts, of strictly mortal contraction; and they lamentably lost caste by exhibiting themselves as the victims, rather than as the scourge, of conscience. A ghost has been known to go to the trouble of haunting a house for the mere purpose of ensuring the payment of a shilling,—an episode that might well permanently compromise the dignity of the entire spectral tribe. Likewise when they acquired the intrusive habit of giving evidence in trials, the original and forceful idea that ghosts were agents of retribution became seriously coarsened. Legally, the fact that the issue of many an actual trial has hinged on ghostly testimony is of extraordinary interest. So far as imaginative terror-literature is concerned, however, the introduction of this matter serves as a mixed and weakened motive, only.

During the later years of the ghost's popularity in literature, it will readily be seen that the greater number of the earliest ghost-motives were outgrown. It is some time, for instance, since the motive of recovering buried treasure through supernatural aid has been able to "carry" the custom of burying treasure having itself somewhat tamely died out. Far more incongruous, even, came to seem the supernatural reunion of lovers, as in the familiar case where the posthumous suitor reappears to bear his still living sweetheart back to the grave with him. Ghosts that are to be understood as the projections of the spirit at the moment of death have always been popular, it is true, but this motive is not in itself strong or picturesque enough to serve as the backbone of a corporate section of imaginative literature.

In short, the only ghost-motive that retained its strength, plausibility, and appeal to the Anglo-Saxon mind was the retribution-motive,—the idea that the ghost's function was to recall, expiate, or avenge a crime. This was impressive; it was terrifying; it had moral and religious significance; it was not subtle; it was susceptible of indefinitely repeated adjustment to time and place. It was the perfect, perhaps the only perfect, ghost-motive for English literature. So valorous is the Anglo-Saxon temper that it scorns or is ashamed to tremble at mere empty shadow-tales. It demands not only to be impressed; there must be an adequate basis for the impression. The clue to the whole matter is that the ghost must not be a wanton and irresponsible power. It must be a moral agent.

Unfortunately, the realization of this simple truth has never been complete. Only subconsciously has the public known what it wanted. As for the tellers of tales, they seem, in those latter days of the ghost's literary existence, to have remained in criminal ignorance of the vital principle of their business. The decay of the ghost in fiction occurred, not through any loss of human interest in the spectral world, but through an indolent misapprehension, on the part of the story-tellers, of the real character of the ghost as we Anglo-Saxons have conceived it. Thus it came about that the ghost, previous to its subsidence, was, as Mr. Lang truly observed, 'a purposeless creature. He appears, nobody knows why; he has no message to deliver, no secret crime to conceal, no appointment to keep, no treasure to disclose, no commissions to be executed, and, as an almost invariable rule, he does not speak, even if you speak to him.'[b] And he adds that inquirers have therefore concluded that the ghost, generically, is 'not all there'— a dreary result of scepticism, indeed! At the same time, what direct and utilitarian folk could put up with a confirmedly inconsequent ghost, even for the creepy fascination of shuddering at his phantom footfall? And could there be, on the whole, a more perfect example of the operation of natural selection in art than that, the ghost of fiction becoming unmoral, superficial, and flabby, it was its pitilessly appropriate penalty to be dropped and apparently forgotten?

A small group of kindred volumes, which have appeared during the past year or so, now for the first time indicate that a perception of the true nature of the literary ghost is returning to the absent-minded craft. Stevenson had, it is true, an admirable perception of the terror-inspiring, and he did not make the mistake of being vague; but his was not the temperament that produces the perfect ghost-story. Mr. Henry James, in that masterpiece, 'The Turn of the Screw' has shown that he can convey a sense of mystery and terror more skilfully than any of his contemporaries; but his work is probably too esoteric to stand as typical, and it remains true that the pattern ghost-tale must be writ large and obvious. If, as now appears, a half-dozen of the ablest writers of the day are realizing this, there is hope for the renaissance of the literary ghost. It has already been proved that the problem of its readjustment to our literature is not insuperable,—that the chambers of our untenanted imaginations stand ready and waiting to be haunted by wraiths that our logic can approve. There may indeed develop with time a regenerated ghosts-literature well worth acquaintance; for, as an essayist of other times has somewhat grandiloquently observed, 'Our inborn proneness to a love of the marvellous and unimaginable, which has originated in our imperfect acquaintance with the laws of nature and our own being, does not appear to suffer diminution as education and culture advance; for it is found to coexist with the highest intellectual development and the most refined critical temper.'[c]

Notes

a. Probably the novelist and journalist Thomas Anstey Guthrie (1856–1934), who wrote humorous novels and stories under the name F. Anstey.

b. From "Comparative Psychical Research," published in the *Contemporary Review* and collected in an expanded version in *Cock-Lane and Common Sense* (1894), an anthropological study of ghosts. For more on Lang, see the introduction to "The Supernatural in Fiction," our next piece.

c. William Carew Hazlitt (1834–1913) in the introduction to *Tales and Legends of National Origin* (1891), a collection of English legendry and folklore.

7. Toward a Horror Genre

In this final section, we turn toward the work of those late authors who began to assemble the pieces of Gothic, mystery, ghostly, macabre, and weird fiction into what would become known as the horror genre. We have already met Andrew Lang as he explored Japanese ghost books. Here Lang begins to define what in the twentieth century was becoming the genre of horror. Lang rightly notes that supernatural fiction—horror—is intimately tied to the rise of science, which explained away the ghoulies and ghosties that plagued the pre-scientific world, and he held out hope that horror fiction would rise from "vulgar" trash to a true art form. "The Supernatural in Fiction" first ran in *The Idler* before being collected in *Adventures Among Books* (1905).

The Supernatural in Fiction[*]
ANDREW LANG

It is a truism that the supernatural in fiction should, as a general rule, be left in the vague. In the creepiest tale I ever read, the horror lay in this—*there was no ghost!* You may describe a ghost with all the most hideous features that fancy can suggest—saucer eyes, red staring hair, a forked tail, and what you please—but the reader only laughs. It is wiser to make as if you were going to describe the spectre, and then break off, exclaiming, "But no! No pen can describe, no memory, thank Heaven, can recall, the horror of that hour!" So writers, as a rule, prefer to leave their terror (usually styled "The Thing") entirely in the dark, and to the frightened fancy of the student. Thus, on the whole, the treatment of the supernaturally terrible in fiction is achieved in two ways, either by actual description, or by adroit suggestion, the author saying, like cabmen, "I leave it to

[*]Andrew Lang, "The Supernatural in Fiction," in *Adventures Among Books* (London: Longmans, Greene, and Co., 1905), 273–280.

yourself, sir." There are dangers in both methods; the description, if attempted, is usually overdone and incredible: the suggestion is apt to prepare us too anxiously for something that never becomes real, and to leave us disappointed.

Examples of both methods may be selected from poetry and prose. The examples in verse are rare enough; the first and best that occurs in the way of suggestion is, of course, the mysterious lady in "Christabel."[a]

> "She was most beautiful to see,
> Like a lady of a far countrée."

Who was she? What did she want? Whence did she come? What was the horror she revealed to the night in the bower of Christabel?

> "Then drawing in her breath aloud
> Like one that shuddered, she unbound
> The cincture from beneath her breast.
> Her silken robe and inner vest
> Dropt to her feet, and full in view
> Behold her bosom and half her side—
> A sight to dream of, not to tell!
> O shield her! shield sweet Christabel!"

And then what do her words mean?

> "Thou knowest to-night, and wilt know to-morrow,
> This mark of my shame, this seal of my sorrow."

What was it—the "sight to dream of, not to tell"?

Coleridge never did tell, and, though he and Mr. Gilman said he knew, Wordsworth thought he did not know. He raised a spirit that he had not the spell to lay. In the Paradise of Poets has he discovered the secret? We only know that the mischief, whatever it may have been, was wrought.

> "O sorrow and shame! Can this be she—
> The lady who knelt at the old oak tree?"

* * * * *

> "A star hath set, a star hath risen,
>   O Geraldine, since arms of thine
> Have been the lovely lady's prison.
>   O Geraldine, one hour was thine."[1]

If Coleridge knew, why did he never tell? And yet he maintains that "in the very first conception of the tale, I had the whole present to my mind,

---

1. Can not the reader guess? I am afraid that I can!

with the wholeness no less than with the liveliness of a vision," and he expected to finish the three remaining parts within the year. The year was 1816, the poem was begun in 1797, and finished, as far as it goes, in 1800. If Coleridge ever knew what he meant, he had time to forget. The chances are that his indolence, or his forgetfulness, was the making of "Christabel," which remains a masterpiece of supernatural suggestion.

For description it suffices to read the "Ancient Mariner." These marvels, truly, are *speciosa miracula*, and, unlike Southey, we believe as we read. "You have selected a passage fertile in unmeaning miracles," Lamb wrote to Southey[b] (1798), "but have passed by fifty passages as miraculous as the miracles they celebrate." Lamb appears to have been almost alone in appreciating this masterpiece of supernatural description. Coleridge himself shrank from his own wonders, and wanted to call the piece "A Poet's Reverie." "It is as bad as Bottom the weaver's declaration that he is not a lion, but only the scenical representation of a lion. What new idea is gained by this title but one subversive of all credit—which the tale should force upon us—of its truth?" Lamb himself was forced, by the temper of the time, to declare that he "disliked all the miraculous part of it," as if it were not *all* miraculous! Wordsworth wanted the Mariner "to have a character and a profession," perhaps would have liked him to be a gardener, or a butler, with "an excellent character!" In fact, the love of the supernatural was then at so low an ebb that a certain Mr. Marshall "went to sleep while the 'Ancient Mariner' was reading," and the book was mainly bought by seafaring men, deceived by the title, and supposing that the "Ancient Mariner" was a nautical treatise.

In verse, then, Coleridge succeeds with the supernatural, both by way of description in detail, and of suggestion. If you wish to see a failure, try the ghost, the moral but not affable ghost, in Wordsworth's "Laodamia." It is blasphemy to ask the question, but is the ghost in "Hamlet" quite a success? Do we not see and hear a little too much of him? Macbeth's airy and viewless dagger is really much more successful by way of suggestion. The stage makes a ghost visible and familiar, and this is one great danger of the supernatural in art. It is apt to insist on being too conspicuous. Did the ghost of Darius, in "Æschylus," frighten the Athenians? Probably they smiled at the imperial spectre. There is more discretion in Cæsar's ghost—

"I think it is the weakness of mine eyes
That shapes this monstrous apparition,"

says Brutus, and he lays no very great stress on the brief visit of the appearance. For want of this discretion, Alexandre Dumas's ghosts, as in "The Corsican Brothers," are failures. They make themselves too common and too cheap, like the spectre in Mrs. Oliphant's novel, "The Wizard's Son."[c] This, indeed, is the crux of the whole adventure. If you paint your ghost with too heavy a hand, you raise laughter, not fear. If you touch him too lightly, you raise unsatisfied curiosity, not fear. It may be easy to shudder, but it is difficult to teach shuddering.

In prose, a good example of the over vague is Miriam's mysterious visitor—the shadow of the catacombs—in "Transformation; or, The Marble Faun." Hawthorne should have told us more or less; to be sure his contemporaries knew what he meant, knew who Miriam and the Spectre were. The dweller in the catacombs now powerfully excites curiosity, and when that curiosity is unsatisfied, we feel aggrieved, vexed, and suspect that Hawthorne himself was puzzled, and knew no more than his readers. He has not—as in other tales he has—managed to throw the right atmosphere about this being. He is vague in the wrong way, whereas George Sand, in *Les Dames Vertes*, is vague in the right way. We are left in *Les Dames Vertes* with that kind of curiosity which persons really engaged in the adventure might have felt, not with the irritation of having a secret kept from us, as in "Transformation."

In "Wandering Willie's Tale" (in "Redgauntlet"), the right atmosphere is found, the right note is struck. All is vividly real, and yet, if you close the book, all melts into a dream again. Scott was almost equally successful with a described horror in "The Tapestried Chamber." The idea is the commonplace of haunted houses, the apparition is described as minutely as a burglar might have been; and yet we do not mock, but shudder as we read. Then, on the other side—the side of anticipation—take the scene outside the closed door of the vanished Dr. Jekyll, in Mr. Stevenson's well-known apologue:

They are waiting on the threshold of the chamber whence the doctor has disappeared—the chamber tenanted by what? A voice comes from the room. "Sir," said Poole, looking Mr. Utterson in the eyes, "was that my master's voice?"

A friend, a man of affairs, and a person never accused of being fanciful, told me that he read through the book to that point in a lonely Highland chateau, at night, and that he did not think it well to finish the story till next morning, but rushed to bed. So the passage seems "well-found" and successful by dint of suggestion. On the other side, perhaps, only Scotsmen brought up in country places, familiar from childhood with the terrors of Cameronian myth, and from childhood apt to haunt the lonely churchyards, never stirred since the year of the great Plague choked the soil with the dead, perhaps *they* only know how much shudder may be found in Mr. Stevenson's "Thrawn Janet." The black smouldering heat in the hills and glens that are commonly so fresh, the aspect of the Man, the Tempter of the Brethren, we know them, and we have enough of the old blood in us to be thrilled by that masterpiece of the described supernatural. It may be only a local success, it may not much affect the English reader, but it is of sure appeal to the Lowland Scot. The ancestral Covenanter within us awakens, and is terrified by his ancient fears.

Perhaps it may die out in a positive age—this power of learning to shudder. To us it descends from very long ago, from the far-off forefathers who dreaded the dark, and who, half starved and all untaught, saw spirits everywhere, and scarce discerned waking experience from dreams. When we are all perfect positivist philosophers, when a thousand generations of nurses that never heard of ghosts have educated the thousand and first generation of children, then the supernatural may fade out of fiction. But has it not grown and increased since Wordsworth wanted the "Ancient Mariner" to have "a profession and a character," since Southey called that poem a Dutch piece of work, since Lamb had to pretend to dislike its "miracles"? Why, as science becomes more cock-sure, have men and women become more and more fond of old follies, and more pleased with the stirring of ancient dread within their veins?

As the visible world is measured, mapped, tested, weighed, we seem to hope more and more that a world of invisible romance may not be far from us, or, at least, we care more and more to follow fancy into these airy regions, *et inania regna*. The supernatural has not ceased to tempt romancers, like Alexandre Dumas, usually to their destruction; more rarely, as in Mrs. Oliphant's "Beleaguered City," to such success as they do not find in the world of daily occupation. The ordinary shilling tales of "hypnotism" and mesmerism are vulgar trash enough, and yet I can believe that an impossible romance, if the right man wrote it in the right mood, might still win us from the newspapers, and the stories of shabby love, and cheap remorses, and commonplace failures.

"But it needs Heaven-sent moments for this skill."[d]

Notes

a. Samuel Taylor Coleridge's vampire poem "Christabel" (1816). For more, see introduction to the excerpt from "A Letter from Geneva," page 77.
b. Charles Lamb, the essayist (See introduction to "Letter to William Godwin," page 66) and Robert Southey (1774–1843), the Romantic poet, historian, and biographer, who created "The Three Bears," the origin of the Goldilocks story.
c. The prolific author Margaret Oliphant Oliphant (1828–1897), whose *The Wizard's Son* was published in 1884.
d. Matthew Arnold, "The Scholar-Gipsy" (1853).

Edmund Gosse (1849–1928) was a British author, poet, and literary and art critic as well as a librarian at the British Museum and later the House of Lords. He was friends with Robert Louis Stevenson, who would stay at his house during visits to London in the 1880s. In "The Abuse of the Supernatural in Fiction," Gosse lays down some rules for writing supernatural fiction and explains the differences between strains of supernatural horror, including tales of the Unexplained, the Explainable Mysterious, and those he considers sensational stories that abuse the supernatural. Among this last group he places Stevenson's *Jekyll and Hyde*. The article ran in *The Bookman* for December 1897.

*The Abuse of the Supernatural in Fiction**
EDMUND GOSSE

The primary object of the story-teller is to attract our attention. He sits down by the fireside and begins to recount something. If it seems to be amusing or thrilling, we listen; if not, we go away. But nowadays there are so many tellers and so many tales that the anxiety of the novelist becomes almost painfully apparent. He is so afraid that we shall not attend to him that he uses every subterfuge to excite us at the outset. If he is a realist, he puts in the squalid details on his first page; if he is a romanticist or a satirist, he tries to do the tricks of his business the very moment that he catches our eye. And as the ground becomes more and more crowded, and the novel situation taken from real life more and more difficult to find, the writer of fiction is tempted to return to the congenial hunting-ground of his forefathers, and try to interest us in what never was and never could be. Within the last two or three years we have seen a revival among us of the supernatural in fiction; we have had quite a crop of notice-

*Edmund Gosse, "The Abuse of the Supernatural in Fiction," *The Bookman: A Literary Journal*, December 1897, 297–300.

able books the plots of which run counter to all existing experience. There is no objection to this practice in principle, but some of the novelists do not seem to perceive what the rules and limitations of it are.

The first law of romantic invention must be not to overstep the boundaries of belief. In the Ages of Credulity it was easy to keep this law. The world was so wide and dim, man's knowledge of it so imperfect, nature

The Haunted Lane. Gosse argued that science had banished the supernatural, but in his own lifetime many believed that ghosts were not only real but could be captured on film. Double exposures, like this staged photograph (1889) of a ghost, were frequently passed off as legitimate, "scientific" evidence of the supernatural. Similarly, in the 1920s, learned men like Arthur Conan Doyle argued for the reality of fairies based on two schoolgirls' photographs of cardboard cutouts (Library of Congress, Prints and Photographs Division, LC-USZ62-49314).

still so mysterious, that if a specially bold man said that he had seen a green dragon chewing little children in his jaws, and puffing flames from his nostrils, he was widely credited. I suppose that there were always some sceptics, but they were likely to be of the class of the sailor's mother, who easily believed in mountains of cake and rivers of rum, but was not to be persuaded that there were fishes which could fly. It was just the absolutely impossible which found an easy path to the mediæval imagination. As experience became wider and calmer, preposterous fancy obtained less and less ready entrance into the mind, but its extravagances lingered among the ignorant. To this very day, in the wilder parts of Ireland, the people will tell you that fairies and witches exist and do marvellous things; they will sometimes aver that they themselves have seen such beings. Here is the mediæval condition in full survival; and to these people, if their fancies were properly approached, nothing too monstrous could be told. They would believe the magic wonders with the simplicity of children. We have to remember that, up to three or four hundred years ago, every one, except a few learned men, was in this condition, in order to realise how facile an appeal was made to terror and awe by the hotch-potch of supernatural romance in the Middle Ages.

But to-day people abide no longer in this ignorance. Science has invaded every section of the world, and there is scarcely a dark corner left into which the imagination can flit like a bat and rest itself in the twilight. Nevertheless, the use of supernatural or extra-experimental elements increases in fiction, and is accepted without demur. Why is this? Primarily, of course, it is because we have accepted the convention of being interested in a story even though we are perfectly aware that it cannot be "true." For instance, there are incidents familiar to every reader of Hawthorne which are outside the limits of prosaic belief. But no reader objects to these, or to the brilliant flights of Oriental magic in Mr. George Meredith's *Shaving of Shagpaf*, or to the monstrous adventures of Mr. Frank Stockton's heroes. The reason is that these authors have the art to awaken in us the curious condition of mind which we may call temporary credence. That is to say, they form such an atmosphere around their creations, and make the movements of the latter so consistent and in such harmony with one another that we resign ourselves, as in a dream, to complete belief as long as the story lasts.

With this must not be confounded the treatment of the Unexplained in fiction. Some of the stories which we most naturally think of in connection with the supernatural really belong to this class, and most prominently the blood-curdling tales of the once famous Mrs. Radcliffe, who has lately found in Professor Walter Raleigh so able a defender. In the awful romances of this lady everything which appeared to be mysteriously sinister was always comfortably cleared up on natural grounds in the last chapter of the book. In the thrilling productions of the first Lord Lytton[a] there is usually a pretence of explaining away or of suggesting a loophole for explanation. But his real successes, and particularly *A Strange Story*, with its splendid invention of the Skinleka or luminous banshee vision, sail boldly away from these safer shores. When I was a child, the author who was most in request forgiving readers "the creeps" was Mrs. Crowe.[b] I suppose that if we were now to read *The Night Side of Nature* and *Light and Darkness* in the garish light of middle life we might find them poor enough. But they thrilled us in the early sixties, and they were pre-eminently stories of the Unexplained. Mrs. Crowe went the length of pretending that they were all "founded on fact," and she usually left herself a chance of escape on physical grounds. Even as a child, I remember being much more impressed by her when she was mysterious than when she made a coarse use of the palpably and revoltingly impossible.

The subterfuge of the Explainable Mysterious has not found much favour among recent English novelists. The great objection to it is that a romance which accepts its aid is obliged to be built up on the lines of a detective story. Under the influence of Gaboriau and Conan Doyle we have come to prefer detective stories that are straightforward tales of crime or social embarrassment. Every now and then the newspapers present us in real life with humble imitations of *The Castle of Otranto*, in which spoons are snatched out of old ladies' hands and coals are showered on babies' cradles by an unseen force. These events, styled "The Macclesfield Mystery" or "Panic in a Shropshire Village," usually turn out in the course of a few days to be the work either of naughty little girls or of rats. They have grown somewhat too obvious and vulgar for the modern romance writer, although they were quite good enough for those old-fashioned favourites of the public, *St. Leon* and *The Mysteries of Udolpho*. Our idealists and romanticists of to-day are anxious to press the genuine supernatural into their service, but they are not all of them sufficiently considerate of the laws that govern this difficult province of constructive art. It is not enough for me, while I am telling a story of middle-class life in Bayswater, because I feel that the plot is getting a little dull, suddenly to say: "As Maria was leaving Mr. Whiteley's shop, with two small brown-paper parcels under her arm, she was somewhat surprised to see that a large blue Unicorn was threading its way between the omnibuses, and that, as it caught her eye, it touched its horn." Yet Miss Marie Corelli is hardly less artless than this in her appeal to the impossible as an exciting element in fiction. The error of this *naïveté* can perhaps be best comprehended by a reference to its opposite, an artful and successful appeal to the incredible.

A little book has just come into my hands which strikes me as exemplifying the right use of the supernatural to a remarkable degree. It is a story by that very interesting young novelist Mr. H. G. Wells, and it is called *The Invisible Man*. This is a pure extravaganza—a young adventurer of science hits upon a plan by which his own living tissues are made absolutely undetectable by human vision. The mode in which the invention of Mr. Wells has worked is obviously this. He has created the notion of a man made chemically invisible by a scientific discovery, and then he has considered how a man in such a condition would act. The poor wretch has no protection for his naked body. He catches a violent cold; he is knocked over in the street; dogs sniff at him and track him; he has to steal clothes and food like a savage, and the clothes he puts on can never hide him sufficiently, even though he wears a false nose, whiskers, blue goggle spectacles, a wig, and copious bandages. Mr. Wells rightly sees that such an existence, though comical at the outset, must become infinitely painful, and must end tragically. So, in fact, we are quickly led to a scene of murderous violence which ends in the death of the Invisible Man, who slowly comes to sight as his life ebbs away.

Nothing of the supernatural order could run more violently counter to experience than this. No man has been or ever will be invisible; the idea is absolutely grotesque. But the author commands our belief while we read, by the consistency and inevitability of his details. We have to grant him one admission—and, of course, it is a huge one—namely, that any chemical action could make the flesh of a living and healthy person inappreciable to vision. But, having made that demand upon us, he makes no more; for the rest of the story he accepts all the responsibility. We are asked to believe no other impossibilities, but, on the contrary, everything is made as easy to belief as possible. Just the same is true of those delightful, grotesque romances of Mr. Frank Stockton, *The Transferred Ghost* and *Negative Gravity*. The imagination has to accept one monstrous outrage upon experience, and then all is perfectly straightforward.

But other modern novelists who use the supernatural do not seem to perceive the importance of thus keeping to the rules of the game. That delightful writer, Stevenson, in a little book which has had hundreds of thousands of readers, *Dr. Jekyll and Mr. Hyde*, missed this initial simplicity. You were asked to believe in the possession of two bodies by a single soul, the good qualities of it inhabiting the handsome frame, the bad ones that which was loathsome and hideous. I do not say that so outrageous a supposition might not have been supported, but I do say that it was not. The little work is beautifully written, and it has a fascinating moral fervour, and it teems with mystery. But that mystery is not legitimately supported. All the cleverness of the author does not make us absolutely credit the occurrences; and when the final explanation comes we reject it. No, we reply as we put down the book, that is no real way out of the extraordinary difficulties which the narrator has raised. The overpowering improbabilities have only been evaded, not really faced, as Mr. Wells, for instance, would have faced them.

A more recent case of the abuse of the supernatural occurs in a clever novel which has been widely read this summer—*Flames*, by Mr. Hitchens.[c] Here we have what purports to be a story of middle-class life in London to-day. There are two friends, one of whom is older and more authoritative than the other, of a cooler temperament, and possessing a will more fully under control. For a reason ill-explained they get weary of the conditions of their friendship and determine to "exchange souls." For this purpose they shut themselves up in a dark room and perform a sort of table-turning on successive occasions, until at last there is a violent nervous crisis, and small blue flames cross the floor in the silence of the night, and we are asked to believe that these are the "souls" of the two young men changing house, like two soldier-crabs in a tidal pool, each creeping into the shell the other has just left. Then follow excited scenes, and a plot, the intrigue of which depends on the temperament expected from the one man manifesting itself in the other, and *vice versa*. I will not charge Mr. Hitchens here with what I think a fatal lack of simplicity, and therefore of credibility, in the succeeding evolution of his story, but I will venture to maintain that this initial incident is an abuse of the supernatural. Why should the temperament—for that is all that Mr. Hitchens means by "the soul"—take the form of a little flame? There is absolutely no reason suggested. And why should this "soul" be limited to one or two of the infinitely complex qualities of which the moral nature of a man is composed? To these questions, and to many others, there is given no reply. We are left vaguely, sceptically, to endeavour to believe that all souls are like blue flames, and could be detached by an effort of the will in a dark room. The initial principle by which an abnormality can be made credible to the imagination—namely, insistence on its being definitely abnormal, has been neglected. The result is that while the careful reader firmly believes in Mr. Wells's *Invisible Man* and shares the agonies of that poor creature's existence, he is apt to toss Mr. Hitchens's *Flames* aside as the mere caprice of a clever, hasty writer.

But no more striking example of the abuse of the supernatural in fiction can be pointed to than is to be found in a book which has just been placed in everybody's hand—*The Martian* of George Du Maurier. In this story a being from the planet Mars is introduced into realistic scenes of every-day life in London and Paris, and is represented as able to endow her favourites with every species of personal charm and executive talent. After she has lived for some years as the wife of one of the characters, whom she has made the most eminent English (and also French) author of his time, she chooses to become reincarnated in the ninth baby of one of her husband's friends, and she starts on another career of fatuous disturbance of the laws of nature and of art. For my own part, I do not see why Mr. Du Maurier should have limited himself to the moral vagaries of his creation. If he had presented to us an image with three heads or a luminous monster without any limbs whatever, we should have been neither more grateful to him nor less. For our belief, our temporary intellectual credence would have been untouched, as it remains untouched by the preposterous Martia. We should have skimmed the pages and have put them down absolutely unenthralled. Yet Mr. Wells and Mr. Stockton, describing things quite as completely foreign to experience, carry us captive with them wherever they will.

A wise novelist will be very cautious how he makes use of supernatural agency to help himself out of a difficulty. No one will blame him if, to heighten the effect of his fable and give it intensity, he introduces what we call incredible incidents with success; only he must remember that we, his readers, will judge success by the degree in which at the time he makes his marvels credited by us. In the old Greek criticism the poets were forbidden to represent the coming of storms in the halcyon days, on the ground that "it would be an affront to the power of the gods to ascribe to them such a force as contradicts poetical probability." Once admit, for special

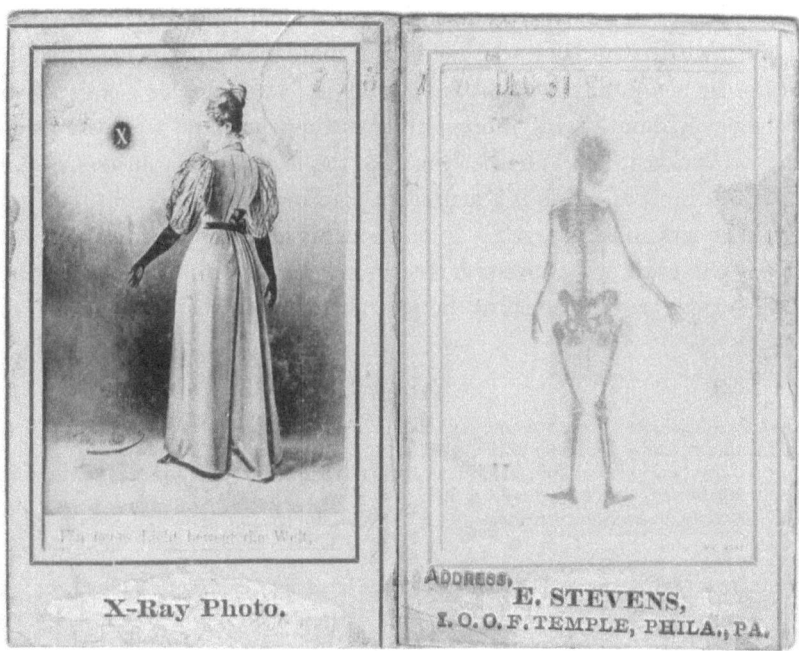

X-Ray Photograph. In 1895 Wilhelm Röntgen discovered that Röntgen rays, better known as x-rays, could be used to see the bones within the human body. This led some to conclude that it was only a matter of time before ghosts were proved real: "A room," wrote psychical researcher W. J. Crawford in 1918, "for instance, may be simultaneously full of light rays, X-rays, wireless telegraphy rays and so on; they may all exist together and our senses will tell us only of the light rays. The rest, without the use of special instruments, will be as though they do not exist for us. So it is perfectly conceivable that the next state may exist in a condition of extreme reality and we be quite unconscious of its presence" (Hints and Observations for Those Investigating the Phenomena of Spiritualism [New York: E. P. Dutton, 1918], 44). Photograph dated 1896 (Library of Congress, Prints and Photographs Division, LC-DIG-ppmsca-12628).

purposes, that such a force as "negative gravity" exists, and there is no contradiction to poetical probability in describing what the effects of its exercise would be on ordinary human beings. Once admit that the tissues of a living man can be made transparent (which seems scarcely more fabulous than the exercise of the Röntgen rays[d] would have seemed two years ago), and there is nothing poetically improbable about the discomforts and adventures of a man reduced to that condition. But to be so unskilful as to have to produce a personage from Mars in order to account for the sudden celebrity of a commonplace man, this is to sin against the laws of supernatural machinery, and to show real poverty of invention.

350   7. Toward a Horror Genre

Perhaps a safe rule would be: Never use supernatural agency to gain an effect which could with the exercise of more ingenuity be produced by natural agency. And a rider on this would be, Never employ a supernatural agency without having thoroughly made up your mind what you mean its exact action to be. Whether you take the reader into your confidence about this limit of action is a matter for your own judgment, but that you should understand it yourself is unquestionably necessary. Many of our latter-day purveyors of the mysterious seem to be as doubtful about the nature of the bogeys they introduce as the most credulous of their readers can be.

Notes

a. Edward Bulwer-Lytton. See note page 102, n.2.
b. Catherine Crowe. See note p. 295, n.3.
c. He refers here to Robert Smythe Hichens, author of "How Love Came to Professor Guildea." See introduction to "Robert Hichens," p. 397.
d. Röntgen rays are better known as x-rays. Wilhelm Röntgen first described them in 1895.

Montague Summers (1880–1948) translated the medieval witch-hunting guide the *Malleus Malleficarum* (1486) into English, and he produced semi-scholarly tomes on vampires, witches, and werewolves, all while claiming his absolute conviction that such creatures were real. He also claimed to be a Catholic priest, though there is no evidence of ordination, and was friend to Aleister Crowley, the well-known occultist.

This particular piece was a review of Dorothy Scarborough's *The Supernatural* in *Modern English Fiction* (1917), of which we shall say more in our last selection. In this review Summers sums up horror down to the end of World War I. This review first ran in volume XIII of *The Modern Language Review*, in 1918.

Review of The Supernatural in Modern English Fiction[*]
MONTAGUE SUMMERS

The Supernatural in Modern English Fiction. By DOROTHY SCARBOROUGH. New York and London: G. P. Putnam's Sons. The Knickerbocker Press. 1917. 8vo. vii + 329 pp.

There are few, none perhaps save the extremest Sadducee and sceptic,

[*]Montague Summers, Review of *The Supernatural in Modern English Fiction* by Dorothy Scarborough, *The Modern Language Review* XIII (1918): 346–351.

who will deny that the supernatural and the macabre form one of the most fascinating realms of fiction. The appeal is universal, and Lafcadio Hearn went so far as to say that "there is scarcely any great author in European literature, old or new, who has not distinguished himself in his treatment of the supernatural."[a] Nor is there any exaggeration in his words. We are nothing surprised then to find Miss Scarborough at the very outset emphasizing the difficulties of her task owing to the enormous mass of material with which she was bound to deal. She very aptly opens her study with a chapter on 'The Gothic Romance,' and here takes occasion to observe that 'the terror novel proper is generally conceded to begin with [Horace Walpole's][b] Romantic curiosity *The Castle of Otranto.*' Walpole's pinchbeck mediaevalism has doubtless come to be an acknowledged landmark of literary history, and it serves this purpose conveniently enough, but none the less it is to be wished that Leland's *Longsword, Earl of Salisbury,* 'a romance of feudal times,' which preceded *Otranto* by two years, were not so entirely forgotten. Even Miss Scarborough has no mention of the earlier book, which in her pages assuredly deserves some recognition, however slight. It is obvious that although the supernatural—the word is used in its broadest sense—as expressed and treated in modern English fiction is the main theme of this study, it was necessary for the writer to trace in some measure the 'terror and blood' which had such vogue in our drama, and hence so marked an influence on the development of the novel. Nor can the tradition of the macabre, as it appears in Latin and Greek classics and in modern literatures other than our own, be wholly ignored, and as link is added to link a stupendous library has to be consulted, an almost incalculable number of volumes examined, for description and citation. Miss Scarborough promises a bibliography which is to comprise over three thousand titles, and which cannot fail to be of permanent value and importance. She has already brought together such an accumulated quantity of material and in this present study discussed so many romances, short stories, chapters, and even episodes that with her copious and painstaking industry it is all the more surprising to note the omission of works which surely rank among the masterpieces of modern macabre fiction. Thus she does not refer to the series of ghost stories from the erudite pen of the Provost of King's,[c] two volumes which have pages so vivid in their description of malignant entities and sinister intelligences, that, when the first tale, *Canon Athene's Scrap-Book,* appeared some years ago in *The National Review,* people were asking if it were not really true, and it was with something like relief we learned that Dr James had invented his midnight demon of the pit. Dr James is of great importance in a study of the supernatural in fiction, and this not only because his stories are consummate masterpieces, but because in his preface to *More Ghost Stories of an Antiquary* he gives us his ideas "how a ghost story ought to be laid out if it is to be effective," and very striking and suggestive these ideas are. He has moreover initiated a certain school of ghost story. Such a book as E. G. Swain's *The Stoneground Ghost Tales* patently and avowedly owes its inspiration to his genius.

Miss Scarborough again has no mention of Mrs Nesbit's[d] sombre little collection, *Grim Tales*, one of the stories in which for sheer gruesome horror it would be hard to beat. Vernon Lee's *Hauntings*, four weirdly fantastic studies of extraordinary power and great literary beauty in a scholarly setting, cannot be forgotten, and Lucas Malet's *The Gateless Barrier* is a novel full of delicate charm, and one which presents no shallow philosophy of the supernatural. *Cecilia de Noël* is famous for its clever characterization and has long since taker its place as a little classic gem of ghost lore. *Raw Edges* by Perceval Landon has several uncanny, and one supremely terrible story, *Thurnley Abbey*, which tells of a building hideously haunted by a foul and carious skeleton. All these, which are of prime importance, and others of lesser note, Miss Scarborough has unwisely omitted to describe in her recent study.

We find moreover only one reference to the name of W. H. Ainsworth, and that casually in a list of some half-a-dozen writers. Ainsworth's faults are great, very great, but he assuredly ought not to be dismissed in so summary a manner. For all his clumsiness and Wardour-street vocabulary, he had parts, and *Auriol*, *The Lancashire Witches*, *Rookwood*, to mention only three of many, are soaked in the macabre. Nor are we at all sure that in such a comprehensive study G. W. M. Reynolds too has not distinct claims to a place however lowly. His works are confessedly ranting melodrama and have worse defects than dubious grammar and grandiloquent bathos. They belong to the slums and alleys of fiction, but Reynolds was prolific and won notoriety in his day. *The Necromancer, Wagner, the Wehr Wolf, Faust* (quantum mutatus ab ilio!)—and a score beside—are very grimoires of cheap diablerie. Far above this *London Journal* romancer stands Sheridan Le Fanu, a writer whose talents are of a very high order. *In a Glass Darkly* (which has sometimes been reprinted as *Green Tea*), is incredibly morbid, horrible, and arresting; *The Dragon Volant* with its tangles and mysteries far surpasses more modern developments of the same theme; *Uncle Silas* is a study which has often been repeated but perhaps never quite so well. There is no account of Le Fanu in Miss Scarborough's pages. An even more astonishing omission is the name of Monsignor Hugh Benson, whose personal interest in the occult was so well known, and whose *Mirror of Shalott* and *The Necromancers* aroused so much discussion a decade or so ago. By reason of those ghastly tales, *The Room in the Tower*, Mr E. F. Benson also has established an undeniable right to inclusion in a study of the supernatural in fiction, where too we might expect to meet with the *Ghost Stories* of E. and H. Heron, a book which has distinctive features worthy of note.

Though none of these are included, and such omissions are serious, Miss Scarborough has nevertheless brought together and compared a very great number of works in which the supernatural has a place, and a study which is so extensive as hers cannot but be of great value and interest. Now-a-days the occult is receiving much serious attention, and it was indeed high time for the entrancing subject of the supernatural in literature to be dealt with at length and in detail. It has been much neglected. Miss Scarborough indeed says 'there has been no previous book on the topic, and none related to it, save Mr C. E. Whitmore's work on *The Supernatural in Tragedy*,' a statement which we are unable wholly to endorse when we recall Thurnau's *Die Geister in der eng. Literatur des 18. Jarhunderts* (1906), a slight yet pioneer contribution in this all-important field.

It is good to find that in her first chapter, 'The Gothic Romance,' Miss Scarborough breaks away from the beaten track and has ample references to little known but entirely characteristic romances such as Charlotte Dacre's *Zofloya, or, The Moor* (1806), and T. J. Horsley-Curties' *The Ancient Records of the Abbey of St Oswyth* (1801), rather than to more easily accessible and somewhat stereotyped exemplars of that school. It will be remembered that Barham in *The Spectre of Tappington* has a good-natured laugh at 'that eminent antiquary, Mr Horsley-Curties,' who described a pointed arch as 'a Gothic window of the Saxon order.' But that unique and unrelated classic, in English literature, *The Ingoldsby Legends*,[e] is not mentioned by Miss Scarborough, and even if it be pleaded that out of some sixty or more pieces only half-a-dozen are prose, yet *The Leech of Folkestone, Singular Passage in the Life of the Late Henry Harris, D.D.*, and *Jerry Jarvis' Wig*, albeit grotesque, are sinister to a degree and told as few writers could have narrated them. For all his mockery and quips Barham (paradoxical as it may appear) treated the supernatural seriously. He well knew that without a vein of grim earnest underlying superficial flippancies and fun the macabre in literature is naught. Even if we do not take the supernatural seriously we must take the treatment of it in literature seriously. This Oscar Wilde appreciated when he ended his 'hylo-idealistic' *The Canterville Ghost* upon a note of deep pathos and exquisite poetry. Although she has frequent references to Wilde, Miss Scarborough curiously enough does not instance this amusing and pertinent tale.

It is obvious that Miss Scarborough completely underestimates the rare genius of Ann Radcliffe; she does not even mention (save in an excerpt from *Northanger Abbey*[f]) that poignant psychological study, *The Italian*, and she entirely fails to appreciate the importance of this great mistress of romance. The faults and follies of a crowd of servile imitators—Horsley-Curties went so far as to name one of his novels *The Monk of Udolpho*—have to some extent obscured the fame of 'the mighty magician of Udolpho,' and blinded by the demerits of her literary parasites, few, if any, critics have given Mrs Radcliffe her ample meed of praise. Miss Scarborough very properly quotes at some length that delightful scene where Isabella Thorpe reads over to Catherine Miss Andrews' famous list of 'horrid' romances, but through some error she counts eight titles not seven. She writes with pardonable pride that she has traced the authorship of 'four out of the eight.' The whole seven however had been identified and examined long before her investigations. Some account of these novels was given by me in a letter to *The Times Literary Supplement*, Dec. 27, 1917, and yet fuller details maybe found in my lecture on Mrs Radcliffe (*Transactions of the Royal Society of Literature*, second series, xxxv, pp. 39—77).

Miss Scarborough, when giving a list of those writers who have made use of the legend of the Wandering Jew (p. 180), ought certainly to have included Lewis. Ahasuerus plays an important part in one of the chief episodes of *The Monk*. The theme of the Flying Dutchman deserves more than a short and superficial paragraph (p. 187), which takes no account of Marryat's[g] fine story *The Phantom Ship*. The werewolf is treated at length, but Baring-Gould's[h] *The Book of Were-Wolves*, first published as far back as 1865, receives no mention. There is too a little-known but exceedingly beautiful fantasy by the late Count Eric Stenbok, *The Oilier Side*, which tells of the loup-garou and the 'wolf-keeper' with his horrible half-human troupe. Attention should have been drawn to this if only to praise the rare loveliness of its literary grace. And surely it is a mistake not to give one of the earliest of all were-wolf stories, the anecdote told by Niceros which made Trimalchio's guests shiver and stare: 'luna lucebat tanquam meridie.

Venimus inter monimenta ... deinde ut respexi ad comitem ille exuit se et omnia vestimenta secundum viam posuit ... subito lupus factus est.'¹ The belief in lycanthropy is, of course, extremely ancient and wide-spread. Amongst other authors, Herodotus; Vergil, *Eclog.* VIII, 95–99; Strabo; Pliny; Solinus; Pomponius Mela; Dionysius Afer; Varro; S. Augustine, *De Civ. Dei*, XVIII; all mention the superstition. Several pages on the supernatural in classical literature would have been highly desirable. It is almost incredible that Miss Scarborough has only one quite casual reference to Apuleius, that past-master of magic and the macabre. Even this reference is third-hand, being taken from Warton's notes on Milton, as quoted by Dyce in his introduction to Peele's *The Old Wives' Tale*.

With regard to the semi–Oriental idea of metempsychosis (p. 189), that the soul may pass into another human body, into an animal, a plant, or even (as used in literature) into some inanimate object, Dr Hawkesworth, who is quoted by Miss Scarborough, probably drew something from *Le Canapé couleur de Feu* (1714), a little fairy tale in eleven chapters, often attributed to Cresset, but in reality the work of Fougeret de Montbron. The hero is first transformed into a dog and then into a sofa. Hence Crébillon le fils drew his inspiration for *Le Sopha; Ah Quel Conte*; and other comic novels, a vein which has been well worked by succeeding writers. In the classics we have Ovid's encyclopaedic *Metamorphoses*.

The Doppelgänger, the double or dual personality, is discussed at some length by Miss Scarborough, and she has collected several very interesting instances. It has been stated that these stones have their origin in Calderon's *El Embozado*, where a man is haunted by himself. I would rather suggest that they are but the presentation in literature of the mystical phenomenon of bi-location, which often appears in modem occultism as the Thought-Body. S. Thomas speaks at length of double personality, and there is much profound matter on the subject in Cardinal Cajetan's *Commentaries* on S. Thomas. According to the Dominican doctor bi-location proper never does and never could happen, but bi-location improperly so called and technically termed *raptus* does occur, and is identical with the double. S. Thomas quotes instances from the Bible (*Ezekiel* viii ; etc.) and from the Lives of the Saints. Calderon, a priest and a theologian, must have been intimately acquainted with this doctrine.

It is doubtful whether on the whole a more comprehensive view of the supernatural in fiction than this given by Miss Scarborough could easily have been contained in one volume. It is true that there are, as we have noted, omissions. There is repetition which is quite unnecessary, and more than one chapter might have been compressed with manifest advantage. But, even as the case stands, the ground which has been covered is very large, and we cannot but give a warm welcome to Miss Scarborough's achievement, which, it is certain, involved long and laborious research. All students of fiction are deeply in her debt. We would caution her however to pay careful attention to the felicities of style. Her own diction, often vivid and modern, occasionally slips into spurious slang, a pitfall to be shunned. That her study will arouse further interest in these investigations is greatly to be desired. We hope that one day the history of that school initiated by *Otranto* and inspired by Mrs Radcliffe will be written in detail. Hardly any branch of literature is less known. The output was tremendous, and the work will be tremendous too, but if the material can be collected—which is in itself a moot point—an addition of prime importance will then have been made to the history of English fiction.

Notes

a. Quoted from "The Value of the Supernatural in Fiction," elsewhere in this volume (see page 267).

b. The brackets are Summers's.

c. Montague Rhodes James (1862–1936), author of *Ghost Stories of an Antiquary* (1904), among others published in the 1910s and 1920s. His work became increasingly popular in the '20s, and his stories were collected as a single volume in 1931.

d. Edith Nesbit (1858–1924), best known as a children's author. Her very adult *Grim Tales* was published in 1893.

e. Supposedly written by Thomas Ingoldsby, *The Ingoldsby Legends* were a series of parodic or humorous ghost stories, legends, and poems that appeared in magazines beginning in 1837 and were collected in book form in 1840 and 1843. They were the work of Richard Harris Barham (1788–1845), a priest. The *Legends* were beloved in the Victorian era but declined in popularity thereafter.

f. Jane Austen's parody of Gothic novels, published in 1817, but written in 1798.

g. Captain Frederick Marryat (1792–1848), a novelist famous for his tales of the sea. *The Phantom Ship* (1839) was a Gothic novel making use of the story of the *Flying Dutchman*, the legendary ghost ship that brings doom to sailors who spy her.

h. Sabine Baring-Gould (1834–1924), the antiquarian and novelist, well known for his two-volume *Curious Myths of the Middle Ages* (1866 and 1868). *The Book of Were-Wolves* (1865) was a non-fiction study of lycanthropy in history.

i. "...the moon [was] shining as bright as day. We arrive at the tombs.... Presently I looked back for my comrade; he had stripped off all his clothes and laid them down by the wayside ... and in an instant changed into a wolf" (Petronius, *Satyricon*, anonymous 1902 translation, later republished in 1930 as the work of Alfred R. Allinson).

Dorothy Scarborough (1878–1935) taught and practiced the art of writing after receiving her Ph.D., for which she wrote a dissertation, *The Supernatural in Modern English Fiction* (1917), later published for the general reader. This work is one of the first book-length explorations of the supernatural in modern fiction, and it contains many useful observations about the development of ghostly and ghastly horror. The following excerpt comes from the conclusion, in which Scarborough sums up her argument and surveys the world of horror from the Gothic to the First World War.

However, Scarborough does not cleanly distinguish the horror genre from fantasy, mystery, or even religious works, as all fall under "supernatural." That distinction would have to wait for Edith Birkhead's *The Tale of Terror* (1921), a study of Gothic horror down to Poe, and H. P. Lovecraft, who would cover the genre up to his own day in his *Supernatural Horror in Literature* (1927), which for the first time attempted to separate horror from other forms of fiction.

Excerpt from The Supernatural in Modern English Fiction*
DOROTHY SCARBOROUGH

...There has been no period in our history from Beowulf to the present when the ghostly was not found in our literature. Of course, there have been periods when the interest in it waned, yet it has never been wholly absent. There is at the present a definite revival of interest in the supernatural appearing in the drama, in poetry and in fiction, evident to anyone who has carefully studied the recent publications and magazines. Within the last few years, especially in the last two years, an astonishing amount of ghostly material has appeared.[...] I hesitate to suggest a reason for this sudden rising tide of occultism at this particular time, but it seems clear to me that the war has had much to do with it.[...]

We have noticed in preceding chapters two aspects of modern supernaturalism as distinguished from the Gothic,—the giving of cumulative and more terrible power to ghostly beings, and on the other hand the leveling influence that makes them more human. The access of horror and unearthly force as shown in the characters described by certain writers is significant. In the work of Bierce, Machen, Blackwood, Stoker, and others supernaturalism is raised to the nth power and every possible thrill is employed. The carrion ghosts of Bierce, animated by malignant foreign spirits, surpass the charnel shudders produced by the Gothic. Algernon Blackwood's Psychic Invasions, where localities rather than mere apartments or

*Dorothy Scarborough, *The Supernatural in Modern English Fiction* (New York: G. P. Putnam's Sons, 1917), 281, 300–310.

houses alone are haunted, diabolized by undying evil influences with compound power, his Elementals that control the forces of wind and wave and fire to work their demon will, are unlike anything that the early terror novel conceived of. Horace Walpole and Mrs. Radcliffe knew no thrills like those of Bram Stoker's Count Dracula who is an immemorial evil, a vampire and werewolf as well as man, with power to change himself into a vampire bat or animal of prey at will. *The Unburied*, by Josephine Daskam Bacon, is more horrific than any mere revenge ghost, however much it shrieked "Vindicta!" The diabolism in Arthur Machen's work reeks obscurely of a Pit more horrible than epic or drama has portrayed. In general, many of the later ghostly characters are more complex, more intense in evil than the Gothic.

While it is true that certain writers show a tendency to create supernatural characters having an excess of evil power beyond the previous uncanny beings, on the other hand there is an equally strong and significant tendency to reduce the ghostly beings nearer to the human. Fiction here, as frequently, seems ahead of general belief, and refuses to believe in the altogether evil. Ghosts, angels, witches, devils, werewolves, and so forth are now made more human, more like to man, yet without losing any of their ancient power to thrill. Ghosts in late literature have more of the mortal characteristics than ever before, as has been pointed out in a previous chapter. They look more human, more normal, they are clad in everyday garments of varied colors, from red shirts and khaki riding-habits to ball-gowns,—though gray seems the favored shade for shades as well as witches,—and they have lost that look of pallor that distinguished early phantoms. Now they are more than merely vaporous projections as they used to be, more than merely phantasmogenetic apparitions,—but are healthy, red-blooded spooks. They are not tongue-tied as their ancestors were, but are very chatty, giving forth views on everything they are interested in, from socialism to the present war. And their range of interests has widened immeasurably. It would seem that the literacy test has been applied to ghosts in recent fiction. Modern specters are so normal in appearance that often no one recognizes them as ghosts,—as in Edith Wharton's story *Afterwards*, where the peculiar thing about the apparition haunting a certain house is that it is not till long afterwards that one knows it was a ghost. The man in the gray suit whom the wife thinks a chance caller is the spirit of a man not yet dead, a terrible living revenge-ghost, who finally takes his victim mysteriously away with him. Modern ghosts have both motions and emotions like men, hence mortals are coming to regard them more sympathetically, to have more of a fellow-feeling for them.

Likewise the angels are now only a very little higher if any than men. Seraphs are democratic, and angels have developed a sense of humor that renders them more interesting than they used to be. The winged being that H. G. Wells's vicar goes gunning for is a charming youth with a naïve satire, as the angels in Mark Twain's story of heaven are realistically mortal and masculine in tastes. They care little for harps and crowns, grow fidgety under excess of rest, and engage in all sorts of activities, retaining their individual tastes. James Stephens's archangel, seraph, and cherub are chatty, cordial souls with an avidity for cold potatoes and Irish companionship.

The demons as well have felt the same leveling influence experienced by the ghosts and the angels. Only, in their case, the thing is reversed, and they are raised to the grade of humanity. We are coming to see, in modern fiction, at least, that the devil is not really black, only a pleasant mottled gray like ourselves. Satan, in Mark Twain's posthumous novel,[1] is an affable young fellow, claiming to be the nephew and namesake of the personage best known by that name. Bernard Shaw's devil is of a Chesterfieldian courtesy, willing to speed the parting as to welcome the coming guest. I have found no comic use of the werewolf or of the vampire, though there are several comic witch stories, yet all these personages are humanized in modern fiction. We feel in some recent supernatural stories a sense of a continuing current of life. These ghosts, devils, witches, angels, and so forth are too real to be cut short by an author's *Finis*.

Another aspect of the leveling influence is seen in the more than natural power of motion, feeling, and intelligence given to inanimate objects, machinery, plants, and animals, in late literature. The idea of endowing inanimate figures with life and personality is seen several times in Hawthorne's stories, as his snow image, Drowne's wooden image, the vivified scarecrow, Peathertop, that the witch makes. The clay figures that Satan in Mark Twain's novel models, endues with life, then destroys with the fine, casual carelessness of a god, remind one of an incident from mythology. The statue in Edith Wharton's *The Duchess at Prayer* that changes its expression, showing on its marble face through a century the loathing and horror that the living countenance wore, or Lord Dunsany's

1. *The Mysterious Stranger*.

jade idol[2] that comes with stony steps across the desolate moor to exact vengeance on four men helpless in its presence, has a more intense thrill than Otranto's peripatetic statue. Lord Dunsany's *The Gods of the Mountains*, of which Frank Harris[a] says, "It is the only play which has meant anything to me in twenty years," shows an inexorable fatality as in the Greek drama.

Science is revealing wonderful facts and fiction is quick to realize the possibilities for startling situations in every field. So diabolic botanical specimens, animals endowed with human or more than human craft— sometimes gifted with immortality as well—add a new interest to uncanny fiction. And the new machines that make all impossibilities come to pass inspire a significant class of supernatural stories. In general, a new force is given to all things, to raise them to the level of the human.

In the same way nature is given a new power and becomes man's equal,—sometimes far his superior—in thought and action. The maelstrom in Poe's story is more than merely a part of the setting,—it is a terrible force in action. Algernon Blackwood stresses this variously in his stories, as where Egypt is shown as a vital presence and power, or where the "goblin trees" are as awful as any of the other characters of evil, or in the wind and flame on the mountain that are elements of supernatural power, with a resistless lure for mortals, or in the vampire soil that steals a man's strength. This may be illustrated as well from the drama, as in Maeterlinck's[b] where Death is the silent, invisible, yet dominant force, or in Synge's[c] where the sea is a terrible foe, lying in wait for man, or in August Stramm's *The Daughter of the Moor*, where the moor is a compelling character of evil. Gothic fiction did associate the phenomena of nature with the moods of the action, yet in a less effective way. The aspects of nature in recent literature have been raised to the level of humanity, becoming mortal or else diabolic or divine.

In general, in modern fiction, man now makes his supernatural characters in his own image. Ghosts, angels, devils, witches, werewolves, are humanized, made like to man in appearance, passions, and powers. On the other hand, plants, inanimate objects, and animals, as well as the phenomena of nature, are raised to the human plane and given access of power. This leveling process democratizes the supernatural elements and tends to make them almost equal.

* * *

2. In *A Night at an Inn*.

Excerpt from The Supernatural in Modern English Fiction (Scarborough)

The present revival of interest in the supernatural and its appearance in literature are as marked in the drama as in fiction or poetry. Mr. E. C. Whitmore, in a recently published volume on *The Supernatural in Tragedy*, has ably treated the subject, especially in the Greek classic period and the Elizabethan age in England. His thesis is that the supernatural is most frequently associated with tragedy, and is found where tragedy is at its best. This may be true of earlier periods of the tragic drama, yet it would be going too far to make the assertion of the drama of the present time. The occult makes its appearance to a considerable extent now in melodrama and even in comedy, though with no decrease in the frequency and effectiveness of its use in tragedy. This only illustrates the widening of its sphere and its adaptability to varying forms of art.

A brief survey of some of the plays produced in the last few years, most of them being seen in New York, will illustrate the extent to which the ghostly motifs are used on the stage of to-day. Double personality is represented[3] by Edward Locke, in a play which is said by critics to be virtually a dramatization of Dr. Morton Prince's study,[4] where psychological apparatus used in laboratory experiments to expel the evil intruder from the girl, a chronoscope, a dynograph, revolving mirrors, make the setting seem truly psychical. But the most dramatic instance of the kind, of course, is the dramatization of Dr. Jekyll's alter ego.

The plays, of Charles Rann Kennedy[5] and Jerome K. Jerome[6] are akin to the old mystery plays in that they personate divinity and show the miracle of Christly influence on sinful hearts. Augustus Thomas[7] and Edward Milton Royle[8] introduce hypnotism as the basis of complication and dénouement. Supernatural healing, miraculous intervention of divine power, occur in plays by William Vaughan Moody,[9] Björnson,[10] and George M. Cohan.[11] Another[12] turns on converse with spirits, as does Belasco's *Return of Peter Grimm*, while a war play by Vida Sutton[13] shows

3. In *The Case of Becky*.
4. *The Disassociation of a Personality*.
5. *The Servant in the House*.
6. *The Passing of the Third Floor Back*.
7. In *The Witching Hour*.
8. In *The Unwritten Law*.
9. *The Faith Healer*.
10. *Beyond Their Strength*.
11. *The Miracle Man*.
12. *The Spiritualist*.
13. *Kingdom Come*.

four ghosts on the stage at once, astonishing phantoms who do not realize that they are dead. Others[14] have for their themes miracles of faith and rescue from danger, though the first-named play satirizes such belief and the latter is a piece of Catholic propaganda.

Magic, by G. K. Chesterton, introduces supernatural forces whereby strange things are made to happen, such as the changing of the electric light from green to blue. *Peter Ibbetson*, the dramatization of Du Maurier's novel, shows dream-supernaturalism, and various other psychic effects in a delicate and distinctive manner. And *The Willow Tree*, by Benrimo and Harrison Rhodes, is built upon an ancient Japanese legend, relating a hamadryad myth with other supermortal phantasies, such as representing a woman's soul as contained in a mirror.

We have fairy plays by J. M. Barrie,[15] W. B. Yeats,[16] and Maeterlinck,[17] and the mermaid has even been staged,[18] Bernard Shaw shows us the devil in his own home town, while Hauptmann gives us Hannele's visions of heaven. The Frankenstein theme is used to provoke laughter mixed with thrills.[19] Owen and Robert Davis[20] symbolize man's better angel, while *The Eternal Magdalene*, a dream-drama, shows another piece of symbolic super-naturalism. Lord Dunsany's plays have already been mentioned.

Yet the drama, though showing a definite revival of the supernatural, and illustrating various forms of it, is more restricted than fiction. Many aspects of the occult appear and the psychic drama is popular, but the necessities of presentation on the stage inevitably bar many forms of the ghostly art that take their place naturally in fiction. The closet drama does not come under this limitation, for in effect it is almost as free as fiction to introduce mystical, symbolic, and invisible presences. The closet drama is usually in poetic form and poetry is closer akin to certain forms of the supernatural than is prose, which makes their use more natural.

The literary playlet, so popular just now, uses the ghostly in many ways. One shows the Archangel Raphael with his dog, working miracles, while another includes in its *dramatis personæ* a faun and a moon goddess who insists on giving the faun a soul, at which he wildly protests. As

14. As *The Eternal Mystery*, by George Jean Nathan, and *The Rosary*.
15. *Peter Pan*.
16. *The Land of Heart's Desire*.
17. *The Blue Bird*.
18. *The Mermaid*.
19. In *The Last Laugh*, by Paul Dickey and Charles W. Goddard.
20. In *Any House*.

through suffering and human pain he accepts the gift, a symbolic white butterfly poises itself on his uplifted hand, then flits toward Heaven. In another, Padraic yields himself to the fairies' power as the price of bread for the girl he loves. Theodore Dreiser's short plays bring in creatures impossible of representation on the stage, "persistentes" of fish, animals, and birds, symbolic Shadows, a Blue Sphere, a Power of Physics, Nitrous Acid, a Fast Mail (though trains have been used on the stage), and so forth.

Instances from recent German drama might be given, as the work of August Stramm, who like Rupert Brooke and the ill-starred poets of the Irish revolution has fallen as a sacrifice to the war. An article in the *Literary Digest* says of Stramm that "he felt behind all the beauty of the world its elemental passions and believed these to be the projections of human passions in the waves of wind and light and water, in flames of earth." He includes among his characters[21] a Spider, Nightingales, Moonlight, Wind, and Blossoms. Carl Hauptmann[22] likewise shows the elemental forces of nature and of super-nature. On the battlefield of death the dead arise to join in one dreadful chant of hate against their enemies. Leonid Andreyev's striking play[23] might be mentioned as an example from the Russian. King-Hunger, Death, and Old time Bell-Ringer, are the principal actors, while the human beings are all deformed and distorted, "one continuous malicious monstrosity bearing only a remote likeness to man." The starving men are slain, but over the field of the dead the motionless figure of Death is seen silhouetted. But the dead arise, and a dull, distant, manifold murmur, as if underground, is heard, "We come! Woe unto the victorious!"

But as I have said, these are literary dramas, impossible of presentation on the stage, so that they are judged by literary rather than dramatic standards. For the most part fiction is infinitely freer in its range and choice of subjects from the supernatural than is the drama. The suggestive, symbolic, mystic effects which could not in any way be presented on the stage, but which are more truly of the province of poetry, are used in prose that has a jeweled beauty and a melody as of poetry. Elements such as invisibility, for instance, and various occult agencies may be stressed and analyzed in fiction as would be impossible on the stage. The close relation between insanity and the weird can be much more effectively shown in the novel or short story than in the drama, as the forces of mystery, the incalculable

21. In *Sancta Susanna*.
22. In *The Dead Are Singing*.
23. *King-Hunger*.

agencies can be thus better emphasized. Ghosts need to be seen on the stage to have the best effect, even if they are meant as "selective apparitions" like Banquo, and if thus seen they are too corporeal for the most impressive influence, while in fiction they can be suggested with delicate reserve. Supernatural presences that could not be imaged on the boards may be represented in the novel or story, as Blackwood's Elementals or Psychic Invasions. How could one stage such action, for instance, as his citizens turning into witch-cats or his Giant Devil looming mightily in the heavens? Likewise in fiction the full presentation of scientific supernaturalism can be achieved, which would be impossible on the stage.

In conclusion, it might be said that fiction offers the most popular present vehicle for expression of the undoubtedly reviving supernaturalism in English literature. And fiction is likewise the best form, that which affords the more varied chances for effectiveness. The rising tide of the unearthly in art shows itself in all literary forms, as dramatic, narrative, and lyric poetry, with a few epics—in the playlet as in the standard drama, in the short story as in the novel. It manifests itself in countless ways in current literature and inviting lines of investigation suggest themselves with reference to various aspects of its study. The supernatural as especially related to religion offers an interesting field for research. The miracles from the Bible are often used, as in Lew Wallace's *Ben Hur*, and Christ is introduced in other times and places, as the war novel,[24] or in Marie Corelli's satire on Episcopacy,[25] where the cardinal finds the Christ child outside the cathedral. The more than mortal elements, as answers to prayer, the experience of conversion, spiritual miracles, and so forth, are present to a considerable extent in modern fiction.

Two very recent novels of importance base their plots on the miraculous in religion, *The Brook Kerith*, by George Moore, and *The Leatherwood God*, by William Dean Howells. I have touched on this aspect of the subject in a previous article.[26]

One might profitably trace out the appearances of the ghostly in modern poetry, or one might study its manifestations in the late drama, including melodrama and comedy as well as tragedy. This present treatment of the supernatural in modern English fiction makes no pretensions to being complete. It is meant to be suggestive rather than exhaustive, and I shall

24. *The Second Coming.*
25. *The Master Christian.*
26. "Religion in Recent American Novels," in the January, 1914, *Review and Expositor.*

Lewis Morrison's Magnificent Faust. *One of the most popular supernatural spectacles on the Victorian stage was the opera* Faust, *based on the German legend of scholar who sells his soul to the devil in exchange for forbidden knowledge. The famous scene on the reputedly-haunted German mountain the Brocken could stand for the popularity of the horror genre, where the author (like Mephistopheles) commands the forces of the supernatural for the audience, who, like Faust, seek after the taboo, the forbidden, and the infernal. This advertisement is dated 1889 (Library of Congress, Prints and Photographs Division, LC-USZ6-457).*

be gratified if it may help to arouse further interest in a significant and vital phase of our literature and lead others to pursue the investigations.

Notes

a. Frank Harris (1856–1931), an Irish-American author and magazine editor, best known for his sexually explicit memoir *My Life and Loves* (1922–1927), which was banned in several countries. Harris shared a residence with the occultist Aleister Crowley in 1924.

b. See note, page 227, n.3.

c. Irish playwright John Millington Synge (1871–1909). Many of his works caused a great deal of outrage for their depiction women and religion. Here Scarborough is referring to *Riders to the Sea* (1904), about a woman who lost all the men in her family to the ocean. In the play, the woman sees a ghost.

Appendix: Timeline of Major Works of Horror

The timeline below lists in chronological order the major works of horror discussed by the critics in this volume.

1764 *The Castle of Otranto*, Horace Walpole
1773 "Sir Bertrand: A Fragment," Anna Aikin (later Barbauld)
1791 *The Romance of the Forest*, Ann Radcliffe
1794 *The Mysteries of Udolpho*, Ann Radcliffe
1794 *The Monk*, Matthew Lewis
1796 *The Castle Spectre*, Matthew Lewis
1801 *Tales of Wonder*, Matthew Lewis
1801 *Tales of Terror*, anonymous
1818 *Frankenstein*, Mary Shelley
1819 *The Vampyre*, John Polidori
1823 *Presumption; or, the Fate of Frankenstein*, Richard Brinsley Peake
1835 "Berenice," Edgar Allan Poe
1839 "The Fall of the House of Usher," Edgar Allan Poe
1841 "Murders in the Rue Morgue," Edgar Allan Poe
1842 *Vileroy; or, The Horrors of Zindorf Castle*, John Malcolm Rhymer (also attributed to Thomas Preskett Prest or Elizabeth Caroline Grey)
1842 "The Pit and the Pendulum," Edgar Allan Poe
1845 "The Raven," Edgar Allan Poe
1845–1847 *Varney the Vampire*, John Malcolm Rhymer (or Thomas Preskett Prest)

1847	*Wuthering Heights*, Emily Brontë
1857	"M. Anastasius," Dinah Maria Mulock
1858	"The Diamond Lens," Fitz-James O'Brien
1859	"The Haunted and the Haunters," Edward Bulwer-Lytton
1859	"What Was It?," Fitz-James O'Brien
1872	"Carmilla" and "Green Tea," J. Sheridan Le Fanu
1886	*The Strange Case of Dr. Jekyll and Mr. Hyde*, Robert Louis Stevenson
1887	"Le Horla," Guy de Maupassant
1889	*Not for the Night-Time*, Theo Gift (Dora Havers)
1890	*The Picture of Dorian Gray*, Oscar Wilde
1890	"An Occurrence at Owl Creek Bridge," Ambrose Bierce
1890	*The Snake's Pass*, Bram Stoker
1893	*My Friend the Murderer*, Arthur Conan Doyle
1894	"The Great God Pan," Arthur Machen
1895	*The King in Yellow*, Robert W. Chambers
1896	*The Three Imposters*, Arthur Machen
1896	*The Island of Dr. Moreau*, H. G. Wells
1897	*Dracula*, Bram Stoker
1897	*The Vampire*, Philip Burne-Jones
1897	*The Invisible Man*, H. G. Wells
1898	*The War of the Worlds*, H. G. Wells
1898	*The Turn of the Screw*, Henry James
1899	"Moxon's Master," Ambrose Bierce
1900	"How Love Came to Professor Guildea," Robert Hichens
1902	*The Hound of the Baskervilles*, Arthur Conan Doyle
1907	"The Willows," Algernon Blackwood
1908	*The Footprint*, Gouverneur Morris
1910	"The Wendigo," Algernon Blackwood
1911	"Fishhead," Irvin Cobb

Index

Ackermann, Rudolph 2, 67, 153
Aikin, Wilford M. 58
The Ancient Mariner 38, 56, 72–73, 87n., 292, 339

Bailey, Alfred 195
Baldwin, Charles Sears 4, 138, 144, 145
Barbauld, Anna 46, 367
Baron de Book-Worms 201, 212
Barrett Browning, Elizabeth 99, 124, 130
Bayne, Peter 105
Beardsley, Aubrey 245, 247, 249–251, 254n.c
Beattie, James 42, 46n.a
Bell, Ellis *see* Brontë, Emily
"Berenice" 138, 139–143, 367
Bierce, Ambrose 4, 6, 152–161, 357, 368
Birkhead, Edith 357
"The Black Cat" 137
Blackwood, Algernon 303–307, 357, 360, 364, 368
Blavatsky, Helena 329
Bloom, Harold 10
Böcklin, Arnold 306
Brontë, Emily 105–107, 136, 215, 368
Brooks, Noah 294
Brownell, W.C. 3, 10, 132
Buddhism 303, 326, 329
Bulwer-Lytton, Edward 100, 102–103n.b, 169, 176, 209–210, 266, 267n.a, 272, 278n.c, 345, 350n.a, 368
Burke, Edmund 2, 18, 19, 225, 325
Burne-Jones, Philip 5, 185, 186, 368
Byron, George Gordon (Lord) 38, 68, 77–78, 103–105, 129, 131, 146, 176

Can Such Things Be? 155
Canby, Henry Seidel 145
Carmilla 4, 182, 207, 291, 368
The Castle of Otranto 2, 7, 32, 54–58, 59, 121, 173, 345, 351, 356, 360, 367
The Centaur 306

Chamberlain, Alex F. 13
Chambers, Robert (*Book of Days*) 3, 122
Chambers, Robert (*King in Yellow*) 122, 299–300, 368
"Christabel" 77–78, 338–339, 342n.a
Christmas 10, 50, 144, 278n.a, 292–294, 330–331
Clark, Ward 5, 301
Cobb, Irvin S. 161–163, 368
Colbron, Grace Isabel 303
Coleridge, Samuel Taylor 38, 57, 72–73, 77, 87n., 292–293, 338–339, 342n.a
Collins, Wilkie 169, 182, 183n.b, 221
Conan Doyle, Arthur 3, 6, 96, 163, 220–223, 224, 243, 343, 345, 368
Conchology 128, 129n.a
Cooper, Frederic Taber 6, 152, 221
Cox, J. Charles 5, 185
Crocker, John 3, 93, 94
Crowe, Catherine 295, 345, 350n.b
Crowley, Aleister 350, 366n.a

Danton, George H. 108
Darwin, Charles 4, 92n.a, 213, 217, 224, 261
Darwin, Erasmus 80, 92n.a
Dawson, W.F. 292
Dawson, W.J. 187
"Death of Halpin Frayser" 157–158
Defoe, Daniel 22
Detective stories 139, 183n.b, 219–220, 223–224, 227
"The Diamond Lens" 144–147, 368
"Dog or Demon?" 326, 329n.b
Doré, Gustave 241, 242
Dracula 4, 6, 103, 200–208, 328, 358, 368
Drake, Nathan 41, 47–50
Dreams 270–278, 341
Dunbar, Olivia Howard 6, 329
The Dweller on the Threshold 307, 312

370 Index

Eagle, Adam *see* O'Brien, Fitz-James
Eaves, A. Osborne 207
"The Fall of the House of Usher" 111, 128, 135, 141, 151, 163, 275, 280, 367
Fantasmagoriana 78, 79n.*a*
Fear 13–14, 18–21, 26–27, 31, 266–267, 275, 280
"Fishhead" 161–163, 368
Flames 308, 312, 347–348
The Footprint 5, 301–302, 368
Frankenstein 3, 58, 66, 71, 77n.*a*, 77, 78n., 79–97, 100, 105, 208, 211, 214, 263, 266, 362, 367
Frost, William Henry 199

Galvanization 71, 77n.*a*
Gautier, Théophile 257–262, 276, 311
Germany 14–17, 39, 52, 59, 60, 62, 66, 67, 69, 77, 78, 79n.*a*, 82, 99, 102, 108–110, 121, 210, 261, 263, 266, 267n.*b*, 275, 294–295, 363, 365
Ghost stories 5, 6, 9, 10, 29, 60, 67, 69–73, 181, 219, 265–336, 351–353, 356n.*e*
Ghosts 2–3, 6, 16, 17, 29–30, 38–40, 42, 44, 47, 48, 49, 51, 66, 67–68, 80, 114, 153, 159, 173, 265–336, 337, 339–340, 357–360, 364, 366n.*c*
"Giaour" 38, 41n.*a*
Gift, Theo 329n.*b*, 368
Gillette, William 297–299
God 25, 26–27, 114, 116, 191, 254, 268, 319
Godwin, William 66, 78, 80, 93–95, 101, 102
Gosse, Edmund 342
Gothic (architecture) 2, 19, 31–36, 55, 58, 254n.*e*
Gothic (literature) 2–7, 18, 19, 37–107, 110–111, 175, 200, 209, 211, 295, 305, 328, 337, 351, 353, 356n.*f, g*, 357–358, 360
Goya, Francisco 271
Grand-Guignol 223
"The Great God Pan" 4–5, 227, 228–230, 243–246, 368
Great War *see* World War I
"The Green Tea" 183, 329n.*c*, 352, 368

Halloween 292, 293
Hamlet 16, 17, 70, 80, 133, 175, 294n.*a*, 339
"The Haunted and the Haunters; or, the House and the Brain" 266, 267n.*a*, 273–275, 278n.*c*, 368
Hawthorne, Julian 206
Hawthorne, Nathaniel 3, 108–121, 139–140, 142, 143n.2, 146, 147, 206, 302, 340, 344, 359
Heard at the Telephone 223–227
Hearn, Lafcaido 31, 267, 271, 351
Heron, E. and H. 353
Hichens, Robert 6, 152, 307–325, 347–348, 350n.*c*, 368

Hoffmann, E.T.A. 60, 108–110, 137, 138, 159, 294–295
Hole, Richard 45, 46n.*f*
Holmes, Sherlock 220, 221–223, 297, 298
"Le Horla" 148, 294, 368
Horne, Richard H. 99–100, 102n.*a*
Horror genre 2, 6–7, 9, 16, 211, 325–329, 337–366
"A Horseman in the Sky" 155–156
The Hound of the Baskervilles 221–223, 368
"How Love Came to Professor Guildea" 6, 307, 313, 350n.*c*, 368
Hunt, Leigh 68

In the Midst of Life 152, 161
The Ingoldsby Legends 353, 356n.*e*
The Invisible Man 214–215, 218, 219, 346, 348, 368
The Island of Dr. Moreau 211–212, 213, 214, 368

Jack the Ripper 199–200
James, Henry 5, 133, 188, 295–297, 309, 335, 368
James, M.R. 351–352, 356n.*c*
Japan 31, 139, 267, 277, 278–292, 337

King, Stephen 9
The King in Yellow 122, 299–300, 368
Kipling, Rudyard 154, 185, 186, 241n., 316

Lamb, Charles 66, 68, 183, 256, 339, 342n.*b*
Lang, Andrew 110–111, 279, 330, 335, 336n.*b*, 337
Lanier, Henry Wysham 5, 295
Le Fanu, J. Sheridan 4, 182–184, 207, 291, 326, 352–353, 368
Le Gallienne, Richard 200
Leslie, Amy 297, 298
Lewis, Matthew 2, 39, 50, 58, 60, 69, 77, 175, 295, 354, 367
London Hermit *see* Parke, Walter
Lovecraft, H.P. 6–7, 161, 217, 242, 271, 357
Lowell, James Russell 126
Lucas, E.V. 183
Lummis, Charles F. 202

Macbeth 38, 56, 91, 93, 137
Machen, Arthur 4–5, 6, 227–230, 243–246, 357–358, 368
Maeterlinck, Maurice 224, 226, 227n.*c*, 268, 278n.*a*, 360
Maeztu, Ramiro de 257
Mansfield, Richard 199–200
Markham, Edwin 158
Marryat, Frederick 38, 354, 356n.*g*
Marvin, Frederick Rowland 148
Maupassant, Guy de 148–152, 155, 163, 294–295, 368
Maurice, Arthur Bartlett 221

Index   371

Miles, Caroline 265
Modern Ghosts 294–295
The Monk 39, 50, 58, 60, 354, 367
More, Paul Elmer 4, 110
"Morella" 139–140, 143
Morris, Gouverneur 5, 301–302, 368
"Moxon's Master" 157, 368
"The Murders in the Rue Morgue" 136, 367
My Friend the Murderer 220–221, 368
The Mysteries of Udolpho 58, 60, 62–65, 67, 121, 173, 345, 367
The Mysterious Stranger 359n.1
Mystery stories 6

The Narrative of A. Gordon Pym 128
Neilson, William Allen 59
Newton, Edward A. 255
The Night-Side of Nature 295, 345
Nightmares 272–278
Not for the Night-Time 329n.*b*, 368

O'Brien, Fitz-James 4, 65, 144–148, 152, 267n.*c*, 368
Occult 84, 207, 228, 329n.*f*, 350, 357, 361–362
"An Occurrence at Owl Creek Bridge" 152, 156, 368
Ossian 43–44, 53

Parke, J. Richardson 205
Parke, Walter 4, 164
Pattee, Fred Lewis 160
Payne, William Morton 214, 218
Peake, Richard Brinsley 97–99, 367
Penny awfuls 4, 164–181
Penny dreadfuls *see* Penny awfuls
Phantasmagoriana *see* Fantasmagoriana
The Phantom Ship 354, 356n.*g*
Phelps, William Lyon 215
The Picture of Dorian Gray 255–257, 260–262, 368
"The Pit and the Pendulum" 135, 136, 367
Poe, Edgar Allan 3–4, 6, 7, 9, 96, 99, 106, 108–152, 154, 159, 160–161, 163, 182, 192, 206, 221, 230, 242, 266, 274, 279, 295, 302, 326, 357, 360, 367
Polidori, John 4, 10, 77–79, 103, 105, 203, 367
"The Premature Burial" 137
Prest, Thomas Preskett 182, 367
Presumption; or, the Fate of Frankenstein 97–99, 367
Prodigal son 25
Puritans 109, 110–121, 237

Quilter, Harry 4, 8, 230, 301

Radcliffe, Ann 2, 3, 50, 54, 55, 58, 60–65, 66, 67, 79, 100, 110, 111, 175, 327, 345, 354, 356, 358, 367

Raleigh, Walter 2, 53, 345
Rankin, Thomas E. 58
"The Raven" 111, 124, 129–132, 151, 242, 367
Reeves, Clara 60
Rhymer, James Malcolm 4, 182, 203, 367
Robertson, Frederick W. 25
The Romance of the Forest 61–65, 367
Röntgen rays *see* X-rays

Scarborough, Dorothy 6, 350–356
School of Terror 58–60
Science 27, 85, 98, 181, 211–212, 213, 214–215, 225, 268, 285, 292, 306, 332, 337, 341, 343, 344, 346, 364
Science fiction 6, 102–103n.*b*, 209–211, 214, 217, 218, 227
Scientific romance *see* Science fiction
Scott, Sir Walter 3, 29, 40, 54, 55, 59–62, 79, 94, 169, 175, 187, 332, 340
Shakespeare, William 16, 17, 39, 41–45, 55, 56, 66, 80, 94–95, 126, 133, 164, 224, 268, 302
Shelley, Mary 3, 66, 68, 71, 77n.*a*, 77–78, 79, 93, 97, 100–102, 105, 208, 266, 271, 367
Shelley, Percy Bysshe 68, 77–78, 79, 80, 102, 105
Shorter, Clement 215–216
"Sir Bertrand: A Fragment" 46, 367
The Snake's Pass 200–201, 368
Society for Psychical Research 279, 281, 312, 326, 331, 332
Specters *see* Ghosts
Spiritualism 5, 9, 27, 28, 220, 221, 295n.*a*, *c*, 305, 329n.*f*, 331, 349
Stedman, Edmund Clarence 206
Stevenson, Robert Louis 4, 187–195, 200, 207, 228, 279, 335, 340–341, 342, 347, 368
Stoddard, Richard Henry 5, 228
Stoker, Bram 3, 200–208, 357–358, 368
Strachey, Lytton 1
The Strange Case of Dr. Jekyll and Mr. Hyde 4, 57, 187, 191–200, 207, 266, 312, 340, 342, 347, 361, 368
Summers, Montague 350
Supernatural 2, 6, 16, 25, 27–31, 37, 41, 44, 45, 48, 56–57, 68, 78, 80, 105, 109, 154, 156, 220, 221, 265, 267–278, 279, 284, 307, 329–331, 334, 337–366
Supernatural Horror in Literature 6, 357
The Supernatural in Modern English Fiction 6
The Supernatural in Tragedy 353, 361

The Tale of Terror 357
Tales of Civilians and Soldiers see *In the Midst of Life*
"The Tapestried Chamber" 40, 60, 340
"The Tell-Tale Heart" 141
Terror 14, 19, 20–21, 25, 27, 28, 30, 51, 53,

57, 58–59, 66, 109, 113, 114, 149, 171, 299, 328, 334, 335, 351, 357
The Three Imposters 227, 368
Traill, H.D. 324
The Turn of the Screw 5, 295–297, 335, 368
Twain, Mark 267n.*b*, 359

The Vampire (painting) 5, 185–187, 368
"The Vampire" (poem) 186
Vampires 3–4, 37–38, 103, 104, 202, 204, 205, 206n.1, 207, 291, 358–359
The Vampyre (novel) 77, 103–105, 367
Varney the Vampire 4, 103, 164, 169–170, 182, 203, 367
Verne, Jules 211, 215, 216, 217, 219
Victorians 1, 7, 8, 9, 10, 27, 37, 60, 102n.*b*, 164, 199, 230, 245, 263, 295n.*c*, 356n.*e*, 365
Vileroy; or, the Horrors of Zindorf Castle 170–176, 182, 367

Walkley, Arthur Bingham 223
Walpole, Horace 2, 18, 32, 54–58, 59, 111, 351, 358, 367
The War of the Worlds 216–219, 368

Weird Tales 294–295
Wells, Carolyn 219
Wells, H.G. 4, 211–219, 346–348, 359, 368
"The Wendigo" 303, 306, 368
"The Were-Wolf" 206
Werewolves 354–355, 356n.*h*, 358
"What Was It?" 65, 144, 146–147, 266, 368
Whitmore, E.C. 353, 361
Wilde, Oscar 249, 254n.*a, c*, 255–264, 307, 309, 354, 368
Wilkins, Mary E. 300–301
"The Willows" 303, 305, 306, 368
The Wind in the Rose Bush 300–301
Witches 51, 112–116, 291, 344, 350, 358–360
World War I 1, 2, 6, 208, 257, 261–264, 350, 357
Wuthering Heights 105–107, 136, 368

X-rays 349, 350n.*d*

Yardley, Edward 37

Zanoni 100, 102–103n.*b*, 212

www.ingramcontent.com/pod-product-compliance
Lightning Source LLC
Chambersburg PA
CBHW051205300426
44116CB00006B/442